Applied Helping Skills

Second Edition

SAGE was founded in 1965 by Sara Miller McCune to support the dissemination of usable knowledge by publishing innovative and high-quality research and teaching content. Today, we publish over 900 journals, including those of more than 400 learned societies, more than 800 new books per year, and a growing range of library products including archives, data, case studies, reports, and video. SAGE remains majority-owned by our founder, and after Sara's lifetime will become owned by a charitable trust that secures our continued independence.

Los Angeles | London | New Delhi | Singapore | Washington DC | Melbourne

Applied Helping Skills

Transforming Lives

Second Edition

Leah Brew & Jeffrey A. Kottler
California State University, Fullerton

Los Angeles | London | New Delhi
Singapore | Washington DC | Melbourne

FOR INFORMATION:

SAGE Publications, Inc.
2455 Teller Road
Thousand Oaks, California 91320
E-mail: order@sagepub.com

SAGE Publications Ltd.
1 Oliver's Yard
55 City Road
London EC1Y 1SP
United Kingdom

SAGE Publications India Pvt. Ltd.
B 1/I 1 Mohan Cooperative Industrial Area
Mathura Road, New Delhi 110 044
India

SAGE Publications Asia-Pacific Pte. Ltd.
3 Church Street
#10-04 Samsung Hub
Singapore 049483

Printed in the United States of America

Library of Congress Cataloging-in-Publication Data

Names: Brew, Leah, 1967– author. | Kottler, Jeffrey A., author.

Title: Applied helping skills : transforming lives / Leah Brew & Jeffrey A. Kottler, California State University, Fullerton.

Description: Second edition. | Los Angeles : SAGE Publications, [2017] | Includes bibliographical references and index.

Identifiers: LCCN 2016009996 | ISBN 978-1-4833-7569-4 (pbk. : alk. paper)

Subjects: LCSH: Psychotherapy—Textbooks. | Counseling—Textbooks.

Classification: LCC RC480 .B697 2017 | DDC 616.89/14—dc23
LC record available at http://lccn.loc.gov/2016009996

This book is printed on acid-free paper.

Acquisitions Editor: Kassie Graves
Development Editor: Abbie Rickard
eLearning Editor: Gabrielle Piccininni
Editorial Assistant: Carrie Montoya
Production Editor: David C. Felts
Copy Editor: QuADS Prepress Pvt Ltd
Typesetter: C&M Digitals (P) Ltd.
Proofreader: Carole Quandt
Indexer: Amy Murphy
Cover Designer: Glenn Vogel
Marketing Manager: Shari Countryman

SFI label applies to text stock

16 17 18 19 20 10 9 8 7 6 5 4 3 2 1

BRIEF CONTENTS

DETAILED CONTENTS

PREFACE

Every undergraduate and graduate program in the various helping professions offers a course (or two) on basic counseling skills and therapeutic interventions. Some would say that this is the most important unit in the program because it forms the foundation for everything else that practitioners do. This is the class where beginners learn the core skills of helping, as well as the essence of what it means to make a difference in the world by transforming lives.

Skills courses tend to be very practice oriented, a hands-on experience in which students not only learn the basics of helping others but also applying these behaviors and interventions in various contexts and situations. The goal is no less than to equip students with everything they need to begin conducting interviews, planning treatments, engaging in systematic assessment and diagnoses, and structuring effective interventions. Most of this helping activity is centered on core skills, but in order to be truly effective, these strategies must be integrated as part of an overall plan for influencing people in positive ways. This text not only teaches students basic interventions but also inspires them to use these skills in the most powerful and ethical ways possible.

UNIQUE FEATURES OF THE TEXT

Applied Helping Skills: Transforming Lives is designed to be an experiential text, one that is highly practical and student centered. It not only includes all the basic skills and core interventions that you need in order to begin seeing clients, but it also presents them in such a way that you can internalize them—make them part of who you are, not just what you do when "the meter is running." The emphasis throughout this book is on ways to apply these skills to your work as well as to your life.

Although much of the book's content includes the "little" stuff, the myriad things that helpers actually *do* to make a difference in the lives of their clients, *Applied Helping Skills: Transforming Lives* keeps the focus on the bigger picture. All too often in texts such as this, students become so bombarded and overwhelmed with the variety of skills, techniques, interventions, strategies, methodologies, and treatment options, they might forget that the primary purpose of all this is to make contact with their clients, to help them feel understood, and to clarify the major issues that trouble them. Some of the most popular skills texts are so overstructured and rigidly sequenced into a series of stages that students must learn a whole "foreign language" just to be able to communicate to one another about what they are doing. In contrast, this text uses a conversational tone and everyday language to help students facilitate change in clients.

Applied Helping Skills: Transforming Lives has these important features:

- The treatment of core skills is combined with issues related to treatment planning.
- A generic model of helping is used that combines features of humanistic, constructivist, and cognitive theories, and will fit a variety of different settings and clinical styles.
- Diversity issues are infused into every facet of the process so that you understand the importance of adapting your skills to fit the unique needs of individual clients and cultural groups.
- Traditional helping skills are augmented with newer, more cutting-edge brief interventions.
- After core skills are mastered, they are applied to specific settings with special chapters on families/couples/children and groups.
- Attention is given not only to what effective practitioners *do* but also how they *think* and *feel*. You will be helped to increase your tolerance for ambiguity, complexity, and uncertainty.
- Case examples and first-person accounts make the material come alive.
- Reflective activities, homework assignments, and application exercises help you personalize the ideas and apply them immediately in work and life settings.
- A narrative voice uses humor, authenticity, engaging prose, practical examples, and very straight talk to communicate the passion, the excitement, and the fun of doing this type of work.
- Beautiful photographs taken by Jeffrey Kottler are included throughout the text.

Web-based resources for students have been created to help students understand the material more clearly. Open-access student resources are available at study.sagepub.com/brew2e and include the following:

- A section to test them on objective information

- A written vignette that demonstrated the skills described in the chapter.

- Common Errors for Beginning Counselors worksheet is a quick and easy resource to use throughout training.

- Types of Responses lists the strengths and limitations of each type of therapist response, especially when overused.

- Basic Reflecting Skills Paper Rubric for paper assignments.

- Video Sessions Rubric for video assignments.

- "Check What You Learned" short answer and essay questions focus on key terms and concepts outlined in the chapters.

- Video clips and accompanying questions demonstrate core concepts in the text and help visualize essential counselor skills. Accompanying video questions reflect and assess the counseling situation presented in each clip.

In addition, this text has a password-protected instructor resources website with the following:

- A course philosophy and structure document

- Editable, chapter-specific PowerPoint slides

- Sample syllabi on how to teach the class with reasoning as to the suggested homework assignments

- A sample final exam that is practice based

USE OF THE WORD *THERAPIST*

This is a book intended for a wide variety of helping professionals, including counselors, psychologists, social workers, family therapists, psychiatrists, pastoral care, and mental health workers, among others. We are sensitive to the differences in professional identity, as well as the specialties of each discipline, however, we believe that there are still universal and generic skills that transcend any particular field. For example, although we were trained in counselor education programs, one of us is licensed as a psychologist (Jeffrey) and the other as a counselor (Leah). We teach in a counseling department that prepares students for practice as family therapists. Our faculty consists of professionals who identify as belonging to four different disciplines.

Certainly, psychiatrists might ask questions differently than would a school counselor, or a social worker might reflect feelings a bit more nuanced than would a crisis counselor conducting intake interviews, but nevertheless the essential and core skills remain similar. As such we have chosen to use the generic term, *therapist* to apply to any professional in a helping role, even though we recognize that particular specialties of those who identify more distinctly with the role of "counselor," "social worker," "mental health worker," "doctor," "teacher," or any other label.

UPDATED EDITION

This new edition includes some more contemporary examples and includes a few more references to issues of diversity and school counseling settings. Resources and references were also updated throughout. We chose to adhere to the classic theories rather than delve into the newer modalities, since they are used as examples. Finally, we worked to make the book more affordable by taking out the photographs and multicolor option for publication. We wanted the book to be affordable for all students.

THE CONTENTS

Each chapter focuses on the skills needed within the many curricular areas taught in training programs. We assume that students will have in-depth courses in all of these areas, but simply introduce the clinical skills needed here for foundational skill development.

In the first chapter, we introduce you to the overall process that is involved in helping people. We talk about what it takes for a client to be willing to change and the conditions under which such transformations can be more easily facilitated. Chapter 2 expands the context under which therapeutic skills are employed to include the individual, social, cultural, and ethical contexts for helping behaviors. This provides a framework for better understanding the kinds of issues and concerns that people bring to sessions.

Chapter 3 summarizes the major "classic" conceptual frameworks from which therapeutic skills evolved. Students receive intensive study of theory in other courses, whereas we think it is important to link therapy applications to these models so that it becomes easier to understand not only what you are doing but why you are doing it.

After this contextual overview, the next series of chapters introduces the major helping skills as applied to building and maintaining relationships (Chapter 4), assessing and diagnosing client issues (Chapter 5), exploring presenting complaints and collecting meaningful information (Chapter 6), promoting deeper understanding (Chapter 7), and moving from insight to action (Chapter 8). The final chapter of this section (Chapter 9) discusses skills for maintaining progress and evaluating the results.

Although there is considerable overlap between the skills that clinicians use during individual sessions, versus those with more than one participant present, there are some specialized strategies, interventions, and helping behaviors that supplement what you have already learned. Chapter 10 covers family therapy, couples, and child therapy skills, and Chapter 11 examines those that are most useful in group leadership. The final chapter brings things to a close and provides structure for further training and development.

Leah Brew
Jeffrey A. Kottler
Fullerton, California

ACKNOWLEDGMENTS

We are sincerely grateful to the students who initially "field tested" this text by providing helpful suggestions that were incorporated into the final draft of our first edition: Jocelyn Frandsen, Lynnette Herrera, Judith Passy, Corrin Reynolds, Rick Thomas, Nichole Walker, and Sarah Walker. In addition, we want to thank the following students for their willingness to share their experiences in this second edition: Kayleigh Soto and Alex Smith.

A number of reviewers, experts at teaching the skills courses, also provided a wealth of experience and wisdom that were crucial in developing the final product. We are indebted to Theresa Benson (University of Illinois at Urbana Champaign), Andrew Bratawidjaja (Kansas State University), Karen D. Cathey (Alcorn State University), Marian Connell (The Academy of Creative Psychological Therapy Ireland), Jane Fried (Central Connecticut State University), Monte Gray (Bronx Community College of the City University of New York), Shane Haberstroh (The University of Texas at San Antonio), Beulah Hirschlein (Oklahoma State University), Carolyn W. Kern (University of North Texas), Patricia A. Heisser Metoyer (Walden University), Marilyn J. Montgomery (Florida International University), Ruth Baugher Palmer (Eastern University), and Chester R. Robinson (Texas A&M University–Commerce).

Finally, we thank our editors, Kassie Graves and Abbie Rickard, for their support and guidance throughout the various stages of this process. We also thank the copy editor Krishna Pradeep Joghee (QuADS).

PART I

FOUNDATIONS FOR SKILLS

Chapter 1

THE PROCESS REVEALED

Three students are sitting in a small clinic room during the second week of class. Adam is in the counselor role, Leslie is in the client role, and Isabella is the observer. They are meeting for the first time in this triad and are expected to practice counseling skills. The student in the client role begins the conversation:

Leslie: (in a sad voice, looking at the floor) I'm not sure where to start. I guess I can start by sharing that I don't belong here. I have huge anxiety problems, and sometimes I feel debilitated by them. During my undergraduate days, I would stare at the computer to begin a paper and nothing would come for hours. My mind would just go blank. People tell me that I look competent, but I fool them all. I'm a perfectionist. I know how to make myself look good, but underneath, I'm a hot mess. I'm desperate to be a counselor, though. I've always wanted to help others, but maybe I don't have what it takes.

What would be the best way for Adam to respond? The typical response from a beginner might be to say something like the following:

Adam: You have to trust the professors who admitted us to the program. They are therapists, and they would know if we could do this or not. I'm sure you'll be fine. You managed to get this far, after all.

How might this type of response affect Leslie? She might feel invalidated, as if her problem isn't important. Adam has good intentions of wanting Leslie to feel better and more confident, but this response would not likely result in that end. Another common response might go something like this:

Adam: I know exactly how you feel! I had a panic attack a few years ago, and I'm really terrified that it might happen again in class!

In this case, Adam can identify with Leslie's experience of being anxious, and by sharing his own anxiety, he may be attempting to help Leslie feel less alone. But by identifying with Leslie, Adam pulls the attention away from her and brings it to himself. What if the counselor took a different approach?

Adam: You're afraid that your anxiety might keep you from pursuing your dreams. You doubt yourself.

This third response is probably the least likely to be said by a beginner to the field, but may have the biggest impact. Leslie (hopefully) feels understood, accepted, and consequently safe to say more. This type of response would likely establish a strong relationship.

Before we talk about skills and interventions that are part of what therapists and counselors do, it is helpful to begin our journey by looking at the overall process involved. In this opening chapter, we introduce you to the subject by covering the main ingredients that are part of most systems currently in use. We begin with a personal look at the magic of this profession through the experiences of the authors. As we will mention consistently, it is important to see the larger landscape that is involved in helping people, even when you are focused on the individual skills and interventions that are part of this complex process.

READING MINDS AND OTHER SUPERPOWERS

When I [Jeffrey] was 12 years old, I spent a significant part of my life reading comic books—*Richie Rich*, *Archie*, but mostly superheroes like *Flash*, *Green Lantern*, *Batman*, and most of all, *Superboy*.

I used to pretend to *be* Superboy when I was a bit younger, launching myself off tables and couches with a towel tied around my neck as a cape. I really believed that if only I tried harder (like Peter Pan), somehow I could fly. Bruised and battered, my parents always scolding me for scuffing the dining room table during my progressively longer take-offs, I abandoned my attempts to leap tall buildings in a single bound but not my search for superpowers.

I next set my sights on x-ray vision, a skill I determined would be far more useful to an adolescent boy who longed to see what girls really looked like. My prayers were finally answered one day, and of all places, in the very comic books to which I was so devoted. There, on the back page, was an advertisement for special x-ray glasses that would permit the owner to duplicate Superboy's feat of seeing through dense objects. I may have clouded memory about this, but I swear there was even an image of a girl whose outline could be seen through transparent clothing.

Five bucks, or whatever the glasses cost at that time, was still out of reach for a kid whose only outside income was shoveling snow for neighbors (this was July). Nevertheless, I begged and borrowed the money from various relatives until I finally had enough for this magical instrument that would reveal all the secrets previously shrouded from me.

Needless to say, the glasses hardly delivered what was promised and they were far too goofy looking to even wear as sunshades. Still, I refused to give up my search for superpowers.

It wasn't until years later, during my training as a therapist, that I finally realized I was developing powers that would allow me to read minds and persuade others to do my bidding. Indeed with lots of instruction, supervision, practice, and experience, I mastered the art and science of picking up cues invisible to others. I learned powerful ways to get other people to do things they really didn't want to do. I learned some tricks of the trade as well, relatively foolproof methods for diffusing anger, confronting others nondefensively, and helping people to feel heard and understood.

When I started teaching others how to do therapy—school counselors, family therapists, psychiatrists, social workers, mental health specialists—I found a whole new realm of secret powers open to me as well. I had to develop ways to keep a group spellbound, to encourage people to take risks and reveal very private things in public settings. I learned to motivate people, as well as to help them overcome fears of failure. As I began writing textbooks for beginners in the field, I figured out how to introduce very complex ideas in ways that could be adapted to a number of practical situations and settings. Then I began doing research, interviewing other therapists and counselors to find out about their own secret powers and favorite strategies.

MY PSYCHIC POWERS

When I [Leah] was an adolescent, I struggled to search for meaning in life while coping with personal problems. I felt terribly unhappy and read texts from different religions, New Age books, self-help books, and anything that would help me understand why pain and suffering were part of life and how to alleviate that pain.

On the journey of this exploration, I stumbled on several books on psychic ability. I was drawn to this possibility, and many of the books said that *I had psychic powers*. Some books simply stated that everyone had the ability but that it was underdeveloped. Other books stated that only certain people had the ability, but since my astrological sign was/is Pisces, I should have it. I was convinced I was psychic. I bought books and started practicing. I visited psychics to understand my ability better, and they frequently told me I had "the gift." I devoted several years to developing this ability.

I imagined that with my newfound psychic ability, I would be able to see the future. I could avoid disasters in my life and in the lives of my friends and family so they and I could avoid pain. I could make decisions more easily since I would be able to see the outcomes to avoid making mistakes. I could know people's thoughts and use them to my advantage. I could understand what's beneath what people present on the surface to respond to them better. I could amaze and astound my friends and family. I would be noticed. I would be special. In retrospect, I now realize that I just wanted to be special, to feel important. Although I am still attracted to understanding the internal experience of others, I certainly don't want to read minds . . . I don't want to know if someone thinks I dress funny or sound stupid or know anything negative without asking first, and I don't want the responsibility of seeing the future . . . too much responsibility!

I never developed my psychic abilities in the way that I had hoped, although at times I convinced myself I had a gift. However, what is most remarkable to me now is that after years of working on the skills required to become a good therapist, and working on my own issues, I have developed some abilities that amaze my friends and family; I appear to be psychic to them. First, I learned to allow myself to get back in touch with my own feelings; I had become very disconnected from myself as a way to cope with early emotional struggles. This helped me to become more empathic with others. I have learned to get my thoughts and my issues out of the way (well, almost out of the way) to see the other person's point of view as much as possible, whereas in the past, I would put myself in the other person's shoes and reflect what I would feel. I have learned how to listen, how to really listen beneath what is being said: the content, the feelings, and the process of how it's all conveyed. I've learned to pay attention to the smallest details in how a person communicates: the body language, the nuances in verbal language, and the voice inflections. I have become more culturally aware, and as a result, even more able to empathize with others. Most important, I have learned to reflect what I see and hear from the other person in a way that seems psychic. All of these skills have helped me to be a better friend, a better teacher, and a better person in all my relationships. I have learned a way to connect with others that is natural to me now. These skills have changed me and saturated every aspect of my life. Now, I finally feel special.

None of the skills taught in the first clinical course were natural to me, although some skills may be natural to some of you. As I said, I was emotionally stiff and disconnected. I knew that I wanted to help people, and I thought that therapy was about hearing the problem and then giving advice to fix the problem. I was well practiced and thought I was good at that. Was I wrong! Therapy is about building relationships, which is best done by really listening and being there for the client in an accepting way.

I had to learn all the skills slowly, with lots and lots of practice. In addition to my university training, I participated in an external training group. I also chose the hardest supervisors during my field experiences and internships to develop as much as possible. I would practice my skills with friends, family, teachers, co-workers, grocery-store clerks, the person next to me in the airplane, with any and all human contact. And now, here I am still developing skills, but they are strong enough to wow my friends, my family members, my students, and even total strangers (if I feel inclined to impress them).

So now I'm writing what I've read earlier. You, too, can become psychic. You can predict the future when it comes to some human behavior, but no, you won't be able to read the future to draw the best lottery numbers. However, with an open mind, a strong conviction, commitment, and tons of practice, you will appear to read minds. Amaze your friends and family. Tell them what's on their mind. You'll be surprised by how much you can know.

SECRETS REVEALED

Client: I'm so overwhelmed right now. My parents tell me that I should become a school teacher because they don't believe I'm smart enough to be a therapist or get a master's degree in this field or any other. I feel so much pressure to do well in my master's program to prove them wrong. I know I'm smart. I always made good grades in school. I work full-time while going to school. I'm in a management position in my job. I've never failed at anything, and in fact, have always done better than most. I'm just overwhelmed managing school and work, that's all.

Therapist: A part of you feels confident in yourself, and at the same time, another part of you is afraid that your parents might be right. That voice in your head tells you that you are inadequate, that you're not good enough.

Client: (with tears forming in her eyes) How'd you do that?

Therapist: Do what?

Client: You know. That thing . . .

Her voice trailed off at the end, as if she couldn't quite capture what she was really trying to ask. This was a woman who was used to being in control. It bothered her already that she had been forced to ask for help about a personal matter, but it was even more frustrating to her that she couldn't figure out what therapy was all about and how it worked. It was as if she was trying to penetrate the smoke and mirrors of an elaborate hoax, or at least a magic show.

"Nothing up my sleeves," the therapist teased her, showing her forearms. She felt very much like the Wizard of Oz who was about to step from behind the curtain of the control room. The therapist didn't like to play games or hide what she was doing with clients. She wanted them to understand *exactly* what they were doing together so that if a time came in the future when clients needed help again, rather than running back to someone like her, they could apply what they'd already learned.

We don't mean to imply that magic and deception don't play important parts in counseling and therapy, because they assuredly do. It is a curious phenomenon that almost nobody pays much attention to us when we are not working under a cloak of expertise. In order to have some degree of influence, it is often necessary to function in a particular setting and context. You may have noticed, for example, that the offices of professional therapists and counselors are designed specifically to display symbols of power—diplomas on the wall and impressive books on the shelves.

Therapists and counselors happen to arrange things in such a way that they increase their sense of power and status in the eyes of their clients. We appear to be magicians and wizards because we seem to *know things* that are beyond mortal beings. We not only can read people's minds, but we can predict the future and get people to reveal things that they would prefer to keep to themselves. We usually know just the right pressure to apply when someone proves reluctant, and when to back off when such efforts are fruitless. We have creative solutions to problems, many of which would never occur to others. We listen extremely well and hear nuances that are beyond awareness. We are able to persuade people to do difficult, risky things they prefer to avoid. We can often confront them with sensitivity and diplomacy so they don't take offense. And when we mess up or make mistakes, we are highly skilled at recovery.

So, when the therapist in the beginning of this section faced her client's persistent inquiries about how she managed to get through to her in a way that nobody else had before, the therapist wanted her to understand the process, but not to the point where it lost the potency. Magic works best when some illusions are maintained.

Of course, counseling and therapy are firmly lodged in science. Almost all of our theories, and the skills that you will learn or are learning, have been developed as a result of empirically based studies that were designed to test their effectiveness and usefulness under various conditions and circumstances. Good therapists do not fly by the seat of their pants, or operate by intuition alone. Every intervention you choose, and every skill you employ, should be supported by a clear rationale that is grounded in the most solid research data available. You will continually consult the literature to determine whether your current practices are consistent with the latest research. And you will conduct your own studies to measure the impact of what you do. So, although there is an element to what we do that might *appear* magical, there is a much larger component that is supported by scientific principles.

Like most professionals, therapists and counselors consider themselves part of an elite guild. We have our secret handshakes, our special language, and our unique rituals. We have our own culture just as any ethnic or religious group. The skills we learn to use in therapy become a part of who we are, a part of our everyday lives and interactions. We are attuned to subtleties in choice of words, the tonality of the voice, and body language in a way that seems invisible to the untrained eye. These skills give clients the impression that we *know things*, that we have *The Answer*, and that we have access to *A Cure*. Instead, we are trained in helping clients find their internal therapist to give themselves advice and trust their intuition. While the perceived power from our credentials on the wall might initially give us power, it's our ability to attune to others that ultimately inspires trust and confidence.

FOR REFLECTION

Either in your journal, or talking to classmates, discuss the extent to which you believe the impact of counseling is mediated by what is currently known through scientific inquiry versus what appears to be magical because the factors are not thoroughly known and understood. As an example that might guide your exploration, consider a time recently in which you experienced some sort of personal change. Try to account for all the reasons and influences that may have contributed to that transformation. Now, consider your level of confidence in those explanations: How certain are you that the changes you experienced did, in fact, result from those causes and not from other things that may be beyond your awareness and understanding?

HOW THERAPISTS ENHANCE THEIR POWERS

I [Jeffrey] have spent some time doing research with witch doctors in the Amazon region of northern Peru, with indigenous healers in the Kalahari Desert of Namibia, with shamans in rural villages of Nepal and in several other regions of Asia. I have been interested in making sense of how it was possible that healers and therapists in so many different parts of the world seemed to operate in such different ways. We're sure you have already heard many of the endless debates among members of our profession about the best way to help people. Some practitioners insist that you must make sense of the past, while others look to the future. There are therapists who work only with thinking patterns, or repressed feelings, or observable behaviors. There are those who think therapy should take a long time and others who see it as a very brief encounter. There are therapists who prefer to work with individuals, or in groups, or with whole families. There are experts who have a style that is confrontational, and others who are nurturing. Some see their role as a teacher, or a coach, or a consultant, a surrogate parent, or a provocateur. The really amazing thing is that there isn't a lot of evidence to support the effectiveness of one of the hundreds of therapeutic approaches over others; they all seem to work pretty well, depending on the situation. Needless to say, we've always found this a bit peculiar. It also makes learning how to do this complex craft extremely challenging when we can't agree on the best way to do it.

So I (Jeffrey) was off in the jungles or deserts observing and interviewing healers to identify some of the strategies that I might recognize in my own work. It occurred to me that in spite of their claims otherwise, maybe all good therapists do essentially the same things. Regardless of what they call themselves, and where they work, there are some universal ingredients that operate in all therapeutic approaches, most of which involve quality helping relationships that meet clients' expectations and particular needs (see Kottler, 1993; Norcross & Goldfried, 2005; Prochaska & Norcross, 2014).

I noticed immediately that witch doctors in the Amazon did not have framed diplomas on their walls (they didn't actually have any walls because they worked on mountaintops), but they did display a stuffed condor, the greatest symbol of power in their culture. On the surface, it appeared as if they were practicing a very different sort of helping than I was familiar with. They led chants and dancing and prescribed the most awful-tasting hallucinogenic cactus pulp that was blown up one's nose through a long tube. They waved wands and old skulls over a person's body, repeating incantations. They kept their clients up all night until they finally agreed they were cured of their maladies.

We might subscribe to a different theory of what causes emotional problems, and might have different methods for working our therapeutic magic, but there are indeed some similarities between what healers do all over the world (Kottler, Carlson, & Keeney, 2004; Pesek, Helton & Nair, 2006). First of all, we all capitalize on a person's expectations by instilling a sense of hope and increasing our power in their eyes. If you act like you know what you're doing, if you believe in your powers to help others, and if you can convince them to believe in you as well, then almost anything you say may be perceived as useful (Sprenkle & Blow, 2004).

POWER AND INFLUENCE

We don't wish to reveal all our secrets—at least right away—but here are just a few of the ways that therapists and counselors enhance their power in the eyes of their clients so as to maximize their influence.

It is one of the most annoying qualities of therapists that we so rarely give direct answers to advice-seeking questions. There are a few possible reasons for this. One is that we may not want to quickly reveal that we feel as lost as the client, especially when we have just met him or her. Doing so could decrease the client's hope. Another reason is that we simply don't have an answer or there may not be an answer.

Client: I've been dating this guy for about two years, but we don't seem to be going anywhere. He says he doesn't believe in marriage, but I do! He wants kids, but without marriage. In this state, I won't have any rights if he leaves me without having been married. I don't know what to do. I love him, he's a good person, and I've invested so much time with him. Maybe I should just get over being old-fashioned. I don't know; it's not how I was raised. Should I leave him?

The therapist's first thought is: "How the heck should I know what you should do? I barely know what's best for me most of the time. I agonize for 10 minutes before I can finally decide between the chef's salad and chicken stir-fry. And I'm supposed to know what you should do with *your* life?"

Third, even if the therapist did know what the client's best course of action should be, it is unlikely that the client would listen, much less act on what was suggested. Our most recurrent fantasy in sessions is imagining ourselves telling clients exactly how they should straighten out their lives—change their wardrobe, lose the glasses, quit their jobs, get rid of that loser of a boyfriend, show better posture, stop raising their voice at the ends of their sentences. People want advice but they rarely take it. Sometimes they don't want to be responsible for making a horrible mistake. At other times, they feel stuck and see only negative consequences to each of their choices. Many times, they are just looking for you to tell them what they've already decided to do. It has gotten to the point that the only time therapists give people advice these days is when they want them to do the exact opposite (this clever strategy is called a *paradoxical intervention*).

Exercise in Advice Giving

With a partner, take turns telling one another about a personal problem or concern that you are currently struggling with in your life. After the person has shared, respond by telling him or her everything that you think he or she should do to fix it. Then reverse roles.

We hope that what you learned from this exercise is that advice that is well intended still doesn't work very well. Even if people do hear what you are saying, they will rarely act on what you've told them to do. And if they do follow your advice, they may end up blaming you if things go wrong, or, worse yet, coming back to you every time in the future when they feel stuck.

So, ask a therapist or counselor a direct question about what you should do, and you'll most likely get a response like the following:

- *"That's a very good question. What do you think?"* Doing therapy is often like Ping-Pong. Keep the ball in the other person's court.
- *"You aren't sure what to do so you're hoping I will decide for you."* This is called a reflection, but is often used as deflection.
- *"Going back to what you were saying earlier . . ."* Changing the subject often works.
- *"What you are searching for has always been within your grasp."* Going mystical is a great way to put the focus back on the other person.
- *"When you leave here today you will find yourself, almost against your will, coming back to some things that were said here that will begin to make more sense, or less sense, than they do now."* We love this one because it makes predictions about the future that, one way or the other, will be confirmed.
- *"A part of you wants to do the one option, but another part of you wants to go the other direction."* This validates their struggle and allows them to give voice to both options.

FOR REFLECTION

Think of a time when you were struggling with a decision, perhaps with a job or to start or end a relationship. As you spoke with your friends and family, did they offer you plenty of advice? Was the advice contradictory? Was it helpful? And think of the many times you followed the advice of others. What has been your experience? Here is some profound advice: "Take my advice, I won't be using it."

We know this sounds cynical, and we don't wish to reduce the important work that therapists do to a bunch of tricks and gimmicks. Most of all, therapy is about a relationship with a person that forms the core for the other skills that you use. Within the context of that trusting alliance, the skilled expert is able to help people to experiment with new behaviors, take constructive risks, learn about new ideas, make sense of the past, and plan effectively for the future. More important, a well-built therapeutic relationship allows clients to explore places within themselves that are too scary because of overwhelming, withheld emotions. It allows them to expose their most vulnerable feelings of inadequacy, as well as to share beliefs that seem taboo or socially unacceptable. This process does *not* take place when the therapist plays games with people; quite the opposite, actually. The therapist goes to great lengths to make him- or herself as transparent, authentic, honorable, and dependable as possible. Ultimately, what I, Jeffrey, learned from my own research with witch doctors and other healers around the world is this: *It is not so much what therapists do that matters as much as who they are.* In other words, personal characteristics are just as critical as their clinical skills. We help people not only through our skills and interventions but also through the sheer power of our personalities, which builds a relationship with the client: the foundation to therapy.

Under ideal circumstances, therapists and counselors are able to model for their clients the same degree of personal effectiveness that is being taught and nurtured in the sessions. This is the real magic of therapy: that two (or more) people can spend time together talking about life difficulties, and within a relatively short period of time, perhaps just a few conversations, the pain and discomfort go away. Sometimes forever.

It isn't magic that heals people, but it is important that clients have strong beliefs in the power of those who help them. This is the first and most important principle to keep in mind in any helping relationship: Unless you can convince others that you know what you are doing, and that you are very good at what you do, your efforts are not likely going to be of much use. Of course, before that can happen, you must first believe in yourself (or at least be able to fake it in your first year or two working with clients).

Exercise in Personal Qualities

Get together with a partner or in small groups and discuss what you consider the most powerful aspects of your personality. This is no time for modesty; you must increase your awareness and understanding of how you impact and influence others.

Each person takes turns identifying the prominent features of his or her personality that have been reported to be inspirational to others. Leah, for instance, has been told that she seems to be open, nonjudgmental, and intelligent. Jeffrey uses his sense of humor and playful spirit.

After everyone has shared what they observe about themselves, then give each person feedback on other qualities that you have observed or sense.

YOU GOTTA BE DESPERATE

Client: The reason I'm here today is to get help holding down a job. My parents say that if I can't keep the next job for at least six months, they'll kick me out of the house. I think I've just had a lot of bad luck. I keep getting jerks for bosses. They're always trying to control me and tell me what to do. They won't get off my back and treat me like a child just like my parents do. It's really not my fault. I was thinking maybe you could help me prove to my next boss and my parents that I'm not a kid any more; I'm twenty-three, after all!

If you wonder how it is possible that people manage to make such stunning changes in counseling and therapy, it all starts with candidates who are very motivated. By the time anyone actually seeks the services of a professional it is likely that many other options have already been tried. Nobody sees a therapist as a first choice, but usually as a last resort after everything else has failed. The person has likely tried sweeping the problems under the rug and pretending they don't exist. He has tried blaming others for the difficulties. He has consulted with friends and family, hoping for attention and sympathy. He has already exhausted every alternative within grasp. With nowhere else to turn, or perhaps being pressured to seek help by others, the client limps into the office feeling desperate.

Exercise in Change

Get into groups of three or four and talk about a time when you made a major change in your life or survived a significant transition that led to some dramatic transformation. Discuss what led up to the change and the amount of courage it took to risk making the change.

Kayleigh: Self-Medication and the Value of Readiness

When I first started therapy, I was going through a break up. I was incredibly depressed, and I didn't believe that I would ever find happiness. Suicide was seeming like a viable option, and I didn't want to do that, so I went to therapy. The only break I could get from the pain was through drinking. In fact, when I had mentioned this to my therapist after the third visit, she told me that it might be better to self-medicate, at least temporarily, if the alternative was killing myself. I was shocked by her giving me permission to continue drinking because everyone else said this was a very bad idea.

I felt like I could now talk to somebody about my pain, and I didn't have to rely on numbing my feelings through alcohol. And I didn't have to hide it. I could be open.

Although I in no way condone alcoholism or binge drinking, I think that self-medication is helpful because it puts you in control (as long as you don't overdo it). I will always remember that session as a pivotal moment in my recovery because my therapist didn't judge me, she helped me and made me feel like I was doing okay. And being okay was major progress.

I realize that my situation is very different from most others in which abstinence is the best option. I'm in no way suggesting that anyone should continue drinking to solve their problems. But I'm just aware that my therapist's patience and (temporary) acceptance of my situation was important before I was ready to make needed changes.

Used with permission of Kayleigh Soto.

Generally speaking, people don't change because they *want* to, but because they *have* to. Nobody walks out of a relationship, quits a job, or relocates to another city when they are feeling quite satisfied with the way things are going. People initiate changes when they are at the end of the line. It all starts with discomfort. Desperation is even better. Unless you are unsettled by the status quo there is little motivation to change anything. When present strategies aren't working, when things start to fall apart, when there seems no other alternative, that's when people seek change. And it ain't pretty.

Change means being awkward and uncertain. It means facing the unknown. It feels like taking a giant leap into thin air, without a net. That is an important secret about the way that change in general, and therapy in particular, tends to work. Most people will get better anyway, over time; a professional guide just makes it happen more quickly. It is the same thing with a therapist. It is not as if most of our clients actually need us in order to get to where they want to go; it's just that we help them to get there a lot quicker, with important lessons learned along the way.

IT'S ALL ABOUT LEVERAGE

When someone is experiencing some personal distress—let's say a moderate case of depression, anxiety, confusion, or loneliness—there is a strong drive to reduce this discomfort. Drugs or alcohol might work for a little while, but they have side effects. People "medicate" themselves with other things as well—excessive sleep, exercise, food, shopping, or work—anyplace to hide from the pain. All of these strategies work pretty well, although they all have significant disadvantages in that they tend to create other problems that are also annoying.

The favored preference, by far, is for the person to deal with the situation so that no big changes are needed. It may be uncomfortable to remain stuck in an empty or unsatisfying relationship, but things could also be far worse.

Once a client realizes that perceived options are limited and favorite coping strategies don't work, he or she may be ready to *consider* significant change. Keep in mind, however, that the client may not be nearly to the point of actually *doing* anything differently, but at least that possibility will be taken under advisement.

When the client realizes limitations, we have "leverage." It is what gives us some starting momentum to get things moving in a constructive direction. After all, it is really the client who does most of the work in therapy, and also it is the client's motivation, commitment, and resources that best predict a positive outcome (Lambert, 2013; Norcross, 2011).

So a very important thing to understand about change is that it is most likely to occur—and last—when people don't see any other choice and when they have hit their own rock bottom in a particular situation. It's easy to walk out of a job or relationship if you can't stand another second of the predicament without imploding. And it is much easier to help someone who feels lost and is willing to acknowledge this state of helplessness.

A FEW THINGS TO REMEMBER

It is difficult to influence anyone in a therapeutic relationship unless the following conditions are in effect:

1. The person is not satisfied with the current state of affairs.

2. The person realizes that he or she can't cope with things on his or her own.

3. You are recognized as someone who can provide needed assistance.

4. You believe strongly in your own power to help.

5. You can convince the other person of your usefulness and instill hope.

6. You are able to deliver on what you promise.

AMATEURS VERSUS PROFESSIONALS

You already have the broad strokes, but there are a few more details to fill in. If the therapy process were as simple as we are making it sound, almost anyone could do it with little training or practice. You would hardly need a whole course on skills, nor would you require a textbook on the subject. In fact, almost everyone *does* act as a therapist at times. Professionals hardly have a monopoly on helping relationships. Taxi drivers, bartenders, hair stylists, family, and friends are also known to engage in helpful conversations with people during times of difficulty. The main difference between amateurs and professionals, though, is that we are far more likely to have a positive impact in the briefest period of time. Also significant is that everything we say and do is intended to be in the client's best interests rather than to meet any of our own needs.

One reason for professional effectiveness is the amount of power and influence we wield in sessions. While these are important tools for helping people, they are also a huge responsibility. Clients take what you say very seriously and assume that you are an expert. This means that you must be careful when providing feedback, no matter how casually it is offered. A boundary exists between you and your clients that must be acknowledged. This is in distinct contrast to the type of boundaries you have with friends and family members where it is never quite clear what personal agendas are operating during helping efforts. But it's also important to note that because you are embarking on a career as a therapist, your advice might hold more weight with friends and family members. So you will have to be cognizant of the responsibility you hold in all of your relationships where others may give you power because of your profession.

Let's take as one example a teenager who asks a friend and a sibling what he should do about his conflicted relationship with his girlfriend. The friend offers the advice that perhaps things have run their course and it is best to end things before they get worse. What is not acknowledged by the friend are his own feelings of jealousy and perceived threat from this relationship. The boy's sister, on the other hand, offers advice that is exactly the opposite—she thinks he should work things out. Also unstated is the sister's strong preference that her brother's relationship continues so she can profit from ongoing affiliation with the girlfriend who is one of the most popular girls in the school. While personal agendas are not always so clearly defined, the examples illustrate the dangers of trying to get therapeutic help from friends and family who are also considering their own needs.

In spite of best intentions, and even high motivation, even well-intentioned people without proper training and supervision can do more harm than good. Contrary to popular belief, helping people is not at all natural. It takes a *lot* of preparation and hard work to put your own needs aside, to focus completely on this other person, and do so with caring and empathy. You must be able to concentrate so intently on what the person is saying and doing that you can fluently decode the underlying meanings that are being expressed. At the same time, you are reviewing a host of options from which to select the best intervention. Students who are learning these skills are often surprised at how tired they feel when they are learning to attend so fully to a client.

For instance, someone says, "I just don't know what I want to do next. It's like . . . I don't know . . . No matter what I do, it's not going to work out."

The initial reaction to this statement is to feel flooded with options. It is not that there is a shortage of possibilities; it is that there are too many. Here are a few possibilities:

1. You could reflect the content of what you hear to let him know that he was heard and also give yourself more time to think of what you might do or say next: *"No matter what choice you make, you still think you're going to end up back in the same place: stuck."* This isn't elegant but, at short notice, it does encourage further elaboration.

2. You could reflect the underlying feelings you hear: *"You are feeling so discouraged and hopeless that you wonder if it's even worth trying. You have faced so many disappointments in the past."* This might seem similar to the previous response but it actually takes the person deeper, exploring some of his or her frightening feelings.

3. You could help this client to examine some thinking patterns that are getting in the way. *"First of all, you are telling yourself that you should know what to do and that you are somehow inadequate because you don't know. Secondly, you are predicting the future based on very limited information."* Now you would be helping the client to look at his or her illogical and self-defeating thoughts that are sabotaging efforts to move forward.

4. You could try a mild confrontation. *"You say that no matter what you do, it's not going to work out, but we've both already seen a lot of progress you've made by taking similar risks in the past. It seems like you are reluctant to risk making a mistake, so you'd really rather prefer to stay stuck so you have an excuse for remaining miserable."* This encourages the person to look at the excuses he or she is giving for avoiding action.

5. For something completely different, you could use self-disclosure. *"I remember a time in my life when I was feeling much the same way that you are. I wanted to give up. I wasn't happy but at least it was familiar. I wondered if that might be better than risking something new that could turn out far*

worse. Then I decided that I couldn't possibly be worse off, took the risk, and then never looked back." This shows the client that he or she is not alone and also gives the client hope that good things are waiting for those who take constructive action.

We could go on at great length and list no less than two dozen other responses that might be used in this situation, but the point is that skilled therapists are trained to sort through the various strategies and select the ones most likely to be helpful. Although this takes years of education, training, practice, and supervision, the basics can be learned and applied rather quickly—even in a single course.

A FEW MISSING INGREDIENTS

Before we get into the actual method of using therapeutic skills, it is important to understand that there are several other ingredients involved in the process. These same elements would be evident not only in therapy relationships, but in any helping encounter.

Altered States of Consciousness

"You're getting very sleepy. It's late. You've had a long day. You've been reading for a long time, and your eyelids are getting heavy. Wait! No! You're feeling very AWAKE and FOCUSED. You're able to absorb this reading without distraction. You're feeling CLEAR and MOTIVATED to continue reading. It's like you just had a cup of coffee!"

If you are thinking about a drug or hypnotic state, you're not far off. There are particular times and situations when people are more open to being influenced than others. What therapists attempt to do is create an environment that is maximally conducive to people hearing and acting on what therapists say. In order to do this, therapists use the setting as a stage and their voice as an instrument of influence to induce a trance-like state with clients. They speak in such a way as to command attention and suggest things in a way that they are more likely to be acted on. Therapists can also resonate with a client and act as a mirror so that clients can see themselves more clearly through the therapist. In that sense, therapy itself is a trance state wherein clients are encouraged to relax, let themselves go, trust in the expert, and then do what they are directed to do.

Some therapists use their voice to calm clients down or get them emotionally activated. The very choice of language is based on what is most likely to match what given individuals will respond best to. The whole object of the encounter is to establish confidence, build suspense, enhance emotional expression, facilitate awareness, provoke insight, motivate action, and then sustain interest. As you will see later, these same stages can be employed in any relationship that is designed to influence another person.

Therapists also enter a kind of altered state of consciousness in which they are hypersensitive and aware of what is happening both before them and within themselves. Once enough confidence is built from hundreds of hours of client contact, the therapist is open to whatever emerges from the client. Agendas are easily released, and the therapist resonates with the client in order to provide empathy and then to shift the client in other directions. Research using EEGs (electroencephalographs) indicates that the brainwaves of the therapist and client become synchronized with one another, which further demonstrates the idea that they are "on the same wavelength" (Siegal & Hartzell, 2004). So, in effect, both therapist and client can go into an altered state of consciousness to facilitate the therapeutic process.

Placebo Effects

"Take two aspirins and call me in the morning. You'll feel much better."

Long ago in medical studies (Beecher, 1955; Caspi & Bootzin, 2002), it was established that the client's own expectations for a cure are often more important than the actual treatment. Give someone a pill, especially a tiny green specimen, and tell the person that it is powerful medicine and, sure enough, the person will likely feel better in the morning. Even if the pill contained nothing but sugar, food coloring, and binding agents, it may still have solid effects if the person believes it is useful. Things work even better if the doctor prescribing the pill believes in his or her own heart that the medicine is just what is needed, and says with utter confidence to the patient, "Take this pill and you will definitely feel better in the morning."

If placebo effects (derived from the Latin, meaning "I shall please") work with medications, they can be equally effective in helping relationships (Bjornsson, 2011). If the therapist communicates confidently that what he or she is about to do is going to be helpful, *and the client believes the therapist,* then the intervention will more likely work quite well. This has extremely important implications for other relationships as well. In any situation in which you want to have an impact on others, it is crucial that you believe in what you're doing. Not only that, you must be able to communicate this confidence effectively.

Compare, for instance, how differently you might respond to the following two introductions to an idea:

1. *"Well, uh, I'm not sure if this will work or not, but let's give it a try. I think it might help, but then again, maybe not."* This kind of covering or self-protection against possible failure also reduces the likelihood that the intervention will prove useful.

2. *"I am about to do something that works very well in these situations. I am certain you will see a significant difference within a short period of time."* Obviously, you wouldn't want to say something like this unless you could deliver on what you promised, but in this confident language the situation is set up in a way to play off others' positive expectations.

So often, results are in the eyes of the beholders. The same outcome can be judged a success or failure depending on others' expectations. If a helper tells you that you are probably feeling better already, and this is said with assurance and convincing evidence, then you will probably start to feel better. This is the case even if the helper didn't do anything other than tell you that you have improved.

On the other hand, you must be careful to whom you tell this. A client may think, "I don't believe I'm doing that well since I cry every day, but if the therapist says I am better, then I must be." If this client has poor boundaries, doesn't trust her own experiences, and surrenders all her power to the therapist, she may experience a state of incongruence and confusion, which can lead to greater dependency on others. Consequently, the client's own power can be reduced. The purpose of therapy is to work ourselves out of a job by helping clients to be their own therapists.

Healing Relationships

"I see you, and you don't seem to like yourself. I hear you, and you want to change. I acknowledge your fears, that change is scary. I understand you and value you, even if you don't always value yourself."

One of the mistakes made most often by beginning therapists is that they think that their job is to learn and then apply the most elaborate, powerful interventions possible in order to provoke changes. In fact, therapeutic techniques and strategies are less important than the quality of the relationship established with the person you are trying to help or influence. If you can establish a close, trusting, accepting connection with another, a relationship in which the person feels valued, respected, and honored, almost anything you try is going to be useful.

Even more important, once you have a solid relationship, you have a lot of flexibility to make mistakes, experiment with new strategies, and take the time you need to discover the best solution. We don't always get things right the first, or even the second time. But that hardly matters if the person we are helping gives us the benefit of the doubt and allows us to work together as a team until we come up with the right combination to set things on the right path. If the therapist gets it right every time, clients might expect that type of mind-reading from everyone in their lives.

If you think about the most successful helping encounters you ever had, whether they were with a counselor, teacher, therapist, coach, family member, or friend, it is highly probable that what the person did or said was less critical than the quality of the relationship you felt with that person. If you felt heard and understood, if you felt safe enough to try new things, if you could risk talking about difficult subjects, if you were pushed and motivated, then you profited from the encounter. Furthermore, the helper could have tried an assortment of different strategies, any one of which may have worked.

This principle is certainly confirmed by your own experiences. In a public forum, you may agonize about the best way to express yourself, rehearse the absolutely perfect lines, but what makes all the difference is the relationship you develop with your audience. The same holds true for any situation in which you hope to have an impact on others. If you can build solid connections with others, get them to trust you and feel confidence in your abilities, what you actually do is a whole lot less important than you think. As stated before, this is one foundation of therapy and one area in which almost all theorists and therapists agree.

Exercise in the Power of Relationships

With partners, or in small groups, talk about the most healing relationships that you have ever experienced. These may be people who have made lasting changes in your life, shifted the course of your life, or helped you through something difficult.

Cathartic Processes

"Just let it out. Don't hold back. Release everything."

Sigmund Freud noted a century ago that people often feel a lot better if they are allowed to tell their story to someone who listens well and allows them to dump all their pent-up thoughts and feelings. This sounds rather simple, but it is actually quite rare that anyone allows you to talk without interrupting, giving advice, shifting the conversation onto themselves, or doing other things at the same time. Other therapists since that time believed that catharsis was so powerful, especially if it involved strong emotions, that this was quite enough to produce a cure. Sometimes it can be, especially with children. However, as it turns out, this is not strictly the case. It may be helpful to be able to talk about your troubles, but it is often not enough without being helped to take things to the next level. This can involve a variety of subsequent steps that will be discussed later, many of which help clients to convert their new awarenesses and insights into constructive action.

The lesson at this point is that if you do nothing else, or perhaps even don't know what to do or say, it is a great first step to encourage the person to simply express him- or herself more fully. This often produces immediate relief and works wonders in establishing the kind of relationship that is so critical to anything else you do. Who doesn't like to be the center of attention and have the safety to say anything without having to filter it while being accepted and heard?

Exercise in Catharsis

Pair up with a partner and each take a turn "confessing" a story that has been bothering you for some time. This should be some incident or event in your life, however significant, that you rarely talk about to anyone else.

The partner in the helping role should refrain from giving advice, implementing any interventions, and should simply (and powerfully) listen with focused, empathic attention. After hearing the story, the partner might respond by thanking the person for trusting sufficiently to share the narrative.

Reverse roles and repeat the process. After you are both done, debrief one another in your dyad or in larger groups.

Consciousness-Raising

"Based upon what you're telling me, you seem to have only two choices: either you continue taking on all the responsibility for your family or you stop taking any at all. You don't seem to see there might be other ways of being with your family."

Listening is great, but not nearly enough for situations when something more is required. All therapies, in whatever form they take, attempt to produce some sort of new understanding. They seek to help people look at the world, their own lives, or themselves in a different way.

Often people who are experiencing difficulties feel stuck because of a perceived lack of choices. They don't see a way out of their predicament, at least a path that is within easy walking distance. Of course, this is not necessarily the case. There may be a hundred alternatives available, not just those that appear possible at the time.

Because there are hundreds of distinctly different kinds of therapies, each one approaches this consciousness-raising in a slightly (or radically) different way. As you are already aware, psychoanalysts approach this task by helping people to understand their past and how it continues to exert influence in current patterns of behavior. So-called cognitive approaches help people to realize the distorted ways they think inside their heads, substituting other, more useful internal strategies. The Gestalt approach believes that the client does not have sufficient awareness or experiencing, so the therapist helps to enhance that awareness. Feminist approaches examine the ways that clients feel marginalized and powerless in their worlds. Some approaches look at the advantages people enjoy for remaining stuck or at the larger implications of their behavior on their whole family "system." Regardless of the form this insight takes, the goal is to increase people's understanding of their situation in a way that leads to new solutions.

Using Intuition

"Listen to that small, inner voice that tells you that you need to slow down or you're going to get a ticket, or that tells you you're working too hard and you'll make yourself sick. There is some part of you that has wisdom that can help your life flow more smoothly."

You have heard of intuition, and experts define what intuition is differently, depending on whom you ask. However, there is something that happens at times where you have something in the back of your head nagging you, you want to say something or ask something, and you're not sure where that's coming from. That's your intuition, and it can be extremely beneficial when you use it wisely. Whether intuition is your brain's ability to assimilate a vast amount of information and deduce new information from those data, or whether you have some ability that science has yet to explain, intuition is something that is helpful in therapy. Every once in a while, you might hear a therapist say, *"I'm not sure why I want to say this or where it's coming from, but . . . ,"* and sometimes whatever that is, it is right on the nose. Intuition helps you to see things or express things that might not be explained through any other means. So, rather than trying to determine the source of it, just appreciate it and use it. That inner voice can sometimes stimulate a powerful process and response in your client.

Reinforcement

"A penny for your thoughts."

All therapies encourage behaviors that therapists think are good for people and extinguish behaviors that are deemed self-defeating or counterproductive. There might be different goals, but the object is to support progress in desired directions.

Behaviorists taught us that there are strategies that can be used to increase or decrease outcomes. The hard part is figuring out what is reinforcing for one particular person, because it may not be all that rewarding for others. This may seem pretty obvious, but you would be amazed how often people fail to do this. Someone does something that we don't like. We respond in a particular way, designed to stop further repetitions of this annoying behavior. Rather than the response having the desired effect, the behavior persists, or even increases. Although it might be apparent that the response so far is not working, and perhaps is even inadvertently rewarding the obnoxious behavior, the individual still fails to alter the strategy by trying something else. As you no doubt have noticed in your own life, some people actually enjoy the attention they get from acting in annoying ways. In order to alter this pattern, you must come up with some other way to extinguish the behavior.

Reinforcement, therefore, can be as obvious as the therapist providing a supportive statement such as, "I'm pleased you were able to take that risk." Sometimes the client needs that external support. At the same time, using this type of reinforcement must be done carefully. We don't want to make clients depend on our approval. If they did, they might constantly seek it out, and if they made a mistake, they might feel shame rather than the acceptance we try to provide.

Perhaps a stronger reinforcing comment would be to say, "You feel really proud of yourself for taking that risk." This reflects the client's internal sense of accomplishment, building self-esteem. In this way, clients are able to become more aware of their inner experiences and seek an internal reinforcement once therapy has terminated.

Another type of reinforcement can be as subtle as, "You feel really sad." which not only demonstrates empathy to the client (if it's accurate), but also implies that feeling sad is okay if said in a gentle way. This encourages the client to go deeper into that sadness.

There are many ways to reinforce a behavior or direction. Everything that the therapist says directs the session. Realizing this, therapists-in-training are able to understand the power of what they say and, consequently, create a desired out-come. Used in this way, reinforcement is a constant in therapy.

Task Facilitation

"Just do it."

It isn't enough to talk about things. You've also got to *do* some things. All good therapies structure ways for people to follow up on conversations by applying what they learned and realized to their lives. In fact, such therapeutic tasks are part of the procedures favored by most healers around the world from witch doctors and shamans to medicine men and sages (Keeney, 1996; Kottler et al., 2004).

You've probably heard enough discouraging stories about people who have been in therapy their whole lives, or at least many years, without any noticeable change in their maladjusted conduct. They may have perfect insight into their unconscious motivations or understand all too well why they do such destructive, stupid things, but they still engage in those behaviors. They still drink too much, or obsess about the future, or pick losers in relationships, or feel depressed. They might perform like trained seals when they are in sessions, saying all the right things, but once they leave, nothing much changes.

The best helping encounters focus less on what people say in a conversation and more on what they do after they reenter their lives. Even if you attended a session every day, 5 days a week, that would still represent a very small percent-age of your waking time. What matters most is how you apply what you learned in the reality demands of daily life.

Talk is cheap. It's action that really matters most.

THE PERFECT COUNSELING STUDENT

Frequently, in our counseling skills classes, we have students practice their skills with each other as clients and therapists. We ask students to discuss real issues and real frustrations so that the student-therapist has an opportunity to develop better counseling skills. In addition, the student-client gets the benefit of becoming more aware of his or her own issues, which may or may not need more work with an experienced therapist. At the very least, the student-client is validated in a way that might not have happened outside of the counseling program. Doing your own work is one of the most important skills you develop as a therapist. For some stu-dents, this can be problematic.

Alex: A New Adventure

Even after 28 years as a recovering alcoholic, I am still prone to attach myself to things that feel good. As a counseling student who is taking her first class practicing therapeutic skills, I love the feeling when I see the light bulb go on for my assigned "client" (another student). There is a kind of spiritual awakening, and I can actually see visible changes, the person melting from sadness and anxiety or showing enlightenment and peace. I am totally addicted to this feeling! It helps me to let go of past discomfort, past weariness, and embrace sacrifice and long hours. Maybe this sounds naïve but it is a total truth for me as I stand at the delta, tying my shoes and readying my backpack for this new adventure.

Used with permission of Alex Smith.

The perfect student is one who is willing to be open to new ways of thinking. If you're really lucky, the professors in your program have very different points of view on how to do therapy. The more diverse your faculty is, the more opportunity you have to learn what fits best for you. The diversity can be based on theoretical orientation, on professors' personal backgrounds (religion, ethnicity, race, gender, sexual/affectual orientation, social class, ability, or other factors), or in teaching style. Being open to all of these differences allows you the variety of experience that's needed to be well rounded and developed. Your openness to new ideas, ways of thinking and being can make all the difference in the world in your development as a therapist. We are more concerned with a student who is not open to receiving supervision and feedback, even if already somewhat talented as a therapist, than with a student who knows nothing but is a sponge, hungry for knowledge and skill-development.

Being culturally sensitive is an important part of your training. You must learn to understand many ways of thinking and living in the world. You can't know them all, but by understanding yourself, you are better able to understand others. You can get many of your own assumptions out of the way. And based upon differences, you can see how there are myriad choices in how to work with clients. We'll talk more about culture in the next chapter.

Inside a Therapist's Head: Processing Skills

What's going on here? The guy seems pretty strung out, as if he is going to fall apart any moment. Look. His hands are shaking. He can't maintain eye contact for more than a fleeting moment. His complexion is wan and his lips are pressed tight. It is almost as if he is hemorrhaging inside, which I suppose he is, at least emotionally.

So, should I let him go on a little longer, finish his story, or interrupt him at this point and offer reassurance? It's not clear yet whether we are dealing with a situational response to stress or a chronic, ongoing personality characteristic. I could reflect his feelings at this point, his sense of terror and hopelessness, but I sense that this would only push him deeper into his despair. And he is already emotionally activated, too much so.

Maybe what I should do next is offer some structure. I can slow him down and we can back up and talk about goals. I bet it would help if we worked one step . . .

Wait! There are tears forming. What does that mean? His voice is devoid of any affect, yet his body is positively exploding with emotional energy that now seems to be leaking out of his eyes. Should I comment on his tears, which will only encourage him to lose even more control, or would things be better if I continue with the plan to introduce structure and incremental steps of progress? He seems like he's the type of man who isn't comfortable expressing his feelings in front of others.

As you readily see and hear from this therapist's internal dialogue, there is quite a lot going on inside a practitioner's head in the course of any interview. It might have seemed to you that therapeutic skills were mostly about what you *do*—your behavior and actions; perhaps you didn't consider the extent to which "doing" can also involve what is in your mind.

So much of what we therapists and counselors do takes place inside our heads. Unlike the work of other professionals, such as physicians, attorneys, architects, and engineers, much of our work is reflective activity.

In a sense, one of our primary jobs is to understand people and then to communicate that understanding. In order for us to be able to accomplish this task, we must have a fairly clear grasp of several things, including the following:

1. What clients are experiencing

2. A comprehensive inventory of their complaints and symptoms

3. A reasonable hypothesis about the origins of their problems

4. A diagnostic formulation that pinpoints the core issues

5. The cultural, familial, and contextual background for the client's experience

6. A treatment plan for what will be done and how it will be done

In the internal dialogue mentioned earlier, you got a sense for the kind of overwhelming pressure that is often felt by therapists, especially during first interviews. We feel tremendous pressure to figure out what the heck is going on, to reassure clients that they will be okay, and to reassure ourselves that we know what we are doing when we often feel some doubt. Unless we can quickly establish trust and a working relationship, we are not going to be able to convince the person to return.

And all throughout the time we are busy doing stuff—listening carefully, asking pointed questions, offering reassurance, reflecting feelings, summarizing content, leading, directing, guiding, following a structured agenda—our minds are racing with ideas. We are sorting out possible hypotheses to account for what we observe. We are accessing our intuition and "felt sense" about what we believe might be going on. We are sorting through complex data, linking what is observed to other things we know, and otherwise just trying to get a handle on the situation. We are so busy on the inside that it is a minor miracle that we ever choose anything to do or say on the outside. But such are the demands on a skilled therapist.

APPLICATIONS TO SELF: INCORPORATING SKILLS INTO YOUR DAILY LIFE

All of this understanding of how therapy works might be interesting, even enlightening, but what good is it unless you take what you learn and do something with it?

Take inventory of your life, including the aspects that feel most satisfying and those you sincerely would like to improve or change. There are likely some relationships that are not going as well as you would prefer, perhaps some conflicts you find disturbing. There are probably some other personal challenges and difficulties that give you trouble. Some of these arise from the daily demands of your family, leisure, and work life; others stem from unresolved issues from the past.

For those of you who have participated in therapy as clients, you may think that you're over that old issue, that you've beaten that horse until it's dead. As you develop as a therapist, however, you may find these old issues reemerge. Some issues never die; we just get better at them. So, don't think that you're not making progress if you've worked on something before and find it emerging again. Just realize you have a new facet of that topic to explore that will help you understand yourself and the nature of therapy better. For those of you who have new issues or issues yet to be worked upon, you may want to think about participating in your own therapy.

If you are serious about mastering the skills of a therapist to apply to your life, the first place to start is with yourself. You can't very well help or influence anyone else if you can't make headway with your own personal struggles. One of the reasons that self-help books and self-improvement efforts often don't last very long (just look at all the books gathering dust on your shelves) is that people take in the ideas they've read, resolve to use some of them, but then "forget" to apply them after the effects wear off. In other words, the new concepts never really became part of them.

In order to behave more effectively in your life, to act like a therapist in the sense of being a model of personal and professional effectiveness, it is necessary to personalize the concepts in such a way that they become part of you. This means that you must find ways to integrate the ideas into your daily thinking and, more important, your behavior. Daily journaling is an excellent tool to begin processing what's often in the back of your mind, hidden from your view, and sometimes a strong facilitator of your behaviors.

In this first chapter, you've read about the process of therapy, the ingredients that are often present, and how it usually works. The question now becomes: So what? What does all this mean to you? How can you use this stuff in the areas of your life that matter most to you?

If you really want these skills to stick, to remain with you for the rest of your life, you are going to have to figure out a way to practice what you learn. For one thing, this means sharing what you are learning with friends and loved ones. We are sure you realize that you can't learn this stuff from reading a book if all you intend to do is rehearse things in the privacy of your own mind. More than any other class you will ever take, the learning of therapeutic skills involves daily practice in which you apply ideas to your work and your life, as well as to your personal relationships.

You must find ways to try out what you are learning, and then get honest feedback on the results. This means recruiting others into your study efforts, describing to them what you are doing, and finding out what is most effective. If our job is to introduce you to ideas that will prove valuable, it is your responsibility to customize and personalize them in such a way that they fit best.

FOR REFLECTION

Take a moment to think about any areas in your life you need to work on. What holds you back? What is it that is difficult to change? What recurring issue keeps getting in the way of your relationships? Now think about how far you've come, and how far you have to go. Think about what you haven't changed and why. Now you understand the position of your clients.

SUMMARY

In this chapter, we have introduced you to some of the secrets and magic behind therapy. We have covered some of the reservations that clients have in coming to sessions, and the tools you will need in order to encourage them to proceed. We have introduced you to the world of being a therapist and, we hope, elicited some excitement about learning the basic skills required to be a good therapist. The next chapter introduces you to cultural sensitivity as well as ethical and legal considerations related to basic counseling skills.

FOR HOMEWORK

Pay attention to the ways in which this chapter has influenced you and the way you think about therapy. You may have been surprised that therapy isn't about giving brilliant advice. As the semester progresses, notice how the ways in which you communicate with your friends and family members change over time. You may find yourself listening with a new compassion and caring, as well as talking less. You may notice nuances in behavior that you never noticed before. You may feel less of a need to direct other people's lives. If you have not already begun a journal to chronicle the personal and professional changes that you are undergoing, now would be a good time to do so. This will allow you over time to measure and track the specific transformations that take place in your thinking, feeling, and behavior.

Skills in Action: The Troubled Wife

Therapist: What brings you here today?

Client: I came to counseling because I'm struggling with my husband. He never wants to do anything but play computer games or watch television. He complains that I nag him all the time to do work, but if I don't ask, then he doesn't do anything. We always seem to fight and never do anything else together.

Therapist: You feel stuck because you don't want to let things go, but at the same time, you don't want to be perceived as a nagging wife either. [Healing relationships]

Client: Yeah! What does he expect me to do, be his mother? I'm tired of it.

Therapist: You resent him. [Healing relationships]

Client: So, how do I get him to do things without asking? Am I wrong?

Therapist: You're angry, but mostly feel unsupported. [Alters state of consciousness by reflecting her sadness]

Client: (crying) I love him, but I just don't feel like he cares. (continues crying for several minutes)

Therapist: (silent with calming and caring presence) [Allowing catharsis; healing relationships]

Client: (still crying) I'm scared that he doesn't love me any more.

Therapist: You're afraid you're losing him. You miss him. [Intuition; altered state of consciousness; healing relationships]

Client: (crying harder now) I think he wants out. I think this is his way of trying to push me away. We don't talk anymore. We don't laugh like we used to. I don't know how to change it.

Therapist: You feel helpless. [Reinforcing her catharsis; healing relationships]

Client: (stops crying) I do. (more silence while the client is thinking, then the client looks at the therapist)

Therapist: Your anger and fear may be holding you back from being loving to him the way you want. Perhaps you could tell me what you do for him that makes you both feel good. [Intuition; healing relationships]

Client: (silent and thinking for a while) That's hard to say. You're right. I have become a nag. I'm ashamed of that.

Therapist: You feel guilty. Perhaps during this next week you could pay close attention to the loving things that you do for him and bring them in to our next session. Notice what you do, his response to it, and how it affects you. [Task facilitation; consciousness-raising; healing relationships]

Client: I'm willing to do anything.

Therapist: You're sad, but I notice you sound a little more hopeful now. [Placebo effect]

Client: I do feel better being able to share this with someone. I've been so ashamed that I haven't shared it with anyone. Thank you for helping me. I will pay attention and be ready to talk about it next week.

Therapist: I look forward to it. I feel like I can help you with this. [Reinforcement of hope; healing relationship]

REFERENCES AND RESOURCES

Beecher, Henry K. (1955). The powerful placebo. *Journal of the American Medical Association, 159*(17), 1602–1606.

Binder, P., Holgersen, H., & Nielsen, G. H. (2009). Why did I change when I went to therapy? A qualitative analysis of former patients' conceptions of successful psychotherapy. *Counselling and Psychotherapy, 9*(4), 250–256.

Bjornsson, A. S. (2011). Beyond the "Psychological Placebo": Specifying the nonspecific in psychotherapy. *Clinical Psychology: Science and Practice, 18*(2), 113–118.

Capsi, O. & Bootzin, R.R. (2002). Evaluating how placebos produce change: Logical and causal traps and understanding cognitive explanatory mechanisms. *Evaluation and the Health Professions 25*(4), 436–464.

Duncan, B. L. (2010). *On becoming a better therapist.* Washington, DC: American Psychological Association.

Duncan, B. L., Miller, S. D., & Sparks, J. A. (2004). *The heroic client.* San Francisco, CA: Jossey-Bass.

Duncan, B. L., Miller, S. D., Wampold, B. E., & Hubble, M. A. (Eds.). (2010). *The heart and soul of change: Delivering what works in therapy* (2nd ed.). Washington, DC: American Psychological Association.

Frankl, V. (1963). *Man's search for meaning.* Boston, MA: Beacon Press.

Keeney, B. (1996). *Everyday soul: Awakening the spirit in daily life.* New York, NY: Ringling Rocks.

Kottler, J. A. (1993). *On being a therapist.* San Francisco, CA: Jossey-Bass.

Kottler, J. A., & Carlson, J. (2015). *On being a master therapist: Practicing what we preach.* New York, NY: John Wiley.

Kottler, J. A., Carlson, J., & Keeney, B. (2004). *American shaman: An odyssey of global healing traditions.* New York, NY: Brunner-Routledge.

Lambert, M. J. (Ed.). (2013). *Bergin and Garfield's handbook of psychotherapy and behavior change* (6th ed.). New York, NY: John Wiley.

May, R. (1953). *Man's search for himself.* New York, NY: Dell.

Norcross, J. C. (Ed.). (2011). *Psychotherapy relationships that work* (2nd ed.). New York, NY: Oxford University Press.

Norcross, J. C., & Goldfried, M. (Eds.). (2005). *Handbook of psychotherapy integration* (2nd ed.). New York, NY: Oxford University Press.

Pesek, T., Helton, L. & Nair, M. (2006). Healing across cultures: Learning from traditions. *EcoHealth, 3*(2), 114–118.

Prochaska, J. O., & Norcross, J. C. (2014). *Systems of psychotherapy: A transtheoretical analysis* (8th ed.). Belmont, CA: Wadsworth.

Rogers, C. (1980). *A way of being.* Boston, MA: Houghton Mifflin.

Siegel, D. J. and Hartzell, M. (2004). *Parenting from the inside out: How a deeper self-understanding can help you raise children who thrive.* New York, NY: Penguin Putnam.

Sprenkle, D. H. and Blow, A. J. (2007). Common factors and our sacred models. *Journal of Marital and Family Therapy, 30*(2), 113–129.

Yalom, I. (2015). *Creatures of a day: And other tales of psychotherapy.* New York, NY: Basic Books.

Chapter 2

CLIENTS IN NEED

INDIVIDUAL, SOCIAL, AND CULTURAL FACTORS

I t often sounds like it is the therapist who does all the work and determines whether the experience is helpful or not. In fact, clients have at least as much say, if not more so, about the outcome. When clients are highly motivated, taught appropriate roles and behaviors, and helped to become actively involved in the process, it is their own self-healing efforts that are as important as anything the therapist does in sessions (Bohart, 2007; Bohart & Tallman, 2010).

You can be the best clinician in the world, with every possible intervention at your disposal, and still not make a dent in a client's situation if he or she is not on board with the negotiated program. Likewise, a therapist or counselor can be an absolute master at applying a particular skill or intervention, but if the effort is not customized to fit the client's unique needs, cultural background, personality, and situation, then the effort is likely to be less than optimally effective.

There are features related to the client's own readiness levels, developmental stages, needs, preferences, attitudes, skills, and personality characteristics that also have an impact on the possibilities for change. A key part of your job involves helping people to make the most of their strengths, as well as strengthening their weaknesses. You should also keep in mind that what might look like significant deficiencies and obstacles could also be viewed as opportunities for learning and growth. Much of the recent research on posttraumatic growth, for example, indicates that even the most harrowing or stressful events in one's life can lead to remarkable insights and personal transformations if processed in a particular way (Calhoun & Tedeschi, 2013; Joseph, 2011; Werdel & Wicks, 2012).

Just imagine how you would help a client with a life challenge or traumatic experience, reframing and reconstructing a narrative in which he or she is heroic rather than a victim. When dealing with any trauma, loss, or life challenge, your job is often to help people to create or construct meaning from the experience in such a way that they feel empowered rather than discouraged from the experience.

CULTURAL CONTEXT OF THE CLIENT EXPERIENCE

In order to make a significant and lasting difference with a client, helping skills are certainly important but rather useless without the sensitivity and ability to appreciate the context of that person's life. There is no way you could help someone with a life-threatening illness or who lost a loved one without understanding the person's cultural background. This may often include not only factors like ethnicity, race, and religion but also include other factors such as geographical location, profession, socioeconomic status, sexual identity, gender, and even personal interests. For each person you will ever see, there is a complex tapestry of cultural themes that play a significant role in shaping that person's attitudes, life experiences, and identified problems (Dass-Braislford, 2012; Fernando, 2012; Grothaus, McAuliffe, & Craigen, 2012).

Exercise in Cultural Identities

We all consist of multiple selves rather than a single, stable identity. For instance, Leah's cultural identity just described may be as a biracial Japanese American, yet there are also other cultural identities that influence her values and behavior. If you were going to see Leah as a client, you would need to know her strong identity as a Texan from a small, rural town. You would also need to understand her strong cultural identities as a professor, a feminist, and a Gestalt therapist. In each case, regardless of the presenting problem she might bring to counseling, her multiple cultural identities would become the landscape for the journey you walked together.

Consider your own strong cultural identities related to your race, ethnicity, religion, socioeconomic class, age, geographical location, hobbies, and so on. In a small group, share those features that would be most important for a therapist to know and understand in order to help you.

CULTURAL SKILLS AND COMPETENCIES

There are certain competencies that are considered essential for culturally sensitive practice (Keyser, Gamst, Meyers, Der-Karabetian, & Morrow, 2014;

Sehgal et al., 2011; Sperry, 2010). Among them are understanding the client's unique worldview, including core beliefs; awareness of one's own biases and values; and an understanding of how methods must be adapted to fit the needs of each person.

Clients present themselves in one way, and their helpers receive them according to their (the helpers') own perceptions. Our perceptions are influenced by our values, our own experiences with people who are similar, our biases and prejudices, and our sensitivity (Tseng & Streltzer, 1997).

According to Tseng and Streltzer, there is

- *The problem as experienced by the client.* This is what the person is feeling, his or her core experience in its most raw form.
- *The problem as identified by the client.* This is what is noticed and labeled. The person takes the raw experience and converts it into verbal and visual images, then gives the problem a name. This identification may or may not be a full and complete representation of all the issues.
- *The problem as presented by the client.* This is what is revealed and told as a story using words. The limitations of language will influence what and how the experience is reported.
- *The problem as understood by the therapist.* This is what is heard by the clinician. Considerable distortions may take place as a result of this "translation." In other words, what the therapist hears may not be closely related to what was said, much less what was experienced.
- *The problem as diagnosed by the therapist.* This is what is labeled by the clinician and what is focused on as clinically significant. The client tells a long, complex, and multitextured and layered story that includes infinite facets. The therapist then must decide what part of this presentation is most important.

Each of these steps is both influenced and distorted by each participant's individual and cultural worldview. The participants in the relationship come from different life experiences that shape what they each understand about one another and how they respond to one another. That is one reason why it is so crucial for you to have a clear grasp of the influences within your own cultural identities and how they impact your beliefs and behavior. Although true objectivity is impossible, this journey of self-discovery will better help you to become aware of your biases, confront your prejudices, and manage your beliefs in the best interests of those you are trying to help.

Exercise in Self-Awareness

Let's start with the assumption that everyone is prejudiced, meaning that everyone makes prejudgments about others based on limited data related to appearance, first impressions, and prior experience. Such behavior is not only normal but sometimes quite helpful: Humans had to evolve some way to make quick and efficient evaluations about whether someone represented a threat or danger.

If you follow this reasoning (you don't have to agree with it), then we all not only have prejudices but certain biases toward and against others, based on our prior experiences.

Either in a journal, or in small groups, talk about some of the prejudgments you have toward people of particular religious, racial, or socioeconomic backgrounds, or other factors such as their labels. For instance, what immediately comes to mind when you consider working with a new client who is a pedophile? Or a member of the Libertarian or "Green" political parties? Or an individual who is transgendered? Or a tax accountant? In each case, you have an initial impression, perhaps one that won't last long after you actually meet the person, but nevertheless you have certain expectations, beliefs, and attitudes, some of which are strongly biased. You would be very naive indeed not to understand the impact your own cultural background and attitudes can have on your relationships with others.

BECOME FAMILIAR WITH CULTURAL DIFFERENCES

Who will your clients be? Most of them will be different from you, whether due to gender, socioeconomic status, sexual orientation, ethnicity, religion, or other cultural differences. That your clients will be similar in all of those areas is highly unlikely. Therefore, embracing differences and educating yourself about cultural issues will help you to provide better therapy. More important, enhancing your awareness of and articulating your own values may prevent you from creating barriers between you and your client.

For example, when I [Leah] was in high school, I had a friend who was ethnically 100% Italian. He was physically just like you see in the movies (olive skin, dark hair, dark eyes, Roman nose), and you would be certain of his heritage except for missing the Italian American accent. I remember going to his house after school one day; it was my first time to visit his home. The place smelled wonderful: garlic and spices—well, you know—like Italian food. His mother was in the kitchen cooking. While I waited in the living room, my friend entered the kitchen to talk with his mother briefly. Then, much to my surprise, I heard lots of yelling and screaming. I didn't know if I should leave. I thought he was certainly in big

Exercise in Confronting Cultural Biases

Make a list of all the cultural groups that you might expect to encounter in your work. Include such dimensions as race, ethnicity, national origin, ability, and religion, but also other cultural identities related to sexual orientation, profession, avocation, geographical location, and so on. Make the list as exhaustive as possible and include almost anyone you might expect to see in counseling.

Circle those groups with whom you have little experience or understanding. For instance, you might have a fair degree of contact with people from the southern region of Vietnam but no experience with the Hmong peoples of the mountain highlands. Or, you might know a little bit about men who identify as gay but nothing about transgendered individuals or women who identify as lesbian. Or, you might be reasonably familiar with middle-class professional African Americans but have had little contact with those who live and work in the inner city.

Now, here's the hard part, because it requires a degree of honesty that is not often politically correct to admit. Put an asterisk (*) next to those groups with whom you feel uncomfortable working. If a transgendered individual came to see you, how would you handle that? What if a new client walked in who was an Orthodox Jew, a devout Muslim, or a Jehovah's Witness? Some of your discomfort may be related to ignorance and lack of experience, but another part may result from prior encounters with particular individuals of a particular culture.

Now the really hard part: Make a commitment to educate yourself about the groups that you circled, and to challenge your biases and prejudices against people of a particular culture. This is not the kind of assignment you will complete in a week, in a semester, or even in the years of your training; it will take you a lifetime.

Exercise in Prejudices (Prejudgments)

Post several sheets of paper up around the classroom. At the top of each page, write down a particular cultural identity, whether it is an ethnic group (African Americans, Asians, etc.), religious group (Christians, Muslims, etc.), sexual orientation (gay men, lesbians, straight men), or any other issue that you think is relevant. Make sure to include middle-class Caucasian Americans. Each student is to walk around the room and then write down particular stereotypes about each group (not personal beliefs). Go around the room as many times as is needed. When everyone has written something, process the experience.

trouble about something. I was frightened for him. Maybe five minutes later, he returned, although it seemed like hours later. We walked silently out of the house and to the car to head to our destination. Once in the car, I nervously asked him if he was in trouble. He looked at me very confused and said, "No, why?" I told him

I heard all the yelling and screaming in the kitchen and didn't know what to do. He said, "We weren't yelling, we were just talking. We weren't even disagreeing about anything. What are you talking about?"

Several areas can be important with regard to cultural differences. Here are some of the most common areas about which new therapists tend to make assumptions. This list is not exhaustive by any means but merely a sample of characteristics that may have an impact.

Socioeconomic Status

Many stereotypes exist based on socioeconomic status (SES). The truth is that all dysfunctions and problems exist regardless of the client's income level. Some common (inaccurate) stereotypes might be:

- High-SES clients will be prompt.
- Low-SES clients are more likely to abuse their children.
- High-SES clients will pay their bills.
- Low-SES clients are less motivated.
- High-SES clients have only superficial problems.

Notice the bias toward high SES having more positive stereotypes and low SES having negative stereotypes. First of all, we can easily mistake people's social class based upon how they are dressed or what car they drive. We must be careful not to make these assumptions but instead ask our clients, if it's relevant. Second, because many middle- and upper-class individuals are models of the dominant American cultural values, we may like them more, excuse them more easily for their faults, or view them positively. We want to be careful to avoid imposing our social class rules on clients of the different classes. It's important to obtain information by monitoring the assumptions and expectations that we hold. For instance, if a lower SES client is constantly late, you might assume that she doesn't care about your time or maybe you assume she's not serious about her therapy. If you take the opportunity to ask this client, you may discover that she has to use public transportation that isn't always on time. You may also discover that she's working two jobs just to make ends meet, and she is unable to leave work early to catch an earlier bus. This knowledge can shift your view of the client and help you to avoid making negative assumptions that will often harm your relationship with your client.

Kim was a counseling student who came from a high SES background. She was privileged by always knowing she would have food on the table, parents to support her, a roof over her head, and many luxuries like her own car and laptop. Kim came to her practicum class worried about needing to contact child protective services after a 12-year-old client reported to her that she was responsible for her family. The child was referred to her by her teachers for constantly being late and not completing all of her homework. The teacher believed she had the potential to be a good student, but assumed that she was just lazy.

However, both the teacher and Kim did not have an understanding of this child's life. She was expected to prepare breakfast for her three younger siblings, get them dressed for school, and walk each one to two different schools before getting to her own classes. After school, she would walk to the other schools to pick up her siblings, walk them home, and then cook dinner before helping each one with homework. She would bathe them, put them to sleep, and then, if she had enough energy, she would complete her own homework. This family often had very little food and almost no parental support. Dad had passed away and mom was working two jobs just to maintain their one-bedroom apartment. Kim believed that this child was being neglected because she was parentified and unable to complete her own homework or get to school on time. Kim didn't understand that families who can work only in minimum wage jobs often have to work multiple jobs just to pay for rent and food. Kim had difficulty understanding that the child's mother was doing everything she could to keep her family together. Kim's exposure to this world was nonexistent.

Even if your clients come from different SES backgrounds, many of their problems can be similar. It's essential to be aware of these incorrect stereotypes so that they do not interfere with your ability to work with your clients. Therapists have the responsibility to educate themselves about cultures other than their own so that they don't impose assumptions based upon lack of knowledge (American Counseling Association [ACA], 2014). With regard to social class, therapists must gain an understanding of the problems that can occur based upon external influences (whether that's knowing the right people or putting food on the table) so that they are taken into consideration when working with clients.

Gender

Have you ever found yourself and your friends saying, "Men are this way," or "Women are that way"? So often, we state or believe gender stereotypes. This is one area where we may already hold assumptions, especially regarding the opposite sex. Whatever assumption you hold, many individuals do not fit your stereotype. For instance, think of people you know who are exceptions to these stereotypes:

- Women are too emotional.
- Men aren't communicative enough.
- Women love shopping.
- Men love sports.
- Women are the victims of abuse.
- Men are the abusers.
- Women are nurturing and supportive.
- Men are assertive and competitive.

Differences obviously do exist between men and women; even our brains develop differently. Nonetheless, we are all thinking, feeling, behaving beings with many of the same wants and needs. Too often, our biases about the opposite sex, or even the same sex, can get in the way of modifying our approach to fit the client.

One common bias that can occur with female therapists-in-training is that men should be as emotionally open and expressive as women. While many therapists do believe that emotional expression can be helpful, men do this in their own way. For example, research indicates that women are more likely to exhibit depression through low energy, sad affect, and expressions of hopelessness. Men, in contrast, will often exhibit their depression by demonstrating feelings of anger (Englar-Carlson & Shepard, 2005; Evans, Duffey, & Englar-Carlson, 2013). Female therapists may misunderstand this anger as simply being angry, when sometimes the male client is expressing his depression in the only way he knows how.

Another potential for cross-cultural misunderstanding is when men or women do not fit culturally determined behaviors for their gender. Men can be nurturing, a stay-at-home dad, a primary care-taker of children, and warmly empathic. Women can be competitive, assertive, and seek higher positions within their organizations. The key point here, which will be explored in greater detail, is that adjustments must be made when working with each gender. Men, in particular, often don't remain in therapy for very long because the very requirements of the process ask them to do things for which they are unprepared and unaccustomed: be vulnerable and express feelings (Englar-Carlson & Stevens, 2006).

Another consideration for gender stereotyping is to understand the rules that each culture has for how feminine or masculine men and women should behave. The lines between being "a man" and being "a woman" is drawn differently depending on the ethnic and religious cultures from which one comes. In dominant U.S. worldview culture, women are allowed to be masculine in a variety of ways.

In corporate settings, for example, women can wear pants, be competitive, be unemotional, or be strong leaders. However, men cannot wear skirts, push for harmony over competitiveness, be weepy, or be "push-overs." A man gets far more criticism for being feminine than a woman gets for being masculine. In many traditional and rural Latin-American cultures, however, the rules for femininity might be more narrow than it is within dominant U.S. culture. In Thailand, gender is so important that men and women speak differently so that the gender of the person you are conversing with is clear. When working with clients, you need to be aware of your own biases about gender roles and behaviors. In addition, you want to be sensitive to people who identify as transgendered. This includes working with the client's own definitions of femininity and masculinity as well as using the pronoun of your client's identity rather than biology.

Alex: My Lesson in the Bridal Shop . . . Oye

My father was a bigoted man, and I didn't understand his sleeping influence over me until I entered into the realm of mental health. I met a woman who was a hermaphrodite for the first time as a salesperson during a bridal gown fitting when, customarily, the bride-to-be is fitted with a corset and slip. Imagine my surprise when she stripped down, and there it all was—breasts and penis. I remained calm, excused myself for a minute, and took a deep breath in the hallway. During that breather I realized that this was a human being who was very excited for this experience, and I wanted no tell-tale sign of panic or prejudice flagging my face to ruin a second of it for her. My father's voice said "freak!" and "run," but I got to put his voice aside and decide that this was her moment, and she was worthy of all my unbiased attention. Now when I think back to that appointment, I see her beautiful, shining face and realize how completely she owned herself and how brave, poised, and magnificent she truly was.

Sexual Orientation

The issue of sexual preference is one that can stimulate a lot of debate among students in counseling. Many people have strong beliefs about homosexuality, some of which can interfere with their ability to provide effective professional care as mandated by our professional organizations. As a therapist, your job is not to decide whether or not your client is acting in what you consider a "normal" or "moral" way, but rather to help your client deal with whatever issues are relevant for him or her. If you are unable to feel respect and regard for your client, you may want to take a look at what keeps you from valuing all people, regardless of who they love.

Three common problems occur with regard to student therapists working with gay, lesbian, bisexual, transgendered, or nonidentifying clients. First, some students, upon discovering a client is gay, will inadvertently or consciously try to convert the client to being straight. Obviously, this can create a significant number of problems for the client and for the therapist's relationship with the client. The client would already have experienced a significant amount of prejudice and discrimination against him, even from his own family. He will be sensitive to any feelings of disapproval. Most therapists don't intend to impose their value of heterosexism, but comments might come out to evidence it. This must be avoided in order to keep from reoppressing the client. Equally important is that professional organizations have determined that conversion therapy is unethical. This is in light of evidence that demonstrates that over time, conversion therapy usually does more damage than good (Flentje, Heck, & Cochran, 2014). As therapists, your job is not to make decisions for your clients, but rather to help your clients make their own decisions based upon their own morality and values. By attempting to convert clients, you reoppress them and cause harm (Hermann & Herlihy, 2006).

A second challenge is when the new therapist believes that all of the client's problems are related to his or her sexual orientation. The fact that your client is gay does not mean that all of his or her problems will necessarily be related to the gender of who he or she loves. In fact, these clients will often have the exact same issues as heterosexual clients: problems with jobs, relationships, or wounds from childhood. So, if you are qualified to help heterosexual clients, you are also qualified to help clients of different affective or sexual orientations.

Finally, student therapists may hold inaccurate stereotypes about gays, lesbians, bisexuals, transgendered, and nonidentifying clients that can interfere with therapeutic effectiveness. The fact that your client is gay does not mean that he is promiscuous (a stereotype for gay men), or that she does not like to wear makeup (a stereotype for lesbians). As with any population, individual differences must be taken into consideration. Accepting your client for who he or she is and responding to him or her in a respectful way is an essential component to good therapy (ACA, 2014; Hermann & Herlihy, 2006; Moran, 1992). By the same token, you would not want to assume that because your male client is effeminate and waxes his eyebrows, or your female client has a mullet haircut and prefers jeans and T-shirts, that he is gay or she is lesbian. Gender behaviors are socially constructed, and individuals do not always fit those constructions in ways that we expect. So be careful about your own expectations for gendered behavior, regardless of sexual/affectual orientation.

Religion

Religious differences are another touchy issue for students. Many students have strong feelings about their own religious beliefs. Furthermore, many religious behaviors are frequently misunderstood and misinterpreted. These differences in values can trigger a therapist who may feel challenged by a client who maintains different values. For example, which of these beliefs stir something up in you?

- Abortion
- Homosexuality
- Eating pork
- Dressing provocatively
- Premarital sex
- Capital punishment
- Divorce due to irreconcilable differences
- Praying to Allah several times a day
- Wearing a hijab (head scarf) or yarmulke
- Wedding vows that require women to obey their husbands
- Going on a mission
- Associating only with others of the same religion

Many religions hold strong opinions about these listed areas, among others. You may find some to be absurd issues whereas others may seem more important to you. However, each major religion, at its core, believes that we should love one another and treat each other the way we want to be treated. So, whatever your opinion, your client has the choice of his or her opinion as well. It is a most challenging skill to support your client's worldview even if it directly contradicts your own.

Valerie is one student who had to deal with a most difficult issue that contrasted with her own religious values. Valerie's practicum was at a high school. She was assigned a 15-year-old client who had just discovered that she was pregnant. Now, Valerie was a very devout Catholic who believed that every human life was to be highly valued, even that of a fetus. Her client, however, had decided with her parents' blessing to have an abortion. She and her family were not religious and valued education; they didn't want anything to interfere with the girl's ability to get through school without incident so that she could earn high grades for college. They didn't think she was mature enough to handle the pregnancy.

Valerie really struggled to work with this client, especially as the client expressed her feelings of sadness for terminating a life and the potential of who that fetus could become. Nevertheless, Valerie provided unconditional positive regard and remarkable empathy for this student. Then, after each session, she would talk with her supervisor, cry for this unborn child who would never get to live, and pray for everyone's soul. Valerie was able to feel compassion for her client and respect her client's perspective even though she was deeply sad about the decision.

So, there may be many times when your client's values contradict your own. Perhaps you are religious and your client is not. Perhaps you are not religious, and your client has fundamental religious beliefs. Or perhaps you come from very different religious backgrounds. In any case, you want to respect your client's values and work within your client's value system. You want to be careful not to inadvertently impose your own values on the process, unless there is an ethical issue such as harm to self or others.

Race and Ethnicity

Race is a construct established by the federal government to put people into categories based upon phenotype (Morning, 2007). However, race is not real and, in most cases, is not an accurate way to understand others in a culturally sensitive way. For instance, try telling a Canadian that he or she is the same as a U.S. American. He or she may never agree with this statement. Do the Germans and the Australians seem culturally similar to you? This is equally true for people who are categorized as Hispanic or Asian or Black. If a Caucasian-South African woman immigrated to the United States and became a U.S. citizen, technically, she would be African-American, but she would not be racially Black. We're just saying that race is a complicated construct and not very culturally nuanced; ethnicity is better, although still can have cultural diversity within the group.

Cultural differences can often be most obvious because of the client's ethnicity. Students can err in two ways when working with ethnically different clients. An error students frequently make is to assume that stereotypes about a client's ethnic group will in fact apply to their client. To assume intelligence, motivation, or anything else about a particular ethnic group can simply be dangerous, and frequently inaccurate. Stereotypes can be helpful, though, when trying to understand others in an efficient way. In a sense, they are shortcuts that have evolved over generations for making quick decisions about who is trustworthy and who is not. Probably for evolutionary purposes, there has always been great suspicion regarding strangers or people "not like us," as they could be a threat. That is one reason why humans hold prejudices, which are "prejudgments" based on prior experience, as well as myths and rumors that may not be valid. Since everyone holds such biases, it is absolutely critical that you become aware of your own and how they influence your perceptions and behavior toward those who are different from you.

On the other hand, students may not be appropriately educated about cultural differences of different groups and may misinterpret a client's behavior (Penchaszadeh, 2001). This is the more common error. For example, you may have a young female client from India come to your office frustrated with her traditional family because they want her to enter into an arranged marriage although she is in love with someone else:

Therapist: So, your parents don't approve of this man because they did not select him for you?

Client: It's not so much that the marriage must be arranged. And that's not exactly why they don't approve of him. It's because he's from a lower caste.

Therapist: What would be the consequences if you did marry him without your parents' approval?

Client: Why would I do such a horrible thing! I must always do as my parents ask.

The therapist in this case made an assumption that the client is trying to decide whether to marry in spite of her parents, when instead she may be coming to therapy to learn how to get over the man she loves. A therapist who isn't careful may find a personal bias in favor of independence creeping in while working with a client who firmly believes in her collectivistic cultural traditions. Therefore, you must not only learn about cultural differences, but respect them.

Another important aspect of being sensitive to other ethnicities is understanding your own ethnic/cultural background and the values that support it. This is also true for *many of you* who identify as White American and who claim you don't have an ethnic culture. This may be true for you because your family has been part of the dominant U.S. culture for many generations, and because when everyone around you thinks like you, looks like you, and behaves like you, you may have difficulty identifying your culture. Such values as individualism, independence, competition, materialism, and productivity are likely to be operative in ways that are distinctly different from the values of people who originate from Asia or Latin America. It would be stereotyping to assume that *all* White/European Americans hold these values since some of them may not apply to you even if you recognize these characteristics within the dominant culture. If you look beneath the surface, you may find that many nuances that define your personal ethnic identity may be based on *your* ancestors' country of origin, as well as other factors.

AN EXERCISE IN AMERICAN CULTURE

If you were born in North America, speak with a first-generation immigrant (someone who was born in another country). Ask him or her to tell you about the differences observed between the home country and what we value in the United States. List as many values as you possibly can. Then review the list for what parts fit you and what parts do not fit you. Pay attention to your reactions as you hear your group being stereotyped. Discuss how this might apply to your work with clients.

Culture Is Dynamic and on a Continuum

Part of the dominant Western worldview is to use rational empiricism as a perceptual lens: Every question has an answer, and there is a box to define everything. But culture doesn't work that way. Whether looking at ethnicity, social class, gender or any other cultural groupings, people move from one end of a continuum to the other. They change based on the context and situation. This is why stereotyping can be so misleading.

Even as you explore your own culture or the culture of your clients, you need to be aware that you and your clients do not fully fit into any one box. We all fit into many boxes, and sometimes the lines between boxes is blurred. Learn about your clients' cultures and then hold those assumptions lightly. Because you cannot simply put people in cultural boxes, no one can be perfectly culturally sensitive. Cultural sensitivity is not a destination, it's aspirational. Because each person experiences his or her multitude of cultures uniquely, one cannot make perfect predictions. We cannot know all cultures because each person nuances his or her expression of his or her culture. So, attempting to be culturally sensitive is also knowing that you will make mistakes, and when you do, own the mistake and heal the relationship with the client once again.

A Note About Cultural Similarity

So far, we have covered some areas of cultural differences, and there are many more. Does that mean if you and your client are culturally similar that you don't have to pay attention to culture? No. Here is where you may risk putting yourself in your client's shoes, imagining how you would feel in his or her position. Taking this approach can be fallible because you lose a sense of who your client is, and instead, project yourself into his or her life. You still need to listen with a critical ear, listening to his or her cues and experiences, and trying to take yourself out of his or her story. Even if you are the same gender, age, race/ethnicity, religion, social class, and everything else, you still have different family cultures, regional cultures, and other cultures that make huge differences in how you view the world.

ASSESS STAGE OF CULTURAL IDENTITY

Now that you've learned that virtually everyone holds some stereotypes about virtually all groups, and that you need to be aware of the stereotypes you hold, how do you assess the client's level of acculturation? Several authors have created stage theories for levels of acculturation (Erchull et al., 2009; Helms, 2015; Leong, Kim, & Gupta, 2011). Although these models have primarily been based upon the African American or Caucasian American cultures, a look at these stages would be relevant for any ethnic group. Loosely described, the stages of cultural identity development proceed through an initial stage of conforming, followed by a certain amount of dissonance and confusion, then attempts at immersion with alternating internal and external resistance. It is hoped that the immigrant eventually reaches a state of integrative awareness in which past heritage is embraced and honored and there is a degree of adaptation to the new country.

You may want to become familiar with these models so you can determine where a client might lie when cultural issues arise. You may also need to explore where you are in these stage models. This is not necessarily a linear process and can occur with any group, whether a White/European American, an immigrant, a second-generation American, or someone who identifies as multiracial. What is consistent is that people often start by valuing one group over another, switch, and then come back to appreciating both groups. Your challenge is to determine what your clients' beliefs are about their own ethnic backgrounds as well as their views about people from other ethnic backgrounds. Then you compare your clients' stages to where you are in your cultural identity development to prevent yourself from negatively influencing your clients.

Check Out Level of Acculturation

A first-generation immigrant in the United States, who has English as a second language and still is steeped in the cultural values and norms of the home country, would be in a different place from a third-generation minority who cannot speak the language of her ethnic background and is steeped in American culture. The former client may be struggling primarily with the adjustment to cultural differences encountered in North America. The latter client may struggle with her parents forcing traditional cultural norms when she does not identify with the culture at all.

Biracial clients can create an even greater challenge: They may not fit in either culture and feel "homeless" (Edwards & Pedrotti, 2004; Vivero & Jenkins, 1999). To further complicate the issue, the parents know only their culture and may be totally ignorant of the specific concerns of being biracial. You can also imagine that this would be an ongoing issue that would be very relevant to bring up with a therapist.

Review Cultural Norms

In order to determine anyone's level of acculturation, you will need to be familiar with cultural norms. You will receive a lot more training in diversity issues throughout your development. This will likely cover the following groups: the gay/lesbian, African American, Native American, and Hispanic/Latino populations; social class; and religion. Even though you're in this early stage of the class (and maybe in your program), you should learn to be mindful of the need to assess cultural norms when working with clients from cultures other than your own. And while you learn about the different cultural norms within these categories, keep in mind that there are some limitations. First, each of these groups includes a great deal of variation. A Mexican American is different from a Cuban American (though they're collectively considered Latino Americans). A Japanese American may be very different from a Vietnamese American (collectively considered Asian Americans). Second, the groups you cover will certainly not be a comprehensive list of all cultures. Many culture classes don't include Western cultures because we assume, as Americans, that the Western cultures are almost identical to each other. Although there is some truth in that, there are many differences. If you have ever traveled or made friends with someone from Europe or Australia, for example, you may be acutely aware of their cultural differences.

With all of this in mind, as you come across clients who are culturally different, you will be delighted that one of the distinct advantages of this profession is that you get to learn almost as much from your clients as they learn from you. With each client, you will want to explore some of the following areas:

- *The value of family.* Some cultures put the family's needs above the individual's, whereas in the United States we believe that self-care has value as well. An awareness of the importance of family can keep you from imposing your own beliefs about how a person should behave with his or her family.

Exercise in Raising Your Personal Cultural Awareness

As we have discussed, culture involves far more than your ethnicity. Depending on your background and experiences, your religious affiliation could be most dominant, or perhaps your sexual orientation, professional identification, geographical location, or even your strong association with a particular thing (i.e., owning a Harley-Davidson motorcycle or being a stamp collector).

Reflect on your most dominant cultural affiliations. Try to think of at least three that have been most influential in your thinking and your development.

Next, list some of the assumptions that you hold that originated from your racial, religious, family, or other cultural heritage. For example, how do you view being on time? How do you express feelings? What feelings are most appropriate or inappropriate for you to express? Is doing what's best for the group or the individual more important? What gender-role stereotypes does your culture hold? What biases, prejudices, and beliefs do others hold about members of your culture? What assumptions do you have that are based upon your religious upbringing? How does your culture view counseling? With what aspect of your culture do you most identify (your cultural home)? How do you treat strangers? Should you always be polite, or should you always be honest and direct?

Then get into small groups and share what you wrote down. Talk about your similarities and differences. Be aware of how you respond when others have different assumptions. Are you offended? Are they wrong? Are they simply different?

By clarifying your own culture and comparing it in a nonthreatening environment with the cultural differences of others, you may be less likely to offend others. You may become more educated about yourself and see others as being different, rather than seeing them as wrong.

- *Individual focus versus group focus.* Related to valuing the family, some cultures believe that an individual must consider the group first and self second; in other cultures, an emphasis on the group is not as essential as self-care.
- *Gender-role stereotypes.* In the United States, we strive for more equality between men and women, but in some cultures different roles are clearly defined. These differences might be especially important when working with couples who are first-generation immigrants.
- *Influence of religion.* The values of Christianity vary from those of cultures that are based in Buddhism, Hinduism, Judaism, or Islam. In some ways, each group's view of life and its purpose can be quite different. If you have a client with existential issues, you'll need to be sensitive to these differences.

- *Social structures.* Unlike in the United States, in some cultures the language or words used are determined by status (authority or age), and in others, language differs for gender. This may appear in the first session with how the client wants to address you or how you should address your client.
- *Emotional expression.* Some cultures value the open expression of emotions whereas others believe expression should be reserved. Be careful not to mis-interpret someone who is emotionally reserved as resistant or someone who is emotionally expressive as unstable, because this may vary depending on the cultural background of your client.
- *High context versus low context communication.* In American culture, we primarily value low context communication. In other words, we expect people to say exactly what they mean as clearly as possible. In many other cultures, high context communication is more valued and considered polite. People in these cultures will seem outwardly to agree, but if you watch body language or hear some hesitancy, they may be trying to tell you they do not agree. The polite way to communicate is through hinting and subtleties.

These are just a few areas that come to mind when thinking about cultural norms. There are others; the list could be virtually infinite. What we most want to convey here is that you must understand the norms of your client's culture before making diagnoses or setting goals. It's vitally important to be sensitive to these values.

FOR REFLECTION

If you were working with a client who told you that he heard voices telling him to do certain things, would you assume he is schizophrenic? Perhaps this client comes from a background where ancestry is important and the voices of our deceased family members help people to cope with difficulties in life. Maybe this client is a shaman within a Native culture who is considered to have special abilities beyond others' daily experiences, and his talent for hearing voices helps him to access his healing power in order to assist others. Another possibility is that this client is sleep-deprived; after some discussion about the voices, he finally reveals that he feels crazy for even acknowledging this experience. Or this client believes these voices to be real, and they tell him what a horrible person he is. Each of these examples comes from a different frame of reference, and you would work differently with each of these clients.

Assess Language Skills

Clearly, if your client has an accent, you will probably assume that English is not his or her first language. And so you might think, *"Am I able to understand this person?"* If you can understand the words, you may think you're off the hook. But you are sadly mistaken. Unfortunately, a lot must be considered if English is the second language of your client. For example, we frequently use idioms or colloquial phrases that are difficult to understand if translated literally. For instance:

- I'm fix'n' to make some notes.
- She's breaking your heart.
- They are flat broke.
- She was fuming!
- He lives over yonder.
- She's so angry that she's going nuts!
- He looks blue today.
- I wonder what's wrong.
- Buzz off!

You see how some of these phrases might be confusing. In fact, some of them are regional, so if you are not from the region that uses it, *you* may not understand it. Imagine how hard it will be for someone who speaks very little English. In addition, some words or ideas cannot be translated at all, which further complicates people who speak English as a second language.

Finally, if your client's English is very weak, he or she may understand very little of what you are trying to convey. You may want to do lots of reflective listening (discussed in Chapter 6, "Exploration Skills") and go very slowly in these cases. The ideal would be to find a therapist who can speak your client's native language. Unfortunately, that isn't always possible. This problem can be further complicated if the culture from which your client comes values externally agreeing with persons in positions of authority, whether or not there is internal agreement. You may never know that your client doesn't understand. He or she won't be able to tell you. So go slowly. Reflect a lot.

Consider Cultural Views of Receiving Therapy

We hope that because you are studying to become a therapist, you value the process of therapy—but you can't assume everyone does. In fact, some of you reading right now believe therapy is good, is valuable, and yet you won't go yourself. You don't think it's good for you, but it's okay for others. Many of your clients from the majority culture will also struggle with what it means to be in therapy. They might be afraid that people think they are sick, that they are incompetent to handle their own problems. Worse, some people may think they have problems! (You get the point?)

Well, in many other cultures, going to a stranger for help is looked on with great dismay and even shame. Some cultures think that you should be able to cope on your own, that focusing on your own problems is self-centered. Other cultures may believe that you should go to family members or other experts within your own culture if help is needed. Finally, still other cultures believe more in a medical type model of healing, taking herbs or going through ceremonies to heal the "sick."

The point we wish to make is that very few of the skills or interventions you will use are culturally neutral; each one reflects particular ideas about what is good for people. It will be your job to make necessary adjustments to what you do, depending on the client's background. For instance, active listening and the reflecting of feelings may be entirely appropriate for someone in the dominant culture who wants to be understood, but may not work very well with someone from a culture that expects you to provide specific guidance as an "expert." Likewise, confrontation may be a very powerful intervention among the majority culture but considered offensive, if not oppressive, among minority members. You absolutely *must* apply every therapeutic skill and intervention through such a culturally sensitive lens.

Respect Client Beliefs

These are only a few areas in which therapists will encounter cultural differences; many others exist. The most difficult challenge is to become educated about cultural differences without become rigid about those beliefs; you do not want your stereotypes or beliefs to prevent you from acknowledging or looking for individual differences. If you learn nothing else about working with culturally different clients, learn this: You must respect your client's beliefs, values, and ways of being in order to provide good therapy. If the client does not feel some level of unconditional positive regard, he or she may not trust you enough to share innermost secrets or to share the parts of him- or herself that the client sees as most repulsive. Without that trust, your contribution to the client's growth is hindered.

The Culture of Therapy

We often talk about understanding and being sensitive to the culture of others, or of being aware of our own culture and its biases. What we may sometimes forget to acknowledge is that the program from which you graduate has its own culture based upon the views of the professors who teach you. The most obvious is the

Exercise in Values

In small groups of five to eight people, rank the following values from most important (1) to least important (9). Your group must come to a consensus, which means that you do not vote, you find agreement. You have 15 minutes to finish this task.

- Patriotism
- Friendship
- Freedom
- Family
- Money
- Spirituality
- Intimate love
- Education
- Competition

After completing the exercise, think about and discuss what this experience was like for you. What was it like to come to a consensus?

value placed on therapy for helping people to overcome difficulties in their lives. In addition, we value respecting the culture of our clients without imposing our own values. This is in marked contrast to the approach taken by religious traditions that do believe that certain values are good for everyone.

Most therapists believe that emotional expression can be helpful and useful in many circumstances. At the very least, the ability to articulate one's problems and reason through them is highly valued. Most therapists try to limit giving advice because the goal is to make clients more resourceful and independent, or to help them become their own therapists. We do not value crossing the boundary from therapist to lover (or even friend). We believe in the laws that require us to report if clients threaten to attempt suicide; harm another person; or harm a child, elderly person, or person with a disability. These are ethical guidelines that are discussed in the next section that create boundaries and limits to our help. First and foremost, the culture of therapy values the client's well-being and avoiding doing harm above acting based on our personal needs or desires.

As students, you are being acculturated to a new way of being, thinking, behaving, and feeling that affects every one of your relationships, not to mention your world-view. You will already have noticed ways that you perceive the world, and yourself, differently as a result of the training you've received. Your friends and family, as well, have likely commented that you seem "different" to them—and they may not altogether like the "new you," who is more assertive, confident, and self-aware.

OVERVIEW OF A CLIENT CONCERN

Now that you are beginning to understand that you need to learn about what to expect from various culturally different groups while remaining sensitive to individual difference, how do you make the most of this information? Imagine a couple comes to therapy who has just moved to this country from Mexico.

Therapist: What brings you to counseling?

Husband: My wife is having difficulty living here without her family.

Therapist: (looking at the wife) Tell me about your difficulties.

Husband: She cries often and is always sad. (the wife is looking down and very sad)

Therapist: (looking at the wife) Can you say something about your sadness?

Husband: She just doesn't know what to do with herself while I am at work. In Mexico, we lived close to her family and she spent most of her time with them. Now she's alone. We have only lived here a few months, and we do not have any friends yet. We know no one here.

Therapist: (looking at the husband) I notice you keep answering questions that I direct toward your wife.

In this case, the therapist did not make any assumptions about why the husband continued to answer questions directed toward his wife. What's *your* first assumption? Your response may tell you something about your biases. There are many possible reasons for this type of behavior:

- The wife does not speak English.
- The husband is controlling.
- The wife is shy.
- The wife reflects on her responses more slowly than her husband.
- This is culturally appropriate behavior.

When therapists simply mention what they have observed, the client is free to respond as to why he was answering for his wife. How he responds may provide some information about their response patterns (and perhaps even her depression, if he is controlling). Therapists who are culturally aware of this population may have assumed that the responding husband is typical of many Latino cultures. However, the therapist cannot assume this, because this couple may not fit the stereotypical, traditional family system. He or she must verify this before moving forward.

Another way in which cultural sensitivity may help you work with clients is to be clear about any value differences you have with your clients. Imagine that a male client comes to your office to work on his marriage. Following is an example where the therapist's agenda can get in the way:

Therapist: You state that you are here to work on your marriage. I think it might be helpful if I see you and your wife together.

Client: We can't do that because I'm having an affair and she doesn't know about it. She accuses me of having an affair, but I won't admit it. So, I guess she kind of knows, but not for certain.

Therapist: Tell me why you haven't admitted to your affair.

Client: It will cause so many problems. I love my wife and don't want to lose her. I don't think this other relationship interferes with my family. If she wasn't so suspicious, then we wouldn't have these problems. I'm tired of listening to her accusations.

Therapist: Of course having the affair interferes with your marriage. There is no way to repair the marriage until you are willing to give up the other relationship and be honest with your wife.

Clearly, the therapist has strong values about extramarital affairs and honesty in a relationship. Although this example is not about an obvious cultural difference, value differences are apparent and can still interfere with your productivity as a therapist. In this example, the client is not likely to return for a second session. A better response would have been, "You believe that your wife's suspicion is the cause of your marital problems, not your affair. Say more about how you experience your wife's suspiciousness." At least this improved response validates the client's experience, and perhaps through further investigation the client may discover his own level of responsibility for his marital problems.

You may use the skill of cultural sensitivity in many ways. Becoming sensitive to specific cultures will help you avoid saying something offensive, which can decrease your power and influence in therapy. Cultural sensitivity may also help you to understand the experience of your client more deeply and clearly. Awareness of cultural differences, especially the values that are held by various cultures, may help you to be clear about your own biases so that they are less likely to interfere with your therapeutic goals. Finally, understanding cultural differences expands the way in which you look at people in general, enhancing your ability to be empathic. This is not something that you do that is optional; sound, ethical practice is grounded in understanding the cultural differences of your clients and responding to them in appropriate, respectful ways.

ETHICAL CONSIDERATIONS IN THE PRACTICE OF HELPING SKILLS

The ethical codes for therapists provide specific information about cultural sensitivity. According to the American Counseling Association (2014), the American Psychological Association (APA; 2010), and the National Association of Social Workers (NASW; 2008), therapists must *be knowledgeable about cultural differences* and respect the diversity of all individuals. Very specific statements are made in all of these ethical guidelines with regard to respecting and understanding diversity. In addition, all of these organizations, plus the American Association for Marriage and Family Therapy (AAMFT; 2012), state that therapists are *to avoid discrimination* based on age, gender, ethnicity, religion, sexual orientation, religion, or any other factor. You may even find nondiscrimination as part of your state licensing law. Therefore, understanding and respecting differences is not just an opinion of the authors but an ethical guideline regardless of the organization with which you are affiliated. That is one reason why you will hear this theme echoed in every one of your classes and mentioned in every text.

Ethical Considerations Applied to Practice

The skills of being ethical are more challenging than you might imagine. Ethics are aspirational, much like being culturally sensitive, and there are very few answers to ethical questions that are the absolute correct answer. Instead, we make ethical decisions based on our own value systems and consulting with other practitioners in the field. Consequently, when you take culture into consideration and how that affects your values and you consult with a few other therapists, you can see why there might not be a correct answer to an ethical challenge. Someone living in the Deep South with conservative Christian values might make very different decisions than someone from Northern California who is spiritual but not religious when deciding whether or not to attend a client's wedding; these two individuals would likely be consulting with very different kinds of people as well.

   Although you will probably take a course on ethical and legal considerations, we want to discuss some common topics briefly that are directly related to practicing therapeutic skills. We wish to introduce them as early in your skills training as possible because they guide everything else you do. There are many excellent resources that you may wish to consult to prepare to conduct yourself in highly moral, ethical, and professionally appropriate ways (see Baruth & Manning, 2011; Corey, Corey, & Callanan, 2015; Remley & Herlihy, 2015; Sue & Sue, 2015; Zur, 2007).

First of all, you may belong to a variety of organizations, each with its own ethical guidelines. In addition, you will have legal guidelines that are prescribed by your state for your particular license. You might assume that these guidelines agree, but in fact, they sometimes contradict one another. When you find yourself stuck in a situation, probably the best thing to do is follow the most conservative guideline. However, if you feel that your client might benefit from something more, we highly recommend that you consult with several of your colleagues (and supervisor) to assure that what you are doing is in your client's best interest. For example, imagine having a client who is HIV positive and is having unprotected sex with his spouse. Some ethical guidelines state that you have a duty to warn the victim if she can be identified, because HIV can be life threatening. Other ethical or legal codes may specifically state that you cannot break your client's confidentiality to warn the potential victim. What would you do? All ethical and legal guidelines agree on one singular fact: Promote the welfare of the client (AAMFT, 2012; ACA, 2014; APA, 2010; NASW, 2008). Just how that is defined may differ with your ethical and legal codes.

Before You Schedule the First Session

Before you see a new client, the first consideration is whether you are operating within your scope of practice. Most state licensure boards have defined the scope of practice for each of the mental health fields. For example, in some states, only psychologists can do a full battery of assessments, while in other states, the licensee must only have scope of competence. You must make sure your license allows you to do the kind of work your client needs.

Next, you need to explore your scope of competence. In other words, are you qualified to work with this particular clinical issue? Although the ethical guidelines make this sound clear and simple, it's a difficult guideline to follow. If you work in a clinic that takes a variety of issues, each client will come in with different backgrounds and circumstances, and you cannot be an expert at everything. The abuses alone are overwhelming: child, elder, or dependent abuse (physical, emotional, and/or sexual); domestic abuse (violence); alcohol or drug abuse. Some therapists have a specific area of interest in which they become experts, working with only a single population. However, many therapists have to be able to work with a variety of clients and situations (individuals, couples, groups, families). In addition, if you are going to use assessment instruments, you must have the competency to administer, score, and interpret them. Therefore, once you have taken all of your required coursework and mastered the basic counseling skills, you will need additional training for more advanced skills as well as training for a variety of populations. Your education will continue for the rest of your career.

When is the situation fully beyond your scope of competence, requiring a referral? That's a difficult question to answer. There are some obvious reasons for referring. First, if you have education/training and have been supervised working with a particular issue, you do not need to refer the person elsewhere. For example, most new practitioners will be qualified to work with a client who comes in because she just ended a long-term relationship. Such a situation would be considered within your scope of competence.

A little more tenuous is when you have the training/education, but have not seen this particular issue under supervision. As long as you get that supervision, you can see the client. One example might be working with a client who not only just ended a long-term relationship, but also is medicated for depression. In this case, if you have not yet worked with a depressed client, you could probably continue to see this client under supervision, assuming you had training in depression.

If you don't have the specific training/education, you may or may not be prepared, depending on the issue. Again, supervision and/or consultation might be a good way to determine whether or not you need to refer the person elsewhere. One example is if your client has a severe eating disorder that has not yet been treated by other mental health professionals or by her doctor. Eating disorders can become life threatening if not treated properly; so you may want to consider referring this client to a specialist.

If you have no training and no supervision, and the topic requires expertise, then refer the client elsewhere. If the issue triggers countertransference issues for you, and you can't seem to separate your own issues from the client's, then refer the person to someone else. For instance, you are seeing a couple whose primary issue is active infidelity, and you have just discovered that your spouse or partner has been cheating on you for the past year with a colleague. You probably will have some difficulty, just after discovering your partner's infidelity, in being unbiased with the "cheating" client partner.

Another consideration is whether you will be using technology as part of the therapy. This is a hot topic in the mental health profession. At the time of writing this book, just over half the states have written legal codes about doing therapy or telehealth across state lines. Most states, so far, are indicating that the practitioner must be providing therapy in the state he or she is licensed and that the client must be in the same state when receiving services. However, each state is different. In addition, there are a set of national guidelines by the HIPAA (Health Insurance Portability and Accountability Act) that ensure client confidentiality. You can't just e-mail a client from any server, provide therapy through texting, use Facebook, or use technology such as Skype. You must use encoded programs that protect the client's confidentiality and let the client know about the many limits of using telehealth in providing mental health services.

Are you ready to schedule your client yet? Not quite yet. You have at least one more primary consideration. Is this client an actual or potential multiple relationship? The ethical and legal guidelines all specify that you are discouraged from providing therapy to clients you know, whether they're as close as a family member or spouse, or as distant as your hairdresser. When you have a potential or existing relationship with a client other than as a therapist, you have a multiple relationship, and having such a relationship can cause many problems (Austin, Bergum, Nuttgens, & Peternelj-Taylor, 2006; Bemak & Chung, 2015).

Exercise in Multiple Relationships

In groups of four or five, discuss the potential problems that might exist in multiple relationships with clients. See if you can come up with at least four reasons why being a therapist to a friend, partner/spouse, family member, or hairdresser (or any other service provider) is a bad idea. Share your ideas with the class.

Your First Session

Okay, you have called your client, who is a total stranger and whom you believe you have the competence to help. You have scheduled your first session, and you are ready to go. Can you just jump right into why the client came to therapy and begin working on the issues as soon as the client walks through the door? You guessed it; the answer is "no." There are a variety of issues that need to be covered, preferably in the first session, and a number of other concepts that you will want to be clear about even before you see your first—or any—client. These issues are covered in general in a later chapter, but for now, let's talk about the legal and ethical requirements. First, the ethical guidelines require that you cover confidentiality and its limits with your client. The client is to be informed that everything discussed in therapy is confidential, with some limitations. It's the ugly truth; you don't have complete confidentiality. Most ethical codes and state laws agree that the client must be informed of these limitations:

- Intended harm to self
- Intended harm to others
- Reports of abuse to a child, an elderly person, or a person with a disability
- If records are subpoenaed by a court of law
- If the client requests information be released
- If you are being supervised and will discuss your client's case with others

- If you are recording the session, the client must be informed of the recording itself and how it will be used
- If your client reports having a sexual relationship with his or her previous or current mental health professional

Some of these limits are further defined. For instance, in some states, physical harm to a person is reportable but harm to property is not; in other states, property is included. In some states, children who are present during domestic violence, even if they are not physically harmed, are considered to have suffered child abuse; other states don't specify this. In many states, the fiscal abuse of a trustee, for example misspending the money of an elderly person or a person with a disability, is considered a reportable offense, even if the trustee is a family member. The category called "limits of confidentiality" is a large area that is covered in more detail in law and ethics classes. We won't go into more detail because these limits often vary somewhat from state to state.

In addition to confidentiality limits, the client's informed consent is required. This is a document stating that the client (or client's guardian) understands the conditions of therapy and is giving consent to participate. In addition, the client must be informed that he or she can terminate at any time. Other common pieces of information on this document might be the agreed-upon fees, a contact number in case of emergencies, a process for complaints, and so on. Many agencies combine the limits of confidentiality with the informed consent in a single form. Typically, the client and the therapist sign these documents, and both the client and the agency or private practitioner keep copies. This document is usually presented in the first session.

Okay, assuming you were able to cover this information at the beginning of the session, you can start to talk about the reason(s) the client came to therapy. Easy, right? Wrong again. When do you speak and what do you say? Everything you say during a session directs the client, even if only minimally, including silence. Therefore, how you respond to your client is critical. As a therapist, your greatest tool is the art of interacting with a client. Although this book covers some basic skills that are considered essential to all theories of counseling, the basic skills may not be sufficient to help your client. Where are we going with all of this?

One theme common to all ethical and legal guidelines is that your job as a therapist is to provide therapy with the best interests of the client at the forefront of everything you do. This seems simple enough, because you came to this field with an interest in helping people, but it's not that simple. Who determines what is the best course of action to help your client? You and your client do. Make sure that you are intimately familiar with the ethical and legal guidelines.

Second, we suggest you keep in touch with the colleagues you meet in school and go to conferences and workshops to meet more people so that you can consult with several other professionals when you are unsure about the appropriate course of action. If for any reason you have to go to court, evidence of consultation (without breaking confidentiality) may go a long way to support your case. Third, many organizations whose guidelines you will be following provide liability insurance in case of a lawsuit. As a result, these organizations sometimes provide free legal consultation in case you have questions. Fourth, to remain congruent with standards of practice, continue to educate yourself about current trends and research for effective therapies. Finally and most important, maintain a strong relationship with your client throughout the therapeutic process by showing empathy. If the client likes and trusts you, he or she will be less interested in litigation and more interested in working through any concerns. Then the only challenge left is to know when to ask for help, and that's left up to your good judgment.

HOW TO BE A GOOD CLIENT

Strangely enough, one of the most important skills of being a good therapist is being a good client. Unless you know how to get the most from therapy in a consumer role, how on earth are you going to teach others to do the same? That is one reason why we believe the single most important thing you can do to prepare for your profession is to gain some experience as a client. You must understand what it's like to sit in the client's chair, to feel the same apprehensions, the same exhilaration. You must understand, from the inside, the games that clients play, the ways they try to keep therapists from getting too close. You must know intimately what it feels like to have someone probing and pushing you beyond the point where you feel comfortable. You can also discover what you like and don't like as a client, so you can modify the way you work with clients to what you think is most effective.

Part of a therapist's job is to teach clients how to behave. Most of what people know about being good clients they have learned from watching television and movies. They think that they are supposed to come and tell you their problems and that you will listen to them and tell them what to do. They assume you will agree with them, or be their friend. They may assume that you will have a magic solution in the form of advice to "fix" their problem. They don't understand how therapy really works, and it is your job to teach them (at least to the degree that you understand it yourself).

One of your first missions will be to teach new clients how to get the most from their experience. You will want to assess their expectations, many of which will be wildly unrealistic. If they were truly honest, they would tell you that they want you to wave a magic wand and fix them, and that they want you to do it quickly. They want you to agree that they are right and others are wrong. Most of all, they want you to be gentle and give them your undivided attention—not just during the session; some would like you to be on call 24 hours a day!

Once you have discovered what they expect (just ask them), you will next correct their misperceptions by telling them what therapy is and how it works. This sounds something like the following:

Client: So, I was hoping you'd tell me what to do with my kid. He's just out of control. I've tried about everything I can think of. That's why the teacher at his school suggested I see you. She said that you could fix things, that you've done this before.

Therapist: I appreciate your confidence in me, but perhaps I should tell you something about what I do and how I work.

Client: Okay.

Therapist: Although I am very good at helping parents deal with problems related to their children, it is not my job to fix things but rather to teach you how to do that.

Client: What do you mean?

Therapist: Just that I don't have a magical solution that I can give you that will make things better. I need to spend some time with you, and your son. I suspect that he has quite a different story to tell about what is going on.

Client: You're not going to take his word over mine, are you?

Therapist: What I'm going to do is help both of you to understand one another better. Then I'm going to help you negotiate better with one another. Obviously, your son is acting up in school for some reason. We have to find out what that is about.

Client: I told you, I already know what the problem is. He just doesn't have any discipline. He needs . . .

Therapist: Yes, I heard what you said. You're frustrated and believe he simply has a behavior problem. And I heard what you want me to do. But what I'm telling you is that I work differently than that . . .

As you can tell from this dialogue, a lot of negotiation goes on during this early stage. Therapists sometimes forget that while we are trying to influence clients and convince them that their dysfunctional beliefs are misguided and counterproductive, they are doing their best to convince us to join their side. There is, thus, an intrinsic conflict in therapy wherein we are trying to get clients to be a way that we think is good for them, and they are trying to get us to be another way that they believe works best for them. As you can imagine, things can become quite conflicted as the two partners in this process struggle for control.

In Part II of this text, we go into more detail about what the foundation for therapy may look like. We spend a great deal of time emphasizing the importance of a strong therapeutic relationship, and this is usually accomplished best by providing empathic responses throughout therapy. When clients feel heard and understood, they are more likely to respond to your feedback, take risks, and make needed changes. In this way, you are less likely to feel any struggle for control. If you feel you are working too hard, or that you are at odds with your client, you're probably not being empathic enough. The best way to handle conflict is in a way that does not feel adversarial but rather as a respectful negotiation of ideas.

FOR REFLECTION

There are many different skills that are involved in being a "good" client. Here are some important ones to consider:

- How to ask for what you want
- How to tolerate painful feelings
- How to talk about thoughts and feelings
- How to be painfully honest
- How to understand and speak therapy language fluently
- How to get the most from sessions
- How to be patient
- How to take risks
- How to convert talk into action
- How to let the therapist know you aren't satisfied
- How to protect yourself from becoming dependent on your therapist
- How to recognize when you are experiencing a setback
- How to know when it's time to stop

DECISIONS, DECISIONS

During or after an initial interview, the therapist is presented with a variety of decisions that need to be made. Often there is paperwork to fill out—progress notes, treatment plans, intake summaries—that provides a structure for some of these. Basically, you will be asked to determine the following:

- *Is the client in the right place?* Are you the best person to work with this person? Can you deliver what is needed? Is there a reasonable match between what the client needs and what you can offer?
- *Does the client require a medical consultation?* Is the client presenting symptoms that could conceivably be the result of a biologically based disorder? Some kinds of depression, anxiety, and other complaints do not respond to counseling alone but may require medication to manage the symptoms.
- *What is the risk of suicide?* If you suspect that clients may be at risk to harm themselves or someone else, your report will start a series of actions that must be followed to safeguard human life.
- *Is this a short-term or long-term case?* You may very well change your mind in the middle of treatment, but you will often be expected to estimate time required to meet the desired goals. Is this a case that will take a few weeks, a few months, or even longer? Is this a candidate for brief therapy?
- *What therapeutic modality is most appropriate?* Is it better to use individual therapy, group therapy, or family therapy? If the latter, which member(s) should be included?
- *What kind of therapy is likely to be most helpful?* Most therapists can work in different ways, depending on the situation and the client. Even practitioners who favor one theoretical orientation are still able to adapt what they do according to their clients' needs and styles. Basically, you will be trying to sort out whether a case is a candidate for relationship-oriented work or perhaps a more action-oriented model. For clinicians who employ a variety of approaches, decisions might be made for one client to use a feminist approach dealing with power issues, another client who is struggling to find meaning in her life might respond best to an existential approach, and still another client with reactive depression might be more amenable to a cognitive-behavioral approach.
- *What style of intervention should you employ?* Does this client primarily need support or confrontation? This is not an either/or proposition because both modes are often helpful at different times.
- *What sorts of supervision and resources will be needed for this case?* Who would be the best person to work with you on this case? What journals, books, and resources might you consult? Who are experts you could consult with as needed? What are some areas of weakness in your ability to work with this case? Needless to say, it is crucial that you be honest with yourself

about what you can and cannot do on your own. In some cases, you might decide it is best to refer the client to someone who has additional training or expertise in areas where you fall short.

APPLICATIONS TO SELF: WHO YOU ARE VERSUS WHAT YOU DO

One of the challenges of becoming a therapist is that the line between who you are and what you do is not always clear. As you develop counseling skills, your communication style will change (and hopefully, improve) in your ordinary life. Furthermore, as you become more sensitive and aware of clients, you will become more aware in your own life as well.

Another way in which "who you are" and "what you do" become blurred is in your contact with clients. You have a strong set of values, beliefs, and ways of moving through life. Concurrently, your client has strong values, beliefs, and attitudes that will likely be different from yours. One challenge is to become vividly aware of yourself. You must be clear about what you value and how you believe others should behave. Once that is articulated, a greater challenge is to accept that the client's way of being, of doing things, is not necessarily wrong . . . just different from yours. Sometimes one of the most difficult aspects of being a therapist is fully accepting your client's differences, or fully accepting where your client is in her or his process of growth. If you push who you are onto the client, you inhibit the client's growth experience.

INTERVIEW EXERCISE

Learning to be a therapist transforms you in a number of ways. You not only master certain professional skills that are useful in building trust when you are at work, but your interpersonal style and personality may also be altered in your personal relationships. Under the best circumstances, you become a far more compassionate and patient listener. You become more sensitive and responsive. You develop a far greater capacity for reading others' internal reactions and communicating at a deeper level of intimacy. Among many other things, you learn how to confront people effectively and how to summarize what you've heard.

Talk to friends and family members you trust to be honest with you. Ask them about changes that they have already witnessed in you as a result of your professional training. What are some aspects about this development that they especially appreciate and value? What about parts that they find uncomfortable or challenging to adjust to?

What can be most difficult is when your client believes or behaves in a way that you vehemently dislike, such as a disowned part of yourself. For example, let's say that your client is from a culture in which it is not acceptable to express emotions in public. As a person, you have struggled with this same issue. You have difficulty allowing your feelings to be not only experienced, but expressed. Because you've been trained as a therapist to honor feelings, you have come to dislike that aspect of yourself. And here you are, working with a client on something you have yet to master in yourself, and even worse, an aspect of yourself that you dislike. One dangerous consequence could be that you don't like your client because he or she is so "cold." Until you become accepting of your own coldness, you may have some difficulty accepting your client's. This is not to say that being "cold" is good or bad. Culture and context might make that judgment more clear, but the idea that you don't like it in yourself is, in itself, the challenge. The line between who you are and what you do is blurred.

Another example of this line-blurring is when the client holds different values than you do. Remember the earlier example of the man who was having an affair? Think about how it might be for you to work with a client like that. Perhaps you are someone who values fidelity. How would you handle this client? Would you refer him out? Would you try to sway him to change his values? Would you find a way to work within his experience? We are not advocating that you give up your values. However, you may have to remember that they are your values, and others have a right to theirs. This can be a challenging task, but it is possible. In this case, you must clearly draw a line between who you are (a believer in fidelity) and what you do (unconditional positive regard for your client). Just make sure and get supervision or consult with someone when these issues arise . . . because they will.

SUMMARY

In this chapter, we have covered cultural factors that must be considered in order to provide effective therapy. In addition, some ethical and legal considerations were presented to add to the formula for good therapy. Both require that you have an awareness of your own values to work effectively with clients and to help you make ethical decisions. And finally, individual considerations such as how to be a good client and which directions to take in therapy were discussed. All of these factors form the necessary foundation for applying the basic skills of counseling. The next chapter focuses on how theory and skills combine in the phases of counseling.

Skills in Action: Student as Client

Therapist: What would you like to talk about today?

Client: Well, I'm a counseling student who just started the master's program. I had to register for an undergraduate class in addition to my graduate classes, which was a prerequisite to the program. I recently learned that I had already taken a comparable class at another institution during my undergraduate degree, and that I don't need this class. I'm really frustrated because I'm already enrolled, and because of how late we are in the semester, I can't just drop; I can only withdraw.

Therapist: You're worried about what a withdraw status would look like on your transcript. [Assessing whether this issue is within scope of practice and scope of competence]

Client: Yeah! I work really hard to make good grades. I don't want people to get the wrong idea. I also don't mind taking the class, but I'm a little stressed about the final exam. I want to do well on my graduate work because it's important to me, but I think it's also important to have my entire transcript look good. What would people think if I had a withdraw? What would people think if I had a not-so-great grade? What will my instructor think if I drop the class? She tells me she understands either way. I also realize that by staying, I'll be more prepared for my graduate level class on this same topic. So, I can benefit from staying, too. (heavy sigh) I'm so annoyed that I didn't learn about this earlier. It's not my fault; it's someone else's carelessness. Why do I have to suffer?

Therapist: You're concerned about what other people would think. I can sense how important it is for you to make a good impression. I imagine you're afraid to disappoint someone. [Providing empathy to build the relationship]

Client: I don't want to disappoint myself. I've worked so hard to get here.

Therapist: It sounds like you're trying to prove something to yourself or someone else. [Still building the relationship; intuition]

Client: Yeah, in school, I always started in lower classes, but then had to be put in higher, honors classes. The teachers wouldn't call on me. They would question why I was in an honors class. I don't know if it was because I was a cheerleader or because I'm Mexican, but clearly they had little faith in me. My parents weren't any better. Everyone around me didn't think I could do much with my life, or that I wasn't very smart. (tears in her eyes)

Therapist: You're hurt by that. Say more about your parents. [Still building the relationship]

Client: Well, my parents always discouraged me about school. They thought my best path was to be a wife and mother, but if I had to work until then, then I should be a schoolteacher. They didn't think I was smart enough, even though I brought home straight A's in high school. I was in honors classes, I got good grades, I was involved in student council, drama, and a cheerleader. They just couldn't see it. I always have to prove myself to them. They would say, "Because you are a Mexican American girl, you can't get very far. Just shoot for something low and realistic like a schoolteacher. It's all you can do." I wanted to prove them wrong! Look at me! I'm in graduate school when no one else in my family has ever gone to college! (crying harder)

Therapist: There's a part of you that really believes in yourself, but another part of you believes your teachers and parents . . . that you may not be good enough. [Identification of potential cultural issues and still within scope of practice and competence]

Client: Yes! That's exactly it. I have to prove to everyone that just because I am a woman, or was a cheerleader, or because I'm Latina does not make me less intelligent. I'm willing to do whatever it takes.

Therapist: You've been given messages about your gender and ethnicity, and even your school involvement that based upon these factors, you are less capable than others. You're deeply hurt by that. I also hear your anger and resentment that you have to prove yourself, that you have to represent each of your groups to overcome these stereotypes. You must be exhausted, always proving yourself. [Clarifying cultural issues as they related to this topic]

Client: I am. I'm always fighting the voices from the past or my parents that tell me I can't do it. I also can't stop. I keep pushing myself to do more. It's never enough.

Therapist: You have told me what other people think about your being a Latina. What does that mean to you? [Assessing level of acculturation]

Client: I can be anything I want, if I work hard enough. I don't believe that my ethnic background or gender can hold me back. I really want to be a therapist, and I will not fail to accomplish this goal. Achieving this degree and working in this profession will give more meaning to my life and prove to everyone, even myself, that I can do it, that I'm smart.

Therapist: It sounds like you are very acculturated, and maybe your parents are not as acculturated as you are. I imagine you have had other struggles between you based upon how traditional they are sounding and how American you sound. [Helping client to articulate acculturation issues]

Client: I never really thought of it that way. You're right. They operate on different assumptions. I have to think about that. Thanks.

Therapist: You're welcome. However, I'm aware that we have drifted from your original issue of deciding whether or not to drop this class. Perhaps you could think about what parts of your decision-making process are based upon proving your capability to others, and what parts are about remaining because you could benefit from the class.

Client: Yeah, I do need to think about it, but I still can't imagine having a "withdraw" on my transcripts. I still have another three weeks, and the professor told me to take some time to think on it.

Therapist: I'm glad you decided to work on yourself as a therapist-in-training. You can understand how hard it is to change. On the one hand, this situation is an incredible growth opportunity for you; by deciding to withdraw, you start to act as if you don't need to prove as much. On the other hand, you can choose to stay, which would either be incredibly helpful to you in the graduate program or cause you unnecessary stress, or both. [Reinforcing the need for her to work on her own issues]

Client: It sounds so simple to just withdraw, but I can't imagine allowing myself to take the easy way out.

Therapist: It's important for you to do the right thing, and you're not sure withdrawing is the right thing to do. Think about it, and we can talk about it again next week . . .

REFERENCES AND RESOURCES

American Association for Marriage and Family Therapy. (2012). *AAMFT code of ethics* [Electronic version]. Retrieved October 23, 2015, from https://www.aamft.org/imis15/Documents/AAMFT%20Code_11_2012_Secured.pdf

American Counseling Association. (2014). *ACA code of ethics* [Electronic version]. Retrieved October 23, 2015, from https://www.counseling.org/resources/aca-code-of-ethics.pdf

American Psychological Association. (2010). *Ethical principles of psychologists and code of conduct* [Electronic version]. Retrieved October 23, 2015, from http://www.apa.org/ethics/code/principles.pdf

Arredondo, P., Gallardo-Cooper, M., Delgado-Romero, E. A., & Zapata, A. L. (2012). *Culturally responsive counseling with Latinas/os.* Alexandria, VA: American Counseling Association.

Austin, W., Bergum, V., Nuttgens, S., & Peternelj-Taylor, C. (2006). A re-visioning of boundaries in professional helping relationships: Exploring other metaphors. *Ethics & Behavior, 16*(2), 77–94.

Baruth, L. G., & Manning, M. L. (2011). *Multicultural counseling and psychotherapy: A lifespan perspective* (5th ed.). New York, NY: Pearson.

Bemak, F., & Chung, C. Y. (2015). Cultural boundaries, cultural norms: Multicultural and social justice perspectives. In B. Herlihy & G. Corey (Eds.), *Boundary issues in counseling: Multiple roles and responsibilities* (3rd ed., pp. 84–92). Alexandria, VA: American Counseling Association.

Bohart, A. C. (2007). An alternative view of concrete operating procedures from the perspective of the client as active self-healer. *Journal of Psychotherapy Integration, 17*(1), 125–137.

Bohart, A. C., & Tallman, K. (2010). Clients: The neglected common factor in psychotherapy. In B. L. Duncan, S. D. Miller, B. E. Wampold, & M. A. Hubble (Eds.), *The heart and soul of change: Delivering what works in therapy* (2nd ed., pp. 83–111). Washington, DC: American Psychological Association.

Brown, L. (2008). *Cultural competence in trauma therapy: Beyond the flashback.* Washington, DC: American Psychological Association.

Calhoun, L. G., & Tedeschi, R. G. (2013). *Posttraumatic growth in clinical practice.* New York, NY: Routledge.

Corey, G., Corey, M. S., & Callanan, P. (2015). *Issues and ethics in the helping professions with 2014 ACA codes* (9th ed.). Boston, MA: Cengage Learning.

Dass-Brailsford, P. (2012). Culturally sensitive therapy with low-income ethnic minority clients: An empowering intervention. *Journal of Contemporary Psychotherapy, 42*(1), 37–44.

Edwards, L. M., & Pedrotti, J. T. (2004). Utilizing the strengths of our cultures: Therapy with biracial women and girls. *Women & Therapy, 27*(1–2), 33–43.

Englar-Carlson, M., & Shepard, D. (2005). Engaging men in couples counseling: Strategies for overcoming ambivalence and inexpressiveness. *The Family Journal, 13*(4), 383–391.

Englar-Carlson, M., & Stevens, M. (2006). Masculine norms and the therapeutic process. In M. Englar-Carlson & M. A. Stevens (Eds.), *In the room with men: A casebook of therapeutic change* (pp. 13–47). Washington, DC: American Psychological Association.

Erchull, M., Liss, M., Wilson, K., Bateman, L., Peterson, A., & Sanchez, C. (2009). The feminist identity development model: Relevant for young women today? *Sex Roles, 60*(11), 832–842.

Evans, M. P., Duffey, T., & Englar-Carlson, M. (2013). Introduction to the special issue: Men in counseling. *Journal of Counseling & Development, 91*(4), 387–389.

Fernando, S. (2012). Race and culture issues in mental health and some thoughts on ethnic identity. *Counselling Psychology Quarterly, 25*(2), 113–123.

Flentje, A., Heck, N. C., & Cochran, B. N. (2014). Experiences of ex-ex-gay individuals in sexual reorientation therapy: Reasons for seeking treatment, perceived helpfulness and harmfulness of treatment, and post-treatment identification. *Journal of Homosexuality, 61*(9), 1242–1268.

Grothaus, T., McAuliffe, G., & Craigen, L. (2012). Infusing cultural competence and advocacy into strength-based counseling. *Journal of Humanistic Counseling, 51*(1), 51–65.

Helms, J. (2015). An examination of the evidence in culturally adapted evidence-based or empirically supported interventions. *Transcultural Psychiatry, 52*(2), 174–197.

Hermann, M., & Herlihy, B. (2006). Legal and ethical implications of refusing to counsel homosexual clients. *Journal of Counseling & Development, 84*(4), 414–418.

Joseph, S. (2011). *What doesn't kill us: The new psychology of posttraumatic growth.* New York, NY: Basic Books.

Kelley, F. A. (2015). The therapy relationship with lesbian and gay clients. *Psychotherapy, 52*(1), 113–118.

Keyser, V., Gamst, G., Meyers, L. S., Der-Karabetian, A., & Morrow, G. (2014). Predictors of self-perceived cultural competence among children's mental health providers. *Cultural Diversity and Ethnic Minority Psychology, 20*(3), 324–335.

Leong, F. L., Kim, H. W., & Gupta, A. (2011). Attitudes toward professional counseling among Asian-American college students: Acculturation, conceptions of mental illness, and loss of face. *Asian American Journal of Psychology, 2*(2), 140–153.

Moran, M. R. (1992). Effects of sexual orientation similarity and counselor experience level on gay men's and lesbians' perceptions of counselors. *Journal of Counseling Psychology, 39*(2), 247–251.

Morning, A. (2007). "Everyone knows it's a social construct": Contemporary science and the nature of race. *Sociological Focus, 40*(4), 436–454.

National Association of Social Workers. (2008). *Code of ethics of The National Association of Social Workers* [Electronic version]. Retrieved October 23, 2015, from http://www.social workers.org/pubs/code/code.asp

Nippoda, Y. (2012). Japanese culture and therapeutic relationship. *Online Readings in Psychology and Culture, 10*(3). doi:10.9707/2307-0919.1094

Pedersen, P. B., & Carey, J. C. (2003). *Multicultural counseling in schools: A practical handbook* (2nd ed.). Boston, MA: Allyn & Bacon.

Penchaszadeh, V. B. (2001). Genetic counseling issues in Latinos. *Genetic Testing, 5*(3), 193–200.

Remley, T. P., & Herlihy, B. (2015). *Ethical, legal, and professional issues in counseling* (5th ed.). New York, NY: Pearson.

Robinson, T., & Howard-Hamilton, M. (2000). *The convergence of race, ethnicity, and gender: Multiple identities in counseling.* Upper Saddle River, NJ: Prentice Hall.

Sehgal, R., Saules, K., Young, A., Grey, M. J., Gillem, A. R., Nabors, N. A., Byrd, M., & Jefferson, S. (2011). Practicing what we know: Multicultural counseling competence among clinical psychology trainees and experienced multicultural psychologists. *Cultural Diversity and Ethnic Minority Psychology, 17*(1), 1–10.

Smith, T. B., Rodriguez, M. M. D., & Bernal, G. (2011). Culture. In J. C. Norcross (Ed.), *Psychotherapy relationships that work* (pp. 316–335). New York, NY: Oxford University Press.

Sperry, L. (2010). Culture, personality, health, and family dynamics: Cultural competence in the selection of culturally sensitive treatments. *The Family Journal, 18*(3), 316–320.

Sue, D. W., & Sue, D. (2015). *Counseling the culturally diverse: Theory and practice* (7th ed.). Hoboken, NJ: John Wiley.

Tseng, W. S., & Streltzer, J. (1997). *Culture and psychopathology: A guide to clinical assessment.* New York, NY: Brunner/Mazel.

Vivero, V., & Jenkins, S. (1999). Existential hazards of the multicultural individual: Defining and understanding "cultural homelessness." *Cultural Diversity and Ethnic Minority Psychology, 5*(1), 6–26.

Werdel, M. B., & Wicks, R. J. (2012). *Primer on posttraumatic growth.* New York, NY: John Wiley.

Zur, O. (2007). *Boundaries in psychotherapy: Ethical and clinical explorations.* Washington, DC: American Psychological Association.

Chapter 3

MODELS OF HELPING

Professional preparation programs are often structured according to two basic approaches. In the first option, you may be studying helping skills before you take a course in theory. It is reasoned that these professional behaviors are so universal among practitioners that it is not necessary to understand their theoretical base before you begin practicing them. Because they take considerable time to learn well and become part of your interpersonal repertoire, the idea is that you should have as much time as possible to master them. Although some of the skills may be learned proficiently in a matter of weeks, mastery of others will take you the rest of your life.

A second training approach requires you to study theories before you learn applied skills. In this approach you postpone learning how to do counseling and therapy until you are fully exposed to the conceptual base that supports practice. Of course, other possibilities are that you are taking both classes concurrently or as part of an integrated unit in which theory and skills are linked.

In any of the scenarios, the outcome is the same: It is necessary to master both the underlying conceptual base of the profession, including the major theoretical approaches (see Corey, 2012; Ivey, D'Andrea, & Ivey, 2011; Seligman & Reichenberg, 2013) *and* the applied interventions that emerged from these models (see De Jong & Berg, 2012). There are distinct advantages and disadvantages to each preparation method and no clear consensus as to which is best.

The purpose of this chapter is to help you understand the ways that theory influences and shapes the application of therapeutic skills in specific ways. This relates not only to choice of which skills are considered most potent and useful, but also when and how they provide optimal effectiveness. One of the guiding principles of our profession is that the choices we make should be informed by evidence-based practice, including empirically supported treatments and those for which there is other reputable literature.

Historically, the evolution of theory in our field has emerged in four movements. You would easily guess that Sigmund Freud's contributions to developing psychoanalytic theory form the first stage. Freud and his collaborators developed the first comprehensive treatment model that explored unconscious motives, instinctual urges, defense mechanisms, and experiences from the past that continue to have an impact on present behavior.

Some of Freud's contemporaries, like Alfred Adler, helped to shape the second wave of psychological theory, which took the form of humanism, an approach later developed by Carl Rogers and others. These theorists emphasized the importance of the relationship in helping encounters, especially the kind of relationship that is characterized by empathy, caring, and respect. Emotional expression is often valued and encouraged in this second set of theories.

The third movement focused more on how current thinking (rather than past experiences or feelings) impacts behavior. These theories value the exploration of thoughts and values that can be changed in order to help clients more easily alter negative emotions.

The fourth movement currently growing that is primarily focused on contextual factors that influence the process of working with clients, such as taking ethnic culture, social class background, and gender into consideration, to name a few. This new approach to theory is influenced by those who seek cultural sensitivity and awareness of social factors that may inhibit a client's ability to feel well. Corollary theorists who are also becoming increasingly influential identify strongly as "postmodern," "constructivist" therapists. All of them share an interest in issues related to marginalization, oppression, social justice, language, and culture as they impact client experiences.

As you increase your exposure to theories, you will find that most practitioners use techniques and skills from all of these theories since they all have something useful to offer. For example, it is reasonable to assume that you might use active listening skills from humanistic theory, challenging and disputing from cognitive theory, reframing from solution-focused theory, re-storying from narrative theory, interpretation from psychoanalytic theory, realigning coalitions from systemic theory, empowerment from feminist theory, and so on. The wonderful thing about a skills training experience is that you will be exposed to all the most important therapeutic interventions that are accepted as being most useful.

Although in this chapter we're using examples from three of the more traditional models, these generic skills are an integral part of the operating strategies of every counselor and therapist. The major differences might include the way these skills are adapted and applied to individual clients and contexts.

THEORIES AND THEIR OFFSPRING

Theories of counseling and psychotherapy provide several distinct uses for practitioners. Theories help you to articulate your values about why clients come to therapy and how clients change. Table 3.1 provides a list of some of the classic or traditional theories and their major goals. You should understand that trying to state a general goal in a single sentence is difficult, at best. You should also be aware that each author who studies a theory may differ subtly in his or her understanding of the theory. All this is to say that the stated goals are subjective interpretations of each of these theories.

Finally, every theory supplies an inventory of techniques, skills, and interventions that become the means by which the model is applied. For instance, you have probably heard that psychoanalytic theory stresses that it is important to help clients uncover their unconscious desires and repressed wishes (Freud, 1936). This means essentially that the therapist's job is to increase client awareness, especially of things in the past that have been buried, as well as internal thoughts and feelings that are not currently accessible. It is reasoned

Table 3.1 Therapeutic Models and Their Major Goals

Theory	Goal
Person-centered	To increase congruence between self and experience by reducing conditions of worth.
Psychoanalytic	To make the unconscious conscious through free association with help from the therapist's interpretations.
Behavioral	To positively reinforce desired behaviors and negatively reinforce undesired behaviors and to use modeling for behavior change.
Cognitive	To recognize cognitive distortions and the underlying schemas, which are changed in order to reduce cognitive dissonance.
Gestalt	To enhance awareness by focusing on polarities and boundary disturbances, and by being in the here and now.
Existential	To create meaning in life by realizing that the client has freedom of choice and the responsibility for his or her life.
Adlerian	To overcome feelings of inferiority in a socially useful way so that the client has a sense of belonging.
Reality	To discover new ways to get our needs met so that we are able to get along with important people in our lives.

that bringing such material into view will help people to come to terms with the unresolved issues of the past that are disrupting current functioning and producing annoying symptoms.

It is one thing for Freud and his disciples to present what they believe are the best ways to practice therapy, and it is quite another when they provide specific methods and skills by which this plan can be carried out. In the case of psychoanalysis, Freud did introduce certain techniques like dream analysis and specific skills like the use of interpretation to increase client awareness of hidden patterns. Most of the other theories you have studied, or will study, have also spawned particular skills; many of these have now become integrated into mainstream practice and are not restricted to practitioners of that one theory. Many therapists and counselors, coming from a variety of schools, now use the skills of interpretation in their work even if they don't apply the skills in the way that Freud first preferred. Interpretation can be used for a variety of other purposes, such as to offer alternative explanations for patterns or behaviors that may seem puzzling to the client.

Although we used a skill from psychodynamic therapy as an example, be aware that many of the other theories have generated skills that have migrated beyond their original territory. For instance, reflective or active listening skills originated from the person-centered approach while challenging someone's internal thought patterns developed from cognitive approaches. Nowadays, these skills are considered generic in the sense that they are employed by every practitioner, regardless of their particular theoretical orientation.

Exercise in Brainstorming Skills and Common Concepts

Those who have taken a theories course or are taking one now can form groups of four or five people and list concepts and skills that are found in each of the theories. See if you can connect some common concepts or skills from one theory to another. For example, the term *projection* is found in both psychoanalytic and Gestalt therapy.

Many counseling skills did not emerge from a single theory, but rather resulted from observing what therapists actually do with their clients in sessions. It is one of the paradoxes of our profession that it is often difficult to tell which theory a clinician is using just by watching what is going on; often, a theory is more an organizing set of assumptions rather than a blueprint for how to behave. Examples of these universal skills include open-ended questions in which you might elicit information, or summarizations in which you tie things together.

What Using a Theory Looks Like

Throughout your studies, you will probably hear how important it is to align yourself with one theoretical orientation. This may seem like a challenging task because so many theories have clear strengths. In addition, you may think that being eclectic can serve you just as well. A theory, however, provides you with a structure, a foundation that explains why people do what they do and how people change. Each theory will offer something useful, and you can actually use any technique in any theory. However, you would integrate a technique from another theory from the frame of reference of your theory of choice.

For example, people often assume that Gestalt theory is primarily about focusing on emotions and works only in the here and now. Some practitioners, however, also work with the client's thoughts and may have clients reflect on the past. Clients who are particularly emotional but do not have a good understanding of why a feeling is particularly intense or seems disproportionate to the situation are encouraged to think back to the first time they first remembered feeling this way. Clients and therapist may explore the beliefs that underlie the feelings as well as the origins of those beliefs. Because this is based on exploring the past, it might sound psychoanalytical. This could also seem to be cognitive since it's based on the exploration of beliefs. A Gestalt therapist, however, would encourage the client to bring that moment into the present and then speak from that experience to gain this knowledge. In Gestalt therapy, the therapist assumes that unfinished business creates an incomplete gestalt. Unless you have studied Gestalt therapy, you might not follow the language, but you still could get the point that techniques from many different theories can be used to help your clients as long as it is theoretically appropriate.

What your instructors and supervisors are advocating when they want you to use a theory (and by the way, many state licensure exams also expect you to align with one) is that you have a direction in therapy. Everything you say directs the session. When a client tells you a story that includes many different important facets, which one do you focus on? Your theory may help you answer this.

To further illustrate the use of theories, we'll conceptualize several models from the perspective of a character that almost everyone will be familiar with: Anakin Skywalker, also known as Darth Vader, from *Star Wars*. As you may recall, Darth Vader was the villain in the original trilogy of these movies. The second set of *Star Wars* films portray him during his younger years, before he "went over to the Dark Side." We look at Darth Vader's life through the lenses of three very different theoretical orientations: psychoanalytic, person-centered, and cognitive. These are by no means the only theories we could have selected, but they are ones that have had a great deal of historical influence.

Darth Vader: A Brief Biography

Many of you may be familiar with Darth Vader from the original *Star Wars,* but that was only after his "transformation." Before he became Darth Vader, Anakin Skywalker was raised by his single mother in an implied immaculate conception. During his formative years he lived in slavery, but had a loving mother who fostered his interests and natural ability to become a talented pilot. At age 9, he was given the opportunity to fulfill his dream of becoming a Jedi warrior, but had to leave his mother behind in order to undergo rigorous training. He left his home and mother in great sorrow, relieved at having escaped his own fate as a slave but still feeling guilty that his mother had been left behind. As you probably realize, 9 years old would have been a rather traumatic time to be separated from your only living parent.

We see Anakin again when he is 19 and still mourning the loss of his mother. In the past 10 years he has found love in the arms of a woman senator, and also found a mentor and father figure in Obi-Wan Kenobi. As much as he loved and respected his mentor, Anakin became rebellious (typical of later adolescence), feeling that Obi-Wan did not appreciate his abilities as a Jedi knight. Meanwhile, Lord Sith capitalized on Anakin's rebellion by convincing him of how powerful he could be if he followed Lord Sith. Anakin's rebellion evolved more deeply into anger after the death of his mother, where we see, for the first time, his rage take control of him. He eventually suffered a traumatic physical injury in a battle against his mentor, Obi-Wan, that resulted in the loss of his arms and legs.

Just before the battle, the love of his life became his wife, and became pregnant shortly thereafter; Anakin was thrilled with the idea of being a father. His wife tried to connect with Anakin, but found him pulling farther and farther away because of fears of intimacy as well as influence from Lord Sith, who felt threatened by Anakin's attachment to another. His wife felt extremely stressed by his erratic behavior. While Anakin was having surgery for his prosthetic arms and legs, he learned that the love of his life had died giving birth. This was too much pain and suffering for him.

Anakin eventually suffered a number of other experiences that moved him farther toward the "Dark Side." He became embittered, filled with rage, vengeful, and in the course of time sustained additional injuries that required mechanical parts. At some point he became more cyborg than man. Anakin eventually "died," and Darth Vader was born, complete with the trademark black mask, cape, labored breathing, and voice of James Earl Jones.

Darth Vader was influenced by his own greed and a hunger for greater power and control. Together with Lord Sith, he attempted to take over the universe for his personal gain.

With that brief synopsis of his history, let's conceptualize his case within the languages of three very different theories.

Freud's Psychoanalytic Theory Conceptualization of Darth Vader

According to Freud's theory, Anakin experienced a strong *oedipal complex* consisting of *unconscious* incestuous desires toward his mother, especially without a father to guide him. These unresolved feelings caused him to be *fixated* in the *phallic stage* of his development. His father figure, Obi-Wan, was considered the enemy, starting with *unconscious wishes* for Obi-Wan's death that eventually became *conscious* and acted upon. His mother contributed to his *narcissism* by indulging him as much as possible during his childhood, enhancing his feelings of grandiosity. Thus, his *ego* was unable to inhibit his strong *id impulses,* enhancing his narcissistic personality.

Anakin/Darth exhibits many of the classic psychoanalytic *defense mechanisms* from the traumas in his life. First, he evidenced *denial* that he could have done something to prevent his mother's death. He *displaced* much of this anger onto the Jedi Council, and especially toward his mentor, Obi-Wan. Furthermore, he *projected* his own undesirable arrogance onto Obi-Wan, completely denying his own inflated arrogance. Anakin *rationalized* his conversion from being good to giving over to the Dark Side because the Dark Side provided him more perceived power, when actually he was trying to *compensate* for his weaknesses. Once transitioning to the Dark Side as Darth Vader, he *introjected* the value of power over good and *identified* with Emperor Palpatine, the creature symbolizing the Dark Side.

If Freud had seen Anakin, he would have had him lie on a couch and *free associate* to make his *unconscious wishes conscious.* Freud would have interpreted his free associations, evaluating *his psychosexual stages of development.* He would have helped Anakin identify *his id impulses* (especially aggression and sexual repression) and helped him develop a stronger *ego.* Eventually, Anakin would have *projected* his issues with his father onto Freud (instead of Lord Sith) so that the therapist could use this *transference relationship* to work on Anakin's *Oedipal complex.*

Rogers's Person-Centered Theory Conceptualization of Darth Vader

Rogers (1961) would have conceptualized Anakin's case very differently: Anakin was held in *high regard* because of his ability as a pilot, creating a *condition of worth.* Anakin believed that being a good pilot made him a worthy person. In addition, when he worked under his mentor, Obi-Wan, his conditions of worth increased because he had to behave according to the Jedi standards. This may have been further complicated by the fact that Obi-Wan was someone he respected early in their relationship so much that he perceived Obi-Wan as a father figure. His need to please his mentor/father figure was *incongruent* with his own wants and needs, enhancing the gap between his *ideal self* and his *self-concept.* Thus, his *organismic valuing process* was externally driven, causing him to have a *regard complex.* As a result, Anakin was unable to *symbolize* positive experiences accurately, causing a *breakdown* and *disorganization* in his *self-structure,* and eventually leading him to feel *confused* and *anxious.* This anxiety and confusion consequently made the Dark Side more tempting with its lure of enhancing his perceived *self-worth.*

If Anakin had been able to express his feelings in a *trusting* relationship where he experienced *unconditional positive regard, warmth, genuineness,* and *empathy,* he might have been able to cope with the loss of his mother and his body image in a more *fully functioning* way, releasing his natural *self-actualizing tendency* to support good, rather than dark forces.

As a result, if Rogers had seen Anakin, he would have provided him the optimal *conditions* of therapy, providing *empathy, caring, respect, and unconditional positive regard* in a *genuine* way. He would have developed *trust* with Anakin (admittedly a very challenging goal) and exhibited *warmth* to enhance the *relationship.* By providing these conditions, the *conditions of worth* would lead to greater *congruence* between his *ideal self* and his *self-concept.* This, in turn, would release a greater actualizing tendency allowing Anakin to become a more *fully functioning* person and to be drawn to good instead of to the Dark Side.

Beck's Cognitive Therapy Conceptualization of Darth Vader

Beck (1976) might have conceptualized Anakin as having several *cognitive distortions.* First, Anakin made an *arbitrary inference* that he could have prevented his mother's death. In addition, he made another *arbitrary inference* that Obi-Wan's intentions were not in his, Anakin's, best interest. Anakin *overgeneralized* his negative experience of his mother's death and the loss of his arms and legs, believing that the world was a bad place where he must become powerful in order prevent feeling hurt. He *magnified* Emperor Palpatine's position and *minimized* the power of the Jedi Council, especially his mentor, Obi-Wan. Furthermore, he *personalized* Obi-Wan's criticisms as trying to decrease his personal value rather than seeing Obi-Wan's influence as educational and helpful. He evidenced *dichotomous thinking* by seeing people in one of two ways: powerless or powerful. Thus, wanting to be powerful, he aligned with the Dark Side. After the death of his mother and the loss of his arms and legs, he probably was clinically *depressed.* His probable *automatic thoughts* with regard to his *cognitive triad* were that *he* was worthless without power; that the *world* was out to get him; and that the *future* would be bleak unless he aligned with the Dark Side. These *beliefs* in his triad and his cognitive distortions were probably related to a *dysfunctional* under-lying *schema* that he must be all-powerful to be worthy of love.

Beck might have started his work with Anakin by developing a *trusting relation-ship* through empathic listening. While Anakin shared his story, Beck probably would have listened for *cognitive distortions,* and would have identified them as Anakin was speaking. He would have amplified Anakin's *distorted thinking* by repeating what he was hearing, and giving Anakin new, more functional language. For example, if Anakin said that he *"had* to become all-powerful," Beck might have said, "you *want* to become all-powerful." This clarity of language would *empower* Anakin to take *responsibility* for his choices and decisions in life. Concurrently, Beck would have attempted to identify the underlying *schemas* that contributed to Anakin's distorted cognitions. He would have worked with Anakin to help him to be more objective about how he viewed *himself,* the *world,* and the *future.*

You may notice a difference in the use of language. You may also observe some commonalities. In all three scenarios, Anakin's negative experiences (mom's death and his own physical injuries) contributed to his angst. Furthermore, he was unable to or not given the right conditions to cope with these losses in a healthier way, leading him to make the poor decision to join the Dark Side. We believe that if he had undergone counseling, Anakin might never have needed to become Darth Vader. But if that had happened, there would have been no *Star Wars* movies, and what fun is there in that?

You may also notice how each of these theories provides a direction for the therapist's work with Anakin. Each practitioner would focus on different aspects of the presenting issue, whether this was the transference and id impulses, the condi-tions of worth and self-concept, or cognitive distortions and schemas. If you were to watch contemporary therapists use these theoretical orientations as they have developed, you would notice a lot of empathic responses, questioning, and clarity of language. They would be thinking in the language of their theory, but, ultimately, they would probably look fairly similar and arrive at similar outcomes.

You can see that although these three theories are quite different in language and what they emphasize, they also use common sense to determine what went wrong with this client, Anakin Skywalker, aka Darth Vader. We hope this encourages you to find a theory or two that emphasize what you think are important contributors to behavior, and we hope that you will become familiar with them so they can help guide you in conceptualization and treatment planning as you work with clients.

Exercise in Beginning Your Theory of Choice

Get into small groups and answer the following questions:

1. Do you believe that you need to focus on the past in order to help most clients, or do you believe that the past is irrelevant and only the present matters?

2. Do you believe that people/clients are driven by their past, are pulled toward a future goal, or have only the present moment in which to make decisions?

3. Do you believe in a structure of personality, or that we are whole and no aspect of ourselves can be separated out?

4. What type of relationship should you have with your client? Are you equal? Do you have more expertise than your client and act in the role of a coach or advisor? Or does the client have the greatest amount of expertise about himself or herself?

5. How active should you be in therapy? Does the client do most of the talking or do you do most of the talking to provide the client with feedback and information?

The Limitations of Some Theories

In Chapter 2, we discussed some of the major cultural constructs that must be taken into consideration when working with clients. One of the challenges when choosing a theory is that not all theories are culturally sensitive. Many of the older theories (the ones we used with Anakin) were developed by Western-European/American men who were raised in privileged backgrounds. If you study their personal histories, you'll realize that much of their theories come from their own experiences, which also include the values of the times. For instance, Freud lived during the Victorian era, which valued the inhibition of sexuality—and all behavior, for that matter. In contrast, some of Rogers's work was developed from the early 1960s to the 1970s, when society's inhibitions and limitations were being challenged. In addition, some of Rogers's theory was in reaction to Freud's work. Add their personal backgrounds to the formula, and you have theories constructed within sets of cultural assumptions. It would be nearly impossible to develop a theory that would work for everyone.

This is why so many of the classical theories may fit privileged individuals—or at least middle-class individuals who are from the dominant Western European culture—very well, especially men. This is the foundation of the fourth wave of psychotherapy mentioned earlier that takes into consideration contextual differences in clients. If you choose one of the more classic theories, you would want to be careful not to pathologize a client's behavior or way of being based on the theory. Instead, modify certain concepts to fit the client.

THEORETICAL FRAMEWORKS AND MODELS OF PRACTICE

Not only are different theoretical orientations adopted by practitioners, but there are several different views on how to apply them even within these schools of thought. If we temporarily put aside the notion that there are more than a dozen major theories currently in use (it has been estimated that there are actually several hundred of them), we can concentrate instead on what clinicians do rather than on their underlying conceptual paradigms. Other courses examine the philosophies and theoretical assumptions that guide therapeutic practice, whereas our job is to focus on skills and interventions.

During the past few decades, a number of authors have developed generic models of practice that formed the basis for the instructional methods. Each of these approaches attempted to integrate what is known about "good practices" and then constructed a systematic method for applying the skills. The goal of these endeavors is essentially to provide beginners with most of what they might need to conduct a helpful interview when a client walks in the door.

In one of the first systematic attempts to teach counseling skills in a sequential, problem-solving way, Robert Carkhuff (1969) combined the skills that emerged from Carl Rogers's person-centered approach with a series of studies undertaken to identify the behaviors most often associated with positive therapeutic outcomes (Carkhuff & Berenson, 1967). The model that emerged from these efforts is one in which helpers were taught a very structured problem-solving approach that moved from one stage to the next, with each stage composed of a series of steps and related skills (Carkhuff & Anthony, 1979).

Thomas Gordon took much of the same material and in 1970 developed a system for teaching parents and later, in 1974, a system for teaching teachers the major skills of helping. Parent effectiveness training and teacher effectiveness training thus introduced a whole generation of nonprofessional "therapists" to the value of active listening and reflecting skills. Students were taught the basics of several specific interventions:

- *Active listening.* This set of skills involves learning how to listen effectively, "decode" underlying affective messages, and then reflect back to the client what was heard. The goal is to promote deeper exploration of issues and lead clients to solve their own problems.
- *"I" messages.* If active listening works well when the client "owns" the problem, then using the pronoun "I" is appropriate when it is the teacher, therapist, or parent who has a problem with what others are doing. If a student is carving his initials in a desk, for example, the teacher might first try saying something like this in a rather stern, scolding voice: "Young man, do you have a problem?"

Exercise in Active Listening

For each of the following statements made by a client, try to decode the message by finishing the sentence, "You feel . . ."

1. "My mother is always telling me what to do! Does she think I'm stupid or something?"

2. "My son is using drugs, and he won't listen to me." (with tears in her eyes)

3. "I really do like this guy, but I'm not sure I can handle that he dates other people."

4. "I didn't get much sleep last night; I kept thinking about the exam I have to take today."

The student, of course, doesn't have a problem at all. He *likes* defacing the desk with his initials. About the only problem that he has is that the teacher is in his face. In fact, it is the teacher who has a problem. And until the teacher is willing to recognize that, any intervention is not likely to be very useful. The teacher can punish the child, send him to the office, make him clean up his mess, but there are considerable side effects of this way of "solving" the problem. Instead, the teacher might have used an "I" message sounding something like this: "Excuse me. I have a problem with what you are doing to that desk. I appreciate that you are expressing your artistic talents, but I am the one responsible for this property. So we have a problem that we need to work out."

This may not sound much different to you from the first statement, but its approach clarifies who owns the problem. If it is the student's problem, then active listening is indicated; on the other hand, if it is the teacher's or parent's problem, then active listening is not going to be particularly helpful.

Note the use of both skills in the conversation that follows between a father and his 9-year-old daughter:

Daughter: No I won't get dressed! I hate this dress. And I hate these shoes. And besides, you said I could stay home and I didn't have to go.

Father: I can see you're really upset right now. You're mad at me for making you do something that you'd rather not do. [Active listening]

Daughter: Well, you told me before that if I didn't want to go, I didn't have to. And I sure don't want to go. So that's the end of it.

Father: So, if I understand what you're saying, this argument isn't really about which dress to wear, but our disagreement about whether you have to go to dinner or not. [Active listening]

Daughter: That's right! I don't want to go. And that's it.

Father: Okay. I'm in a bit of a bind and I need your help. I did tell you that you didn't have to go if you didn't want to. You're right. But if you don't go to dinner, then I can't go either. And then your mother and brother will be pretty disappointed. So, I wonder if there is something we can do to help me with my problem? ["I" message]

You can see in this brief interaction that the father starts out by resisting the urge to scold, to use power and discipline to enforce his will over his daughter. Instead, he decides to listen carefully and compassionately to her, trying to sort out what is really going on. He reflects back to her what he hears her saying. Once he thinks he has a handle on what might be going on (since this is only a tentative hypothesis, it must be checked out), he then "owns" his share of the problem. Notice he does not become defensive or accusatory. He does not argue with his daughter. He does not yell at her. He simply maintains an active listening stance until the point that he realizes that he is the one with the problem, and until he articulates this reality, he isn't going to get much cooperation from his daughter.

The models introduced by Carkhuff and Gordon revolutionized the ways that counseling skills could be taught. A very complex process was reduced to a few basic skills and a half dozen progressive stages. This made it possible to teach a method previously restricted to psychiatrists and psychologists to a host of other helping professionals: nurses, crisis intervention workers, supervisors, teachers, parents, and more. It also made it possible to take a similar systematic approach to teaching skills for therapists and counselors.

AN INTEGRATED MODEL

There are many existing skills manuals that rely primarily on a particular theoretical orientation. They might emphasize specific interventions that are part of constructivist/narrative, solution-focused, cognitive, or person-centered theories. We have synthesized many of the different models that have been used over the past few decades into a generic outline that we believe most practitioners could live with. What you need most at this point in your development is a framework that helps you accomplish several critical tasks:

1. *Assess what is going on with your clients.* This includes but is not limited to their presenting complaints, other symptomology that is operating behind the scenes, family history and background, cultural identities and personal values, and anything else that helps you to understand their worlds.

2. *Formulate a diagnosis and treatment plan.* This becomes the outline for organizing the work you will do. Diagnoses can be developed according to a number of different models, which might concentrate on personality attributes, behavioral descriptions, developmental functioning, systemic patterns, or other factors. The treatment plan addresses systematically whatever you identified as clinically significant in the diagnosis.

3. *Establish a solid working alliance.* This is the therapeutic relationship that allows you to develop trust and reach treatment goals. The relationship may be structured differently depending on client needs and preferences, the nature of the presenting complaint, the length of the treatment, and the particular stage in which you might be operating. Therapeutic relationships evolve over time according to what is needed.

4. *Make good choices about which skills and interventions to use in which situations.* As we have said before, the major problem you will face is not a scarcity of choices but far too many to sort out in the time you have available. A client says or does something and you must respond—immediately. You need some way to simplify and organize your choice efforts.

5. *Figure out where you are in relation to where you wish to be.* Regardless of which model you are following, you still will need some way to assess

accurately the impact of your interventions. In any given moment you must have at least a rough idea of the stage you are operating in and what your goals are. It is also a very good idea to have a defensible rationale for anything you do or say, one that you can explain if called on by a client or supervisor.

Of course, the kind of model you use to organize your work depends on your own stage of development as a professional. These stages are represented in a series of questions related to a beginner's fear of failure:

1. *Stage 1: What if I don't have what it takes to be a therapist?* Hopefully, you are now past the point where you question constantly whether you have the stuff it takes to make it in this profession. You may have some doubts and insecurities about how good you will be as a practitioner, especially when you compare yourself to others who seem more poised, confident, and experienced, but deep in your heart you trust that with sufficient training, practice, and hard work, eventually you will reach a point where you can do somebody some good. On a good day, you will notice a few things you do very well; on a not-so-good day, you will question all over again whether you made the right career choice.

If you are still feeling stuck in this very first stage because you are having serious reservations about whether being a therapist is a good fit for you, then the helping model you choose should be one that is very basic and simple to operate. You already have enough to worry about without adding to your stress by making things unnecessarily complicated.

2. *Stage 2: What if I don't know what to do with a client?* Once you are comfortable with your ability to function as a relatively skilled practitioner, you'll reach the stage of being afraid of making a mistake. The usual fantasy is that you will say or do the wrong thing, resulting in the client becoming so distraught by your ineptitude that he or she immediately jumps out the window, cursing your name all the way down.

As a beginner, of course you won't know what do with a client. We [Jeffrey and Leah] have been doing this work for many decades and we often still don't know what to do a lot of the time. Doing therapy means living continuously with ambiguity, complexity, and uncertainty. Just when you think you might be helping someone, you discover later that the effects didn't last, or that the person was just deceiving you and himself. Other times you will be sure that you have screwed up big-time only to discover later that what you thought were misguided efforts turned out to be a brilliant strategy. Then there will be other times when the client thanks you profusely for your masterful interventions—only you will have no recall whatsoever of what you supposedly did. The question is not whether you will feel uncertain at times, but rather how you will handle these doubts.

3. *Stage 3: What if my treatment harms a client?* If in the previous stage you are wracked with doubts about not knowing what to do in a given situation, in this stage you are concerned more with the consequences—most of them negative—of making a huge mistake. At this point you recognize the awesome power of what you have learned; your concern is how to harness this power.

If you get inside the head of a therapist at this stage, you might hear something like the following:

Therapist: Where would you like to begin? [What a stupid way to say that. I should have just asked what he wants to talk about today.]

Client: Um. I don't know.

Therapist: You don't know? [What am I, a parrot? All I can think of to say is to repeat what he says?]

Client: Remember last time what I was talking about things my supervisor said?

Therapist: Sure. You were talking about how angry you were feeling because she wasn't being fair to you. [Oh no. I'm putting words in his mouth. I don't think he was saying that at all; rather, that was where I wanted to lead him.]

Client: I was?

Therapist: Um, so what would you like to talk about then? [I'm such an idiot! Now what did I do?]

This therapist is obviously being unnecessarily hard on herself but it gives you a sample of how concerned any of us can be with making mistakes. If there is an overriding fear of failure, the clinician is going to proceed in a way to minimize risks and errors.

4. *Stage 4: What if I'm not really doing anything?* More experienced therapists, who have been practicing for some time, eventually reach this stage. Once you have mastered the basics and become comfortable with the major skills, you have time to wonder about the relative value of your work. Are your clients really changing, or maybe just pretending to change?

One of the most challenging, and at times frustrating, aspects of our work is that we can never be certain about the impact of our helping efforts. Clients lie about what they report in sessions. Sometimes they tell you that things are going great when nothing really has changed in their lives. Other times they will complain that the therapy isn't working even though they really are making significant changes. Even when clients do appear to have profited from the therapy, the effects often don't last long—clients relapse without ongoing support.

Therapists who have been in the field for many years, especially those who work with the most intractable problems (personality disorders, substance abuse, impulse disorders, psychotic disorders), often wonder if they are really having much of an impact on their clients. Without good supervision, collegial support, and an ongoing commitment to personal growth, burnout can easily ensue.

5. *Stage 5: What if my life's work doesn't really matter?* Here you are trying to transform lives, but perhaps none of this really matters.

Given the stage of development in which most readers might be currently operating (somewhere in the first three stages), we have organized the process of helping (and this text) according to four basic stages. We believe that this outline for understanding the therapeutic process is neither needlessly complicated nor simplistic. It represents our best efforts to preserve the wonderful complexity of what we do, yet does not (yet) burden you with things you probably don't need at this stage.

The Beginning Stage

Think through this logically and analytically. A new client walks in the door. What are the first things you need to do and the first tasks you must accomplish in order to get any productive work done?

This is not rocket science. It isn't a lengthy, hidden formula that needs the combined efforts of brilliant minds to figure out; it is all quite obvious: Unless you can get clients to respect you and like what you are doing, they won't come back, and that makes it very difficult to help them. So your first task is to inspire some sort of trust and confidence. You must establish rapport and a working relationship that is designed to elicit the information you need and that also helps the client feel comfortable and safe enough to talk about some very threatening and personal issues.

You have four main tasks to accomplish in this first stage:

1. Establish a working alliance.
2. Complete an assessment and formulate a diagnosis.
3. Conduct a treatment plan.
4. Negotiate a contract and mutual goals.

The major skills that you will be learning and using that are linked to this stage include questioning and reflective listening. These are behaviors that are specifically designed to elicit information efficiently, as well as to develop relationships with clients that build trust, intimacy, and respect.

This is what the beginning stage looks and sounds like in the middle of the first session with a new client, about 20 minutes into the interview.

Therapist: When did you first begin to notice that you were having difficulty sleeping? [Open-ended question to elicit more information on the symptoms of anxiety]

Client: I can't really recall. It seems like it's always been like this.

Therapist: So your sleep has been disrupted for some time. [Restatement]

Client: I guess so. I don't really know. All of this is just so overwhelming that I can't remember things anymore. I don't even know what I'm doing here.

Therapist: You're having some doubts about your decision to come for help and you're feeling like things may be hopeless for you. [Reflection of client's most terrifying feelings]

Client: (nods head) So, what do you think I should do? Can you help me or not?

Therapist: I think that your decision to seek help at this time is a sign of your resilience and strength. [Reassurance and support] You have been feeling so alone and already you will notice that some of that has diminished. [Instilling confidence and planting favorable expectations] Yes, I can help you. I've worked with issues like this many times before. Before we proceed further, I'd like to ask you: What would you like to have happen as a result of our work together? [Question about expectations and treatment goals]

The therapist is trying to accomplish several things simultaneously. At the same time, he or she is learning as much as possible about the client's symptoms and when they occur, while also offering support and reassurance. There is a lot more the therapist will want to explore: what the anxiety feels like, when it first occurred, what has worked and not worked in dealing with it, whether these symptoms have occurred before, whether there is a history of this disorder in the family, what the consequences are of having these symptoms, and so on. Yet gathering all this important information to satisfy the therapist's curiosity and needs is worthless unless the client feels heard and understood. It is absolutely crucial that the initial exploration of the problem is balanced with sufficient efforts to build a good working relationship.

Building a good working relationship involves reflecting—reflecting not only the content and the feelings expressed by the client, but the meaning and emotions beneath what is presented. We are not the only people who believe that a good working alliance is a necessary condition of therapy. All of the primary theorists believe it is the foundation of therapy. As stated before, if clients do not like you or have confidence in what you do, why would they be motivated to return for more sessions? It is difficult enough for most clients to make it to the first session. If they can find an excuse not to return, they may not. This means you have to create a strong working alliance and maintain this relationship throughout the therapeutic process.

Exercise in Building the Relationship

Get into pairs and have one person talk for 5 minutes about an emotionally charged issue, either positive or negative (client role). The other person (therapist role) is to reflect a feeling and some content, in a single sentence, of what is most essential about what the "client" said. Have the client respond with agreement or a correction, and repeat until the reflection is accurate. When complete, switch roles.

Exploring and Understanding

What you began in the first stage is continued as things develop. The relationship is deepened. More and more data are collected about the client's presenting complaints and annoying symptoms, preexisting conditions, relevant family and cultural background, and other important areas of personal functioning. Essentially, you are exploring what is going on now and what has been going on in the past. This is not an activity that is taken solely for the therapist's comfort and curiosity; rather, the very process of getting significant background information is also related to helping promote greater awareness and understanding in the client.

Just as you might expect, there are as many ways of promoting this understanding as there are approaches to therapy. Some systems—like behavior therapy or brief treatments—minimize this stage, believing that insight is at best needlessly time-consuming and irrelevant, and at worst is downright dangerous. We would certainly agree that the realities of contemporary practice sometimes require us to shorten treatment to a few sessions. However, we also find that when it is feasible to include some component of insight, even such efforts often help clients to generalize what they learned to other areas of their lives.

Before facilitating insight, you might want to explore the clients' readiness for moving in this direction. Do they have the emotional resources to explore painful memories at this particular time? Do they have a support system in place so they can talk with someone between sessions? Are they already so overwhelmed with work and home responsibilities that they don't have time or inclination for self-care? Evaluating client readiness is often essential when working with clients who have experienced trauma.

Insight can be promoted in a number of different ways, depending on your own therapeutic style and theoretical allegiances. Cognitive therapists concentrate on helping clients understand that problems are the result of distorted and irrational thinking patterns. Insight work is focused on helping clients identify the dysfunctional beliefs that are getting in the way and teaching them to substitute alternative perceptions that are more reality based.

Once a strong working alliance is established and maintained, many therapists help clients explore the current problem by looking for patterns of behavior that were established in childhood. Once an awareness of where the patterns originated is reached, the client can choose to see self, others, or the world in a more realistic way and act accordingly. Some theorists would say that true insight is not reached until awareness, cognitive change, *and* behavioral change occur.

A classical psychoanalytic therapist might encourage the client to free associate in hopes of bringing about a catharsis. This process allows the client to bring unconscious material into consciousness, enhancing his or her insight into what has driven the client unconsciously in the past (Freud, 1936).

In Gestalt therapy, one of the assumptions about what brings people to therapy is that they have not fully experienced something. They feel resistant and fearful of going deeper into a certain experience, such as pain or despair. They are stuck, at an impasse. A Gestalt therapist, then, would help the client move into those feelings (or thoughts) in a way that allows a deep immersion into those experiences and the freedom to express what the client has previously feared to release. Once the client has moved through the impasse and experienced and expressed what was lying underneath, an insight usually occurs that helps the client understand what has kept him or her stuck.

The type of insight that is promoted depends not only on therapist preferences but also on client needs and time parameters. One of the first questions we like to ask in the early stages of treatment is: How much time do we have together to work this out? Obviously, you would structure therapy differently with a client who was coming for only one meeting versus another who was committed to attending sessions for several years. So if the first question you ask is, "How can I help you?"—one of the next things you will wonder about, if not ask aloud, is, "How much time do we have?"

Compare the different ways you would manage the Insight Stage according to these client responses:

- "Look, I'm kind of in a hurry. I'd prefer that we finish this thing today, but if you really think it's necessary, maybe I could come back another time."
- "I understand that therapy takes a long time, maybe years. I'm not looking for a quick fix. I really want to get to the bottom of things and I'm prepared to do whatever it takes to make this happen."
- "My kids are both sick. I'm out of money. I've got nowhere else to turn. I just think that I might as well give up. I think everyone would just be better off if I wasn't around anymore."
- "I've been sent here by my probation officer. I'm here to serve my six sessions and then get on with things."
- "I keep getting myself into these awful relationships. I dump one loser and then end up living with another one who is worse than the one before. It's almost like I can't help myself."
- "I'm really not satisfied with my life. I'm in my mid-thirties and I can't keep a steady job. I don't have a career, a family, or anything to show for myself. I feel like a loser."
- "Look, my parents think I need to be here just because my grades aren't perfect in school. I don't have a problem; they do. I'm just busy with hockey. That's all."

Exercise in Insight

With partners or on your own, develop a plan for the kinds of insight that you might promote for each of the clients presented in the above scenarios. Role-play each scenario.

We don't wish to give the impression that we are "selling" you insight as a necessary and sufficient condition for change to take place. The phrase *necessary and sufficient* was exactly the wording Rogers (1961) used in his research, where he believed that it was quite enough to help clients access, understand, and express their feelings (i.e., insight). However, like Rogers, many of the great theorists believe that insight is an important condition of therapy. For example, Freud proposed that "good" therapy helps people to understand their pasts as a way to free them from dysfunctional behavior in the present (Freud & Gay, 1989). Rogers believed that most of the action took place in the realm of feelings, while Freud was far more concerned with understanding unconscious and repressed desires. Cognitive therapists also subscribe to the philosophy that insight is critical for change, but, as we mentioned, they are concentrating on underlying belief structures (Beck, 1976). Existential therapists also place high value on insight, but they are interested in uncovering the meanings of life (May, 1953; Yalom, 1980). Gestalt therapists are interested in enhancing awareness so that clients can fully experience an incomplete gestalt, creating an insight not only at a cognitive level, but at a full mind, body, and spirit level (Perls, 1969). Within individual psychology, insight is the final stage of therapy where a change occurs not only in awareness, but also in the way a person thinks and behaves externally (Adler, 1963).

It is our position, and the one we take throughout this book, that insight is important and valuable but it is often not sufficient to promote lasting changes. You probably know several people who have been in therapy for a long time, may understand perfectly why they are so screwed up, but still persist in their self-defeating behavior. It is therefore entirely possible to understand what is going on but still be unable to do much to change the situation. A particularly good example of this has to do with addiction. A substance abuser *knows* that doing drugs or drinking all the time is not a good thing to do, but he or she is still unable to stop. An even more common example has to do with smoking. Every smoker today understands all too well the health risks of continuing to engage in this behavior. Most people would love to break this habit, but they still can't stop.

When there is time to foster some kind of insight, this stage offers a number of advantages:

1. It satisfies the human urge to make sense of life.

2. It can facilitate an awareness of the origins of maladaptive behaviors, normalize it, and thereby reduce the feelings of stigma associated with these behaviors.

3. It helps people to generalize what they learn to other areas of their life.

4. It teaches skills for working systematically to deal with problems in the future.

5. It can sometimes foster change.

Given the variety of ways that different therapeutic systems use insight and understanding, you can appreciate that there is a wide variety in the skills that are used most often. If the skills in the previous stage are centered around exploration, then the ones at this juncture are designed to increase awareness and help move clients to a different level of understanding of themselves and the world. This means that people often must be provoked and challenged before they will give up comfortable but ineffective coping strategies in favor of others that are more fully functioning. The major skills employed include confrontation, challenging, reflecting discrepancies, and information giving.

In the following vignette, some of the major features of the insight stage are evident.

Client: I guess the anxiety that I've been feeling is nothing new for me. When I was much younger—I think when I was in elementary school—I had problems going to school. And my parents tell me I was always afraid of strangers.

Therapist: So what you are experiencing right now is part of an ongoing pattern in your life that began when you were quite young. The risks that you avoid at work, and in your most important relationships, represent your best efforts to protect yourself from being hurt.

Client: Yeah. I'd say that is probably true.

Therapist: You think of yourself as rather fragile, as if you can't take much stress or you'd fall apart.

Client: (nods head)

Therapist: But if that was really the case then how could you possibly have learned to live with your anxiety for so long?

Client: What do you mean?

Therapist: I think you are a lot tougher than you give yourself credit for. You are amazingly resourceful in the ways you have learned to live with your fears. Somehow you've managed to keep your job and your friendships. You strike me as pretty competent in a lot of areas—in spite of your handicap.

Client: You really think so?

Therapist: Well, what do you think? Let's look at the evidence.

This gentle confrontation is intended to help the client examine alternative ways of looking at his or her situation. The therapist is introducing another way of viewing the situation: Instead of weakness, things have been reframed as a kind of strength. The client has not yet agreed to this interpretation, but this conversation is typical of the negotiations that take place in therapy. In part, our job is to teach clients alternative ways of looking at their lives. We do this through an assortment of different skills that are all designed to challenge thinking, clarify feelings, and provoke people to consider alternative viewpoints that are more helpful. And all of this must be accomplished while still being mindful of the relationship with the client.

Exercise in Exploring the Limitations of Insight

In pairs, talk about something in your life that isn't working. Maybe you need to quit smoking or maybe you drink too much. You may eat unhealthy food, or may need to exercise. Perhaps you need to end that unhealthy relationship. You could want to be nicer to someone important in your life.

Think of at least one or two of your life habits. Discuss what you believe you should do, and what you believe keeps you from doing it. This may help you to appreciate the limitations of understanding in making a change.

Action Stage

This component of the process is more about how clients may act than about how they think or feel. The bottom line for clients is the question: "Based on what you now understand, what are you going to *do*?"

Like the previous stages, this part of the process is interpreted according to the practitioner's favored theoretical orientation. One therapist might explicitly ask each client about structured homework assignments after sessions, each of which is designed to build specific behaviors and work toward established goals. Another therapist might interpret action to include things that the client will think about between sessions.

Although some of your clients will be less interested in making specific changes in their lives than in just spending some time understanding themselves better, the vast majority of your caseload will have rather annoying symptoms they wish to eliminate. Your job is to help them to do so by making continual small steps toward their preferred goals.

An adolescent boy has been talking for several weeks about his interest in making more friends. The counselor helped him to look at the origins of this problem, how being a loner became an established pattern when his younger brother was hospitalized and his older sister went away to college. He was also helped to look at his fears of rejection and the consequences of this protective strategy. In this fourth meeting with his school counselor, he is pressed to translate what he now understands into some form of action.

Client: So, what I was telling you is . . .

Therapist: Excuse me but I see we're almost out of time today.

Client: Oh. Sorry.

Therapist: No problem. I just wanted to bring that to your attention so we could save some time to think of some ways that you could apply what we have been talking about to your life.

Client: I'm not sure what you mean.

Therapist: Just that we could talk about this stuff on and on, but unless you make some changes in the way you do things, nothing much is going to be different. You're still not going to have many friends.

Client: So, what do you want me to do?

Therapist: The question isn't what I want you to do, but rather what you would be prepared to do.

Client: Go on.

Therapist: That's just it. Talk is great but my question for you is what you intend to do about the things we've been discussing.

Client: You mean I should just go up to people and ask them to be my friends.

Therapist: You could try that, of course, but it isn't likely to work very well. I had in mind that you start out with something that might be a small step in that direction. What could you do between now and next week when we next talk? Ideally, this would be something small but important, something that would make you feel like you are making definite progress in the right direction.

The major skills used in the action stage are those designed to increase client motivation and momentum, as well as provide structure for reaching goals. Although some theories—such as psychoanalytic, person-centered, and existential—pay less attention to an action stage, many of the theories specifically address this process. In individual psychology, the final stage of therapy is insight (as stated earlier), but insight is not only an understanding of the problem, it's practicing new ways to be in the world or with others. With Gestalt therapy, the client frequently experiences the action stage in a therapy session aimed at enhancing awareness, such as the empty chair technique, where a client might imagine speaking to her father. In cognitive therapy, action is seen in the homework that might be assigned to clients to increase their awareness of how they think and react in certain situations, and then finally how to change the thoughts or cognitive distortion in the moment. Behavioral therapists might challenge the client to make changes in session and, subsequently, out in the world once a certain level of confidence is built. Both cognitive and behavioral changes are expected to occur within reality therapy and rational emotive behavior therapy.

One primary challenge at this stage is that the client has to be ready, the relationship has to be solid, and the way in which you invite change must be done so that the client doesn't feel invalidated. In the above example, if the therapist had been this confrontive before the relationship was fully established, or before the client was ready, the client may have felt that the therapist didn't really understand. He may have felt hurt and scolded, as if his parents were telling him to *do something.* So, as they say, timing is everything. If, by chance, you take a risk like this and it goes sour, then you use this opportunity to help your client work through conflict. The session might look like this:

Client: I don't think you fully appreciate how terrified I feel. You don't get me at all!

Therapist: You're angry with me.

Client: Yes, I'm angry with you. How could you push me like this? Aren't you listening? I'm scared.

Therapist: You're angry because you feel like I don't understand your fear of people. You're not ready to take this type of action, yet.

Client: Exactly. Thank you.

Therapist: Since our time is running short, maybe we could talk about how angry and hurt you feel because of my eagerness to help. I imagine that your feeling misunderstood by me is part of what you're afraid of in developing new friendships.

In this way, the therapist can use the conflict and misunderstanding as a metaphor for what happens in the client's life. This example is a different way of taking action, by using the relationship between the therapist and the client as a model for how to be outside the session.

The reality of being a therapist is that you will be accountable not only to yourself and your client for evidencing change, but also to the agency you work for and any insurance company or health maintenance organization (HMO) that might be helping to pay for your client's sessions. Although insight can be wonderful, actual change in the client's behavior or experience *must* occur in order for therapy to be deemed successful in the opinion of most agencies and insurance companies/ HMOs. Sadly, we have also heard that many insurance companies are less interested in healing than in getting clients to a level of functioning that does not interfere with their work. The behavior change is to "be better," not necessarily well. Therefore, regardless of your theoretical orientation, you will need to define goals and have some sort of evidence of reaching those goals in order to proceed with therapy. In the above example, the goal may simply be for the client to accept his fear of making friends without believing that eliminating that fear is necessary. We have to be careful not to impose our own goals on clients, even if we feel absolutely confident that we have the answers. Of course, there is an exception to this rule of setting goals. If you have the luxury of working with a client in a private practice and the client is self-paying, then you can do whatever is comfortable for you and your client. You will find, however, that as you gain more experience as a therapist, you will want to see evidence of change as confirmation that your interventions are helpful to your client. After all, that's what you came to this field to do: transform lives.

Exercise in Action

Using the scenarios role-played earlier, see if you can generate specific goals for each and role-play a technique that might move the client toward that goal.

Integration

As things move toward closure, clients are helped to prepare for the end of treatment. Concerns and apprehensions are addressed. An assessment is made to determine the extent to which original goals were met. Clients are taught to apply what they have learned to other areas of their lives. They are encouraged to have relapses so they can practice recovering from them. They are prepared in every way possible to be their own therapists in the future.

In the following conversation you can see the integration stage in action:

Client: That's about it for now. So where do we go next?

Therapist: It sounds like we are moving to a point where you can imagine a time when these sessions will no longer be needed. You've been making some solid progress and we're almost done with our work, or at least the goals that we originally established.

Client:	Are you kicking me out? (laughs)
Therapist:	No, not at all. We can keep talking as long as this is helpful to you. I just want you to be able to do more and more of the stuff we've been doing on your own. All along, you've been learning how to be your own therapist.
Client:	I guess that's so. But I'm just worried that once we stop I'll revert back to the way things were.
Therapist:	That's not only possible but highly likely.
Client:	Excuse me?
Therapist:	Of course you will have slip-ups. I can see how anxious you look even thinking about that possibility, but consider that when you do have set-backs you can simply apply what you've already learned. In fact, I think that a good place for us to go next would be to arrange for you to mess up deliberately so we can see how you handle that kind of situation.

The therapist is implementing a strategy in which he or she is prescribing a relapse in order to improve the client's confidence and ability to resist deterioration once the therapy ends. This client's fears are entirely reasonable. During this final stage, the therapist's job is to help the client handle whatever might come up in the future. Even after the treatment ends, follow-up sessions can be scheduled on a monthly basis to make sure that the momentum continues. Frequently, therapists see clients over the course of years. The client may come for six or eight sessions, terminate for a year, and then reappear when a new challenge occurs. Therapy does not have to be something static with a single beginning, middle, and end; rather, therapy can be something dynamic that's taken when needed, like aspirin for a headache.

So when does therapy end? That's a good question. If you are in training, it could end at the end of the semester. It could end when the HMO or insurance company stops paying, which is sometimes after six sessions. Therapy could end once a concrete goal is reached. However, the ending is usually more vague and nebulous. Termination is something that is agreed on between the client and therapist and should always include an invitation to return, if needed, in the future.

A Note About Stages

As we stated earlier in this section, stage theories have developed in myriad ways. Many were developed with the assumption that when one stage was completed, the client would move into the next stage. While that is a possibility, it is more likely that stages are rough estimates of how things flow. You may start in the beginning stage with a strong relationship, but find that the relationship becomes compromised and must be repaired. This can happen at any time; you have to go back and reestablish the relationship. You may have an assessment of what's going on with the client, but then after six sessions, the client finally feels safe enough to disclose the real issue, which is much different from the presenting problem. You may even get as far as the action stage, where the client experiments with new behaviors, and find that this experience brings up some repressed information that must be understood in order for the client to continue the new behavior. In addition, you are always working on the relationship, always assessing and diagnosing as the client changes, and always shifting and adjusting goals. The point is this: The stages aren't clearly delineated, and many stages must be reexperienced, massaged, or readjusted completely. Keep this in mind as you work with clients. The process is not linear; it is more like a spiral—each time you touch back on a particular stage, you do so from a better understanding and with greater clarity. No two clients work in the exact same way. No two therapists work in the same way, either, even if they are using the same theoretical orientation. Individual differences often make therapy a messy and complex experience. Yet, we believe that the process of working with clients is a most rewarding experience once we let go of our preconceived notions.

APPLICATIONS TO SELF: CHOOSING AND USING A THEORY

Many programs require that you choose a theory to use before you begin working with clients. Some state licensure boards require proficiency in at least one theory, and most licensure exams require some familiarity with all of the primary theories. The question is: How do you choose a theory?

Before discussing how to choose, let's start with your resistance to this process. One common response from many students is that they like several theories and find many techniques useful from all theories. They feel frustrated that they must choose one and prefer, instead, to be eclectic. The problem is, in order to provide good therapy, you must have a rationale for applying certain interventions, an underlying structure that motivates the direction of mutually negotiated goals. Without that structure, you will have difficulty justifying what you do. Even if you choose to be eclectic, you are likely to have some beliefs about how to treat each client, a foundation from which to work. Thus, you are still using a theory, a theory of eclecticism. It's difficult to escape the fact that using an underlying structure or theory is necessary.

The good news is that research indicates that which theory you choose is far less important in determining therapeutic outcomes than your ability to use it effectively. Therefore, choosing a theory to learn well is what's most essential, because there is no right or wrong theoretical approach; rather, the best theory is the one you feel most comfortable with (for now). Remember, you can always change if it doesn't fit. You aren't stuck with it for life.

In addition, we have found that good therapists all look basically the same, but differ in how they explain what they do. Most theories essentially focus on the same task—finding underlying causes of behavior that must, usually, be understood and then consciously changed. That's why we presented our eclectic stage theory as a way to provide a structure for *what* you do. The primary theorists give the motivations for *why* you do what you do.

Okay, let's assume you have, reluctantly or not, agreed to choose a theory. Let's talk about how you choose, before discussing the best way to use your theory. First, you must think about what brings people to therapy and how people change.

If you believe that clients come to therapy because of unconscious drives and can change once those drives are made conscious, then psychoanalysis might be the theory for you. On the other hand, if you believe people feel discouraged because their feelings of inferiority are overcome in socially useless ways that inhibit their ability to feel a sense of belonging, and that learning socially useful ways of striving for significance is the key, then individual psychology (Adler) might be your theory. Existential therapy might be more your cup of tea if you believe that people come to therapy because they lack meaning in their life, and change can occur once they realize they have the freedom to choose meaning and take responsibility for their lives. Or you may be attracted to person-centered therapy, which focuses on how the client's ideal self and perceived self are incongruent due to conditions of worth; and once the appropriate conditions of warmth, empathy, genuineness, and unconditional positive regard are provided to the client, the client will be able to realize his or her actualizing tendency to become a more fully functioning person.

If you believe that individuals get stuck at an impasse because they feel fearful of fully experiencing something painful, and by fully experiencing that pain through some sort of expression they could increase their awareness and change how that pain is experienced, then Gestalt therapy might be more interesting to you. Another possible paradigm that might parallel your belief system is cognitive-behavioral therapy, where people come for help because they have cognitive distortions, and once the schemas that hold those distortions are confronted and changed, clients' affect and behavior also change. Finally, if you believe that all of our problems are contained within a system and can be changed only by working within that system to reveal alliances, then family systems therapy might be more appropriate for you.

You may have noticed that in each of the descriptions just given, a special language was used to say that the client comes to counseling because of some problem (i.e., unconscious drive, discouragement, lack of meaning, conditions of worth, impasse, cognitive distortions, or systemic dysfunction), that an exploration must occur to gain insight into that problem (i.e., the techniques of each of these theories), and finally, that some kind of change will occur once a shift takes place (i.e., unconscious material made conscious; courage and belonging; responsibility; fully experiencing; changing schemas; or change in a system). And the beauty of it is that you can use any technique you want as long as you can rationalize how you are using this process within your theoretical framework. So the hard part is exploring your value system, and then studying each of the theories that you think might best align with your values. After learning the top two or three really well (we're talking about reading more than what your theory textbook describes), you are more prepared to choose one and learn to use it. In addition, we recommend talking with practitioners or professors who align with the theories that interest you to gain a deeper understanding. This brings us back to how best to use your theory of choice.

Once you master (if that's possible) the basic counseling skills, especially of building a solid relationship with the client, you will need to do other things with most clients to bring about change. Your theory helps you to understand why your client is experiencing this problem. Once you are able to conceptualize your client's problem and identify the consequent goal, you use your theory to help explain why you say what you say to the client, why you apply certain interventions with the client, or why you suggest a certain homework assignment. Your theory provides you with a rationale and direction for therapy. Theory is one of your best tools for understanding the therapeutic process, which you must usually share with your supervisor(s), teacher(s), or HMO/insurance company in the form of case notes and other paperwork. Therefore, although identifying your own values and studying the theory that matches you best is a daunting task, you will be better prepared to serve your clients effectively.

SUMMARY

In this chapter, we have discussed how skills and theory work together within the therapeutic process. We talked about the fact that many theories have specific stages in their process, and that several writers have worked to create an eclectic model for working with clients. Finally, we examined our own model for conceptualizing the therapeutic process with four primary stages: beginning, conceptualization and understanding, action, and integration. These stages are broken down in the following chapters, which give more detail to help you work with clients more effectively.

Skills in Action: The Phobia

Therapist: Where would you like to start today? Shall we pick up with talking about your mom? [The beginning stage]

Client: As I told you before, I'm going on a trip, and I'm really excited about it, but I'm also really scared. I'm, well, I'm embarrassed to tell you, but I'm afraid to fly. It's a new thing! I've flown many times, but only recently have I had this fear. I don't know where it comes from. I meant to come here to talk about my mom's illness, but I'm losing sleep over this. I don't understand it.

Therapist: You sound surprised and ashamed to fly. You sound like your mind is obsessing over it. What do you imagine will happen? [Empathy; exploring and understanding]

Client: I'm flying with the other passengers, and all a sudden, the turbulence gets out of control. Then I hear the engines shut down, one by one. People are screaming. I know it's going to be a long and painful death. We have several minutes as we nosedive to our deaths. I'm helpless, I can do nothing.

Therapist: You're helpless. [Empathy]

Client: Yes! I can't protect my wife. I can't save my own life. I just have to wait for my death and feel the fear of pain and dying.

Therapist: You're afraid to die. [Empathy]

Client: I suppose everyone is, but it's that I'm *sure* that I'll die in a plane crash. What's wrong with me? Am I going crazy?

Therapist: Let's see if we can figure this out, since you're worried you might be going crazy. I'm aware that you are afraid of a plane crash even though I assume you know it's safer than driving. [Instilling hope; empathy; exploring and understanding]

Client: I'm not going to die driving. I have control. There are lots of ways to die, but if a plane crashes, then I can't do anything about that! If I'm sick, I get help. You know what I mean?

Therapist: Control. Now you have said that twice, in a way. You feel helpless to protect your wife; you have no control. Tell me about the last time you flew and were comfortable, and then the first time you flew that you were uncomfortable. [Exploration and understanding]

Client: Okay. When I was in college, I flew all the time. I went to school here and would fly home to Oregon to see my folks every few months. The last time I flew and wasn't worried about it was six years ago. Then, the next time I flew, for a delayed honeymoon, about four years ago, I was terrified. We went to Fiji, and the vacation was wonderful, but the flight was like a horror movie in my mind. Since then, I have worked really, really hard to avoid flying. But this is an awesome opportunity to fly to New Zealand, and I don't want to pass it up.

Therapist: I'm struck that there was a two-year window between flights. I wonder if there was anything that happened during that time where it was important for you to be in control. [Exploring]

Client: I got married. That happened. Control? Well, I guess I feel responsible for my wife, to protect her.

Therapist: Protect your wife. From what in particular? [Probing]

Client: From everything. She is my responsibility now. I need to care for her, make sure she's safe, help her get her needs met.

Therapist: That sounds like quite a responsibility. Any ideas where you might have gotten that belief? [Probing]

Client: No, not really. It's true, isn't it?

Therapist: It sounds like you believe that. I wonder if you see her being equally responsible for you. [Probing]

Client: No. Not really.

Therapist: Okay, now we're getting somewhere. [Instilling hope]

Client: Really? I'm lost. Weren't we talking about my phobia?

Therapist: I can't help but think there might be some connection. Indulge me for a moment and tell me about your parents' roles with each other. [Exploring]

Client: I'm not sure how this will help since I've worked on my past, but I'll answer. My dad is addicted to pain killers and my mom is a saint. She took care of us and him. I never understood why she didn't leave him.

Therapist: Your dad wasn't the kind of dad you wanted. In fact, I imagine your dad still isn't the kind of dad you deserve. [Facilitating insight]

Client: True, but I understand. He's an addict. I've studied addiction, and when I look at his past, I'm surprised he doesn't do worse. He did the best he could.

Therapist: A part of you knows he did the best he could and feels understanding. Another part of you is angry that he wasn't the father you needed. [Reflecting discrepancy]

Client: That's true. He wasn't there for any of us.

Therapist: When I bring that into the present situation, I can imagine that you feel responsible for your wife because the worst thing you could do is be the kind of husband and father your father was. [Interpretation; intuition]

Client: I have to admit that. I don't want to be anything like him.

Therapist: Now, I'm really going to take a guess. Please feel free to tell me if any part of this or the whole thing doesn't fit for you. I think that you feel a strong sense of responsibility as a married man to care for your wife, your family. The most horrible thing you could do is not follow through on this responsibility. And when you fly, you have no power to save her life or help her. You like having control. I say this not only because of what you said before, but also because of how you dress and hold yourself. You're also very careful with your words. You like control. Is that accurate or is there any part that doesn't resonate with you? [Interpretation; intuition]

Client: Um (long pause) I think that does fit, really well actually. I do like control. It's a good thing.

Therapist: It must be helping you in some way, to have control. [Exploring]

Client: Well, yeah. I'm not like my dad. I keep a job. I take care of my responsibilities.

Therapist: And control can be really helpful. At the same time, you don't want to face that you can't control everything. So much of life has chaos that's beyond you. When I say that, what's that like for you to hear? [Preparing for action]

Client: I feel anxious (pause) lots of anxiety.

Therapist: Yeah. It's almost as if by acknowledging any lack of control, you resemble your father. [Interpretation; intuition]

Client: That makes a lot of sense. Now, I don't feel quite so crazy.

Therapist: Now when you think about flying, how is it? [Assessment]

Client: (long pause) There's still some anxiety, but not nearly as bad. I don't think that fixes it, but it sure helps.

Therapist: I wish this insight were enough to get you over your fear of flying, but you also have to make some changes. I would like you to think about taking a risk in the near future. Go to a movie without knowing what's playing. Or go to your favorite restaurant and let your wife or if you're really feeling brave, let the chef choose your meal. [Action]

Client: Whoa! That sounds really scary.

Therapist: What might be a little risky for you? Let's take it one step at a time. In our past conversation, you seemed to really care about not looking like a fool. I wonder if you would have any difficulty going to a playground with your wife and swinging on a swing set. My thought is that maybe the carefree child in you could come out and play. I imagine he's been hidden for a while. [Action]

Client: That would be really weird, but I'd be willing to do it. How will this help me?

Therapist: I think if you can begin to let go of control of some little things, that eventually you may not need to control so much. I'd also like to teach you some deep breathing before you go. That way, when you begin to feel anxious, you can practice your breathing and talk yourself down. [Action; integration; homework]

Client: Sounds good to me. I'll do anything I can.

Therapist: Great, and by the way, I will follow up on how the swinging went. (smiling) Now let's get started on your breathing . . .

REFERENCES AND RESOURCES

Adler, A. (1963). *The practice and theory of individual psychology.* Paterson, NJ: Littlefield Adams.

Beck, A. (1976). *Cognitive therapy and the emotional disorders.* New York, NY: International Universities Press.

Berant, E., & Obergi, J. H. (Eds.). (2009). *Attachment theory and research in clinical work with adults.* New York, NY: Guilford Press.

Bowlby, J. (1978). Attachment theory and its therapeutic implications. *Adolescent Psychiatry, 6*, 5–33.

Carkhuff, R. R. (1969). *Helping and human relations.* New York, NY: Holt, Rinehart, & Winston.

Carkhuff, R. R., & Anthony, W. A. (1979). *The skills of helping.* Amherst, MA: Human Resources Development Press.

Carkhuff, R. R., & Berenson, B. G. (1967). *Beyond counseling and therapy.* New York, NY: Holt, Rinehart & Winston.

Corey, G. (2012). *Theory and practice of counseling and psychotherapy* (9th ed.) Pacific Grove, CA: Brooks/Cole.

De Jong. P., & Berg, I. K. (2012). *Interviewing for solutions* (4th ed.). Pacific Grove, CA: Brooks/ Cole.

Freud, A. (1936). *The ego and mechanisms of defense.* New York, NY: International University Press.

Freud, A. (1954). The widening scope for indications of psychoanalysis: Discussion. *Journal of the American Psychoanalytic Association, 2*, 607–620.

Freud, S., & Gay, P. (Ed.). (1989). *The Freud reader.* New York, NY: W. W. Norton.

Gelso, C. J., & Bhatia, A. (2012). Crossing theoretical lines: The role and effect of transference in nonanalytic psychotherapies. *Psychotherapy, 49*, 384–390.

Greenberg, L. (2014). The therapeutic relationship in emotion-focused therapy. *Psychotherapy, 51*(3), 350–357.

Ivey, A. E., D'Andrea, M., & Ivey, M. B. (2011). *Theories of counseling and psychotherapy: A multicultural perspective* (7th ed.). Thousand Oaks, CA: Sage.

Kottler, J. A., & Blau, D. S. (1989). *The imperfect therapist: Learning from failure in therapeutic practice.* San Francisco, CA: Jossey-Bass.

Maroda, K. J. (2012). *Psychodynamic techniques: Working with emotion in the therapeutic relationship.* New York, NY: Guilford Press.

May, R. (1953). *Man's search for himself.* New York, NY: Dell.

Perls, F. (1969). *Gestalt therapy verbatim.* Moab, UT: Real People Press.

Rogers, C. (1961). *On becoming a person.* Boston, MA: Houghton Mifflin.

Seligman, L., & Reichenberg, L. (2013). *Theories of counseling and psychotherapy* (4th ed.). New York, NY: Pearson.

Yalom, I. D. (1980). *Existential psychotherapy.* New York, NY: Basic Books.

PART II

SKILLS TO USE WITH INDIVIDUALS

Chapter 4

SKILLS FOR BUILDING COLLABORATIVE RELATIONSHIPS

Although this is a chapter about relationship skills in a therapeutic context, we want you to know from the outset that building relationships with people involves far more than applying a few helping behaviors. Although it is true that some of these actions are conducive to constructing closer connections with people, human intimacy and trust develop in far more complex and mysterious ways. You can do all the right things with a client, apply your relationship skills with perfect mastery, and still fail to establish any sort of meaningful connection.

YOUR BEST RELATIONSHIPS

Think about the most powerful and influential relationships you have ever experienced. Aside from your parents, who were the teachers, coaches, and mentors who made the greatest difference in your life?

As you reflect on these relationships, now consider: What was it that these powerful individuals did that helped you the most?

Our strong hunch is that some of the following attributes played a prominent role:

1. *You felt safe.* You were allowed to make mistakes and learn from them. You were not manipulated, abused, or taken advantage of. You felt essential trust.

2. *You felt respected.* You were treated with essential kindness and caring. Even if the mentor was a strict taskmaster, you still felt that this structure was enforced for your welfare.

3. *You felt valued.* You were treated as if you were important and as if what you thought and felt and did really mattered.

4. *You felt understood.* It was clear to you that this mentor heard you, responded to your needs, and demonstrated high levels of empathy.

FOR REFLECTION

Go back in your mind to elementary school or high school. Think about someone in your life who picked on you or treated you in a way that hurt you. What were some of the ways in which this person behaved that hurt your self-esteem? What was missing in the relationship?

Now think about a person who had a strong positive impact in your life. How was that person with you? What quality or behavior of that person meant the most to you? How did you feel about yourself with this person?

These are the qualities that therapists try to exhibit, in genuine and caring ways, with clients. For some clients, having a therapist who is fully present and understanding is all that is needed.

USES OF THE THERAPEUTIC RELATIONSHIP

It might seem to you as if the only function of your helping relationships with clients is to build sufficient trust so that they will tell you what is really bothering them, but that is only a small part of what is possible within this alliance. It is certainly true that without a solid relationship it would be hard for you to accomplish much. You must keep in mind, however, that there are very different sorts of relationships that can evolve and prove useful, depending on such factors as (a) what the client needs, (b) what the client would respond best to, (c) your personal style, and (d) the stage of counseling that you are operating within. Keep in mind that in the very beginning of your contact one sort of relationship is appropriate, whereas in the latter stages you would wish to construct a very different sort of alliance.

Imagine, for instance, that you are greeting a therapist for the first time. What would you like from this person to help you feel most comfortable? You would probably want someone who is polite, careful, reassuring, validating, supportive, and who makes it clear that things will move at your pace. Yet once you have established some degree of rapport and trust with this person, you might very well be open to a more directive, confrontive, and perhaps less structured interaction. The ways you use the relationship with your clients thus depend on where you are in the process and which treatment goals are currently being addressed.

You would probably create a different relationship with a client who presented himself for treatment because he was shy, withdrawn, and friendless than with a client who was embroiled in conflicts because she was overly verbal, gregarious, and controlling. In the first case, you might try to allow the client to take more responsibility for the process in order to bolster confidence and teach assertive skills, whereas in the latter instance you might wish to install more structure and boundaries and to offer constructive feedback.

The dialogues below illustrate what we mean. Let's assume the client starts the session by saying the following:

> I'm struggling through a divorce with my husband. Our son is only six months old, but I don't want my husband to have any custody. My ex borders on being abusive to me, and I've seen him be verbally abusive to others. I don't trust him. He's so unaware of child development and expects our baby to meet his needs. I'm afraid he'll do permanent damage. I don't know how to prove to the judge that he's not fit to be a parent, especially to an infant.

If this was the very first session with the client, the therapist might respond with something like this:

> You sound really frightened about the consequences if your ex-husband gets some level of custody. You're also feeling really helpless and uncertain about how to protect your son.

This type of response does several things simultaneously. First, it validates the client's experience. Second, it helps the therapist make certain that she understands the situation and the client's meaning. Third, it invites the client to talk more about her thoughts and feelings, exploring them on a deeper level.

As with any other moment in therapy, there are innumerable interventions that could be chosen and implemented. Although this reflective response is certainly a valid option, the therapist could proceed in a slightly different way that first acknowledges what was said, then probes in the area that the therapist thinks is most important:

> You're afraid of your ex-husband's potential abusiveness. Tell me more about the ways in which you experienced him as abusive.

Once the therapist has developed a more solid relationship in which the client feels safe and trusting, the therapist has more latitude to explore at a deeper level without the client feeling threatened. In addition, if this topic has come up before and the therapist has already validated the client, then it may be time to get more details to understand the client's experience better.

As another example, imagine that the therapist has been seeing this client for a year and knows that the client has a tendency toward drama. Furthermore, from this prior experience, the therapist has developed and maintained a strong alliance characterized by mutual respect and a high degree of trust. In this case, the therapist might respond as follows:

> We've talked before about how toxic your relationship with this man was. You've shared before about how extremely angry you are at him. But I'm concerned that your use of the word *abusive* is really about putting him down and taking away his power so you can hurt him back. I think we need to talk more about your anger so that your son is not harmed by the relationship between you and your ex-husband.

In this situation, the therapist may have more information and a strong enough relationship with the client to be able to introduce this relatively mild confrontation. However, if this was attempted very early in the relationship, before sufficient trust was developed, it is entirely possible that the client could feel sufficiently offended and threatened that she might not return. With some history, background, and experience, the therapist can be far more direct and probing. It is still possible that the client could become offended, but if so, the therapist would know the client well enough to process that conflict in the session. Such negotiations could strengthen the relationship even more.

Relationship as a Diagnostic Aid

How a client behaves with you in session offers clues as to how this person interacts with people in the outside world. You can observe very closely the patterns with which your relationship evolves and how the client responds to you, and use this valuable information to generate hypotheses about what may be happening in other relationships.

A client says to you that he wishes to have more intimate relationships with people. You invite him to tell you more about how this isolation feels to him. He then becomes angry with you for being intrusive and withdraws into a pouting posture. When you attempt to draw him out, he lashes out and calls you incompetent. There may, of course, be many reasons to account for this conflict, but one possibility is that this behavior is characteristic of how he deals with personal overtures. Perhaps, you surmise, what he has just done with you he does with others. You will have to check that out, naturally, but your close observation of the ways your clients establish relationships with you gives you time to consider ongoing patterns in their lives. As mentioned previously, you will also have to look at the relational style within the larger cultural context of the client's background and experience.

Interpersonal Engagement

Your relationships with clients can act as powerful vehicles for influencing them in a variety of ways. One of your jobs is to impact clients in as many ways as you can within the limited time you have together. This is a daunting mission, given all the other influences (many of them counterproductive) in the client's life, the short period of time you spend in sessions, the client's fears and apprehensions, and the client's tendency to backslide to old, familiar habits.

Through your engagement with clients, you develop the leverage to influence them in ways that you think would be good for them. By establishing a strong, safe relationship, your clients will be more likely to reveal the most shameful parts of themselves. They will trust you to not judge them critically and be willing to tell you about themselves and their choices. Without such a strong relationship, clients tend to hold back how they really feel about themselves and what they are doing in their lives, compromising your ability to help them. As they share more about their life experiences, their concerns and difficulties, their strengths and resources, you get a clearer picture about what keeps them stuck and prevents them from making desired changes. Then, when it's later in the therapeutic process, they are more willing and able to change because you understand them better, can precisely tailor your treatment to their needs, and they trust you more to take the risks you suggest.

Sometimes, despite taking your time and trying to proceed at the client's preferred pace, you find that sessions remain stagnant. You might be tempted to push faster or harder. Keep in mind that clients often become defensive for very good reasons—to protect themselves from perceived threats or to buy themselves time until they are ready to make changes.

Unfinished Business

Sigmund Freud and his psychoanalytic legacy were instrumental in sensitizing us to the power the past can have in shaping present behavior. People respond to others in particular ways not just because of what is happening right now, but because of what has happened earlier. We sometimes don't see others as they are but how we imagine them to be. These perceptions are often distorted or exaggerated. They are also "grooved" as a result of patterns that were established long ago, often during childhood.

Clients will sometimes respond to you in ways that may seem out of proportion to reality. Called *transference,* these reactions represent client fantasies about who you are. As an authority figure, as someone in a position of power in their lives, you may resemble others they have known (parent figures, other helpers) in the past. You may do or say something that evokes an extreme response. When you replay the scene, you are puzzled by why the client reacted so negatively and even why the client has attached himself so closely to you. After all, you hardly know this person. Here are some examples of the forms that transference might take:

- The client acts in a deferential way that is inconsistent with his behavior in other environments.
- The client assumes you are trying to control, manipulate, or coerce her when you haven't even made a suggestion yet.
- The client dislikes you before you spend 5 minutes with him.
- The client instantly likes you because you and she seem similar in age, appearance, and ethnicity or you remind him of someone he knows and likes.
- The client reacts to you the way he describes acting toward his mother.
- The client assumes you don't like her and that she's your least favorite client.

Countertransference reactions, that is, the distorted ways that you see your clients based on your own fantasies and past experiences, further complicate matters. In fact, one of the lifelong challenges you will have as a therapist is to recognize when you are having a strong personal reaction toward your client. Many therapists believe that you have countertransference with every client since you can't help reacting in some way, even if positive, but it's only the strong reactions that are likely to impede your work. The most dangerous situation is when you don't know you are experiencing countertransference and react in counterproductive ways.

How do you know if you might be experiencing countertransference? Here are a few examples:

- You feel a strong attraction or aversion to a client you've just met.
- You are less effective with this client than with others you see.
- You dread seeing this client each week and hope she cancels her appointment.
- You find yourself reacting to the client as if she is your mother or he is your father.
- You feel deeply hurt, resentful, or angered by something the client said that wasn't intended to be taken personally.

If you combine a client's transference reaction and your countertransference reaction to the client, you have a big mess. Supervision can help you sort through some of the major issues. If supervision isn't enough, your own therapy might be helpful in adjusting how you perceive your client.

Once you can accurately read and identify the ways that unfinished business from the past plays itself out in sessions, you can use your relationship as an instrument of healing. Imagine, for example, that a client has never had a positive relationship with an authority figure before, but has always suffered as a result of her misplaced trust. No matter what else you do to help this person, your relationship with her, if it is structured in a way to help her to feel safe, can help to restore her faith in others who may serve in an authority role in the future.

TRANSFERENCE EXERCISE

In pairs, have one person role play the therapist and the other person the client. The client will talk about a positive experience. The therapist will negate everything the client says and look at the dark side, becoming the pessimist. Do this for 5 minutes, then process the experience.

What was it like for the therapist to be negative? What was it like for the client to be faced with that negativity? Did this remind you of someone in your own life? Some students may not have a reaction, and that's okay; they will have different transference buttons. Other students may have strong negative reactions that may indicate an area where countertransference could occur. Share your experience with the class.

Problem-Solving Collaboration

Some approaches to therapy, especially the brief and cognitive therapies, construct relationships that are based on a collaborative model. Partners in this process both work together to sort out what is going wrong, and then put their heads together to figure out what can be done instead. The role of the therapist is structured more as a consultant rather than as benevolent parent figure or expert teacher.

Regardless of the kind of work you do, there will be times when you slip into this role of consultant and structure a relationship that is more egalitarian, with shared responsibility for content and process. In the example of the woman unhappy with her job, the clinician first tried direct intervention but encountered resistance. He then decided to abandon this kind of relationship as ineffective and redesigned an alliance in which they would work together as collaborators on a problem that was "externalized" to make it feel less threatening to the client.

"Let's approach this situation as if the problem is not yours," the therapist begins, "but instead belongs to someone else. How might we tackle this challenge?"

Note that in the use of the pronoun "we," the therapist is making it clear that this is a partnership, a relationship in which they will work together to solve a problem in a systematic fashion.

With some clients and in some situations, this approach really helps clients to become more objective about their situations. This might be enough. At other times you may need to slow down to find out what's missing before you can get back to solving the problem. This process is seldom necessary with most high-functioning clients (meaning they have fairly positive self-esteem and have at least average or above average intelligence). In contrast, clients who are lower functioning (whether from an intelligence perspective or due to severity of pathology) may need much more guidance of this kind from you as the therapist. That means you will need to assess your client's strengths and weaknesses before becoming too focused on solving a problem.

Personal Support System

It would be difficult to overestimate the importance of our role as a source of support in clients' lives. Apart from anything else you do, any interventions you use or any techniques or skills you employ, standing in a person's corner provides immeasurable benefits. Clients too often feel isolated and alone in their pain. They lack confidence. They are dispirited and demoralized. They feel little hope for the future and sometimes want to give up.

One of the most important things we can do to help clients is offer consistent support for their efforts to change. We communicate, as strongly as possible, the following messages:

- "I am here for you."
- "No matter how bad things get, you can always count on me."
- "Even if I don't approve of some of the self-defeating things you do, I still support you as a person."
- "I am utterly reliable and dependable."
- "I will never take advantage of you or deliberately do anything to hurt you."
- "I have no vested interest in the choices you make; my only job is to help you to get what you want."

It feels wonderful, more comforting than words can ever describe, to be involved in a relationship with a professional who is completely trustworthy and supportive. We inspire faith. We teach people that it is indeed possible to be involved in a relationship with someone who will cherish you. Although our commitment is professional, we hope our clients will become so used to this sort of relationship that they will expect support from others in their lives. Keep in mind that many people, and especially those who come to therapy, may not have experienced very many healthy, supportive relationships. If you do nothing else, providing this net is essential.

Modeling

The way you are with your clients teaches them how to be with others. It's a parallel process. As your clients develop a relationship with you, they learn how to be in healthy, honest, authentic, relationships that are characterized by mutual respect. They learn to take responsibility for their reactions, and learn to articulate their feelings more clearly and to see the benefit of sharing those feelings, both for catharsis and for making changes. They experience what it's like to be treated with care, and consequently, will look for others who treat them this way. They learn from you, the therapist, how to treat others with compassion and kindness.

Whether intentionally or not, you are a model for your clients in how to be with others. This includes the ways you express yourself, the ways you process the world and make sense of things, the ways you handle yourself during challenging situations (such as when a client confronts you). The only difference is that clients will want to seek reciprocal relationships rather than the one-sided relationships that therapy provides. This is where group therapy can be especially helpful because it allows clients not only to observe fully functioning behavior in action, but to try out those new behaviors in an experimental laboratory where refinements and feedback are available.

Novel Interaction Experience

Once support and trust are established, it becomes possible to use the relationship to experiment with alternative ways of functioning using immediacy. Let's say, for example, that a client has trouble asserting herself with others, especially older, authority figures. Characteristically, she has allowed herself to be steered in whatever directions others have wanted, silently fuming to herself, building resentment over time. In one session, you notice that she seems a bit reluctant to go along with a suggestion you have made that you think would be helpful. Knowing her history, you could back off at this point and nudge her along slowly. Instead, you decide to use your relationship as an opportunity to practice new behaviors.

"No," you tell her, "I must insist that you do this. I really think this will be good for you."

"Well," the client hesitates. "I don't know."

You can see that she is becoming angry at your prodding but she is far too polite and deferential to say no in a direct way. You decide to push her further and even exaggerate things to the point that she will have to confront you. Finally, with her back against the wall and her resentment boiling to the surface, she tells you in no uncertain terms that she has had quite enough of this. You will please respect her wishes and stop pushing her.

The therapeutic moment has arrived. You applaud her courage and reinforce her strength in standing up to you. You make the point that if she can do this with you, if she can set limits within therapy, she can do so in other areas of her life with her husband, her children, and her coworkers. This novel interaction with you is the beginning of a new pattern of assertiveness that the client is learning. Before employing a technique like this, though, you want to make sure you have a strong relationship and that you're being culturally sensitive. Perhaps the client appears nonassertive when in fact she's from a culture that relies on high-context communication. Clients from high-context cultures (meaning that it's polite to communicate information indirectly) need to understand about how the communication style of their home culture may be different from the environment in which they live. You can work with them to understand the difference and then help them modify their communication style to get their needs met.

Enforcement of Boundaries

Some people come to you with more severe personality disorders or extremely irritating, controlling interpersonal styles. With diagnostic labels like borderline, narcissistic, or sociopathic personality, these are individuals who are used to controlling and manipulating others to get their way. They are often very self-centered and sometimes exploitative. They seem to have a strong sense of entitlement.

Even some clients with less extreme forms of full-fledged personality disorders will play lots of games to test the limits of what they can get away with. They will come consistently late to sessions and then expect you to accommodate them by running over into your next session. They will not pay their bills and then argue about the charges. They will cancel appointments at the last minute. They will call you at home with constant emergencies. You may feel them get under your skin in a variety of ways, haunting your fantasies, invading your sleep. You will notice yourself spending a disproportionate amount of time thinking about these very few individuals.

In such cases, a very different sort of therapeutic relationship is called for. Specialists who work with such "disorders of self" believe that the primary instrument of treatment is a special sort of relationship that includes a *holding environment* and clearly enforced boundaries. This means that although you might ordinarily be flexible and adaptive with your clients, in some cases it is absolutely imperative that you establish very structured rules that are enforced without exception.

Take, for instance, a client who fits the description of a borderline disorder, meaning that she exhibited characteristics of vulnerability, instability, volatility, and intense emotional states that could be, at times, very manipulative. Imagine that a therapist had seen her for several sessions. As one particular session came to an end, she asked if she could send a note during the week summarizing what she got out of the session.

The therapist may think that this is a fabulous idea. It shows how motivated the client is to work on herself and to reflect on the work between sessions. The therapist may be keen to get ongoing feedback from her about what was getting through to her and what was not working at all. The therapist may even think that this might be a good thing to try with all clients.

The therapist sensed a warning buzzer going off in his head but he chose to ignore it even though this woman previously had tried many other ways to get him to demonstrate to her that she was his most valued and important client. For example, she would save her best stuff for the last 5 minutes of the session to see if he would give her more time. She would threaten suicide to see if he would spend extra time with her. She would call the therapist's office occasionally in immediate crisis to see if he would see her outside of her scheduled sessions. Ordinarily, therapists can be extremely responsive to any of these requests from most clients, but with this woman the therapist had learned the hard way how important it was to stick to agreed-upon rules. As is so often the case, he found that she was improving not so much due to his brilliant interventions but instead by the enforcement of these boundaries, which helped her to realize that relationships could indeed be dependable. The therapist "held" her in an environment that was safe and predictable, yet was impervious to her manipulations—that is, until this ploy.

Sure enough, the two-page summary of the session came in the mail. She was insightful, concise, and entirely on target in identifying the main themes they had covered in their previous session, what she had learned, what she was working on, what helped most and least, and a review of the assignments she would complete before they saw one another next. Needless to say, he was quite pleased with this new development.

When after the next session the client asked if she could again mail him a summary of what she learned, he again agreed. Frankly, he was enjoying this process. Of course she knew that, and knew exactly how to get him to make exceptions to their contract of no contact outside of regularly scheduled sessions. When her next letter arrived a few days later, it was again extremely impressive.

This time it was four pages long. This concerned him a bit, and again a warning bell chimed in his head, but he was already planning how he was going to write this up for an article.

I'm sure you know where this is going. The next week, the letter was 12 pages long and no longer appropriate in either length or content. When the therapist told her in the next session that he would no longer accept or read these letters, she became hurt and indignant. "But I don't understand," she accused him innocently, "at first you said this was okay and now you are changing your mind. I thought you said that you would be consistent with me, that this was part of my treatment."

She got him.

We are not including this story to warn you to mistrust your clients, but rather to alert you that there are some cases, such as personality disorders, that require a different relationship than what you might ordinarily construct. In such situations you will want to use the relationship as a way to teach these clients how to live within boundaries. This is a task many of them will find very difficult, and they will test you in every way possible. Just remember, they are doing the best they can in a world that seems scary and unpredictable to them. Perhaps that will make it easier for you to be stronger in enforcing boundaries (for those of you who have difficulty with this).

Authentic Engagement

Last but hardly least, Carl Rogers (1951) was among the first to advocate the value of therapeutic relationships to provide genuine human encounters between people. People have always lived in groups and been nourished and sustained by these interactions. Among all the things that therapists do to be helpful to people, one is to use the therapeutic relationship to provide caring and love. We are not talking about love in the romantic sense, of course, but rather as the genuine and real affection and respect that we feel for those we help. We are communicating to them in many ways that they are important to us, that they are not "just" clients but real people who are involved with us in real relationships.

It is true that you will work with many clients you won't like very much, and you will certainly not like some of the crazy, hurtful things that they do, but you will nevertheless come to care about them deeply. There are other clients you will see with whom you will have among the most intimate relationships that you will ever experience in your life. They will tell you their deepest, darkest secrets. They will show a degree of honesty and openness that you will rarely experience in any other relationship in your life. If you think about it, even your closest relationships with family members and friends rarely (unfortunately) involve meeting on a weekly basis (without interruptions!) to talk about feelings and innermost thoughts.

Remember, in therapy sessions, almost everything is private, secret, and confidential (unless someone exhibits dangerous behavior or potential). There are no interruptions or distractions. You listen to one another with perfect, hovering attention. You talk about the most important things, all of them very personal. You become a perfect confidante and listener for your clients, and they feel very grateful to you for this. They will tell you a lot about how much you matter to them. And you will reciprocate.

The nature of the authentic engagement between clients and therapists makes for some very intimate, powerful encounters. In some ways, your clients will be among the most cherished people you will ever be privileged to know. Authentic engagement is an extremely powerful process, not only for your clients, but for you as well.

ABOUT EMPATHY

The glue that holds everything you do in your therapeutic relationships together is *empathy*. It is the state of entering into other people's experiences and sensing their worlds from their points of view. It is when you can see, hear, feel, and sense what someone else is going through, yet at the same time you are able to preserve your own sense of self. You can feel what another is feeling at the same time you can feel yourself.

Economist Adam Smith was actually one of the first writers to sort out empathic reactions (Sugden, 2002). Although what he called "fellow feelings" were more closely aligned to sympathy, Smith believed that this uniquely human state occurs when two conditions are met. One is the observation of someone else in the midst of emotional arousal, whether that is elation, despair, or frustration. The second is having the imagination necessary to share this affective experience.

Empathy originates from the German use of aesthetic transcendence in which observers project themselves into the object of beauty. American psychologists borrowed the term, translating it into English in order to describe what happens when one person experiences another person's emotional reaction to stress.

There has actually been considerable debate among psychologists and philosophers about what constitutes empathy. Is it a cognitive process in which thinking and interpretation are involved, or solely an emotional reaction? Like so many intellectual debates, it probably doesn't matter as much as the theorists believe.

You may experience empathy in your head, your heart, or more likely in both places. You are moved at a profoundly personal level and are also making sense of this experience with your senses and mind.

What we do know is that empathy is a uniquely human experience. At its most primitive level, infants only a few days old are known to cry in response to others' distress. It turns out that humans have developed the capacity for empathy for a number of reasons that ensure our continued survival:

1. Increased sensitivity to others' moods allows us to predict their behavior or avoid direct conflict.

2. Empathy allows us to recognize and anticipate others' needs, making for a more cooperative society.

3. It allows for mutual support and help-giving when one person is in distress and benefits from assistance from the "tribe."

4. Empathy creates interpersonal bonds that are useful in community action.

5. It is a vehicle that elicits altruistic behavior in which one sacrifices personal safety for the greater good of the community.

When it comes to empathy, we are definitely not created equal. And when we say "created," we don't mean just the capacity you are born with but also how you are trained. There are, in fact, vast individual differences, in which some people bleed emotionally at the slightest provocation of another's discomfort and others feel nothing at all in the presence of human suffering. They feel no pity, no sympathy, no concern, not even any guilt and shame if they were the cause of others' pain (these people are often called sociopathic).

First and foremost, empathy must be applied to yourself before turned toward others. How can you tell what other people are feeling if you don't recognize such states inside yourself? Awareness of the world and its inhabitants thus begins with the self. Sometimes this is one of the most difficult tasks for individuals to learn. In order for you to be more in tune with your client, you have to be self-aware, which engenders feeling pain, sadness, despair, anger, fear, and myriad other unpleasant feelings we so frequently like to avoid.

Protect Yourself

When sensitive people like therapists get close to others, especially to individuals who are wounded and bleeding emotionally, it is hard not to become profoundly affected by the experience. It is important that you are able to open yourself up to feel the pain and express it, but without identifying with it as if it were your own. You need to be able to leave the experience in the room with your client, although you may still feel sadness. It's important that you don't allow the wound itself to become yours. All you should keep is compassion for your client after the session. This is certainly a concern that many therapists-in-training have. How many times, when you've told someone that you want to be a therapist, have they said, "I could not do that, listen to people's problems all day. How do you keep from taking it home with you?" So how do you do it?

First, you must become clearly aware of your own feelings and reactions toward others. Learning to differentiate between your own feelings and what someone else is experiencing is essential. One way to establish these boundaries is to take in the feelings of others so that you will be able to reflect them back, and, at the same time, be aware of your response to what that person experiences. This helps you to differentiate your feelings from your client's.

Second, enforce those boundaries. Each time you interact with individuals, and especially clients in pain, be mindful of your boundaries, of what's yours and what's the other person's stuff. Remember, the client is ultimately responsible for his or her own life. Clients have to make their own decisions and live their own consequences. Your job as the therapist is to provide support and enhance their understanding so they can make their own choices. Let go of feeling responsible for your friends and family, and any feelings of responsibility for clients will follow. Work hard not to let that guard down until it becomes second nature to you. It may seem like a lot of work, and that's because it is. However, in time, you will not need to be as mindful of it as often.

Additionally, confront your own need for distraction. We frequently use distraction to avoid uncomfortable feelings. First, you have to be willing to feel your own emotions without distraction before you are receptive to the emotions of others. Then you have to get yourself out of the way; you must put aside your needs (of hunger, of feeling tired, of wanting to talk about yourself) and fully listen to your clients. Once any distractions are put aside, you will be more fully able to feel what the client is expressing without identifying with those feelings. As long as you are not clear, you run the risk of taking on what the client feels as if it were your own.

Exercise in Empathy

With a partner, talk about a time when you could feel the emotions of another person or other people when you walked into the room. Students can usually report feeling tension in a couple. Talk about how you identified the feeling and realized where it came from. This will help you do the same with clients.

RELATIONSHIP SKILLS

The skills for building relationships are the same ones needed to communicate effectively. The various behaviors are divided into several successive stages. First we cover the skills required to read nonverbal behavior; then we address the skills required for good attending.

You Are Watching the Client: Reading Nonverbal Behavior

Before clients even open their mouths, your observational skills kick into gear. You note their dress and appearance, the way they carry themselves, the way they walk. You observe how they present themselves and form a first impression. You listen to the sound of their voices. You feel the firmness of their handshakes. You note which chair they take in your office. You observe their posture, their gestures. And inside you, there is a whirlwind of reactions going on that might sound something like this:

Nice haircut. But what's with that pink hair? Why does she keep touching her hair? Is that a nervous gesture or more a grooming thing?

Interesting that she wore such a short dress. Is that the usual way she dresses, I wonder, or rather a seductive gesture? Or perhaps this is my own projection? She seems rather feminine in her mannerisms but she could be overcompensating. Bet she's having relationship problems.

Careful now. Don't jump to conclusions. Wait to hear her story.

She seems kind of passive, waiting for me to take charge. Is this a pattern in her life? Does she characteristically defer to men?

Her voice is rather throaty, as if she has a cold. Maybe she's a smoker. She does look rather nervous, even for a first session.

I like this woman. I wonder what that's all about? There is something about her that is instantly endearing. Could it be a vulnerability or is it something deeper? Must watch my reactions in this area.

She is smoothing her dress, as if she is ready to begin. But she is still waiting for me. Her foot is moving, a nervous gesture. It seems coordinated with her hair grooming. Should I let her off the hook or wait for her to begin? My sense is that she wants me to start. Okay. Here it goes.

In this brief example, which lasted about 20 seconds in the therapist's head, you can begin to get a sense of the observational skills that are used to begin the therapy process. It all starts with reading nonverbal behavior accurately.

Skills in Reading Body Language

The first information at your disposal includes what you notice and observe about the ways clients present themselves. In those first few minutes, you will be paying close attention to any cues you can read from how clients stand, walk, sit, and conduct themselves. The face alone presents a staggering 5,000 different expressions, many of which can be recognized as far away as the length of a football field. And there have even been studies (Gottman, 2014) in which a couple's divorce can be reliably predicted based on watching only a minute or two of nonverbal behavior, especially subtle facial expressions of contempt.

Although there are cultural variations in what nonverbal cues can mean, as well as the possibility of deception (fake smile), many human facial expressions such as smiles and anger are universal.

Body language can be grouped in several categories:

- *Facial expressions.* What can you read in the client's face? Smiles, head nods, frowns, tiny movements in the mouth, eyes, cheeks, and brows all signal internal states.
- *Gestures.* Look for hand movements that accompany speech. What do they communicate that supports or contradicts verbal speech?
- *Body movements.* Notice restless feet, wringing hands, or any other movements that may be significant.
- *Posture.* Is the client's body tense? Relaxed? Slumped?
- *Visual orientation.* This includes eye contact and movement.
- *Physical contact.* Handshakes, hugs, pats.
- *Spatial behavior.* How does the person position him- or herself? How close or far is the person standing or sitting? In family sessions, how do members position themselves in relation to others?
- *Appearance.* Clothing, grooming.
- *Nonverbal vocalizations.* Uh huhs, ums, exclamations, sighs.

Cultural variables make reading nonverbal signals more complicated. Some cultures value stoicism and restraint of emotional expression. You might assume that a client is cold and repressed because so little is revealed nonverbally. Or another client may smile all the time, demonstrating politeness within his culture, even though it is not at all representative of what is going on inside of him. It is for this reason that you don't want to inadvertently misinterpret behavior simply because it's not a part of your cultural norms. On the other hand, the fact that someone comes from a particular cultural background doesn't necessarily mean that he or she will behave in ways that are consistent with what might be expected. Each family has its own cultural values, which may or may not reflect the dominant culture or the culture from which the members were born.

BODY LANGUAGE EXERCISE

Get together in small groups. Take turns expressing some internal state using only nonverbal behavior and vocalizations. The other members of your group will try to guess what you are feeling inside.

Take turns telling a story that involves some emotional response. Frame your body language so it is inconsistent or incongruent with the way you are really feeling as you relate this story. For instance, if you were actually feeling quite anxious inside, you would say that you handled the situation quite well and felt no nervousness whatsoever. In fact, you are still feeling quite calm about the situation. All the while you are saying this, your behavior is showing agitation (wringing hands, darting eye contact, nervous foot tapping).

What are you looking for and what are you thinking about when you observe clients systematically? Here are some general guidelines:

1. *Assessment of general mood:* How does the person appear to be feeling? Check energy level, emotional states, and variation of affect.

2. *Clues as to inner states:* What does nonverbal behavior tell you about what the person might be feeling inside? How does what you observe fit with what the person reports is going on?

3. *Mental status:* What is the person's relative functioning level in terms of memory, behavior, and control?

4. *Verbal and nonverbal congruency:* What are the discrepancies between what you see and hear?

5. *Signals of distress:* What are overt and subtle symptoms of acute distress? (See Table 4.1)

6. *Elaboration of verbal expression:* What is the person's communication style?

7. *Unconscious reactions:* What are some things the client is doing about which he or she may be unaware?

8. *Communication of underlying meaning:* What are some of the symbolic and metaphorical communications that are accompanying the surface messages?

9. *Evidence of deception:* This is a difficult area to recognize (see Table 4.1). Even professional police investigators can tell when suspects are lying only about two thirds of the time. In our work, we aren't as concerned with finding out the "truth" anyway because this is a relative concept strongly influenced by people's imperfect memories and perceptions.

The Client Is Watching You

Think about what happens when you meet a person for the first time. Now imagine that this stranger has come to you for help. He or she takes a seat in your office and tentatively begins to tell you what is desired. As this scene unfolds, the very first thing you do is observe the individual and form some initial impressions. Remember that your clients are doing exactly the same thing. They are watching you carefully and asking themselves several questions:

- Will I like this person?
- Will this person like me?
- Can I trust this person?
- Does this person know what she is doing?
- Will this person judge me harshly?
- Will this therapist agree with me or give me a hard time?
- Will this person make me do something I don't want to do?

Table 4.1   Reactions to Stress

Physical	Cognitive	Emotional
Fatigue	Poor concentration	Guilt
Sleep disruption	Obsessive thoughts	Helplessness
Lethargy	Flashbacks	Anger
Appetite changes	Violent fantasies	Depression
Lowered sex drive	Memory disturbance	Moodiness
Headaches	Self-blame	Numbness
Hyperactivity	Poor reasoning	Irritability
Startle responses	Irrational thinking	Fear
Muscle tremors	Impulsive decisions	Anxiety

All of these observations are based on nonverbal cues. The client is looking at your dress and manner, the way you furnished your office, the diplomas on the wall, the books on your shelves, the way you sit, your voice and manner, your posture, all the innumerable ways that you present yourself. Do you convey a sense of confidence and essential competence? Do you seem attractive and trustworthy? In these first moments, clients are still trying to make up their mind about whether they want to continue this enterprise.

FIRST IMPRESSIONS EXERCISE

In small groups, get together and share your first impressions of one another the first day you met. Talk about the personal reactions and opinions you formed during that first contact and what shaped most of those impressions. Mention the ways that clothing choices, hairstyles, posture, voice tone, and body language all provided cues.

Discuss the impressions you presented to others compared to the ways you see yourself.

Discuss the values and limitations of first impressions. For instance, such quick, instinctual reactions are programmed into us as a way to react quickly to perceived danger.

What's Beneficial About These Listening Skills?

You would be amazed how much information you can collect and how well you can develop a relationship with clients by relying solely on listening skills. Keep in mind this is not "listening" in the usual sense of its practice. Most such listening in the "outside world" takes place while people are distracted and multitasking. Rarely is anyone given the kind of focused, undivided attention that therapists routinely employ. In addition, in the outside world, the listener may be more interested in responding than hearing all of what the first person has said. Such a posture communicates intense interest, caring, and respect, saying to the client: "I am totally and completely with you in this moment. I am listening (and observing and sensing) so carefully to what you are saying (and doing) that I can hear (see) things that would otherwise remain buried or ignored. Based on this intense empathy, I hope you will feel understood in a way that you have never experienced previously."

Listening skills let you accomplish the following tasks:

1. *Help clients tell their story.* You are encouraging clients to share a narrative about who they are, where they came from, and how they ended up where they are now. Using probes and reflective skills, you draw out the story looking for patterns, themes, and deeper meanings.

2. *Draw out appropriate background and contextual information.* You are exploring the cultural and individual context of clients' experience. You are collecting relevant information about their family of origin, their presenting complaints, their medical history, their cultural background, and so on. You are doing this not only to formulate a diagnosis and treatment plan, but also to facilitate deeper understanding of the client's experience.

3. *Communicate understanding.* Listening is by no means a passive enterprise. It is not nearly enough for you to listen, hear, and understand, unless you are able to communicate this back to clients in such a way that they feel like they have been making sense to you. They also want to know that you are not judging them critically and disrespectfully, that you feel caring and compassion toward them, even after they have confessed their deepest secrets and hidden desires.

4. *Facilitate deeper level exploration.* Based on the exploration that takes place during this listening stage, a number of more advanced skills and interventions are used to help promote insight and to move toward constructive action.

5. *Make connections.* Throughout the listening process you are not only collecting information, but also trying to make sense of what you are hearing and understanding. This often involves identifying recurrent patterns and themes, as well as making connections between (a) what clients are experiencing in the present versus what they have lived in the past, (b) the problems they are encountering versus those that already exist within their families, (c) what they are doing and saying in sessions versus what they do and say in their outside worlds, and (d) what clients are saying they want most versus what they have been actually doing.

6. *Demonstrate empathy.* Throughout every aspect of this process of data collection, listening, and meaning making, the single most important task is to demonstrate empathy. It isn't enough merely to feel it yourself; the client must also feel understood. Empathy is demonstrated most effectively when you reflect their current feelings.

Attending Skills

Now that you have an idea of how to read the client's nonverbal behavior, you must use this knowledge to let your client know you are listening. This is going to be a lot harder than it looks. We are talking about those nonverbal behaviors with which you *communicate* your complete and total interest in what the client is saying. Sounds simple, doesn't it? What's the big deal? You just look at the person and nod your head a few times.

The truth is that most people don't have the slightest idea about how to attend fully to others. Watch others (even more educational: watch yourself) during their conversations and you will see people who are engaged in multiple tasks at the same time. They are nodding their head in acknowledgment all the time they are looking around them, fumbling with notes, glancing through pockets for lost objects, signaling to passersby, or trying to interrupt.

Exercise in Attending

Get into triads: a client, a helper, and an observer. While the client talks for about 5 minutes, the helper should try to attend to the best of his or her ability without talking. The helper should practice attending as much as possible and at the same time, be aware of how thoughts, feelings, and other distractions seem to get in the way of the ability to fully listen (Are you hungry? Do you need to scratch an itch? Do you want to talk about yourself?).

The observer should observe the helper (not the client who is talking). Pay attention to body posture, eye contact, facial expressions, and acknowledgments/minimal encouragers.

After 5 minutes, the helper should talk about the experience of attending, followed by the client sharing his or her experience. Finally, the observer can talk about what was noticed during the interaction. Rotate until everyone has played each role.

Even when they are giving their full attention, you would never know it. It is important not only that you are attending fully to what others are saying but that you also appear to be attentive. The difference may elude you at this point, but it won't do you much good to be concentrating on others if they think you aren't listening. There must be congruence between what you are actually doing and what you appear to be doing.

What does someone look like who is attending effectively?

- *Body posture.* You will notice body positioning and posture that signal attention. This means facing the person fully, often leaning forward, using your whole body to communicate intense interest. Arms and legs aren't crossed in a way that blocks the client.
- *Eye contact.* You will observe that the person is making relaxed but focused eye contact.
- *Facial expressions.* Your face shows appropriate responses to what is communicated.
- *Acknowledgments/minimal encouragers.* Head nods and other gestures communicate nonverbal encouragement.

You may notice that these are precisely the same skills that you use to read your clients. Obviously, the message you convey is just as essential as what you are observing from your client. Therefore, even though you haven't even opened your mouth to say a word, you are still using every part of your being to say to the client:

I am hanging on your every word. There is nothing else that exists for me in this moment except for you and what you are saying. I am using all of my concentration and all of my abilities to listen intently to everything you say. I am picking up the slightest nuances of what you are expressing.

One question that occurs to many beginners when attempting to listen fully is about eye contact when talking. It's quite normal to look away while you're talking. Frequently, you or your client will be searching for the right words. It's also fairly normal to be more internally focused, especially for an introverted, less social person rather than someone who is externally focused. At other times, clients may look down because of feelings of guilt or shame. It all depends on the client and the circumstance. We don't want you to obsess about eye contact, but rather to be aware of when you may be distracted and to redirect yourself to your client.

Exercise in Observation

Spend an evening watching reporters on television conduct interviews. Watch the ways they use their bodies and gestures to communicate to their interviewees (and the viewing audience) that they are attentive listeners. Note which things each interviewer does well in addition to weaknesses you observe.

Exercise in Feedback

Ask people who know you well what they like best and like least about the ways you listen to them. It is going to be difficult to get people to be really honest about this, so in order to get useful feedback you need to impress on them the importance of giving you specific suggestions.

Passive Listening

So far, we've talked about establishing a relationship with someone by demonstrating solid listening skills, and have covered the skills involved in this process. You may have noticed that we haven't even gotten into the realm of speaking aloud, and we won't for a bit longer. Before covering active forms of listening, you must first master passive listening, which includes all the nonverbal things that we cover in this chapter, to encourage and to keep the client speaking.

Make sure that you are positioned so you can listen and respond effectively. Try not to have any big objects (like a desk) between you and the person you are helping. Face the person fully but in a relaxed position. Make eye contact in a natural way. Of course, once again, culture may play a role in this. Clients from some cultures will be more comfortable with some object between the two of you, so try to assess whether this is a cultural difference or a way of avoiding connection.

With a clear mind and gentle spirit, allow your face to be as animated as possible, to let the person know you are tracking appropriately what is being said. Your face shows sadness or delight or concern, depending on what the client is trying to convey at the time.

Head nods are particularly important. In a natural way, you nod your head up and down (or side to side if you are in parts of Asia) to let the person know you are hearing what is said. You smile when appropriate (when the content is happy, not if you feel nervous). And you use verbal encouragers like "uh huh" to keep the person talking.

Exercise in Passive Listening

Sit opposite a partner. Your partner talks about something, anything, for about 5 minutes. During this one-way conversation you are not permitted to speak. No questions. No prompts. Use only passive listening skills to track the conversation. Obviously, this is not what you would do during a normal session, but it is a valuable first step. Once you're able to do this, you can move on to more complex skills. A good analogy is learning the proper grips for holding a tennis racket before proceeding on to the correct way to strike the ball.

This will feel awkward and even silly, but it is important to get into the habit of practicing sound listening skills. Besides using your eyes, facial expression, and body posture to communicate your interest, you are allowed only to nod your head and say, "uh huh."

After about 5 minutes of this (which is about all you'll be able to take), switch roles.

Technology Skills

Technology is increasingly being integrated into the therapeutic process, sparking a number of ethical, legal, and practical challenges that must be addressed. Many therapists use mobile devices as their business phones, and clients can often rely on text messages to communicate to their therapists. Some therapists use e-mail or use websites that appear to e-mail therapists to correspond with clients about their issues or manage appointments. Historically, therapists have conducted sessions using the phone, which has now evolved to conducting sessions as video conferences on HIPAA (Health Insurance Portability and Accountability Act) compatible systems. With each of these venues, the ability to read nonverbal language is decreased because there are fewer visual cues. Utilizing video has fewer problems than using other forms of communication, but this may still provide inconsistent audio or visual information; this lack of fluidity can at the very least lead to frustration and at worst lead to misunderstandings if important words or expressions are lost. Written communication through text, e-mail, or instant messaging can be even more deleterious. Nuances of tone of voice, facial expressions, and other cues may be lost, leaving only the receiver's projections about how the message was meant to be conveyed.

Ideally, you will want to establish a strong relationship with your client before using telehealth (using technology as a means to deliver therapy). This decreases the chances of misunderstandings; your client can hear your voice. In addition, you can make guesses about the client's nonverbal behavior as well based on past experience. However, many therapists conduct all sessions, from the first to the last, using telehealth. Consequently, the therapist should frequently take the time to check in with the client to make sure nothing important was missed or misunderstood.

Internal Assessments

The empathic attitude described earlier in the chapter would now be applied full force. With your attention focused and your listening skills brought to the forefront, your main job at this point is to stay with the client.

To start, you must listen to your own heart. Put yourself in a state of maximum receptivity so you are fully open to what is coming from the client. Open your eyes, your ears, your senses, and most of all, open your heart. This means that before you sit down with your client, you should feel and exhibit the following characteristics:

- *Be confident.* Your client needs to have confidence in you, and that cannot occur unless you have confidence in yourself. You may feel like you still have so much to learn, even after receiving your degree, and you do—that learning never ends—but regardless of where you are in your program when you see your first clients, you still know more than they do about therapy. You know how to attend and how to build a strong relationship.

- *Be flexible.* One of the most valuable skills a therapist can develop is flexibility. Any opinions you have formed about your client should change easily with new information. Your preferred way to work may not work with one particular client. You must be flexible enough to try something different. You may set goals that later seem inaccurate or inappropriate as you develop your relationship with your client. You must be willing to adjust the goals negotiated with your client. No matter how set you might become in your ways, you will inevitably need to change at some point since individuals are unique.

- *Be assertive.* Many people who come to the field of counseling really want to be liked and can sometimes neglect to assert themselves in exchange for popularity. However, as a therapist, you must sometimes be willing to assert yourself, even if it upsets your client. You must set boundaries for appropriate behavior in therapy, especially with couples, families, and groups. You must almost always end your sessions on time, even if your client was late. You must sometimes assert yourself by confronting your clients. Finally, asserting yourself is an excellent way to model this important life skill to your clients.

- *Be nonjudgmental.* As discussed in Chapter 2, you will find that being nonjudgmental can be difficult at times, especially when your values are substantially different from your client's. If you are aware of your own values and biases, you will be better prepared to handle all kinds of client issues. Furthermore, realize that values are not necessarily objectively correct or incorrect; rather, values are things we decide are right for us. If you can perceive values as choices we all make, you should find it easier to accept value differences. Finally, accept that clients are ultimately responsible for their own lives. Your job is not to make decisions for or judge the client. Instead, your job is to provide a supportive and fostering environment. You must trust that the client has the ability to find his or her own solutions in a way that is best for him or her.

- *Be focused.* In the first chapter, we discussed a little about how you attempt to put your client in an altered state of consciousness. You can only do that if you are focused. That's why it's a good idea to take a deep breath before beginning. If your mind is wandering about what you'll eat for dinner or your last client, you aren't really fully listening to your client. This is a skill that can be difficult to learn at first, and as you encounter personal problems while trying to do therapy, focusing can be quite difficult. However, you must work to develop your ability to give your attention fully to the client. Otherwise, you might miss something important!

- *Be caring and compassionate.* You may like your client; you may not like your client. In either case, you must care for your client and be interested in

Exercise in Testing Your Listening Skills

Now that you have been introduced to observing and attending skills, let's see how you are doing. Sit with a partner so you are facing one another. One of you tell a story about something personal that happened recently. Pause at least every minute or so, selecting spots that lend themselves to transitions. The listening partner will then summarize what was heard thus far while using observation skills and demonstrating good attending skills. The storyteller will then fill in any details that were left out before continuing with the narrative.

After doing this for about 5 minutes, switch roles so that each of you has the chance to practice listening.

Talk to one another afterward about what this was like.

his or her welfare. You must maintain a loving attitude and feel compassion as a parent would for a child, but without the responsibility. When you care deeply for your client, your loving attitude comes across, and the client feels valued. Clients who feel valued also feel safe and therefore are able to explore unpleasant aspects of themselves. What's more, experiencing that caring can enhance their self-esteem.

Related to this internal assessment process, your job is to carefully check out how well the relationship appears to be going. This allows you to make adjustments as things proceed. Here is a list of questions you might wish to consider at this time:

- How is the relationship evolving so far?
- How am I reacting internally to this person? What are my own reactions?
- What have I done so far that seems to be working well? What have I tried that has not worked that well?
- What is the client avoiding? What am I avoiding?
- Before I respond, what do I know and understand so far?

You have not really been allowed to say much yet. So far, all the skills you have learned are designed to position you so you can demonstrate maximum receptivity and sensitivity. Although most people in the "outside world" associate helping with giving people advice—telling people what they are doing wrong and what they could do—instead, the professional concentrates as much on listening as on talking. In fact, the skills you learn in this chapter account for more than half of the counseling skills you will use in your work to build collaborative relationships;

add a few responding skills to your repertoire (which are covered in Chapter 6, "Exploration Skills"), and you will be amazed at the results you will get.

BEFORE YOU BEGIN

When you begin an interview, or any conversation, the first thing you must do is clear your mind of all distractions. This is very much like what happens during the practice of meditation, yoga, or the martial arts. The goal is to gently push aside anything going on within you or around you so that you can remain fully present with the person you are facing.

In yoga, a ritual called a "cleansing breath" is used to begin any activity. You close your eyes for just a moment and take a deep breath through your nose. As you exhale slowly through your mouth, you focus on the sensation of the air moving out of your body. You then allow yourself to breathe normally, increasing your awareness of the sensations of your breath moving in and out of your body (the heat as you exhale through your mouth, the coolness as you inhale through your nose, the rise and fall of your abdomen and/or chest with each breath, etc.). As you do this, you will find your mind wanders or that other sensations in your body interfere with your breath awareness. Acknowledge the interruption without judgment and gently turn your attention back to the task of breathing. Let us warn you: Concentration on a single task is difficult to accomplish, and those who do it well practice for hours each day for years and years.

Exercise in Meditative Listening

Several times throughout the day, notice how your attention wanders when you are speaking to someone on the phone or in person. Each time you observe yourself "leaving" the conversation, thinking about something else, gently return yourself to the present. Close your eyes for a moment and take a "cleansing" breath in order to remain focused.

In this preparation phase to begin helping, your goal is to lead yourself to an "altered state of consciousness," a place where you will be acutely aware to what you hear, observe, and sense. You do this by following five steps:

1. Clear your mind.
2. Resist both internal and external distractions.
3. Stay neutral and centered.

4. Focus your concentration.

5. Take a deep breath.

6. Be gentle with yourself each time you fail and get distracted, because you will.

PITFALLS AND COMMON MISTAKES

In Part II of this book you will learn specific skills related to being a therapist. As you learn each skill, you may be prone to making some common beginner's errors. In the next several chapters, we present lists of these pitfalls. Following are some mistakes related to observation and attending skills. Perhaps by our presenting these pitfalls, you will be more conscious of them and more able to avoid them.

Using Minimal Verbal Encouragers and Nodding Too Much

Earlier in the chapter, we recommended the use of minimal encouragers and nodding to let clients know you are following what they say. However, there are a few caveats. First, avoid nodding too much or overusing "uh huh," as this can sometimes convey that you feel impatient. If you record yourself listening to someone, fast forward the video as you watch it. You will quickly be able to see if you nod too much. Listen to the session for 5 minutes, and if you hear yourself frequently saying "uh huh" to the client, you know it's too much. Finally, some therapists say "right" or "good" as minimal encouragers. Although these may be intended to be neutral, they imply a judgment that increases a client's external locus of control. In other words, when you say judgment-like encouragers, the client may think you approve and begin interacting with you in a way that seeks approval. Your goal is not to judge or approve of your client; instead, your goal is to provide understanding and caring regardless of what your client says.

Maintaining a Stoic Face

Some therapists are focused so intently on listening that their face remains stoic. We recommend that you practice making faces in the mirror if you tend to be serious. Practice your sad face, angry face, happy face, and compassionate face. Spend time with infants and toddlers because for some reason, we seem to parallel the expressions of infants naturally (probably because language is not yet developed). Make your face congruent with the client's topic so he or she feels more understood. Record yourself talking with someone to see what you do.

Making Your Face Too Animated

A problem similar to the stoic face is a face that's too animated. If you appear overly happy or overly sad, your expression may not match what your client is feeling. As a result, the client may not experience accurate empathy. The best way to develop appropriately modulated expressions is to record yourself in a conversation with someone, and then make the appropriate adjustments.

Closed Body Language

We all have habitual ways of sitting. Pay attention to how you sit in your office, when waiting for something, and in the passenger seat of a car. When you feel chilly or if you are feeling angry or sad, you may cross your arms in front of you and cross your legs. Ask someone to sit like this in front of you and notice your reaction. Most likely, you will perceive that person's body language as closed. Arms and legs crossed may communicate, "Stay away, I want to be alone," or "I'm feeling vulnerable and afraid." Learn to be aware of what your body says. We also suggest you always bring a jacket in case your office gets too cold to avoid needing to cross arms and legs.

Sitting Too Relaxed

Habitually slouching in your chair or leaning on something may convey to clients that you aren't interested in them or that you're too tired to listen. You are a professional, and as such you must convey a demeanor that presents professionalism and confidence. That's not to say that we want you to sit perfectly straight with your feet on the floor and your hands on your knees; rather, be comfortable, but be professional. You are not selling an object; you are selling yourself as a service to your clients.

Staring Too Much

You have read above that maintaining relaxed eye contact with the client indicates good attending behavior. What does that mean? Well, it doesn't mean staring at the client without ever looking away or blinking. You may find that when people listen, they tend to make stronger eye contact as compared with when they talk. When people talk, they tend to look up when they think or down when they feel.

So it's okay to look away when you are talking, but only on occasion. It's also okay to look away briefly now and then while the client talks to avoid staring. Prolonged eye contact can be interpreted differently in different cultures.

Exercise in Staring

Choose a partner and sit facing each other. For 3 minutes, stare into each other's eyes without talking. Afterward, talk about your experience. You may find that you had difficulty not laughing because of feeling embarrassed. You may have found that staring was quite intimate. You may have been aware of thoughts about what the other person sees when she or he looks at you. You may have been aware of your thoughts about the other person based upon that person's appearance. You may have noticed your mind drifting to avoid the discomfort of such intense contact.

Matching the Client's Face Rather Than the Content

As stated before, socially we tend to smile when people laugh or smile, even if the content of the information is sad or serious. This is to match where the other person wants to be. It's polite. In a therapy session, however, the rules for politeness are different. In order to help clients connect with their feelings, match the content of their conversation rather than what their face or tone of voice projects. During a first session, you may want to smile a little and make a mental note of this incongruence. Eventually, though, you will want to match the content. If the client still tends to be incongruent even when your face and tone are matching content, then let the client know he or she does this. For example, "I notice that when you talk about something difficult, you tend to laugh a lot." The client is avoiding feelings; you may serve them better by gently helping them to connect with those feelings.

APPLICATIONS TO SELF: THE EFFECTS ON ALL YOUR RELATIONSHIPS

"So, what is the client trying to say? What does that facial expression mean? Is my facial expression appropriate? Am I leaning forward to show that I'm attentive? How am I reacting to what the client says? How can I convey empathy while facilitating the client's emotional expression?"

Learning how to focus on so many aspects of the client while still attending to your own reactions may seem like a daunting task. That would be because it is.

Fortunately, you don't have to learn all of these skills in one class that meets for a mere 3 hours per week. These skills are something you can practice every day in all of your relationships, in all of your interactions with others. Each time you interact with a person, whether or not it's someone you know, pay close attention to his or her nonverbals and what he or she is attempting to convey. Practice listening to others while expressing good relationship-building skills, such as appropriate minimal encouragers, focusing your attention fully, using appropriate nonverbal expressions, and so on. The more you practice, the better you will become. Eventually, most of the time, most of these tasks will become second nature.

At this point, we recommend that you start recording some sessions with a partner to practice these skills. If you are not already assigned a client, find a classmate with whom you can practice these skills. Meet with him or her each week to record a 15- to 20-minute session. Then immediately review your tapes to see if you are applying the skills you will learn in the following chapters. Most of the skills you learn will be cumulative. Now that you have been introduced to nonverbal attending skills, you should evaluate your progress in this area until the end of the semester.

We also recommend that you save the videos you make so you can compare your early sessions with later ones. As you start to feel a little overwhelmed, it helps to look at earlier work in order to see your progress and, we hope, build your confidence. In fact, an exercise at the end of the book is designed to compare three videos: your first, a middle video, and one of your last videos.

Practice at home. Practice at the grocery store. Practice in class. Practice on tape. Review your progress, and you will find that some skills will become second nature.

SUMMARY

In this chapter, we introduced the various uses of the therapeutic relationship. We covered the important concept of empathy, its definition, its facilitation and advantages, and the risks associated with it. We also introduced you to how to listen— listen to your clients as well as yourself. If you begin to practice your nonverbal listening skills, you will be better prepared to learn how to respond verbally (Chapter 6, "Exploration Skills"). Finally, we presented a perspective on how you can use these skills in your daily life.

The next chapter introduces you to the intake process. At the same time you are building a solid, collaborative relationship with your client, you are also collecting relevant information and assessing what's going on with the client. In order for this to proceed in an efficient and helpful way, your relationship skills must be finely tuned so you can better respond to client needs during session while you also attempt to meet the needs of treatment planning to provide you with direction.

Skills in Action: Ambivalent Intimacy

Therapist: Have a seat. You look like you have a spring in your step this week as compared to last week. You're smiling more and you even look like you're standing up straighter. You're dressed more fashionably today, too. [Noticing nonverbal behavior]

Client: I do feel good today. Thanks for noticing. I had a good week. Jill and I decided to take a week off from talking or seeing each other. Jill made that decision and I think it was a good one. I need to make a decision about whether I want to stay in this relationship with Lisa, and having time away from Jill helped.

Therapist: You're pleased with these results. What happened? [Reflecting feelings; probing]

Client: It's amazing. I wasn't any different, but Lisa was different with me. She was much more affectionate and attentive. She was happier, and I really enjoyed spending time with her. It's like it was ten years ago when we first met.

Therapist: You sound so relieved and hopeful. [Reflecting feelings]

Client: Yeah, I definitely am. What do you make of it?

Therapist: You know I'm always honest with you, and I would like to challenge you here. [Authentic engagement]

Client: Okay. Shoot.

Therapist: I don't believe it was an accident that Lisa was different with you. I'd like to challenge you to think about how you might have been different without daily interactions with Jill. [Authentic experience; problem-solving collaboration]

Client: Hm. (pausing for a moment) I suppose I was less distracted with whether or not Jill would call and how I would catch the phone if she did. Come to think of it, I guess I was probably more attentive to Lisa, as well. Maybe that's why she was attentive back. I felt close to her again.

Therapist: By investing in Lisa, you felt closer to her, and believe that she was closer to you. [Reflecting content]

Client: Exactly. I guess I was different. I think that we're good now, that we should be safe.

Therapist:	I appreciate how optimistic you feel. I'm also aware that we've been through a cycle like this before, where you felt willing to invest in Lisa and to give up Jill. Something always pulls you away from Lisa.
Client:	(looks down and whispers) So you're saying it's my fault.
Therapist:	You sound defeated. [Attending to the nonverbals of low voice and lack of eye contact] I'm saying that you may have a role to play in it. Some part of what happens in your relationship is you, and some part is Lisa's. Lisa isn't here, so let's try to figure out your part. [Authentic engagement; problem-solving collaboration]
Client:	Touché. What do you think is my problem, Ms. Expert?
Therapist:	You sound angry with me. [Immediacy; authentic engagement]
Client:	Oh, I supposed I'm really angry with myself. Really, what's my issue?
Therapist:	We've talked about how you have wavered back and forth between being close to Lisa and not. In some ways, you've even done that with Jill. I also notice how you do that with me. If you have a single good week, you're ready to end our relationship, and when things get too intimate, you cancel the next session.
Client:	Really? I never realized it, but you may be right. I get it. I can't seem to stay close to anyone for too long. I don't have a clue what that's about.
Therapist:	Go back as far as you can, and tell me the first time you ever remember feeling unsafe in a relationship. Maybe you were in college, in high school, maybe you were a little kid. [Probing for possible unfinished business]
Client:	(thinking for a moment) I suppose it was when my mom left us. I was only four years old. I don't know why she left, but my dad told me it wasn't my fault. I guess I just didn't trust women after that. I mean, what kind of woman leaves her own children! (talking louder) That's so wrong. We must have been pretty awful for her to leave us like that.
Therapist:	You're still hurt and angry. I notice that you said that you just don't trust women now. I wonder if you don't trust me. [Interpersonal engagement; novel interaction experience]
Client:	I suppose not, based on what you're telling me. I do cancel a lot. And it's true, you will eventually abandon me.

Therapist: I'll abandon you. [Parroting; seeking clarification]

Client: Well, yeah. You won't be my therapist forever.

Therapist: You can't imagine our relationship ending or changing in any way except that I might abandon you. [Reflecting content; authentic engagement]

Client: Ouch! When you put it that way, I sound pretty stupid.

Therapist: I sense you feel vulnerable and unsafe when you get close. [Reflecting feelings; redirecting]

Client: Yeah. I'm not sure how to change that.

Therapist: Let's start with you and me. What might be some other ways in which our relationship might continue or end? [Problem-solving collaboration]

Client: I suppose you'll always be here if I ever need to come back.

Therapist: True. I have many clients that leave therapy for several years and then come back when something new comes up. What else? [Validating; instilling hope]

Client: I guess I could end the relationship rather than you.

Therapist: In fact, you kind of do that in small ways all the time. What might be the way you would like our relationship to end when the time comes? [Miracle question]

Client: That I feel like I'm ready to be on my own because I've gotten what I want out of therapy. So, I tell you, and then we say goodbye, or maybe, goodbye for now.

Therapist: Now we're getting somewhere.

REFERENCES AND RESOURCES

Brammer, L. M., & MacDonald, G. (2002). *The helping relationship: Process and skills* (8th ed.). Boston, MA: Allyn & Bacon.

Chen, M. W., & Giblin, N. J. (2002). *Individual counseling: Skills and techniques.* Denver, CO: Love.

Ciaramicoli, A. P., & Ketcham, K. (2000). *The power of empathy.* New York, NY: Dutton.

Cooper, M. (2013). Experiencing relational depth in therapy: What we know so far. In R. Knox, D. Murphy, S. Wiggins, & M. Cooper (Eds.), *Relational depth: New perspectives and developments* (pp. 62–76). New York, NY: Palgrave Macmillan.

Courtois, C. A., & Ford, J. D. (2013). *Treatment of complex trauma: A sequenced, relationship-based approach*. New York, NY: Guilford Press.

Feltham, C. (1999). *Understanding the counseling relationship*. Thousand Oaks, CA: Sage.

Geller, S. M., & Porges, S. W. (2014). Therapeutic presence: Neurophysiological mechanisms mediating feeling safe in therapeutic relationships. *Journal of Psychotherapy Integration, 24*(3), 178–192.

Gelso, C. J., & Hayes, J. A. (1998). *The psychotherapy relationship: Theory, research, and practice*. New York, NY: John Wiley.

Gottman, J. (2014). *What predicts divorce?* New York, NY: Psychology Press.

Hoglend, P. (2014). Exploration of the patient-therapist relationship in psychotherapy. *American Journal of Psychiatry, 171*(10), 1056–1066.

Howe, D. (2013). *Empathy: What it is and why it matters*. New York, NY: Palgrave.

Moyers, T. B. (2014). The relationship in motivational interviewing. *Psychotherapy, 51*(3), 358–363.

Muntigl, P., & Horvath, A. O. (2014). The therapeutic relationship in action: How therapists and clients co-manage relational disaffiliation. *Psychotherapy Research, 24*(3), 327–345.

Okun, B. F. (2007). *Effective helping: Interviewing and counseling techniques* (7th ed.). Pacific Grove, CA: Brooks/Cole.

Razzaque, R., Okoro, E., & Wood, L. (2015). Mindfulness in clinician therapeutic relationships. *Mindfulness, 6,* 170–174.

Rogers, C. (1951). *Client-centered therapy: Its current practice, implications and theory*. Boston, MA: Houghton Mifflin.

Rogers, C. R. (1980). *A way of being*. Boston, MA: Houghton Mifflin.

Staemmler, F. M. (2012). *Empathy in psychotherapy: How therapists and clients understand each other*. New York, NY: Springer.

Stark, M. (2000). *Modes of therapeutic action: Enhancement of knowledge, provision of experience, and engagement in relationship*. Northvale, NJ: Jason Aronson.

Sugden, R. (2002). Beyond sympathy and empathy: Adam Smith's concept of fellow-feeling. *Economics and Philosophy, 18*(1), 63–87.

Tryon, G. S., & Winograd, G. (2011). Goal consensus and collaboration. In J. C. Norcross (Ed.), *Psychotherapy relationships that work* (pp. 153–167). New York, NY: Oxford University Press.

Chapter 5

SKILLS OF ASSESSMENT AND DIAGNOSIS

A new client walks in the door and sits down. In your most caring, compassionate voice, you ask what's going on?

"I'm not sure really," he tells you after a long pause. "I've been having some problems concentrating lately. And I feel out of sorts. Not just depressed, but also sad all the time. I don't really know why. And I've been having some physical issues, like these headaches that aren't so much painful as they are just annoying. Oh, and one more thing, I sometimes feel like I'm losing my mind. So, what do you think this all means and what's wrong with me?"

If you are like us, and most other therapists, your first reaction with a new client is panic. You can't possibly know what's going on with a new client after just a few minutes, or even a few sessions. Yet you will be pressed for definitive answers—not only by the client who wants a name for whatever is happening but also your supervisors who insist on you presenting a coherent narrative about the presenting complaints, differential diagnosis, and treatment plan. So you take a deep breath, stall as long as you can, and dig for as much information as you can possibly collect in what will always be limited time.

Among the first things you must do in a new relationship with a client is figure out what the most important issues are to deal with and to develop a plan to address them. This is a collaborative effort in which you enlist the client's help to determine desired goals and treatment objectives. It is also a process that uses a number of structures to help you to organize your efforts.

In this chapter we present a number of skills that will be useful in conducting assessments, formulating diagnostic impressions, and planning treatment strategies with your clients. There are several different structures that are currently in use, depending on the setting (i.e., hospital vs. school vs. crisis center), the professional identity (family therapy vs. psychiatry vs. psychology vs. counseling), or even the theoretical orientation of the practitioner (i.e., cognitive-behavioral vs. psychoanalytic vs. existential vs. constructivist). Rather than confusing you with all the various possibilities at your disposal, we will concentrate on the assessment skills and strategies that are somewhat universally employed. The most commonly used such structures originally evolved from medical practice, especially in psychiatric units.

THE MENTAL STATUS EXAM

In medical and mental health settings, a standard clinical examination is often used to assess mental functioning. This is especially important for clients who are manifesting extreme symptoms of disorientation or unusual behavior. Although you may not be required to use this assessment structure (it is more universally applied by psychiatrists, medical practitioners, and psychologists), it is still helpful to understand the various areas that are covered. Even if you are specializing in adjustment and developmental disorders, it is helpful to examine client behavior systematically.

- *Appearance:* How does the client present him- or herself? Look at hygiene, clothing, nutrition, weight, and alertness.
- *General behavior:* Examine characteristic mannerisms, facial expressions, eye contact, voice tone, and general attitude. Take into consideration gender, cultural, and individual differences in the ways these mannerisms are manifested.
- *Mood:* Assess the types and intensity of moods displayed. Are these emotional reactions appropriate to the situation?
- *Flow of thought:* Note the rate and rhythm of speech. Is there a flight of ideas, incessant rambling, disjointed thoughts?
- *Content of thought:* Is there evidence of delusions and hallucinations that might indicate psychotic thinking? Are obsessions present in thought? Is there suicidal ideation?
- *Orientation:* Make sure the person is oriented to time, place, and person. This means that the person knows where he or she is, what day it is, and what he or she is doing in your company.
- *Language:* Note comprehension and fluency of language. If there is some concern about whether the person understands and speaks well. Check out the first languages used in the home.
- *Memory:* Assess both short- and long-term memory functions. Simple exercises are available for this process.

- *Attention and concentration:* Is the person able to track the conversation appropriately?
- *Abstract reasoning:* Can the person grasp symbolic or metaphorical ideas?
- *Insight and judgment:* Does the person appear to have the capacity for self-reflection and insight?
- *Cultural background:* What are the client's dominant cultural identities and how might they influence the behavior previously considered?

The question remains: What do you do with the information you've collected so far during a mental status exam? Let's say that you are pretty skilled at asking good questions according to the format just presented. The most important part involves using these data to help you formulate a clearer notion of the client's presenting problems and underlying processes. This is crucial for creating a sound treatment plan.

Imagine that you are faced with the following client during an initial interview:

A woman in her thirties walks into your office, looking down at her feet. She's wearing a gray sweatshirt and green sweat pants with beat-up-looking flip-flops. She's pale and dangerously thin. Her hair, originally gathered in a ponytail, is now askew. Her shoulders are slouched, and she slumps into the couch rather than sitting. You notice that she leans away from you and balls herself up in the corner of the couch. As you go over the informed consent and limits of confidentiality, the woman still seems enamored with her feet, wiggling her toes as if she is not sure they belong to her. She nods and grunts for answers as you check for her understanding of the situation. You invite her to talk about why she is there.

Therapist: So tell me what brought you to see me today?

Client: (in a quiet voice) I'm tired. I'm alone. I hate my job. Even my friends don't come around as often as they used to. I don't know. My boss threatened me saying that if I didn't come to therapy, I'd lose my job. (tears form in her eyes)

Therapist: You sound like you're afraid of losing your job, but even more than that, you sound really down.

Client: (talking to her feet) Yeah. (sighs) I don't know. I guess I've always been this way. When I was a kid, I didn't have many friends then, either. They always picked on me. (more animated now) I never understood why. I just never fit in. I don't even fit in at the grocery store. Just yesterday some checkout girl gave me a hard time. I didn't do anything! Does that ever happen to you? It happens to me all the time. (deep sigh) Anyway, how much time do we have? I'm not sure I could talk for more than a few minutes. I'd bore you to death if I did. Who wants to hear my life story? Even I don't want to hear it. There's really nothing to tell. I get up. I work. I go home. I sleep. Sometimes I eat in between.

MENTAL STATUS EXAM EXERCISE

First, write down what you notice about this brief introduction. Start with objective data and then write down your best guess about what each of these observations might mean. Take 2–3 minutes to do this.

Get into pairs and compare notes. Notice what you have observed that is similar versus what you have found that is different.

With another pair, form groups of four and compare your observations. You may notice several obvious commonalities that everyone picked up on, as well as several interpretations that reflect your own perceptions.

Talk to one another about ways that collaborations such as this might help you to develop and refine your assessment and diagnostic skills.

The mental status exam is only a quick, relatively crude initial evaluation of a person's mental, emotional, and cognitive functioning. Its highly structured format allows you to compare responses to a rather large database and determine the extent of impairment in certain areas. A more extensive intake procedure is needed to get a more in-depth picture of what is going on. As you gain more training and experience, you'll be able to consult helpful sources to guide your assessment process (see Sommers-Flanagan & Sommers-Flanagan, 2015).

THE BASICS OF CONDUCTING AN INTAKE INTERVIEW

Although a mental status exam is a fairly structured process for assessing cognitive as much as psychological functioning, other procedures are used for general practice. Basically, you might ask yourself what you need to know in order to help someone.

REFLECTIVE EXERCISE

Imagine that you could only ask a new client three questions. Based on the answers you get to those queries, you would have to construct a plan for being most helpful. In small groups, or on your own, settle on the three most important questions that you would want to ask.

In this section, we teach you the mechanics of how to do a first interview and illustrate the steps with sample dialogue from a beginner who is meeting a client for the first time. You will wish to customize these steps to fit the needs of your clients, clinical style (as it evolves), and work setting.

Phone Contact

So, this is your first meeting with a client. You may feel a bit excited and nervous. Many clinicians feel that anticipation each time a new meeting occurs. Your client will also likely be very anxious about meeting you, so it is essential that you help the client feel more comfortable. This is a challenge, though, because you need to collect a significant amount of information while trying to convey empathy, concern, and hope.

Several approaches exist for conducting the intake interview, and you will have to develop your own style. However, there are some basic guidelines that might be helpful to get you started (see Sommers-Flanagan & Sommers-Flanagan, 2015). First, when contacting clients by phone, you may want to let them know that the first session will be a little different from the others and to arrive early to fill out any paperwork prior to meeting with you. Because so much of the first session can be occupied by completing forms, you might schedule the first meeting for an hour and a half—if you have the liberty to do so—to give clients more time to talk about what brought them to therapy. In addition, you may want to review the cost of services at the agency. Before you hang up, reiterate the day, date, and time of your session, and say something like, "I'm looking forward to meeting you."

Keep in mind that the therapy begins with this first phone contact (actually it began as soon as the client first considered reaching out for help). Some clinicians even use this first conversation to begin the work by planting a favorable prognosis, instilling a sense of hope, and encouraging the person to think about how to use the time in the most efficient way possible.

Other clinicians are very careful not to touch on any topic about why the client is coming to therapy for fear the client will want to have a session on the phone.

Oftentimes, clients are so nervous about coming to therapy that they have a nearly rehearsed introduction that's just bursting to come out. In addition, some clients have difficulty with boundaries and may not appreciate that the phone is not an appropriate venue for talking about issues, especially in an age of cordless phones and cell phones in which anyone might be listening (accidentally or on purpose). In any case, pay close attention to the very first things clients say during this initial contact, as they can be very revealing.

The Greeting

Beginning with the first impression you present to your clients, we intend to describe some of the most gritty, specific details that are involved in first meetings. It is hardly necessary to follow these instructions to the letter. We just want to give you some idea of all the nuances that are considered when you begin with a new client, even if you eventually adapt the ideas to fit your own interpersonal style, agency or school policies, and client needs.

When you first meet a client you will of course wish to introduce yourself. Tell the client what you would like to be called (i.e., by your first name, by your title, etc.), and ask what your client would like to be called. It's best to ask because clients from different cultural backgrounds may have certain expectations about how to address one another. Therefore, if you suggest that your client call you by your first name, but she chooses to call you by a more formal name, just go with it. The one possible exception is if your client wants to call you "doctor" but you are not a doctor.

We recommend that you don't begin any conversation while in the waiting room but rather wait until you get into the therapy room to continue. Waiting is not only important during the intake interview but during all sessions, as sometimes clients begin the session right in front of other people. Waiting will assure your client's confidentiality. (The one exception might be if you have a long walk to your therapy room from the waiting room, you may want to ask your client not to say anything until reaching the therapy room.) Remember, your client will most likely be unfamiliar with your procedures and the layout of your clinic. Many clients don't know how to be clients (except what they have seen on television or in the movies), so it is your job to teach them the appropriate behaviors to get the most out of the experience.

The Opening

After reaching your office, ask the client to sit anywhere he or she feels comfortable (that choice may provide you with interesting data) and close the door. Some clients will sit very close to you; others will sit far away. If you're seeing a couple, notice whether they sit close together or far apart (all of these actions reveal useful data). After sitting down, begin to help your client feel at ease. You might start with telling him or her what to expect from this session that may be different from other such interactions. In addition, we do not recommend starting this session (or any other session) with "How are you?" because that statement frequently elicits a social atmosphere rather than a therapeutic one. Here is an example of an opening conducted by an intern:

Therapist: Hi, Maria. I'm pleased to meet you. This conversation may be very different from others you have experienced before with friends you have talked to, with doctors, or other professionals. I will start by telling you about some of our agency procedures and some of your rights as a client. After we get some paperwork completed, we can talk about what brought you to visit us. During all other sessions, we will be spending our time together working on helping you achieve your goals.

Although this opening is somewhat formal and follows procedures, which we recommend for beginners who want to be certain they cover all the necessary steps in the process, sometimes it just isn't possible to stick to the agenda. Clients in crisis or those bursting to tell their stories may immediately launch into their presenting problems. This scenario might unfold as follows:

Therapist: Hi Maria. I'm glad we could schedule this time together.

Maria: Yes, I've just been so busy lately, so anxious about things, about this meeting. That's part of my problem, that I feel so out of control. I just get so worked up that I can't seem to think straight. My memory is shot too. My kids tell me it's because I'm getting old. (laughs) But I've been wondering if there might be something seriously wrong with me. I didn't used to be so upset over such little things all the time.

At this juncture, the therapist has dozens of questions and areas to explore: Just how anxious does Maria feel? When and how often does she experience symptoms? What sets her off most consistently? What are her specific symptoms? When did things change for her, considering she says it wasn't always like this? She has children—how many and what ages? Is she taking medication for her symptoms? How has she been managing things so far?

In spite of all these legitimate areas to explore, the therapist takes a deep breath, realizing that in these first crucial sessions there will be enough time to gather more information. First, however, she needs to reassure her client, and then she can introduce a bit of structure.

Therapist: Maria, I can see that you are really ready to get going. You have been struggling with your anxious feelings for some time and seem very motivated to do something about this. I am eager to help you with those feelings of being out of control. Before you tell me more about what is going on in your life, there are a few things we need to get out of the way.

The therapist is acknowledging the client's feelings, providing some reassurance, but also implementing some structure so they can take care of business details. Although we have provided two examples of an opening in therapy, there are limitless ways this may be done. Keep in mind that first impressions are critical, so you want to make sure that you present yourself as confident, relaxed, and in charge (even if you won't exactly feel that way).

Taking Care of Ground Rules

Telling clients what to expect can help them be more comfortable with the process of therapy. Informing them that this session is different is also essential because they may think that every session will be like this one. If you don't make it clear how this first session is different, clients may not want to come back. After all, you will be doing the majority of the talking and structuring during this first session, which does not necessarily help clients reach their goals. The intake continues with:

Therapist: I would like to start by informing you that all of our sessions will be confidential, but there are a few limitations to that confidentiality. For example, you need to know that all of our sessions will be recorded. I am a graduate student and my experience here at this clinic is the final part of my education. Because I'm in training, my supervisor and this agency require the use of recording devices to provide you with the best possible services. That means you will get the benefit of my supervisor's experience as well as my own. Once a session has been reviewed by my supervisor, I will erase it immediately. Therefore, my supervisor and I will be the only people to view your session, and my supervisor is bound by confidentiality just as I am.

If you are recording your session, it may be helpful to start with that information, especially if the video camera is in full view. Stating, with confidence, that the video is required by the agency for your and the client's benefit will decrease the amount of resistance the client has for recording. However, if you sound unsure or lack confidence, your client may become reluctant and apprehensive. The session continues:

Therapist: Another limitation on confidentiality is if you inform me that you will hurt yourself or another person. Your safety is essential to me, and I am bound by my ethical guidelines to report any harm you intend toward yourself or others. In addition, if you reveal any abuse of a child, an elderly person, or a person with a disability, I am legally bound to contact the authorities. Furthermore, if you request that your records be released or if your records are subpoenaed by a court of law, I will release your records to the appropriate person(s). Do you have any questions? [If your client does not] Well, if any come up, please do not hesitate to ask. Here is an informed consent form that I need you to sign. It states that you are coming to sessions of your own free will, and that either one of us can terminate at any time. However, I would like to have a final session prior to terminating, regardless of the reason. I have one copy for you and one copy for our agency files. After you've taken a moment to read it, let's both sign them.

You will need to first know your state's laws with regard to the limits of confidentiality. Once learned, we recommend you memorize the list. Practice it with a few friends before you sit down with your first client. This will help you feel more confident and help you remain thorough in discussing these important limitations to confidentiality. Now you have covered your limits of confidentiality and informed consent. Starting with this will let the client know immediately that some limits exist. If you have agency policies, this might be a good place to cover those. For example:

Therapist: I would like to meet with you each week at this same time for our sessions. Our sessions will be between forty-five and fifty minutes. If you notice me checking my watch, it's not because I'm bored, but because I need to make sure we finish on time since this room is used immediately after our session. If you need to cancel, please provide me with twenty-four hours' notice. The agency phone number and

> my name are on this form. Our agency requires that you pay the fee
> if you do not show without canceling. Another agency policy is that
> if you do not appear for three consecutive sessions, your time will be
> given to another client, and you will need to call us for a new day and
> time. This policy is in place to assure that I obtain my training hours
> and to provide as many clients as possible with services. If you have
> an emergency, our agency is not available twenty-four hours per day.
> We are open from eight in the morning to nine at night, Monday
> through Saturday, so you will need to call 911 or contact the suicide
> hotline listed here on this form. Do you have any questions so far?

Perhaps your agency will not have these policies, but if they do, you need to
cover them explicitly. You will want these policies, as well as your name and the
agency's phone number and address, to be on forms that your client signs. We
recommend keeping one signed copy in the client's file and giving another to the
client to take home. We do not recommend giving out any personal information
such as cell phone numbers or e-mail addresses for a few reasons. First, some
clients have poor boundaries and will contact you several times a week. Second,
you cannot guarantee confidentiality on either of these technologies. It's best to
use only the agency's phone number and let clients know which days you are in
the office and can return their calls.

Checking and Correcting Client Expectations

The next section may help eliminate some confusion about the counseling process,
especially if your client has never been to therapy or has previously received
counseling from a therapist or agency that did things differently. What is it we're
leading up to? Checking out the client's expectations about your role as a therapist.
For example:

Therapist: Before we talk about what brought you here, I would like to find out
what you expect my role to be as your therapist. In your mind, what
do you think is my role as therapist and your role as client?

Sometimes clients believe that your role is to provide advice or concrete
answers to their problems. Sometimes clients believe that you will be "psychoana-
lyzing" them. Once your client responds, reflect what you heard, and then make
any corrections to how you see your roles. You may want to use your theory to
help define your role here, or you can be more general. For instance:

Therapist: You believe your role is to tell me your problems and that I will provide you with solutions to those problems. [If the client says yes, then . . .] Well, my style is a little different. I believe that clients come to therapy when they feel stuck and are unsure of how to proceed in their lives. They may feel depressed, frustrated, or any variety of emotions. I believe that my role is to help facilitate your exploration in order to clearly identify the source of your problems, and that source may not be as obvious as you might expect today. I believe that once I help you to clearly identify those emotions or thoughts that cause you to feel stuck, then we can work together to find the best way for you to cope with your situation. I may be reflecting some of what you say to make sure I understand your position, and I may ask you some questions to help you explore deeper. In addition, I may have you do some activities in or out of therapy to help enhance self-awareness. How does that sound? [Wait for client response and reflect if necessary] Any questions?

Exploring the Presenting Complaint

Once your clients are a little clearer about how you do therapy, they will be ready to explore what brought them to therapy and what to expect from your sessions together. However, if you are required to complete a structured interview, you may need to proceed with that paperwork. If not, an open invitation to talk about what brought them to therapy would be appropriate now: "We have covered the basics, and I would like to invite you to tell me what brought you here today."

During this first session, whether structured or unstructured, practice your feeling and content reflections (covered in the next chapter). Even if you have many questions for your interview, taking the time to reflect not only assures that you are hearing what your client is saying, but also helps the client to feel your empathy and consequently establishes a strong therapeutic bond between you and your client.

INVENTORY EXERCISE

Team up with a partner or two. One of you agree to be the client; another agree to help take inventory of all those areas of your life that could profit from some sort of reflection, deeper exploration, and possible constructive action. Using some simple open-ended questions and reflections, help the "client" to review all the ways that he or she might use counseling to improve personal functioning.

If time allows, do not be afraid to get into deep material during this first session (sometimes one session may be all you have to make a difference). Beginning practitioners often feel hesitant to explore things in great depth when the relationship is so new. Trust the client. He or she will not go any deeper than feels safe, especially if you respect his or her pace and moderate your own impatience. As long as you display good empathy, you can frequently help the client with something during the first session. Clients who feel that something has been accomplished, who feel valued, and who also like you, are more likely to return.

Discussing the Treatment Plan

After reviewing the situation, the presenting problems and primary issues with the client, you will want to discuss plans for future sessions. This is a negotiated process; the client may want you to do things that you are unable or unwilling to do ("I want you to tell my wife that she is wrong and agree with me that she is the problem" or "I want you to tell me what I should do"). Likewise, you may have expectations for your client that he or she is not amenable to ("I think it's important that we explore some early experiences that may be contributing to your problem").

Treatment plans include both short-term goals (those to be worked on before the next session) and long-term objectives (those targets that are to be worked toward before therapy ends). Don't be surprised if long-term goals often evolve over time. What you and the client believe is the problem in the first session may only be a symptom of something more that you discover as your relationship grows and you both learn more about the client. Both short- and long-term goals will be established collaboratively.

We wish to emphasize that this part of a first session does not involve simply telling the client what you think is going on and what you have in mind to make things better. There is often a negotiation involved in this process. The client has one set of objectives in mind and you might have quite another. Note in this dialogue how the therapist attempts to find common ground between their discrepant goals for treatment.

Therapist:	Given what we have discussed so far, what is it that you would like to accomplish before our work is done?
Client:	Well, that you'll be able to straighten out my kids and get them to stop acting up.
Therapist:	Yes, I heard quite clearly that you are frustrated and unsatisfied with the way your children are behaving. Rather than me doing the work

to fix them, though, my job is to teach you the skills to handle things much better.

Client: You mean you are going to tell me what to do with them?

Therapist: I will certainly work with you to develop some more effective parenting strategies, but ultimately you are the one who lives with them every day, and you are the one that your children love and respect.

Client: Sometimes I'm not so sure about that.

You can see that the therapist and client are trying to come to agreement about the work to be done and which roles each will play. It is quite important, before you end your first session, to make sure that you both (or in the case of family therapy, all of you) have reached a consensus.

Closure

When you have arrived at your last 5 minutes, let your client know that your time together is almost over. Check to see if your client has any questions before you end the session. Finally, some therapists and counselors like to take the last 5 minutes to solidify the relationship and reiterate any goals. For example:

Therapist: Well, our time is about up. Before you leave I want to check with you to find out if you have any more questions. [If the client says no] It sounds like you want to improve parenting skills. I believe we could work well together to help you with this goal. How do you feel about us working together? [If the client feels good about it] Good. Then I will see you next Monday at two in the afternoon. It was very nice meeting you today, Maria.

Then take the client to the door or the waiting room, but be sure not to allow the client to continue the session outside the room. If you can, stay in the room after the client leaves to prevent any further conversation; if not, just walk to the waiting room silently and show your client out.

Some clients have a lot of difficulty with the end of sessions. They may save their best stuff for the last 5 minutes. One way to end the session gently is to say, "I'm glad you brought that up. You're really scared your husband might be having an affair. Because we're out of time for today, I'd like to start there next week." Then stand up and walk to the door. Of course, this is only for clients who won't leave, and this problem is not an unusual one. That's why we believe it's very important to give clients a 5-minute warning. This gives them an opportunity to prepare themselves to leave the room and sets clear boundaries for clients who need them, as discussed in the previous chapter.

An example of a disclosure and informed consent statement is shown in Figure 5.1. Each agency is likely to have developed its own specific form that you will be asked to review with your clients.

- *Agency contact information:* This gives clients the necessary information to contact the agency or you once they leave.
- *Qualifications:* Believe it or not, but stating that you're a graduate student is impressive to most people, especially since you'll likely be providing services based on a fee reduction.
- *Experience:* This section is more relevant once you graduate and gain some experience, assuming you didn't have any experience prior to your education.
- *Nature of therapy:* It's important to use everyday language as much as possible. You don't want to talk about "transference" or "projections" or "schemas." Use language clients will understand. Can you guess what theory is used in these examples?
- *Therapy relationship:* This clearly establishes the boundaries of the relationship between you and your client. This may be helpful if clients later want to become friends, act in a social way, or want to date you.
- *Effects of therapy:* This section helps clients understand that unanticipated changes may (and probably will) occur. Clients may forget this, but it's a way of informing them without scaring them.
- *Client rights:* This language empowers clients to take responsibility for their termination and provides a process should there be any problems.
- *Referrals:* This lets clients know about the referral process, the clients' responsibilities, and any potential termination based on the ending of your contract with the agency.
- *Fees:* This provides written evidence of the fees. If your agency doesn't handle insurance, this section informs clients of that policy.
- *Cancellation:* This lets clients know about any charges for missed, late, or cancelled appointments. It also spells out that the client must cancel with at least a 24-hour notice to avoid being charged for the session.
- *Records and confidentiality:* These are the limits of confidentiality that you will learn. You will also want to include whether or not you have a "no secrets" policy when working with couples.

Now let's explore some information that might be covered in a structured intake, as well as any diagnostic information.

Figure 5.1 Informed Consent and Professional Disclosure

Informed Consent and Professional Disclosure

Agency Name

Agency Address

Agency Phone Number

PROFESSIONAL DISCLOSURE STATEMENT

Qualifications: I am a graduate student in Counseling working toward the completion of a master's degree. I am qualified to counsel under the supervision of a faculty member of the (your university) counselor education program and/or a licensed mental health professional. My formal education has prepared me to counsel individuals and groups.

Experience: (This section may be more useful once you graduate and are completing your internship hours. Be sure to include any special populations or techniques.)

Nature of Counseling: I believe people come to counseling because they are discouraged, which can come from feelings of not belonging and/or misguided feelings about self, such as "I am worthless," or about life, such as "life is unsafe." I believe in holistic counseling, meaning that the personality cannot be broken down into parts. A client must be seen in terms of how he or she moves through life. Therefore, the goal of counseling is to identify patterns that are being repeated throughout life to determine what is causing discouragement. Once insight about the reason(s) for discouragement is attained, I work with my client to create cognitive and/or behavioral changes. My style of counseling incorporates various techniques, depending on the needs of the client. Some example techniques are acting "as if," which is pretending to behave a certain way; task setting, which is accomplishing certain tasks; or catching oneself, which is trying to be consciously aware of a certain thought or behavior. These and other techniques are sometimes used exclusively in the counseling environment, but are more often used as homework assignments to practice new behaviors in real-life settings.

INFORMED CONSENT

Counseling Relationship: During the time we work together, we will meet weekly for approximately forty-five–minute sessions. Although our sessions may be very intimate psychologically, ours is a professional relationship rather than a social one. Our contact will be limited to counseling sessions you arrange with me except in case of emergency when you may contact the agency by phone. Please do not invite me to social gatherings, offer me gifts, ask me to write references for you, or ask me to relate to you in any way other than the professional context of our counseling sessions. You will be best served if our sessions concentrate exclusively on your concerns.

Effects of Counseling: You may at any time initiate a discussion of possible positive or negative effects of entering, not entering, continuing, or discontinuing counseling. While benefits are expected from counseling, specific results are not guaranteed. Counseling is a personal exploration and may lead to major changes in your life perspectives and decisions. These changes may affect significant relationships, your job, and/or your understanding of yourself. Some of these life changes could be temporarily distressing. The exact nature of these changes cannot be predicted. We will work together to achieve the best possible results for you.

Client Rights: Some clients need only a few counseling sessions to achieve their goals; others may require months or even years of counseling. As a client, you are in complete control and may end our counseling relationship at any time, though I do ask that you participate in a termination session. You also have the right to refuse or discuss modifications of any of my counseling techniques or suggestions that you believe might be harmful.

I assure you that my services will be rendered in a professional manner consistent with accepted legal and ethical standards. If at any time and for any reason you are dissatisfied with my services, please let me know. If I am not able to resolve your concerns, you may report your complaints to my supervisor, (name and phone number of supervisor).

Referrals: Should you and/or I believe that a referral is needed, I will provide some alternatives, including programs and/or people who may be available to assist you. A verbal exploration of alternatives to counseling will also be made available upon your request. You will be responsible for contacting and evaluating those referrals and/or alternatives. I most likely will be available to be your counselor at (agency name) until (date of your practicum/internship ending). If you wish to continue counseling beyond that time, I will provide some referral options.

Fees: In return for a fee of $_____ per session, I agree to provide counseling services to you. If the fee represents a hardship for you, please let me know. The fee for each session will be due and must be paid at the conclusion of each session. Cash or personal checks made out to (agency name) are acceptable for payments. The agency does not file for reimbursement from health insurance companies.

Cancellation: In the event that you will not be able to keep an appointment, please notify the agency secretary at least 24 hours in advance, if possible. My opportunities to gain experience depend upon your attendance. Therefore, if you are absent two weeks in a row, I will ask to be assigned to a new client and your name will be placed at the end of the waiting list. Likewise, if you intend to discontinue counseling, please inform me or the agency secretary as soon as possible so that I may be assigned another client.

Records and Confidentiality: All our communication becomes part of the clinical record. Records are the property of the agency. Adult client records are disposed of seven years after the file is closed. Minor client records are disposed of seven years after the client's 18th birthday. Most of our communication is confidential, but the following limitations and exceptions do exist: (a) I am using your case records for purposes of supervision, professional development, and research; in such cases, to preserve confidentiality, I will identify you by first name only; (b) I determine that you are a danger to yourself or someone else; (c) you disclose abuse, neglect, or exploitation of a child or an elderly or disabled person; (d) you disclose sexual contact with another mental health professional; (e) I am ordered by a court to disclose information; (f) you direct me to release your records; or (g) I am otherwise required by law to disclose information. If I see you in public, I will protect your confidentiality by acknowledging you only if you approach me first.

In the case of marriage or family counseling, I will keep confidential (within limits cited above) anything you disclose to me without your family member's knowledge. However, I encourage open communication between family members, and I reserve the right to terminate our counseling relationship if I judge the secret to be detrimental to the therapeutic progress.

By your signature below, you indicate that you have read and understood this statement, and that any questions you had about this statement were answered to your satisfaction, and that you were furnished a copy of this statement. By my signature, I verify the accuracy of this statement and acknowledge my commitment to conform to its specifications.

_____   _____
Client's signature   Counselor's Signature

_____   _____
Date   Date

Exercise in Practicing an Initial Interview

Take turns with different partners conducting a 15-minute initial interview. In this limited time, try to collect as much information as you can about the presenting complaint and relevant background.

You may want to take notes during the process. We'll discuss note-taking later in this chapter.

One hint: You get more information by listening than by talking. So, limit your questions, reflect some content and feelings (you'll learn this more in Chapter 6), and really listen to not only the details of the client's story, but also the way in which the client tells the story.

When you are done, consult with your "client" about things you did well, as well as important things you missed.

Exercise in Obtaining Information

Using the categories described in this section, conduct a conversation with someone in which you attempt to get background information in each of the areas. For now, don't worry about the skills you use to elicit this information; just try to get some experience in what it's like to assess areas of someone's life.

After you are done with the interview, write up the results as a case report that follows this outline.

- *Family history.* Who lives with the client? Who is the client close to and/or in conflict with? What are the intergenerational patterns, support systems available, sibling positions, coalitions, and power balances? Who else has a vested interest in the outcome of the counseling?
- *Presenting problems.* What are the initial complaints? When did they begin? What happened right before the onset of the symptoms? When, where, how often, and with whom do the symptoms occur? When do the problems not occur? What are the client's accompanying thoughts, feelings, and reactions to the problems?
- *Expectations for treatment and goals.* What does the client expect from treatment? What are the desired goals and outcomes?
- *Treatment history.* What were the client's previous attempts at getting help? What were the types, kinds, and lengths of treatment? What has worked best and least? How does the person engage in self-medication? This includes illicit drugs, exercise, stress reducers, and perhaps self-defeating coping strategies.
- *Behavioral description.* How did the person behave and respond during the interview? What stands out most to you? What are your overall impressions?
- *Summary and recommendations.* In this final section you summarize the main points and themes of the case. You also specify the kind of treatment recommended—short or long term? Group, family, or individual sessions? Is a medical consultation needed?

STRUCTURED INTAKE INTERVIEWS

Some theoretical orientations, like cognitive-behavioral therapy and Adlerian therapy, have structured intake interviews. Many other clinical settings will also require you to follow a standardized procedure for conducting first interviews with clients (such as a mental status exam). These protocols are designed to help you collect background information in an organized and systematic fashion. If a specific form must be completed that requires you to ask lots of questions, make sure to do some reflecting along the way to establish a good working relationship with your client. Typically, such structured intakes include the following components that can also be used to write up case reports.

- *Identifying information:* This category includes the client's name, marital status, occupation, interests, and cultural background.
- *Background information:* Include educational and work history, developmental history, and how and why the person was referred for help.
- *Medical history:* List physical symptoms present, sleep and eating patterns, and any relevant medical conditions. Include all medications that are taken regularly.
- *Mental health history:* Included might be any information regarding the client's previous mental health diagnoses as well as any family history of mental health issues.

SPECIAL CONSIDERATIONS IN ASSESSING ADDICTION

There are a number of issues to look at with any high-risk client population. For instance, substance use and abuse present some special considerations for clinicians that must be reviewed. Substance use and abuse can include alcohol, prescription or illicit drugs, and/or over-the-counter drugs used in an illicit way. Some researchers include gambling, sexual addiction, and even eating disorders in this category because similar processes occur in the brain with regard to dopamine (Stevens & Smith, 2012).

You would want to assess client behavior in several domains:

- Behavior patterns: acting out, self-control, consequences, relapses
- Health status: accidents, injuries, illnesses
- Psychiatric disorders: depression, anxiety, personality disorders, psychotic symptoms

- Social competence: social skills
- Family system: conflicts, parental supervision, marital quality, family history of addiction
- School performance: adjustment, grades
- Work adjustment: competence, motivation
- Legal issues: driving under the influence (DUI) or other actions resulting in litigation as a consequence of using
- Peer relationships: social network, gang involvement, friendships, support system
- Leisure activities: recreation, hobbies, outlets, interests
- In addition, it is critical that a detailed substance use or behavioral history be collected so you can determine which substances are being used or what behaviors are being abused, how much, how often, in which circumstances, and with what effects. Clients will often minimize their use, so be skeptical internally while externally validating the information they give you.

Some populations have a higher likelihood of substance abuse. Clients who come from cultural backgrounds that are typically oppressed are strong candidates, such as racial and ethnic minorities, sexual minorities, or clients from low-SES backgrounds (Huebner, Thoma, & Neilands, 2015; Stevens & Smith, 2012). Furthermore, different cultures view the use of substances, especially alcohol, in different ways depending on the community, norms and peer pressure, socioeconomic class, and other factors. What's agreed upon, though, is that if the use of a substance, or engaging in certain behaviors, interferes greatly with work, friendship, family, or other aspects of a person's life, then it's most likely a problem in need of attention.

All of this would be taken into consideration in formulating your treatment plan. For instance, it is unlikely you will wish to treat clients who are actively abusing a substance with only weekly one-hour therapy sessions. You may decide that inpatient treatment is indicated or, at the very least, use of a 12-step program such as Alcoholics Anonymous or Narcotics Anonymous.

You will want to establish that the use of any substances in session is prohibited, and you may want to assess whether or not you're qualified to work with a client who has these issues. If the client is actively using, you may need to refer him or her to a treatment facility to become clean and sober before starting therapy.

SPECIAL CONSIDERATIONS IN ASSESSING PHYSICAL OR SEXUAL ABUSE

You will be required by law in most jurisdictions to recognize, identify, and report evidence of abuse of children, the elderly, people with disabilities, and in some cases, spouses. This includes sexual abuse, physical abuse, neglect, or emotional maltreatment. This also can include the abuse of another's finances. For example, you may have a client who is taking care of his mother and is the trustee of her retirement money. If he chooses to buy a new car instead of providing her with necessary medical treatment, this is considered abuse in most states, and is reportable. Spousal abuse is not necessarily reportable unless there are children in the home who can hear or witness the abuse; again, this depends on state law.

Most programs will require you to go through specific training to develop the skills to identify and report abuse. In most states this means that if you have reasonable suspicion of any abuse going on, you *must* report it in a timely way to Child or Adult Protective Services or a law enforcement agency. You are usually protected from breaching confidentiality in such circumstances and given immunity from legal action. It is when you fail to report such suspicions that you will be accountable to your licensing board, as well as put others at risk of further harm.

There are several things you should look for in assessing possible abuse (Table 5.1). None of these symptoms by themselves signal that abuse is taking place, but in combination, or if part of a consistent pattern, you would wish to investigate matters more carefully.

SPECIAL CONSIDERATIONS FOR HIGH SUICIDE RISK

Another important assessment that must be done is for the risk for suicide. You are obligated ethically and by law to protect your client from self-harm. Most counseling or social work programs will offer classes that provide a more thorough description of how to assess suicide risk. Nevertheless, we cover the topic briefly here because of its obvious importance.

First, many applications and/or assessment instruments screen for suicide risk. If you don't have the luxury of those tools, or even if you do, start your assessment by identifying whether your client seems depressed. Is his or her affect sad, energy low? Does the client seem to have a sense of hopelessness and helplessness about life? In fact, hopelessness was found to be one of the greatest

Table 5.1   Indications of Abuse

Emotional Symptoms	Physical Evidence
Sadness	Poor dress and grooming
Guilt	Bruises or injuries
Fear/anxiety	Bandages
Irritability	Camouflaged or excessive clothing in warm weather
Anger	Ligature or binding marks
Behavioral Indications	Systemic Factors
Seductive behavior	Overly clingy behavior
Inappropriately sexualized behavior	Isolation in family
Phobic reactions	Scapegoat
Regression	Exploitation of power
Aggression	

predictors of suicide ideation (Kuyken, 2004). You might even ask if the client has thought about dying as an escape from his or her pain. In this way, you introduce the concept of suicide without mentioning the word to avoid insulting your client. If the client has considered dying, then ask if he or she has considered harming himself or herself. During your first experience, you may want to freak out (using a technical term here), but try to remain calm. Make sure to practice your reflecting skills a lot here. More than anything else, it's essential that your client feel understood at this point.

If your client has considered suicide, ask if he or she has a plan. The more detailed the plan, the greater is the likelihood of suicide. Does the client know what method he or she will use? "I will run the car in the garage until I die from the fumes." How lethal is the method, such as taking aspirin versus shooting oneself? Does the client know when he or she will do it? "I will do it after everyone has just left for school and work so that I have plenty of time alone." If the plan is detailed and the method highly lethal and the client has the means to do it, then at the very least you may want to have the client sign a written contract with you that the client will call you (or a suicide hotline) if he or she feels that hopeless. You may want to come to some agreement or plan for the client if his or her feelings seem out of control.

REFLECTIVE OR DISCUSSION EXERCISE

Most people, at some time during their lives, have considered suicide, or at least entertained fantasies of not waking up in the morning. Of course, contemplating suicide and actually following through with a plan may be two quite different things. Nevertheless, there may have been a time in your own life when you were feeling despair and hopelessness, when the prospect of putting an end to the pain seemed very attractive. Either in a journal, or in a discussion in small groups, talk about what this experience is like. In other words, start to become more comfortable talking to people about deep, uncomfortable feelings. Of course, you will want to use sound judgment regarding how much you share with others, depending on the level of trust.

In any case, providing lots of empathy and understanding can be very beneficial to a depressed client. We find it helps to acknowledge how the pain seems so devastating that death may seem to be the only escape, but death is permanent and the pain does not have to be. Many times, validating the client rather than trying to talk him out of suicide will provide greater comfort and support. After you have validated the client's sense of despair, it is usually helpful to lead toward hope for the future: "A part of you feels hopeless, but another part of you feels hopeful and wants to live."

In some cases, the client may be so deeply depressed that hospitalization is necessary. At the very least, a psychiatric evaluation might be recommended to determine if antidepressant medication might be indicated. You will want to remember that it is difficult for even the most experienced and expert therapists to predict whether clients are truly at risk for harming themselves or others. When in doubt, seek consultation and supervision immediately.

SPECIAL CONSIDERATIONS FOR CRISIS SITUATIONS

The skills used for regular, weekly therapy are quite different than when clients are faced with an event or a disaster. In regular therapy, exploring the past or going deep into feelings may be appropriate. When working with clients who are in the midst of or have survived trauma, seeking stability and recovery is the initial goal, followed by efforts to find meaning in the aftermath. Whereas many years ago, the modest objective was only to help clients regain previous levels of function, new research on posttraumatic growth helps us reorient our approach to focus on the gifts and growth that can occur as a result of difficult challenges (Calhoun & Tedeschi, 2013; Werdel & Wicks, 2012). This has changed the way we routinely respond to traumatized clients, helping them adopt roles not as victims, or even survivors, but rather as heroes or heroines who have flourished as a result of adversity.

A client, for example, begins the first session by sharing, "I've just been through a tough time. There was a major fire in our area, completely destroying our home and all our possessions. We barely escaped alive. Unfortunately our dog died as well and now we have to scramble to find somewhere else to live and rebuild our lives from scratch."

Your responses could be one of the following:

a. That must have been so terrible for you, and I can understand why you would be so distraught.

b. You feel such despair and frustration, the injustice of it all that your whole life was destroyed.

c. What was that like for you?

Although so far in this book we have been prompting you, whenever possible, to respond to client statements with reflections of feelings, such as the options for (a) and (b), it seems that sometimes we make assumptions about client experiences that are not necessarily accurate or valid. In this case, if you tried the first two responses, you'd likely encourage the client to talk more about all of his negative feelings and difficulties, which would certainly seem appropriate and indicated under the circumstances. But because we now know and understand that whereas one third of those who survive trauma, whether an earthquake, combat, or catastrophic accident, do experience lingering symptoms of posttraumatic stress, another third recover and move on with their lives, and still another third report incredible growth as a result of what they experienced. They report feeling more engaged with life, value relationships more than ever, and have discovered new meaning and greater appreciation for every day (Joseph, 2011).

In our example, if you chose to ask the more neutral question, "What was it like for you?" or "How are you dealing with things?" you might very well hear an unexpected response:

"Well, it really has been a challenging time for all of us. There has been a lot of anguish and certainly annoyances. But this fire also got my attention in ways nothing else has before. I used to think that having nice things was so important, and I'd spend so much time thinking about crap that I wanted to buy but now I know that none of it really matters. It's my family and friends who are everything. And I feel so incredibly grateful that so many people have come to my aid. I intend to make some new choices about how I spend my time in the future."

Clients definitely need the freedom to tell their story in their own way. The ability to tell their story helps them adapt to the crisis and create a cohesive narrative, which could reduce the chances of posttraumatic stress disorder from emerging later on. It's important to assess for basic needs such as shelter, food, and clothing. You may find yourself doing more social work practice rather than therapy to help find these resources, which are needed for stability. Clients may have safety issues, may be unable to find friends or family members, or may be faced with the loss of important people in their lives. Your nonjudgmental compassion is important to their stability as well.

We recommend that you seek training for crisis counseling before engaging in this specialized modality. Several organizations such as the Red Cross provide training and have an infrastructure established in which you can participate. Regardless of whether you ever become involved in disaster relief work you will certainly see your fair share of clients recovering from abuse, neglect, and trauma, which kicks in some rather specific procedures for helping stabilize clients and aid in their continued recovery.

OBJECTIVE AND SUBJECTIVE SOURCES OF INFORMATION

In order to supplement subjective perceptions and the information you gather during clinical interviews, you will also wish to use psychometric and more objective assessment tools. Such tests and measures may be far more reliable (consistent) than reliance on your own perceptions; at the very least, they provide additional data to consider in forming your diagnostic impressions. In addition, each instrument has a distinct "way of thinking" that may emphasize more standardized, empirically based administration that helps you to maintain a certain distance and objectivity. It is important to realize, however, that such supposedly objective instruments may be biased regarding members of various minority groups who were not part of the normative group with which the instruments were developed.

There are a number of assessment tools at your disposal, including objective personality tests like the Minnesota Multiphasic Personality Inventory (MMPI) or Beck Depression Inventory, subjective personality tests like the Thematic Apperception Test (TAT) or Rorschach tests, or other measures like the Draw a Person or Bender Gestalt. You might also use genograms for a systematic assessment of clients' family history and configurations.

Even if you do not become trained in the administration of most psychological instruments (or choose to use them), you must still become familiar enough with what they can offer so they might guide your practice and help you make sound clinical decisions. You may receive reports from previous therapists or need to refer a client to an expert who can use these tools. Therefore, a basic understanding is necessary.

In one sense, such tests represent just another sample of client behavior, one that is offered in a normative context that helps you obtain information beyond your expectations. At the same time, instruments are not to be used in isolation without getting to know the client. Even though such instruments have their limitations and biases, they are still valuable tools for assessing client functioning. You will also have to consider that instruments like the MMPI and projective measures (TAT, Rorschach) are to be administered and interpreted only by advanced-level practitioners with specialized training in the use of these instruments (usually with a PhD in psychology). A more common tool used by counselors, marriage and family therapists, and licensed clinical social workers is the genogram.

A genogram plots the relationships among and between family members, both in the current family and in the family of origin. Such information as ages, marital status, names, occupations, degree of conflict and/or affiliation can be included. Genograms help clients to see and understand patterns in their life, which can lead to less self-blame. Like in any new system, genograms or family diagrams have their own unique symbols and language. Gender is noted by circles (females) and squares (males). In other genograms, the relative strength of relationship might be represented by the number of lines, conflict indicated by jagged lines, and so on. For further information, there are manuals you can consult that teach you the method and its applications, as well as software packages and Web sites that provide templates for you to follow when inputting data about your client's life.

MODELS OF DIAGNOSIS

So far we have looked at some of the practical aspects of what therapists and counselors do to launch an effective therapeutic relationship and collect necessary information. All these data must somehow be processed in a meaningful and constructive way in order to formulate a diagnostic impression of the case.

Therapists conceptualize their work in so many different ways. You might think that there is universal agreement on a diagnostic system, but there are actually several such models, depending on one's professional identity and theoretical orientation. These are just a few:

- *Medical:* categories of psychopathology, uses a disease model and a biologically based perspective, mental disorders
- *Psychodynamic:* a disease model as well, ego functioning, defense mechanisms and coping styles, looking at past, unconscious, diagnosing
- *Developmental:* stages of growth, assessment of current levels of functioning in all dimensions

- *Phenomenological:* complex descriptions of person, relational skills, personal strengths and weaknesses, freedom, autonomy, responsibility
- *Behavioral:* specific descriptors of behaviors, reinforcers, consequences, specific goals
- *Systemic:* contextual dynamics and family structures, power, coalitions

Each of these diagnostic models can be applied in different ways, depending on the clinician's perceptual filter. For instance, a client complains of frequent stomachaches that are believed to be brought on by excessive stress. Working backward from the list of diagnostic options, a systemic model might conceptualize things in such a way that the identified client is a scapegoat in a dysfunctional family system. Because of weak boundaries between interfamily coalitions, a chaotic system of communication between members, and an inappropriate power hierarchy, the client's symptoms represent a call for help to realign the family system. Given this conceptualization, the treatment plan would attempt to address these issues.

A behavioral model, on the other hand, would focus specifically on the presenting problems, identifying as clearly as possible what is bothersome and when, where, with whom, and in which situations the behavior occurs. You would be looking for ways this behavior is being rewarded—in other words: How are the stomachaches helpful to the person? You would attempt to define, in very specific terms, exactly which behaviors are going to be targeted, what the behavioral goals will be, how they will be reached, and the consequences that will result from each prospective outcome.

A phenomenological model is far more global and encompassing. Rather than seeking to reduce a person to a diagnostic label, the intent instead is to retain the essence of a person, who is far more than his stomachache. The presenting complaint would be only one small facet of the total picture, and the goal would be to describe (and conceptualize) what is going on, using the language of the person. Behavioral and systemic models focus on the presenting complaints; this model is concerned with the client's experiences and perceptions of these symptoms. This approach is favored by not only a phenomenological model but also by so-called constructivist models that look at presenting problems in a much broader cultural/ social/political context.

Developmental diagnosis refers to the identification of a client's functioning in a host of areas including physical, emotional, cognitive, social, cultural, moral, spiritual, work-related, and gender dimensions. If you can accurately diagnose the level at which a person is currently functioning, you predict where the person needs to go next. The treatment that follows is to design experiences that will help facilitate movement to the next stage of development. For instance, if the stomachaches are seen as an example of low-functioning coping skills in dealing with social situations, then efforts may be directed to help the person move to the next stage of developmental functioning in that area.

Current psychodynamic models evolved from psychoanalysis. This diagnostic approach focuses much more on patterns originating in the client's past: How is what people are experiencing now related to their current or childhood relationship with their primary caregiver? Diagnostic impressions thus include characteristic defense mechanisms and an assortment of other coping strategies.

The medical model is the one that has given rise to the diagnostic system now favored in the mental health system. When it is combined with a few of the other systems just described, you will have at your disposal an assortment of powerful tools for conceptualizing cases and making sense of what you encounter. All of these diagnostic models provide some useful structures for exploring, investigating, and finding meaning in what clients present.

Learning the *DSM*

Other courses will teach you how to use the *Diagnostic and Statistical Manual* (*DSM;* American Psychiatric Association, 2013), which has become the "bible" of our profession. Regardless of the setting in which you will eventually work, whether in a school, mental health center, hospital, community agency, or private practice, you will still be expected to master the nomenclature and structure of the *DSM* (American Psychiatric Association, 2013; Barnhill, 2013).

Most human problems that can show up in therapy are sorted and classified into one of several different categories and then further divided into subclasses. Because the *DSM* was authored primarily by psychiatrists, it is consistent with a medical model, a very different kind of approach from the other diagnostic models described in the previous section.

A *DSM* diagnostic assessment looks something like this:

296.32 Major depressive disorder, recurrent, moderate;

305.00 Alcohol use disorder, mild;

Hypertension;

V62.9 Unspecified problem related to social environment.

The client seemed to have difficulty maintaining friendships and reported that she did not have any friends in her state of residence with which she could talk.

She is in school and has a part-time job, but she fears graduation next fall because she reported being afraid to fail. The client stated that she would be happy living in a forest with animals, with little or no human contact.

You can see from this example that the *DSM* classification system is useful in assessing the client's presenting problems in a host of areas covering all facets of human functioning. As another example, let's take the case of a young man who presents himself to you complaining of chronic stomach problems. There are a number of possible sources for these problems. Perhaps there is some genuine organic problem that is contributing to the symptoms. The pain could also be the result of extreme anxiety as a result of an upcoming exam or perhaps a cry for attention as part of an ongoing manipulative interpersonal style. It would be important for this case, and all others that you work with, that you proceed with caution and consider many different dimensions of the difficulty.

You should also be aware that there are certain biases associated with the use of the *DSM*. As we have already mentioned, it is clearly slanted toward a medical model and favors approaches used by psychiatrists, and to a certain extent those of psychologists. Because it is empirically based, it may also take some work to make it fit those who prefer a more constructivist or humanist orientation—examples of theories that downplay labeling and prefer to operate within the client's frame of reference.

The cultural and gender biases of the *DSM* are not unlike those of any diagnostic system or choice of therapy. That is why it is so critical that you take a client's cultural background, gender, ethnicity, spiritual beliefs, and other factors into consideration when assigning any diagnostic labels. What may be auditory hallucinations in one person might very well be a transcendent religious experience in another. Or what might strike you as antisocial behavior in one adolescent might very well be entirely normative within another person's peer group. That is why all of your thinking and internal processing should take place within the cultural context of the clients you are seeing.

REMEMBERING WHAT YOU SEE AND HEAR

One of the most important aspects of developing your skills for conceptualizing cases and evaluating the impact of what you do is related to keeping accurate, comprehensive, descriptive, and meaningful records. Basically, after every intake interview you will want to write extensive notes that include a diagnostic impression, a detailed treatment plan, and working guidelines for future sessions.

In this first session and all succeeding sessions, you will need to maintain case notes on what occurred. Keeping records of your sessions can be helpful for remembering details that could be forgotten from week to week. For example, referring to last week's notes prior to meeting with the client can jog your memory as to what you might want to follow up on, such as homework assignments. In addition, sometimes the details of two similar clients in a large caseload can become confused early in the process. Keeping notes will help you to avoid the blunder of mixing up client information.

Some therapists choose to take notes during the session while the client is talking. This can be helpful in that you will retain all the details of the session, forgetting nothing. However, there's a serious disadvantage to doing this. If you are taking notes while your client is talking, you can't listen as effectively.

Exercise in Note Taking

Get into triads: The talking person tells a story with lots of details, the second person takes notes on the story as a therapist might, and the third person listens as a therapist might but without taking notes. After 5 minutes, both listeners make detailed notes about the speaker's content, the essence of the content, the client's process, and any nonverbal messages. Compare notes. Then get feedback from the speaker about what he or she preferred: the person taking notes or the person just listening. Rotate until everyone has played each role, and then discuss the experience overall.

After completing this exercise, you may find that taking notes can interrupt the client's process. The client might slow down his or her story to give you time to write down all the details, staying in his or her head to tell the story and thus avoiding emotions. In addition, an inattentive therapist taking notes may miss important nonverbal information, such as the formation of tears. And finally, believe it or not, when you get so involved in taking notes, you sometimes don't really attend to what's being said. Think of a time when you have been so busy taking notes in class that you have no idea what you just wrote down. If you feel it's important to get the details, you may want to record the session; it's less invasive. A good therapist is more interested in the process than in the content. How does the client convey his or her story? Does he or she do so without feelings? Is the client animated while telling the story? Do you see any patterns from previous stories? Rarely will the details like names, ages, or cities be important to the overall problem.

Whether or not you decide to take notes during the session, you will need to make some notes afterward. The amount of detail is up to you or the agency for which you work. Some therapists prefer to take notes just on processes, such as,

"The client seemed to be gaining insight about why she chooses domineering men." Other therapists prefer to report only the facts, such as, "The client discussed the relationship between her mother and father, and stated that her father seemed to be 'controlling' with regard to her mother and her." A classic and popular format is known as SOAP: subjective, objective, assessment, and progress. In the subjective section, the therapist records information about how the client was dressed, client's overall mood, or anything else that is perceived or observed. In the objective section, the therapist notes the content of what was discussed during the session. The assessment section might include an interpretation of how the client is doing; it's the section where you'd be most likely include information based on your theoretical orientation. The final section, progress, includes how the client is doing relative to meeting short-term and long-term goals and prognosis (see Figure 5.2).

We have a few pointers in keeping case notes. First, especially during training, you may want to write only the client's name at the top of the page in case you need to duplicate the progress notes for your supervisor or professor, or insurance company paying for sessions. This way you can cover the name to conceal the identity of the client. Second, when stating information that is not factual, you may want to use tentative language because you are only speculating. Finally, you want to keep your information secure and safe from harm. If you keep hard copies, the file cabinet should be locked at all times and fireproof. If you keep notes on the computer, the diskette, thumb disk, or CD should be locked up or, if on your hard drive, your computer should have a password that is changed monthly to assure security. You may not want your computer to be connected to the Internet, to prevent hackers from breaking into your files. Keeping the records confidential is required by your ethical guidelines; and each state requires that you maintain your client notes for a certain number of years.

The preceding example is just a sample format for keeping case notes. If you work for an agency, as you most certainly will during your practica and internship experiences, the agency will likely have a format for you to follow. State and county agencies are known to have extensive systems for keeping case notes. In addition, your supervisor may have specific requirements about record keeping, because case notes are a vital part of how the supervisor provides feedback. The good news is that your supervisors should be evaluating and critiquing your case notes weekly to help you develop an appropriate format. What is most critical is that you are following the standard of care for your profession and the region in which you live. Each state and each profession has a different set of expectations. Finally, you will want to be consistent in your record-keeping, maintaining the same format for all of your clients.

Figure 5.2   SOAP

SOAP
Counseling Services Agency, Inc.
Client Name: <u>Jane Doe</u>   Therapist: <u>Rae Me</u>
Date: <u>January 21, 2016</u>   Session Number: <u>6</u>
Subjective: The client came in dressed much nicer than usual. She wore makeup and seemed unusually cheerful. Her energy level was high, and she smiled frequently.
Objective: The client reported that she had just met a man this past weekend. She discussed how he was different from her ex-husband and previous boyfriends in that he had a full-time job and a home. She reported how they met and how they have spent every day together since meeting last weekend. She stated that she was hopeful that this relationship could be different from all her previous relationships. She talked of hopes of marriage.
Assessment: The client seemed to have a lot of positive self-talk with regard to this new relationship. However, she also seemed to have unrealistic expectations about the future by hoping for marriage after knowing him only one week. The client has evidenced this pattern of belief before. When confronted about this pattern of wishing for marriage after one week, the client denied ever having this experience before and was quite defensive.
Progress: The client may be making progress toward meeting her short-term goal of wanting to meet more people. However, the client does not seem to be meeting her long-term goal of getting into a healthy relationship at a slower pace. She seemed to be making decisions about the future in a short period of time, as she has done in the past.
_____ Therapist Signature
_____ Supervisor Signature

MAKING THINGS FIT YOUR STYLE

In this chapter, we have provided you with an abundance of information to prepare you for the beginning phase with your client: the mental status exam, the intake interview, the assessment instruments, and the *DSM*. How you perform your intake interview may be predetermined by the agency in which you work. They may require a very structured intake process. In other agencies, someone else might complete your intakes. However, most agencies give you the freedom to obtain relevant information in whatever way you see fit. In any case, you will need to develop a style that fits your personality and your values and that works with your unique qualities. When you sit down with your client for the first time, you will have to figure out what works best for you. We hope we have given you some tools that you can choose from to adapt to your personal style. In the next section, we alert you to some traps and errors that you will want to watch out for as you learn to conduct assessment interviews.

PITFALLS AND COMMON MISTAKES

As with any new skill, mistakes are made by new practitioners. By exposing you to some of the more common mistakes and pitfalls, we hope you can avoid what we have come to realize does not work.

Thinking Too Much Instead of Listening

As we've said before, the experience of doing counseling (in case you haven't noticed) is one of feeling confused and overwhelmed. In any given moment there are at least a dozen things you could do or say, and no matter which one you select, you will wonder what you should have done instead. The client is speaking. You are doing your best to demonstrate solid attending and listening skills. You are trying to figure out the underlying meaning of the communication: What is the client *really* saying by this? You are making connections between what is being said and things the client has talked about earlier. You are considering how what is going on fits within your overall scheme of things. You are planning where you are going to go next. You are reviewing options in your head, rejecting some, choosing others, then making adjustments as the client changes directions. Something the client says sparks a recollection of something you must do later in the day. This reminds you of something that you forgot to do earlier in the morning. Then you think about the client you saw last hour, and the one you will see in the next hour. Then you realize that for the last several minutes you haven't been really listening to what the client has been saying.

You can ask the client to summarize what the main points were—this is a clever way to catch up when you have been falling behind—but the main goal is for you to stay centered and focused on listening above all else. At least a dozen, maybe even a hundred times, in any session you are going to find your mind racing, darting backwards and sideways. You will have the most brilliant realizations and insights—about the client, about the world, about yourself, about the meaning of life. You will be juggling so many different ideas, theories, and revelations at the same time. And all this time you are nodding your head, *pretending* to listen to the client. Remember that you can't help clients very well if you are not paying close attention to what they are saying. All your amazing theories and insights are useless if they do not correspond with where the client is at any moment in time. Listen now and save your thinking for later.

Failing to Engage the Client

As a beginner, you may be so focused on your diagnostic and assessment skills that you forget that being with the person is as important as what you actually do. Unless you manage to create strong connections with your clients, relationships in which they feel valued and understood, nothing else you do is going to work very well. We are giving you fair warning that there will be times when you have the most accurate, comprehensive, and utterly brilliant diagnostic grasp of what is going on with a client, yet such conceptualizations will be utterly useless if the person doesn't return. You will be left with your detailed case notes and your meticulous clinical judgments, all of which will get tucked away into a case file and eventually thrown out. Almost all other mistakes can be forgiven *if* you have built good relationships with your clients.

Being Judgmental

We humans have a natural tendency to make assumptions or judgments about people when we meet them. Making these presumptions is our way of organizing the world. We even study cultural stereotypes to help us be more sensitive with our clients. If your judgments about your client, whether negative or positive, are rigid or inflexible you will not be able to see him or her clearly. You will have difficulty demonstrating empathy and consequently difficulty building a strong therapeutic alliance. Therefore, although it may be necessary for you to develop some theories about your client, make them just that: theories. Theories are flexible and require supporting evidence. They can change, and we can assure you that some of your first assumptions about most clients will change over time.

The best way to manage being judgmental is to first become aware of the critical voice inside your head. You must become more comfortable with nuances of right and wrong, with ambiguity, and with changing your mind. Each session should be a process of discovery for you, one in which you learn new things not only about your client, but also about yourself and the world.

In order to strengthen your relationship with the client, you need to separate the person from his or her behaviors. You need to see each and every person, no matter how toxic, no matter how bad the behaviors, as a good person who is doing the best she or he can. If you believe that people are basically good, this will be much easier for you.

Trying to Do Too Much

The problem that most beginners have is not in doing too little, but in trying to do too much. People come to you in pain and you want to do something to take away their suffering. You may even have your own issues with feeling some level of intolerance toward your own pain or the pain of others. You have visions of being a healer, of saying a few magic incantations, and voila!—the person is cured. We are not saying that quick relief is out of the question, especially in this era of brief therapy, but rather that you must honor the pace of your clients. When you force things, when you push too hard, that is when clients can be hurt or fail to return. And remember, if you don't get clients to come back, you can't help them!

The more work you do in the sessions, the less there is for the client to do. That is a problem in many couples' relationships in which one partner complains that the other is too passive in social situations or in other areas. In such situations, the goal is to get one partner to back off so the other can step up and become more active and involved. This same analogy holds true for counseling relationships.

How do you know if you are pushing the client too hard or working harder than your client? You experience a lot of resistance from the client. The resistance indicates either that you are wrong, or more often that you are way ahead of your client. Your client is not ready to see what you are presenting or to do what you are suggesting; more work needs to be done right where the client is stuck.

When you catch yourself working very hard to convince a client of the merits of your brilliant interpretation, and you notice that the client isn't buying it, then back off. In most situations where you observe that you are working furiously while the client is sitting back watching the show, it is time to make adjustments so those roles can be reversed. In spite of what you have been led to believe, in therapy it is the client who does most of the work.

Neglecting to Offer Help

The opposite problem of the one just discussed is not doing what is needed. Let's say that a client comes to you in the midst of a crisis. There has been a recent tragedy and this person is experiencing profound grief and loss. She is barely holding things together. You quickly find out that she is acutely depressed and unable to manage the most ordinary daily tasks. She clearly needs immediate relief and crisis intervention.

Instead of responding to the immediate situation, you persist in the usual data collection that is part of an assessment interview; after all, you have forms to fill out and procedures to follow. Through dedication and Herculean effort, you manage to get the information you need while keeping the client focused on the task at hand. The session ends and you have what you need—but the client is still just as lost and distraught.

We'd like to repeat one more time the most important thing to remember in doing a first interview: *The object of a first session is to get the client to come back for another one.* Unless you can do this, all the information you have collected and diagnoses you have formed will be worthless. This means that you must deliver some constructive help during the session, even though your own goal is to get the information you need to create an intelligent treatment plan.

Failing to Collect Relevant Information

Another common mistake is believing that the more information you collect, the better. You can fill volumes of notebooks with data on your client, but unless these details are clinically meaningful and relevant, you have just wasted a lot of energy and time. Throughout the interview, keep in focus where you are going and what you need to get there.

Your principal job during the initial contact is to find out what is bothering the client the most and what is desired from the treatment. That is the big picture. The subgoals are to find out (a) when, where, and how the problem started; (b) what has already been tried with what results; and (c) how what is being presented connects with other facets of the person's life. There are indeed other things you will want to learn about the client, many of which have already been discussed, but keep in mind that time is very limited. You have only 45 or 50 minutes in a first session, so you must be disciplined and find out the basics as efficiently as you can. Many times this involves listening rather than asking questions because clients will tell you what is most important if you let them.

For school counselors and crisis intervention specialists, who don't operate in neat time segments, you will have to be even more focused in your assessment efforts. There are times when you might have only 15 minutes to figure out what is going on and create some sort of intervention. In some cases, this might be your only contact with this client. Plan the assessment according to the time that is available and the realistic constraints that are in place. Remember that you can almost always make modifications and adjustments to your initial assessment.

The most common way that beginners get lots of irrelevant data is by asking too many questions. Questions are very important, but in the initial session, once you finish with the informed consent/disclosure statement process, you will want to do more listening and allow your client to do most of the talking.

Thinking That What You Missed Was Important

After you complete the interview and reflect back on what you did (and didn't do), you may very well find that you missed a lot more than you captured. This is not only normal, but just what you should expect. A first contact is just that—the initial attempt to figure out what is going on and to start building a collaborative relationship.

One exception is during those instances when you might be seeing someone for a one-time session. Although you might question the value of just one consultation, you may be surprised how often some clients get what they want from a single meeting. There are even approaches that are specifically designed to be implemented in one face-to-face session, augmented by an initial phone/video prescreening and a follow-up call (Hymmen, Stalker, & Cait, 2013). Unless you are doing single-session therapy, or are limited to very brief therapy (less than three sessions), you will have plenty of time to fill in gaps.

In addition, the client will first present what is most relevant at the moment. You cannot force the client to talk about anything until he or she is ready. When supervising new therapists, we have found that many clients keep going back to the same topic, the topic that is most essential to them at the moment, no matter how often the beginning therapist goes off the primary topic to explore some tangent. You might as well give in and allow the client to lead. By reflecting well, you will obtain an abundance of information.

The beauty of the pace of therapy is that you usually meet with clients once (or even twice) per week. After they walk out the door, you have plenty of time to reflect on the session, consult with supervisors, and do your homework in preparation for the next meeting. Anything and everything that you missed the first time, you can usually pick up the second or third or eleventh meeting. It is very important that you have realistic expectations about what you can do, and what you cannot do, or you will set yourself up for failure.

Forgetting to Find Out How You're Doing

Never forget that clients are your customers. They pay your salary directly, or indirectly at taxpayer expense. Clients, or those who referred them in the case of involuntary participants, must be satisfied with the way things are going or you will be "fired."

Despite your zeal to conduct your assessment, you must keep in mind that clients (as well as their parents, significant others, and referral sources) must have confidence in your plan. If they have any doubts, they will go somewhere else or, worse, simply abandon their efforts to seek help.

You are not expected to read clients' minds, even with your advanced skills in reading body language and discerning underlying meaning in their communications. You are not only permitted but encouraged to find out how you are doing. Such an inquiry might look something like this.

Therapist: Now that our session is over, I'm wondering what this has been like for you.

Client: Excuse me?

Therapist: How did you find this conversation?

Client: Oh. It was fine.

Therapist: What I'm asking is, what about this meeting was most helpful to you? I am very interested in making sure that what we do together meets your needs. In order to do that, I need feedback from you—not just now but all along the way—about what you liked most and liked least about what we are doing. Specifically, I'd like us to spend the last few minutes reviewing what we did today and then figure out how we could best proceed in the future. That means it would be helpful to hear what your reactions were to the session.

This was a fairly realistic glimpse into how this conversation might go. Clients don't know what we are looking for and often don't know how to respond to your queries. In your efforts to conduct ongoing assessment about progress and satisfaction with services you must teach your clients how to give you feedback as honestly and clearly as possible.

There is nothing more frustrating than having a valued client unexpectedly cancel an appointment and refuse to reschedule, and you never learn what happened or why. What did you do to drive the person away? What did you neglect to notice and respond to? Or perhaps the person didn't return because she had already gotten what she wanted from the sessions. Unless the person returns for a future session, you will never know.

Misdiagnosing

A diagnosis represents a clinician's perception of what is disturbing to clients, but there is always potential to misread the situation. Under the best possible circumstances, even among very experienced clinicians, there is often disagreement about what the "real" problem is. You have seen this in the medical profession, of course, but in our own field the potential for error is even greater because what we are observing and measuring is often elusive and imprecise. Sometimes even clients can't say exactly what is bothering them.

A client says that he is depressed, but that can mean a whole assortment of things. Is this a temporary or chronic situation? Was there a precipitant to the symptoms or did they begin without a particular stimulus? Might the depression be masking other conditions? In other words, is the depression the problem, or is it the result of what is really most bothersome? Is the depression biologically based or is it sparked by something in the person's life? In addition, there are at least a half dozen kinds of depression (dysthymia, reactive depression, major depression, bipolar disorder, etc.) that might be operating, and each one might involve a different treatment.

Complicating matters is the way in which culture plays a factor in diagnosing. Some men, for instance, often exhibit their depression through anger, while many women tend to exhibit a sad affect. So, these men might be misdiagnosed as having problems with anger, when in fact you should be treating the depression (Englar-Carlson & Stevens, 2006). Many Asian cultures value the inhibition of expression of emotions to keep from affecting other people negatively; they might not look depressed at all. You might be completely baffled about how they are feeling. Individual differences make diagnosing an inexact science.

If even experienced therapists struggle with formulating accurate diagnoses, then imagine how difficult it will be for you. The good news is that a diagnosis is only a working hypothesis that will be altered in light of new data. The key feature is to make sure that you don't become so vested in your reading of the situation that you fail to make adjustments as things develop.

Trying to Fix the Problem

There are some styles of practice, especially some forms of brief therapy, where the therapist's job is defined as identifying the presenting problem and then fixing it in the shortest, most efficient period of time. This is often how managed care organizations describe our preferred roles—we are problem solvers.

We leave it to other courses for you to resolve this dilemma as to what your main role is to be—problem solver, consultant, teacher, confidant, surrogate parent, mediator, or perhaps a combination of all them. Frankly, much will depend on where you work and what the mission of that health care organization is.

For our purposes in this class on basic helping skills, we would like you to learn sound procedures for *not* getting in the habit of fixing other people's problems for them. There are several good reasons for this. Number one: If your efforts to "cure" or fix the problem are unsuccessful, you will be blamed. In fact, positive outcomes are most likely the result of what *clients* do or don't do; *they* are the ones who primarily determine the outcome. Granted, we can do a lot to improve their motivation, resilience, and strategies, but ultimately, *their* efforts will influence the result.

Because many clients don't want responsibility for their lives and choices in the first place, they will be delighted to blame you when things go wrong. The implicit message is that you failed them because of your incompetence or inadequacies. We much prefer to communicate a very different message to our clients; it goes something like this:

Client: What we talked about last time didn't work at all. I'm worse off now than ever!

Therapist: What is it that you did this week and how did that work out?

Client: I just told you: What you told me to do didn't work.

Therapist: I'm a little unclear about what I told you to do. What I remember is that you said that you wanted to try approaching things with your mother a bit differently. You said that you were tired of arguing with her and that you were going to try backing off a little to see how that worked instead. I told you at the time that this first strategy of yours might not be as successful as you'd like, at least the first time you tried it. I also told you that I could help you to come up with some other things that you might use to work things out. So, let's figure out where things fell apart, and what you did that wasn't all that helpful. Also, let's look at what you did that you liked and might want to continue doing.

FOR REFLECTION

Reason through why you think we claim that giving "good" advice could be dangerous. After all, if you tell someone what to do, and it solves the problem, haven't you done what you're paid to do? What could possibly be wrong with that?

To understand the reasoning behind our point, consider the consequences of giving someone good advice. The person comes to you, feeling helpless, frustrated, at a loss as to how to proceed. He tells you what is wrong and you say, "Hey, no problem. Have you thought about trying this?" The client goes home, uses your advice, and it works out beautifully. Now, what has the client learned from this experience?

Notice the way the therapist continues to emphasize the pronoun *you*. It is what the client did, or did not do, that matters. The therapist does not directly argue with the client about who is at fault but instead turns the conversation to a review of progress. This continues to reinforce the idea that the client is the one who fixes his or her own problems; the therapist is the guide, the consultant, the partner along the way.

The second reason why trying to fix the client's problem is generally a bad idea (except when using paradoxical directives that are the kind of advice designed to be disobeyed) is that what you tell the person to do might work out. You heard us right: Giving good advice could be even more dangerous than giving bad advice.

When you tell people what to do with their lives, you are essentially saying that they don't know what is best for themselves and they need someone like you to figure it out for them. They are either too stupid or too inept to sort this out for themselves so they need someone like you, an expert, to fix things. You have just reinforced their own inability to take care of themselves.

Because things appear to have worked out so well, they have now learned to come back to you, or another expert, the next time they have problems. They have not only learned to distrust their own problem-solving ability, but have learned very little about the process of taking care of themselves. In contrast, clients who do not take your advice may feel too ashamed to return the next week. They may feel that you will not approve of them because they did not take your advice.

The final reason for not giving advice often is that nine times out of ten, the client is not going to follow it anyway. Think of how many times you gave great advice to your friends. Did they really listen and do what you told them to? Not that often. And how many times did you ask for advice or were told exactly what to do? Did you do what you were told? Not that often. Most people aren't really looking for advice unless they want to avoid responsibility. Most people need support and a greater understanding of themselves so that they can make their own decisions. When did you ever leave a relationship because someone told you that you should? You leave when you're ready to leave.

These points are the reasons why it is so important to choose your language very carefully. Following are some examples of how you might intervene in response to some client statements:

Client: You really helped me last week with that suggestion.

Therapist: You mean that you really helped yourself by adapting what we talked about to that situation.

Client: Thank you so much for all your help!

Therapist: You're quite welcome. But I want to remind you that you are the one who did all the work. You are the one who took the risks and tried so hard to change this pattern.

Client: That idea you gave me last time worked perfectly.

Therapist: Tell me, how did you take what we talked about last time and make it fit this situation?

Client: I'm really going to miss you when these sessions end.

Therapist: I will miss you as well. Remember, though, that what you have managed to do here you can continue to do once we stop these meetings.

Note that in each of these responses, the therapist continues to reinforce the idea that it is the client who solves his or her own problems, with the able assistance of the therapist.

Liking or Disliking the Client Too Much

A final common mistake we would like to mention is related to the countertransference reactions discussed earlier. At a rather basic level you will find yourself having personal reactions to your clients. Some you will find immediately attractive and others may repulse you. Some you would enjoy as friends and others you would hope never to run into again. You may have vivid sexual fantasies about some clients—when you are with them in session and when you have idle moments on your own. All of this is normal, natural, and part of what comes with the territory of being a therapist. On the other hand, if your fantasies are frequent and persistent, then you have to consider a pattern that could be dangerous to the people you are paid to help.

You are probably well aware that your personal reactions, if left unchecked, can wreak havoc on your work as well as other people's lives. At this beginning juncture, just as the relationship begins, you will want to make sure that you present yourself as warm and accessible without being perceived as seductive. Depending on the client's age, cultural background, and individual style, you will wish to adapt your demeanor to match that of the person you are helping.

The warning we wish to issue is that although it is permissible, even desirable, to like your clients, you don't want to like them so much that you enable their manipulative behavior or disrupt your own life by thinking about them when you are off duty. Likewise, when you must work with individuals whose behavior you find abhorrent (sex abusers, murderers, partner batterers, obnoxious people), you will want to protect yourself against your strong negative reactions so they don't compromise your work. In spite of what you might believe, you will often not have the luxury of referring elsewhere people to whom you have a negative reaction. Not only does this send a strong message to your supervisor about the nature of your biases, but it suggests that you have a hard time accepting people who come from different backgrounds.

This is where supervision is really helpful. If you have a supervisor to talk to about these extreme feelings, whether good or bad, then you can process it to keep it at bay when you're with the client. When you like someone too much, it's usually because he or she has a quality that you like in yourself, or one that you wish you had more of. By the same token, you often dislike people or qualities that you dislike or deny in yourself.

A supervisor will help you to identify these issues and gain some balance. In some cases, you may even discover that you need to go to therapy to work on them a bit more. Part of being a therapist is constantly doing your own work. The most important thing is that you recognize when feelings about your clients are more intense than usual so you can work on them.

Conceptualizing Client's Presenting Problem

If only therapy were as easy as simply asking what is bothering clients and then proceeding to fix things just like an auto mechanic or a surgeon. Unfortunately, even when clients do articulate clearly what most bothers them (and that is usually not the case), we still can't be certain that this is the core issue that must be addressed. At times, clients may wish to test you first, find out if you are trustworthy and competent before they trot out their *real* concern. In other situations, they genuinely don't know what is wrong. They might just feel uneasy or depressed or unhappy but can't point to the source of the difficulty. Sometimes they will come up with some explanation just because they know it is expected. Finally, clients sometimes present the *symptoms* of some underlying issue. Remember, what is presented is usually not the problem, but the symptom of some pattern that was developed earlier in life but isn't working today.

Before doing anything else, the therapist must come up with at least a working hypothesis and structure for figuring out what is going on. This is often called case conceptualization and treatment planning and involves the mental activity of gathering needed information, synthesizing the data, and generating reasonable assumptions about what is most likely occurring. It involves generating hypotheses about what caused the problem, what precipitated it, and what continues to maintain it. Based on these hypotheses, the therapist's next job is to plan what needs to be done and how this can be best accomplished.

APPLICATIONS TO SELF: DIAGNOSING IN A VARIETY OF SETTINGS

The skills you develop from this chapter will be helpful in a variety of ways, both professionally and personally. The ability to build a relationship while collecting information as thoroughly as possible in a limited amount of time is essential in the helping field. You can use these skills in a variety of environments, such as private practice, agencies, schools, universities, at work, or at home. You can use these skills with a variety of people, such as with individual clients, couples, groups, families, organizations, colleagues, or with your friends and family. You can use these skills with a variety of roles, such as therapist, mediator, consultant, friend, or family member.

Let's start with how diagnosing skills are helpful in various environments. You may assume that once you graduate you'll open a private practice. The reality is that you will probably work in more than one setting. Some individuals work in a private practice while having a connection to an agency. Others consult with schools while maintaining a private practice. It does not matter what kind of office you work in, you will need to develop a proficiency in obtaining information and organizing it while maintaining a good relationship with the individuals in that environment.

You might also assume that you will use these skills only in the context of individual therapy, but you can and will use them with many populations in many roles. For instance, your client types may include individual adults, children, groups, families, or couples. In all cases, diagnosis will be a necessary beginning to the process of therapy. You may choose to work as a consultant or a mediator with organizations. In these situations, you will still need to develop a thorough understanding of the problem while being mindful of the relationship to establish trust and to inspire confidence in your clients. Furthermore, you will most likely consult with colleagues and interact with coworkers in ways that require strong diagnostic skills. Finally, these skills may be helpful in your personal life. We are all social animals, and life is full of problems. Whether you have a conflict with someone or just happened to be a shoulder for a friend to cry on, you will probably find that you use these skills every day once you learn them. In your life, you will have personal challenges, and developing these skills with clients helps you to work on your own issues, an essential component of becoming a good therapist.

SUMMARY

Our goal in this chapter was to introduce you to the first steps involved in your initial client meeting. We provided an overview of some concepts that you will likely learn more thoroughly in other courses, such as the Mental Status Exam, assessing for special conditions of abuse or suicide risk, different methods of diagnosis, and the *Diagnostic and Statistical Manual*. All of these subjects are relevant to the intake interview. We attempted to provide you with an overview of that process and to give specific examples. Finally, we introduced some mistakes commonly made by beginners so you can be conscientious about avoiding them during your first meeting with your client. The next chapter introduces you to the exploration phase of therapy.

Skills in Action: After the Intake Interview

Therapist: You appeared a bit frustrated as you were filling out the paperwork that's part of this intake process. [Reflecting feelings]

Client: Yeah, I guess I was. I've just been having a hard time with everything lately. I just don't have much patience.

Therapist: You said that as if something happened recently, that at one time you had more patience.

Client: Well, it has been almost a year since I lost the love of my life. The pain is as bad today as it was last year. I wasn't able to go to the funeral and I'm not able to get any support from friends or family. No one wants to hear me talk about it. No one knew him, really, some knew about him, though.

Therapist: You feel all alone. [Reflecting feeling; building the relationship]

Client: I do. If only I had one person. He and I were in it alone. No one understood how much we loved one another. No one who knew about him approved of our relationship. And now, I don't have him anymore either. I just feel so lost without him. This stuff with your paperwork—I just wonder if this will help either.

Therapist: So you have some doubts about whether therapy can make a difference. Over the last year, you've lost a lost of hope for the future. [Reflection of feeling and content] I'm also struck by what you said, that no one approved of your relationship. [Seeking clarification]

Client: It's true. No one supported me before, and they certainly aren't supporting me now. I'm just so lonely. (crying)

Therapist: (silence) [Offering support by not interrupting]

Client: (looking up)

Therapist: (in a soft voice) You miss him. [Reflecting feelings; Building the relationship before seeking more information]

Client: (crying) I do. I don't know how to live without him. He meant *everything* to me. We spent so much time together; I don't even know how to be without him. We worked together. We played together. We leaned on each other. He was my whole life. Now, I have nothing. I just can't seem to get any better. (still crying)

Therapist: You feel so much sorrow, and you feel hopeless about ever feeling good again. [Reflecting feelings; building the relationship; beginning to assess for suicidality]

Client: Exactly! I didn't know where else to turn since I can't speak about this with anyone else. You're my last chance.

Therapist: Last chance? [Assessing for suicidality]

Client: I don't want to live like this any more. I'd rather be with him.

Therapist: By last chance, you mean being dead? I'm concerned for you. I'm wondering if you have had thoughts of harming yourself?

Client: Of course. I've gone through a thousand scenarios. No one would care.

Therapist: Say more about your scenarios. [Assessing for suicide]

Client: Well, I thought I would take these pills I got when I broke my leg. They were really strong painkillers. I thought I'd take these pills with some Scotch and let myself fall asleep. Then the pain would be over.

Therapist: You're tired of being in pain. You can't imagine that it will get any better. [Aware that the client has the means and a plan that is lethal; reflecting feelings and content first to continue building the relationship]

Client: (crying) I can't. I just don't want to live like this any more. You have to help me.

Therapist: A part of you feels hopeless, but another part of you brought you here and believes that maybe, with help, you can feel better. [Reflecting discrepancy; instilling hope]

Client: I suppose you're right. I really do *want* to move on, I just don't know how.

Therapist: I would really like to try to help you do that. In order for me to help you, though, you need to give our work together a chance. [Instilling hope; beginning an informal countersuicide contract]

Client: I can do that. Oh, I don't think I'm ready to take those pills yet. In some ways, I feel better already. You really seem to understand me. Or at least you listen to me, which nobody has done in a long time.

Therapist: I notice that you have stopped crying for a moment. [Reflecting process]

Client: I guess I finally feel understood for the first time in over a year. Thank you.

Therapist: You're welcome. I'd like to ask you something difficult, if you think you're ready to answer it. If not, just tell me. [Preparing a gentle confrontation]

Client: Go ahead.

Therapist: I notice you haven't told me the reason others didn't approve of this relationship. You seem to love him so much. [Seeking information; reflecting feelings]

Client: I was afraid you would judge me, too, but I think I feel okay to tell you.

Therapist: You can wait until later if you would like. [Empowering the client]

Client: No, I'd like to tell you. John was married . . . but not to me. (looking up expectantly)

Therapist: I see. Your family and friends didn't approve of you being in a relationship with a married man. You look worried that I might think negatively of you. [Reflecting content then feelings/process]

Client: You don't?

Therapist: I can see that you loved him very much, and still do. I'm not here to judge you. I want to help you feel better about yourself and where you are headed for the future. [Instilling hope]

Client: I'm so relieved. (sighs) So, what's next?

Therapist: First, I would like your reassurance that you will not harm yourself.

Client: I promise, I won't.

Therapist: Our time is about up, so in closing, it seems like you have a few things to work on. First, you feel socially isolated, at least with regard to this lost relationship. Second, you seem to be experiencing complicated bereavement. I'd like to refer you to a friend of mine who is a psychiatrist. You can talk with him about whether or not you would like medical treatment to help you through this. [Closing; summarizing; referral for further assessment]

Client: I'm not crazy!

Therapist: I don't see you as crazy. Sometimes, though, we need a little help to get back on track after experiencing deep pain. You don't have to take the medication, but I'd like you to talk with the doctor if you're willing, and then make the decision. I think it might be helpful as we work through some of your pain. I have his card here. (passing the card to her) [Self-disclosing; offering some education]

Client: Okay. I'll check it out.

REFERENCES AND RESOURCES

Abendroth, M., & Figley, C. (2011). Vicarious trauma and the therapeutic relationship. In J. C. Norcross (Ed.), *Psychotherapy relationships that work* (pp. 111–125). New York, NY: Oxford University Press.

American Psychiatric Association. (2013). *Diagnostic and statistical manual of mental disorders* (5th ed.). Washington, DC: Author.

Barnhill, J. (2013). *DSM-5 clinical cases.* Washington, DC: American Psychiatric Publishing.

Calhoun, L. G., & Tedeschi, R. G. (2013). *Posttraumatic growth in clinical practice.* New York, NY: Routledge.

Englar-Carlson, M., & Stevens, M. (2006). Masculine norms and the therapeutic process. *In the room with men: A casebook of therapeutic change* (pp. 13–48). Washington, DC: American Psychological Association.

Halstead, R. (2007). *Assessment of client core issues.* Alexandria, VA: American Counseling Association.

Hersen, M. (2006). *Clinician's handbook of adult behavioral assessment.* San Diego, CA: Elsevier Academic.

Hood, A. B., & Johnson, R. W. (2007). *Assessment in counseling: A guide to the use of psychological assessment procedures* (2nd ed.). Alexandria, VA: American Counseling Association.

Huebner, D., Thoma, B., & Neilands, T. (2015). School victimization and substance use among lesbian, gay, bisexual, and transgender adolescents. *Prevention Science, 16*(5), 734–743.

Hymmen, P., Stalker, C. A., & Cait, C. (2013). The case for single-session therapy: Does the empirical evidence support the increased prevalence of this service delivery model? *Journal of Mental Health, 22*(1), 60–71.

Joseph, S. (2011). *What doesn't kill us: The new psychology of posttraumatic growth*. New York, NY: Basic Books.

Kuyken, W. (2004). Cognitive therapy outcome: The effects of hopelessness in a naturalistic outcome study. *Behaviour Research and Therapy, 42*(6), 631–646.

Lee, C. (Ed.). (2007). *Counseling for social justice* (2nd ed.). Alexandria, VA: American Counseling Association.

Paniagua, F. A. (2001). *Diagnosis in a multicultural context: A casebook for mental health professionals*. Thousand Oaks, CA: Sage.

Seligman, L. (1998). *Selecting effective treatments: A comprehensive, systematic guide to treating mental disorders* (2nd ed.). San Francisco, CA: Jossey-Bass.

Simeonsson, R. J., & Rosenthal, S. L. (2001). *Psychological and developmental assessment*. New York, NY: Guilford Press.

Sommers-Flanagan, J., & Sommers-Flanagan, R. (2015). *Clinical interviewing* (5th ed.). Hoboken, NJ: John Wiley.

Stevens, P., & Smith, R. (2012). *Substance abuse counseling: Theory and practice* (5th ed.). New York, NY: Pearson.

Welfel, E. R., & Ingersoll, R. E. (Eds.). (2005). *The mental health desk reference* (3rd ed.). New York, NY: Wiley.

Werdel, M. B., & Wicks, R. J. (2012). *Primer on posttraumatic growth*. New York, NY: Wiley.

Chapter 6

EXPLORATION SKILLS

S o, the client begins the second session, "I was wondering where we go next?" Good question, you think, considering what direction to proceed. "What were you thinking about since our last conversation?" You ask this partially to stall, but also to get a sense of what has transpired during the intervening week. It is important to get an accurate reading on the current situation rather than make assumptions that may no longer be valid.

"I felt better after our talk. I mean, it feels good to know you can help me and all. Last time you said some interesting things about what might be going on. That all sounds good to me. So, what do we do next?"

AN OVERVIEW OF THE EXPLORATION STAGE

With the working diagnosis in place and a basic assessment process completed, the next step is to learn more about what is going on, study relevant background, and help facilitate a deeper-level exploration of the problem and its meaning in the client's life. Several questions may immediately come to mind:

- Why is this problem occurring now?
- How is the current issue related to other issues in this person's life and other themes in the person's past?
- How is this problem connected to other things going on within the client's family?
- What cultural influences maybe affecting the client's current struggle?
- What feelings and thoughts are going on of which the client may be currently unaware?
- What unconscious motives and forces might be operating?

- What hidden agendas might be in play?
- How can I help this person to understand his or her story in a way that is more personally meaningful and clinically useful?

You may recognize the theoretical roots to some of the questions that reflect the assumptions of a particular orientation. For instance, wondering about unconscious desires is part of psychoanalytic theory, or wanting to know about underlying thinking patterns may stem from cognitive therapy, or constructing the client's story in a more helpful way may be an extension of narrative therapy or constructivist therapy. Almost every other therapeutic approach has its own priorities concerning what material is considered most important to explore. Yet regardless of where you go, and what paths you take, there are still a few generic skills that will be most useful to you.

You should know that including some skills in this chapter on exploration and other skills in the next chapter on promoting insight was somewhat arbitrary. All of the skills used in the search process are also part of deepening a client's understanding. Delving into a client's background allows connections to be made, new ideas to be generated, and greater self-awareness initiated. Likewise, exploration is hardly restricted to the beginning stage of helping, but cycles through again and again as new material is introduced. So, although we are talking in this chapter about a half dozen skills that are usually associated with exploration activities, you should know that you will use them in all other stages of the process.

STRUCTURING THE CONVERSATIONS

Exploration is not something you do *to* a client, but rather *with* a client. It is a mutual process of searching for valuable and useful information and collecting important background information. When at its best, this process proceeds in a systematic, progressive, and logical fashion, but also at a pace and direction that is fluid and flexible. At its worst, it comes across as an interrogation in which the therapist fires one question after another at the client.

Compare these two examples of a structured exploration:

Therapist: Can you tell me when this problem first started?

Client: I'd say about a week ago.

Therapist: Would you say that was, what, about last Monday?

Client: Yeah. About then.

Therapist: And did the symptoms begin gradually, or all of a sudden?

Client: I'm not sure. Maybe gradually?

Therapist: This is the first time you've experienced anything like this?

Client: I think so.

Therapist: And how would you say this has been affecting your life? Would you say that you are having difficulties sleeping and eating?

Client: Uh-huh.

You can see that this therapist is going after some very critical information, but is doing so in a way in which he retains full control. The client is reduced to providing brief responses and is clearly not involved except as a reluctant participant. You may recognize this pattern as similar to a physician asking a series of rather specific yes–no questions: "Do you have pain here, or here? Would you say the pain is radiating or centralized? Does it hurt when I do this?" Such questions are appropriate when you are trying to find very specific answers to questions that help with differential diagnosis, but they are not especially useful in counseling settings when you are trying to foster a spirit of mutual responsibility for the outcome. In addition, problems that emerge in therapy are not so easily repaired.

You can pay attention to interviewers on television or in newspapers or magazines to see how common this type of conversation is. There is an erroneous assumption that if you want to keep the conversation going, if you want to find out as much information as possible, you ask lots of pointed questions. In a typical media interview, the reporter asks a series of rapid-fire, closed-ended questions that produce just about the same result you can expect if you try this with your own clients:

Q: Did you think you were going to die there?

A: No.

Q: Were you trying not to show that you were in pain?

A: Of course.

Q: Do you feel lucky?

A: I do.

Q: Has this all affected your view of women in the military?

A: Not really.

Q: Do you follow what's going on in Iraq now?

A: Not too much.

In this next example, a clinician goes after the same information as demonstrated above, but in a less interrogative, more open way.

Therapist:	Talk about what has been bothering you most and when it first began.
Client:	Um, I guess about a week ago, more or less. I was visiting my parents and I started to feel uneasy, like I couldn't catch my breath. I felt dizzy and, I don't know, kind of funny.
Therapist:	So this really took you by surprise and scared you.
Client:	Yeah, you could say that for sure. And I wasn't sure what to do. I didn't know what was happening to me.
Therapist:	It sounds like you felt particularly upset because this was a new experience for you.
Client:	Well, once before something like this happened, but it was in a different situation.
Therapist:	This wasn't completely unfamiliar to you but you still felt caught off-guard.

Notice in this second example that the therapist is not even asking questions to elicit information and encourage exploration. Instead the therapist is reflecting back both the content and feelings of what he or she hears. This preferred way of proceeding encourages a mutual process of exploration while showing empathy for the client's situation.

OPENING WITH A STORY

Typically, therapy and counseling begin with clients telling their stories. They talk about what is wrong and their theories about how these problems started. There is a history within the story. There are antagonists and supporting characters. There is a complex plot and there are many subplots. There is a beginning, a middle, but no end in sight.

During the exploration phases of therapy, your job is to help the client tell the story well. This includes richness of detail and texture. It means including as many details and as much context as possible. Most of all, it means helping the client to feel comfortable during this process.

It could be said that even if you do nothing else, helping people to tell their stories can be intrinsically therapeutic. It capitalizes on what Freud and other psychoanalysts described as catharsis—the emotional release of pent-up energy. It feels good to tell one's life story to someone safe. If you have ever been in therapy or counseling yourself, then you know how wonderful it is to have an attentive audience for hearing how you ended up in your current situation.

Inviting the storytelling is just about the easiest thing you can do. People have seen enough movies and television shows about therapy that they pretty much know what is expected. They will come in fully prepared to dump the sad tale on your lap; it takes little to get things going other than the opening prompt: "How can I help you?" or "What's on your mind?" or "What would you like to talk about?" or "Tell me your story."

More than ever before in daily life people rarely get the chance to share their stories without interruption. Everyone is distracted by their mobile devices. Most of the time people ask, "How are you doing?" they really don't care; they are just being polite. Even visiting a health professional for attention is often an exercise in frustration considering that the average amount of time that a patient has to tell the story of what is wrong is about 18 seconds before he or she is interrupted. Ninety percent of patients are never allowed to finish their story before they are sent off into the world with instructions that they don't really understand (Levine, 2004).

The truly difficult part, which includes advanced skills covered later, involves several structuring actions to keep clients on track, to prevent digressions and rambling, and to elicit depth and as much useful information as possible. You will do this with a few good questions, but mostly with reflective skills described later in the chapter.

ASKING QUESTIONS

Beginners ask far too many questions. Questions represent a direct but inelegant way to collect information, probe particular areas, or invite exploration. It is certainly direct to say to a client: "What were you thinking when that happened?" As you will learn, there are other options at your disposal that are more indirect and therefore more inclined to let the client lead things. After all, you don't want to get in the habit of being defined as the one who does all the digging with the client in the role of reluctant participant. In addition, the client does not feel heard when you are shooting off question after question. Reflecting helps the client feel heard and, consequently, continues to strengthen the collaborative relationship.

When to Ask Questions

There are specific times when asking questions is not only unavoidable but highly desirable. This would be in the following situations:

- *When the session first begins:* "Where would you like to start today?" or "How can I help you?" or "What would you like to talk about?"
- *When you need more clarification:* "I wonder if you could say some more about that?" or "What do you mean by that?"
- *When you need to get things back on track:* "Earlier you talked about this recurring problem with avoiding new situations. What is a recent example of that?"
- *When you want to check out how things are going:* "What are your reactions to what we've been doing today?"
- *When you want to bring focus to present-moment reactions:* "What is this like for you right now?"
- *When you must find out specific information:* "What help have you sought in the past for this problem?"
- *When you want to make connections:* "How is this related to what you were talking about earlier?"
- *When you want to bring attention to a significant point:* "What were you thinking and saying to yourself right before you backed down?"
- *When you want to clarify goals:* "Given the various things you've mentioned, what do you want to focus on most?"
- *When you want to move the person to take action:* "What are you prepared to do about this right now?"
- *When you need to assess for crisis situations:* "Have you had thoughts of harming yourself?"

These examples highlight the ways that questions are actually used in every phase of the therapeutic process. They not only gather information and foster exploration, but they can also be used as subtle forms of confrontation and goal setting.

Good and Bad Questions

There are effective and ineffective ways to ask questions, just as there are times when they are most and least appropriate. For instance, you wouldn't want to interrupt someone in the middle of an important story to ask about a particular detail.

A HOMEWORK ASSIGNMENT

Listen to your favorite talk show hosts on television, radio, or podcasts conduct interviews. Now that you are more familiar with what it takes to ask good questions, as well as what makes for lousy inquiries, notice how spectacularly unskilled and ineffective most talk show hosts really are. They ask a series of closed-ended questions ("So, did you find the experience making this film rewarding?"). They follow written scripts, often without even listening to the previous answers. The only reason they are able to elicit any entertaining interaction whatsoever is that their subjects are so highly motivated to promote their products. It doesn't even matter what the interviewers ask, or how they ask it, because the celebrity authors, actors, or athletes have already prepared their canned self-promoting answers.

Start paying close attention to good and bad interviews in the media. Notice what professionals do best, as well as their common mistakes.

While Jeffrey was working on this chapter, he was driving in the car with a friend. She was telling him about some recent problems she was having. This was how the conversation went:

Friend: So I've been carrying more than my fair share of work lately. That's why I am always in such a hurry.

Jeffrey: What has been going on with you?

Friend: Well, my husband has been out of work so the burden fell on me to carry the load.

Jeffrey: Oh, what kind of work does your husband do?

What is wrong with this? Why did Jeffrey kick himself afterward for making such a simple error in judgment, especially when he was in the process of writing about how questions can get in the way?

You will notice that the first question, a probe, was appropriate and useful: "What has been going on with you?" It is leading and somewhat general and ambiguous. These are often good characteristics of leading questions because they allow the person to interpret the question in various ways. Sometimes you will find that how the person interprets the question is as revealing as how it is answered. That's one reason why therapists respond in that maddening way when their clients ask them, "What do you mean?" and they respond, "What does it mean to you?" We are not playing mind games by being evasive but rather allowing the client to go wherever seems most important.

Back to the questions. The first leading question was appropriate: "What has been going on with you?" Jeffrey patted himself on the back for that one. It is concise, to the point, and very inviting because it's open and can be answered in greater detail. It creates space for the other person to elaborate, and yet does so in a way that allows a lot of latitude. Sometimes (like with friends) you don't want to be intrusive. So far, so good.

Then the friend shares a very emotionally laden statement about her stress and pressure supporting her family because her husband is out of work. Rather than following up on this disclosure, or even acknowledging that he heard her, he instead asks a question that is irrelevant and distracting. At the time, of course, it made perfect sense to follow this up because Jeffrey was curious (and he wasn't in the role of a therapist). But the price paid for this needless and mistimed question is that the conversation remained superficial (which is maybe where he unconsciously wanted it to stay).

Other options might have been:

- "You're feeling overwhelmed."
- "You're worried."
- "You hope this won't last long."
- "Carry the load . . . in what way?"

The lesson implicit in this story is to make sure that the questions you ask do not distract the client from the central story or ignore important feelings and thoughts that should be explored further. On the other hand, if a part of you wants to stay superficial with friends, the guy next to you on the plane, or with anyone except a client, ask lots of questions, especially closed questions. That will do the trick every time.

Ask "Why" Questions Carefully

Why, you ask, do we want to avoid "why" questions? Because most of the time people don't know why they do things. The most common answer you will get after asking someone why is: "I don't know."

Teacher: May I ask why you carved your initials on the desk?

Student: [Shrugs] I don't know.

What the student is really thinking is something along the lines of:

Because it was fun. Because it felt wicked and naughty. Because I could express my artistic talents. Because I wasn't really thinking one way or the other. Because I wanted to piss you off. Because I'm mad at this school and I can't fight back any other way. Because I don't value furniture the same way you do. Because I just felt like it.

Yet the most likely answer you'd hear is, "I don't know," which is always the easiest way to evade the query.

The truth is that most of the time people don't really know why they do things, or don't do things. If we asked you why you wait until the last minute to do your studying for class, what would you answer? If we asked you why you remain stuck doing certain things that don't work for you, what would you say? We are sure you would come up with some sort of intelligent answer or explanation, but that doesn't mean it is meaningful.

Another reason asking "why" can be less than desirable is that your client may misunderstand your question and take offense, as if you think he or she was doing the wrong thing. You could read and interpret most of the below "why" questions in two different ways—sarcasm or innocent curiosity:

- "Why won't you leave your husband?"
- "Why won't you change your job?"
- "Why don't you confront your mother about that?"
- "Why are you so stubborn?"
- "Why won't you change?"

Each of these can be heard in a way that sounds accusatory, as if the client should leave her husband, should change her job, should confront her mother, shouldn't be so stubborn, or should change. And that if she won't do these things, then something must be wrong with her. Each of these questions could easily be framed as reflective statements:

- "You seem reluctant to leave this relationship even though you're unhappy."
- "You sound afraid of changing jobs."
- "I sense a part of you would like to confront your mother, but another part of you feels held back."
- "You have a great deal of tenacity, which can be helpful at times and a hindrance at times."
- "You have been telling me that you want to change, but another part of you doesn't want to. Tell me about that part."

You may notice that these responses validate the client's experience, which builds the relationship, and yet still encourage the client to say more about what is holding things back. That isn't to say that there are not times when you can and should use "why" in your questions, just that it is ordinarily not very useful compared to the other options available. Some exceptions might include when you are provoking exploration but not really expecting a definitive answer: "I wonder why you keep involving yourself in situations you have trouble getting out of?"

Open Versus Closed Questions

A closed question is one that can be answered with a single word, usually yes or no, or very briefly, such as a time, a place, or a short phrase. Such questions tend to cut off communication and set up a pattern wherein the client becomes a passive respondent. Listen to the following conversation between a parent and her young child who just came home from school.

Parent: So, did you have a good day in school today?

Student: Sure.

Parent: Would you say you had a good day or a bad day?

Student: Pretty good.

Parent: Did you go on that field trip?

Student: Yup.

Parent: And did you get to sit next to Lisa like you wanted to?

Student: Uh huh.

Parent: Were you able to talk to her like you wanted to about coming to your birthday?

Student: Not really.

Parent: The time didn't seem right to you?

Student: Yeah.

Parent: Um, okay then. Can I make you a snack?

Student: Okay.

This parent will now complain that her child was uncommunicative and resistant. So much depends on how you probe, the questions you ask to open up the interaction. One way to probe is by using open-ended questions, the kind that cannot so easily be answered with one word.

Table 6.1   Open Versus Closed Questions

Original Question	Open-Ended Version
"So, did you have a good day in school today?"	"What was your day like today?"
"Would you say you had a good day or a bad day?"	"What was the best thing that happened in school today?"
"Did you go on that field trip?"	"What was the most interesting thing that happened on your field trip?"
"And did you get to sit next to Lisa like you wanted to?"	"What things did you do and talk about on the bus?"
"Were you able to talk to her like you wanted to about coming to your birthday?"	"How did Lisa respond to your birthday plans?"
"The time didn't seem right to you?"	"I remember you said you wanted to talk to Lisa. So, what happened?"
"Can I make you a snack?"	"What would you like to do right now?"

Compare the closed questions that were asked with how they could have been framed, as shown in Table 6.1.

With a particularly uncommunicative child, even these new questions might not elicit much more information or facilitate deeper exploration, but they certainly increase the probability of a more balanced conversation. Closed-ended questions create an atmosphere in which the therapist is the expert, the authority, the problem solver, the one controlling the proceedings. They also elicit very limited information. Closed questions also stop the flow of conversation. When you get into the habit of conversing like this, you may find that you run out of questions and the client has nothing to say in response. The client is simply waiting for your next question. Because closed questions can disrupt the flow of conversation, you want to limit these questions as much as possible, especially in the early sessions.

This may sound very basic to you and easy to learn, but we can tell you from years of experience watching counselors, teachers, and therapists in action that most professionals have the very bad habit of asking closed questions. Check this out for yourself.

It is difficult to catch yourself asking closed questions, and to remind yourself to rephrase them, unless you monitor yourself very closely. Do you understand what we mean? (Closed question.)

See what just happened? (Closed question.) Oops, we did it again. We asked both questions in ways you could answer with "yes" or "no." It would have been far better to ask, "What about this confuses you the most?" or "What just happened?"

As with any rule, this one has exceptions. As we already mentioned, there are indeed times when closed questions are useful, especially when you need rather specific information. Let's say that someone says that he has trouble sleeping. You ask what he means by this, because the kind of sleep disruption could signal a variety of problems that may be treated in different ways. Early-morning wakening is different from trouble falling asleep, which is different from frequent awakenings in the middle of the night. It might be entirely appropriate to ask: "Would you say you have more trouble falling asleep or staying asleep?"

The use of closed questions might also occur when there are indications of suicidal ideation or intent. In such situations it is crucial that you assess very specifically such things as: "Do you have a plan for carrying out this fantasy?" "Have you tried to kill yourself in the past?" "Has anyone else in your family ever tried to kill themselves or succeeded in doing so?" You will notice that these questions elicit yes–no responses, but for this purpose that is entirely appropriate. However, it's helpful to follow up on the responses with some type of reflection so that the client doesn't feel interrogated. A suicide assessment might look something like this:

Therapist: You sound like you feel hopeless, like your life will never improve.

Client: Yeah, I'm so sad all the time. I've been stuck here for years. It keeps getting worse and I don't know how to escape.

Therapist: Have you had thoughts of harming yourself in any way?

Client: I sometimes wish I would just not wake up in the morning. Well, I guess I have thought about taking a bottle of pills to just go to sleep.

Therapist: You're tired of hurting. A part of you feels like giving up. I want to make sure you're safe, so please tell me if you've thought about what kind of pills to take and if you have them.

Client: Sleeping pills, and yes, I have them.

Therapist: So, this is a very real possibility for you. How do you imagine the situation might go?

Client: Not really. I only fantasize about it when I'm really feeling down, but I'm scared to do it.

Therapist: You're scared.

Client: I am. With my luck, I'd end up doing some sort of permanent damage, but living through it in some way.

The conversation could continue with the therapist alternating between validating the client's experience and obtaining the necessary information. You can see that the therapist still needs to ask a closed question ("Have you thought of harming yourself?"), but does so in a way that does not damage the relationship. The moral of this story is that you want to avoid closed questions as much as possible, but when you have to use them, use them wisely.

How Does That Make You Feel?

When you watch movies with therapists, this is the one question that seems to be asked most often. In fact, if you ask this question when talking with friends or family members, they will accuse you of doing that "psychobabble stuff" with them. Clients also might be expecting you to ask a question like this. Before we proceed farther, we'd like to ask you a question about this (even though it's a why question): Why would you never ask someone: "How does that *make* you feel?" Note: the italics are a hint.

There are several possible reasons that might occur to you. First of all, it is certainly a cliché. A second problem with this question has to do with the word *make.* One of the most important tools you have as a therapist is the understanding of how language influences the way we think. As touted by the cognitive therapies (Beck, Freeman, & Davis, 2014; Ellis & Ellis, 2011), implying that someone or something outside yourself can "make" you feel anything is distorted, illogical, and irrational. Except for instances of extreme physical threat, people may have more power to *make themselves* feel whatever they choose than they know, based on how they interpret situations.

How many times have you heard (or said yourself):

* "He makes me so mad."
* "She makes me feel stupid."
* "You make me do things I would never do."

Yet how often has someone actually "made" you feel anything? This may seem like we are nit-picking words, but the language used, whether internally or out loud, is what leads us to feel powerless. If you believe that someone or something outside yourself controls your emotions, you are going to feel pretty helpless when you are upset because those feelings would not be under your control. If, on the other hand, you choose your own emotional states, then you can make different choices about how you might react if you are sufficiently prepared to do so.

With clients, then, you want to be especially careful with the language you use. There is thus a big difference between saying, "He makes you so angry" and "You feel angry when he does that." In the second example, you are acknowledging the client's feelings, but are doing so in a way that doesn't imply that they are caused externally by the other person's behavior. An even more forceful example of this point could be made with a third alternative: "You are really *upsetting yourself* over what he did."

A final reason not to ask clients how something makes them feel is that the question could demonstrate your lack of empathy. In a sense, you are admitting to the client: "I don't have a clue what you are experiencing right now so I have to ask you directly to fill me in."

FOR REFLECTION

Note in this example of a dialogue that the therapist does exactly what we are saying not to do.

Client: I just don't know what to do. Every time I try to assert my needs with my father, he just won't listen. He always has to start a fight. I get so angry with him.

Therapist: How does that make you feel?

What are some alternative responses you could have made to this client? Possible answers appear at the end of the chapter.

As you will learn with reflective skills, it is far better to guess what you imagine the client is feeling than to ask directly. That is the beauty of these skills: Even when you are not on target, you still encourage the client to go deeper.

Client: I just don't know what to do. Every time I try to assert my needs with my father, he just won't listen. He always has to start a fight. I get so angry with him.

Therapist: You say you're angry with your father but I sense that you are really disappointed in him.

Client: No, it's not that at all, really. I know that he has tried to do everything he can. It's not that I'm disappointed in him as much as I am frustrated with myself.

Impressive the way that works, isn't it? And it does work in the sense that you almost always encourage clients to explore their thoughts and feelings on a deeper level, even if it is to clarify a reflection you offered that was not on target.

REFLECTING SKILLS

Therapists often act as mirrors for what their clients are saying or doing. Our job is to listen carefully, take in what we hear, and then reflect back our understanding in a way that fosters a deeper awareness and understanding. This might look easy, but is one of the most difficult helping skills to master.

Reflecting skills have two primary applications; one focuses on the content of the message and the other on the underlying feeling. Both are important.

The following verbalization has both content and affect, or to say that differently, there is a surface message and an underlying or deeper one.

Client: I am not really sure how this fits together with what I already know. It seems confusing to me. I think you are trying to cover too much material and too many things in one semester. How am I supposed to learn all of this? Besides, I've got a lot of other things going on in my life right now. You act as if I've got nothing else to do but focus on this one thing. I just don't think your expectations are very fair. And I don't like it.

Whether you are sympathetic or not to this student's point of view, certainly you can understand the source of these thoughts and feelings. In this brief but rich communication, there is a lot of information. Some of it involves the content of the message and the rest contains the essence of the person's feelings. Although in actual situations it would neither matter nor be useful to focus only on one dimension or the other, for the purposes of learning the skills involved, it is helpful to label and respond to the different parts. This is especially the case with reflecting feelings because this is so much more difficult than reflecting content.

In the preceding example, what are some of the major areas of content that were expressed? In other words, on the surface, what was the person communicating?

1. I don't know how this fits.

2. I'm having trouble integrating the material into my life.

3. I'm very busy and overscheduled.

4. Your expectations of me are unreasonable.

If you chose to focus on the content, these might be some of the parts of the message to home in on and reflect back to the person, and the conversation might sound something like this:

Student: I am not really sure how this fits together with what I already know. It seems confusing to me.

Teacher: So, you've having trouble getting a handle on what we've covered so far.

Student: Yeah, I think you are trying to cover too much material and too many things in one semester. How am I supposed to learn all of this?

Teacher: You don't find that the expectations are realistic. You're having serious doubts about whether you can manage all the work with other things you have going on.

This brief dialogue gives you a sense of the natural rhythm that takes place during a reflective conversation. The teacher is listening carefully and then responding with what is understood so far. This lets the student know that she has been heard and, it is hoped, encourages a deeper level of exploration into what might be going on.

There are also a lot of emotions and underlying feelings expressed in the communication. If you chose to identify and reflect back this affect-laden material, what might you select?

1. I'm confused and frustrated because I don't feel in control.

2. I'm feeling very anxious and overwhelmed in my life right now.

3. I'm angry because you are expecting more than I can deliver.

4. I'm feeling helpless because I don't know how to sort things out or center on priorities.

5. I'm feeling better already telling you how I feel.

6. I'm unhappy with the way this is going so far.

If during the same conversation the teacher instead chose to go deeper than the content and reflect the person's feelings, this is what it would look and sound like:

Student: I am not really sure how this fits together with what I already know. It seems confusing to me.

Teacher: You sound really frustrated because you can't seem to catch up with what you think I expect, and what you expect of yourself.

Student: Yeah, I think you are trying to cover too much material and too many things in one semester. How am I supposed to learn all of this?

Teacher: You're upset with me because I don't seem to appreciate many of the other things going on in your life. You also sound pretty anxious because you aren't sure how to catch up.

In this second scenario, the teacher responds by reflecting the predominant feelings expressed. The goal in this case is to lead the student to examine, in greater depth, what he is feeling and what this might mean in the larger context of his life. Perhaps the problem actually has little to do with school at all, but rather is an overture to get into other areas. Or maybe the student's frustration has been building for some time and is really related to something that happened weeks ago. Or suppose the student is just using this problem as a way to get to know the teacher better. Any and all of these possibilities would reveal themselves as the conversation proceeds.

Reflecting Content

We are going to teach you how to reflect content in a way that will strike you as both artificial and awkward. The rationale behind this method is to introduce you to some very basic behaviors and then slowly build on them, not unlike what we did in earlier chapters on attending and listening skills.

The very first step is called "parroting" because you will sound very much like a parrot that mimics what it hears. You would not actually ever do this in real life (except if you go brain dead), so rest assured that any discomfort you might feel in learning this "skill" will be short-lived. It is intended only as an intermediate step toward a more complex, advanced set of behaviors.

With parroting, all you do is repeat back exactly what the other person says. Believe it or not, many people can't do this, especially partners in the midst of a conflict. They don't listen to one another because they are so busy preparing to dispute whatever the other says. An exercise therapists often use with couples is to require each partner to repeat back exactly what the other person said, to that person's satisfaction, before being allowed to respond with his or her own thoughts and feelings. This might sound rather silly to you—except that many people can't do it!

In learning to parrot, all you have to do is follow these steps:

1. Attend fully to the other person, putting into practice what you have learned so far (remember your body posture, eye contact, facial expression, and cleansing breath).

2. Listen carefully to what the person is saying. Concentrate with all your energy and focus. Gently push aside any distractions that interfere with your attention.

3. Repeat the content of what was said (which we hope is the same as what you heard).

Here is an (annoying) example of what this is like:

Talker: I've been having a bit of trouble with my car lately. That's why I'm late.

Helper: You've been having trouble with your car and that's been causing you to be late.

Talker: Yeah, I think there's something wrong with the fuel injection system. I need to take it into the shop.

Helper: You think the problem is with the fuel injector and you intend to get it fixed.

Talker: That's what I just said! Are you deaf or just stupid! (gets up and walks out of the room, shaking his head)

Just kidding.

Remember, you wouldn't actually repeat exactly everything your client says; this is just practicing the rhythm and pace of a reflective frame of mind.

Exercise in Parroting

As with all helping interventions, you always start with that cleansing breath (or whatever you do to focus your concentration).

With a partner, take turns practicing parroting one another. One of you agrees to talk for a minute or so (that's about how long you can last without laughing) about something. The other will listen and repeat back exactly what was said, word for word.

Reverse roles so that each of you can practice parroting and being parroted.

As we've said, you would rarely use parroting in a real session, except when you can think of nothing else, but it is a necessary first step in your reflective skill development. You might be surprised to learn, however, that if on occasion you did repeat just what the other person said, it would hardly be noticed. Most of the time people are concentrating so hard on what they are saying that they rarely listen to what anyone else is saying. We offer this as a reminder to those of you who are unduly hard on yourselves for the frequent mistakes you will make. However, there is one time where parroting can be most effective: When you want to emphasize an interesting word or phrase that the client says rather flippantly, repeating the exact word or phrase can slow the client down enough to elaborate on feelings:

Client: I can't believe I locked my keys in the car again! I'm so stupid for doing such an idiotic thing. What's wrong with me?

Therapist: Stupid.

If the therapist repeats such a strong word, the client will often not be able to ignore it but will slow down and think about what you just said. At the worst, he'll look at you funny and continue ranting and raving. However, you will probably have the opportunity to repeat the word again, and after enough repetitions, the client will not be able to avoid your reflection any longer. In the best scenario, he'll elaborate on feeling stupid, which may be an underlying theme of most sessions.

Okay, you are now ready to move on to the next step. Thank goodness, huh?

The next skill, which you will use a lot, perhaps more than anything else in your work, is called rephrasing or reflecting content. This is where you do essentially what you just tried with parroting, but this time you use different words to convey what you've heard and understood. You are taking in what was said, making sense of the essential messages, and then reflecting back what you understand. This accomplishes several tasks simultaneously:

1. It lets the client know that you are listening carefully.

2. It checks the accuracy of what you heard.

3. It helps the client to hear better what he or she is saying, especially the core themes.

4. It helps you to remain actively involved in the conversation.

5. It takes the discussion to a progressively deeper level, at least with respect to the content.

6. It encourages the client to keep going in a particular direction.

In the following interaction, the therapist uses rephrasing almost exclusively to keep things going and track what is going on. Notice that the tone remains on a content level throughout.

Client: I can't seem to concentrate on my studies. I just get distracted so easily.

Therapist: You are losing focus, unable to stick with your work even though you think it is important to do so.

Client: Well, it is important. I agree. But I can't seem to find the time to get the work done. (laughs) Maybe it isn't that important.

Therapist: You are beginning to question your priorities. You have believed that school was more important than anything else, but now you are reevaluating that value in light of other things in your life that are also important to you.

Client: Yeah, like my friends for instance. I hardly ever have time just to hang out, you know, relax, have a beer, listen to music. My friends kid me about that but I know they feel hurt, too, that I'm ignoring them.

Therapist: You are noticing in many ways that you have been neglecting the people who matter most to you. Even though they say they don't mind, you can tell that it is becoming a bigger problem. And you're wondering what to do about that in light of other commitments you've made.

It is (we hope) evident that this deceptively easy skill of rephrasing helps the client to explore further what is going on. At first, it seems like a relatively simple matter of poor study habits. But as the two people get farther into things, they discover (through the reflections of content) that there are deeper issues involved. This is the beauty of this method. It also has several other advantages you should be aware of:

1. Although potentially quite powerful, it is also relatively benign. Even if you don't help anyone much with reflections of content, you also won't hurt anyone. This should be reassuring to beginners who are afraid they will do or say the wrong thing and somehow provoke a psychotic episode or deep depression.

2. It keeps the conversation progressing at a gradual rate, building steadily on what was just said.

3. It is easy to learn in theory. Crisis intervention phone counselors or student peer counselors can learn to use this skill in just a few hours.

4. A skilled and experienced helper can lead someone to very deep levels of awareness and understanding. You do this by holding up a mirror and allowing the person to see and hear him- or herself.

5. It is culturally sensitive and easily adaptable to different client preferences and styles.

Exercise in Rephrasing

As in the previous exercise, meet with a partner—the same one or not. Take turns with one of you being the speaker and the other the listener/reflector. Each of you will spend about 5 minutes talking about something and the other will listen carefully and then rephrase what was said using different language.

Exercise on Your Own: Take This Skill Home With You

There is nothing that can change your life faster and create more intimacy in all your relationships than the skills of reflection. The fact of the matter is that in most conversations with people you are not listening to them and they aren't listening to you. Reflecting skills provide a structure for constant, hovering attention. You not only listen carefully, but prove you understand what was said. You can't imagine the difference this makes to people.

Try using rephrasing with the people who matter the most to you. Don't restrict these skills to your work. That is the truly amazing thing about this job: Everything you learn not only makes you a better practitioner but also a better person.

Several times during the day—with family, friends, coworkers, fellow students, neighbors, even strangers—make an effort to use rephrasing to let the person know that you are listening and to communicate what you heard. Note the effects.

We warn you that some people will tell you—in jest or seriously—"Stop using that counseling psychobabble with me," but most people are secretly delighted to have the attention. Just keep in mind that this is such hard work that we ordinarily don't like to do this for very long unless we are being paid to do so. We feel exhausted by always listening intently while avoiding giving advice or asking questions out of curiosity. Sad but true.

One other warning is that you need to do this when you have time to listen. If you don't, you'll find it's difficult to stop people because they want to be heard so badly. We've been amazed at how strangers will tell you the most intimate details of their lives in a nontherapeutic setting when all you do is reflect.

Reflecting Feelings

We are now going to go deeper, *way* deeper. We warn you that, at first, reflecting feelings will not seem any more challenging than reflecting content (which you have to admit doesn't seem that hard). Indeed, it *is* pretty easy to learn the basics of this skill, a matter of following a simple formula. Yet even after decades of practice, you will still not be able to do it as well as you would like.

The procedure is not unlike what you have already learned:

1. Listen to what was said.

2. Ask yourself what the underlying message is.

3. Reflect that back.

This time, however, rather than focusing on content you are decoding the underlying feelings expressed. Because emotional reactions are so complex, their nuances so diffuse, it is extremely difficult to identify what people are feeling. Then, once you can find a label for the feeling, you must ask yourself what it might mean. Then, just as challenging, you have to figure out a way to reflect this understanding back so that the client will hear you.

Consider that there are five basic feelings or emotions that include being mad, glad, sad, fearful, and guilty. Feelings can also include sensations like "feeling down" or "feeling pressured." Experiencing and expressing feelings often makes life rich, and each feeling has a purpose. Anger is a feeling that often covers other emotions such as hurt or vulnerability. Anger sometimes mobilizes energy to stand up for yourself or make needed changes. Happiness is a natural reaction that helps us feel balanced and take positive action, although recent research indicates that sometimes the compulsive pursuit of happiness makes people pretty unhappy, which is why the term *well-being* is used instead. Sadness is a normal reaction to loss or pain and often facilitates a healing process if it does not become chronic. Fear, if appropriate, provides protective functions. Guilt in moderate doses can also have useful functions in helping us behave in moral ways. Thus, feelings are neither intrinsically good nor bad until such time that they become so severe and overwhelming that they compromise normal functioning. Certainly, how feelings are expressed is important to maintain relationships with others, and timing is critical as well. You wouldn't want to go to a job interview feeling sad—or at least visibly revealing what is going on.

Like the reflecting of content, the skill of reflecting feelings has several powerful effects:

1. Letting the client know that you understand his or her experience at the deepest possible levels.

   Client: My mother criticizes me so much. I don't feel like I can do anything right with her. I can't please her. I wish I could do something right.

   Therapist: You feel worthless.

2. Bringing attention to previously unacknowledged internal reactions.

   Client: (in a soft voice) I knew the relationship would have to end eventually. He was no good for me. I wasn't myself. In some ways I feel relieved.

   Therapist: A part of you feels relieved, and another part of you feels sad and misses him deeply.

3. Fostering exploration of underlying feelings that may be hidden from view.

   Client: . . . so that's about it. I have a really amazing relationship with my mom, and it's just my brothers that get on my nerves. With her declining health, I need to find a way to deal with them better since we'll be spending more time together.

   Therapist: I notice you talk so positively about your mom, as if she's an angel. I notice that you seem jealous that your brothers got privileges that you didn't, and you blame them for that, rather than your mom. You seem afraid to betray your mother by giving some of the responsibility to her.

4. Slowing the client down so he or she can fully experience the feelings being evidenced or reported.

   Client: (speaking in a rapid and loud tone) . . . and I just don't know what to do with him. My son gets into trouble all the time. He doesn't listen to me. I have no authority over him. My husband says that I'm too overprotective, but I know what kind of trouble he can get into. I just want to protect him from getting into serious trouble but . . .

Therapist: I'd like to interrupt you for a moment. (pauses; speaks slowly and softly) You're scared. You're afraid you won't be able to protect your son.

5. Demonstrating that feelings are appropriate to express, at least in therapy.

Client: I'm sorry. I don't mean to cry. I'll try to stop.

Therapist: You're worried that I will be judgmental about your crying. You're so sad, of course you're crying. In here, it's safe to cry.

6. Deepening the relationship with the client.

Client: No one has ever understood my pain the way you have. I feel less alone now.

Therapist: You've missed the support you've needed, and you're relieved to feel understood.

Building on what you have already learned, your task is now to listen on multiple levels to communication. You are not only attending to the nonverbal messages and the surface, content messages, but also to the feelings beneath the surface. Once you grab hold of some affective material you then reflect back what you sense, feel, observe, and hear.

1. *Step 1.* Listen and look for feeling. In order to go beyond content, you must sensitize yourself to what people are feeling inside. You look for cues in their behavior, their voice tone, manner, nonverbal mannerisms, and certainly the ways they communicate.

2. *Step 2.* Select the label that best fits the feeling. There are limitations to language in trying to describe inner states. Depending on the vocabulary available, you might say that someone is merely annoyed, or perhaps there's a more intense manifestation of anger: The person is enraged or furious. In order for this to work, you are going to have to expand your vocabulary of feeling words (see Table 6.2).

Table 6.2   Sad, Mad, Glad Vocabulary Exercise

For each of the three emotion states below, brainstorm (alone or with others) as many other feelings as you can that fit into the category.		
Sad	Mad	Glad

3. *Step 3.* Find the meaning in the feeling. Once you have identified what you believe is the dominant feeling being expressed, decide what the particular meaning of it is in the context of this person's experience.

4. *Step 4.* Decode the source of the feeling. You may have settled on anger as the most likely emotional force currently being expressed in the client's words and behavior. But what is the source of this anger? Sometimes it isn't enough to simply reflect that the client is angry; it is far more helpful to highlight the origins of the feeling. Instead of merely saying, "You're really angry," you might say, "You're really angry because your friend won't respect your privacy."

5. *Step 5.* Reflect the feeling that you hear or sense, supplying the source of the reaction.

It is a good idea to practice reflecting feelings by progressing in small steps. Let's start with the next logical step after using rephrasing. Use the stem sentence, "You feel . . ." to respond to the following client statements:

1. "I am just so tired of all this crap. I wish I could just give up." "You feel _____."

2. "Did you see the grade I got on this assignment! I mean, wow, I really aced it!" "You feel _____."

3. "If he gets on my case one more time, just one more time, I'm going to make sure it's the last time he ever treats someone that way." "You feel _____."

There are several choices possible for these client statements. Here are a few possibilities:

1. Frustrated, helpless, discouraged.

2. Excited, proud, surprised.

3. Angry, resentful, homicidal.

We're just kidding (again) with that homicidal option in number 3 (we just want to make sure you are paying attention). You can see, however, that there is not a single correct answer so much as there is a general area to explore. In other words, you don't have to hit the bull's-eye, just the target. This should take some of the pressure off doing this stuff perfectly. That is an amazing thing about these reflective skills; it is certainly better to be on-target every time, but in this work you get credit for trying, even if you miss what you are trying to hit. When you miss, the client will introspect to correct you and give you the right feeling. In addition, if you were right every time, the client might expect others to be right all the time. It is important for clients to be able to tolerate the occasional empathic failure, or error in reflecting feelings, to be able to have healthier relationships.

In the following example, notice that even though the therapist's skills are not particularly accurate, the client is still able to keep exploring at a deeper level.

Client: If he gets on my case one more time, just one more time, I'm going to make sure he never treats someone that way again.

Therapist: You are so upset you want to punch him.

Client: Well, not that angry. It's just that he has so little respect for me, or anyone else.

Therapist: You wish he would treat you with more respect. It pisses you off that he treats others differently.

Client: I'm not really that special, to tell you the truth. He treats everyone else the same way.

Therapist: So, you feel better about that at least.

Client: I don't feel good about any of this. I just wish I could get him to stop acting the way he does.

Therapist: You are feeling helpless because you don't know what to do next.

Client: I do know what to do, I'm just afraid to do it.

Every single one of this therapist's interventions was off target. In each case, the client corrected the reflection by stating how she really felt. That is what is so amazing about this skill: Even when you are wrong, you still help the client to explore more deeply. Of course, if you are wrong every time, or most of the time, the client is going to wonder if you are in fact understanding what is going on. If you keep missing the client's feeling, you also have to wonder about calibrating your empathic attunement.

Here is what reflections of feeling look and sound like when things are going well:

Student: I'm still having trouble figuring out how all this fits together.

Teacher: You're feeling impatient because this isn't coming together as quickly and as easily as you had hoped.

Student: When you use these skills, they look so easy and effortless, but when I try them I feel like an idiot. I'm waiting for the person to slap me for being so clumsy and transparent.

Teacher: You are comparing yourself to me and then feeling inadequate. Part of you wants to give up, but another part is feeling more determined than ever.

Student: Well, what do you think it takes for me to get this stuff?

Teacher: You are asking me for the answers, but you sense that only you can work this out for yourself. Although this is hard for you, and perhaps you are not used to this sort of challenge, you recognize that you are going to have to be more patient.

In this 1-minute conversation, the teacher tries to reflect back what she senses and hears in the student who is obviously frustrated. Notice how she deftly avoids the "trap" at the end when the student asks for advice. Nine out of 10 inexperienced helpers would answer that question with some advice or platitude like, "You need to be more patient and realistic about what you can do." Instead, the teacher continues to reflect back what she understands.

Try It Yourself

With these next client statements, reflect the feelings that you hear coming through by (a) selecting the feeling word that you think best fits the emotion, and (b) supplying the paraphrased content. Follow the pattern of the first example.

Client: I haven't been able to sleep well at night. I just keep thinking about stuff.

Helper: You've been feeling anxious because you're worried about some things.

Client: No matter what I do, I just keep tossing and turning.

1. *Helper:*   You feel _____ because _____.

   Client: I think I know what's bothering me, but I don't know if I want to talk about it quite yet.

2. *Helper:*   You feel _____ because _____.

   Client: This is kind of difficult for me. Even kind of embarrassing. It's just not something that I've ever talked about before. Do you know what I mean?

3. *Helper:*   You feel _____ because _____.

   Client: I've tried to talk to a few friends about this but they act like they'd rather not get into it.

4. *Helper:*   You feel _____ because _____.

In the Helper Response 1, you could have said something like: "You feel frustrated (or uneasy or helpless) because you feel out of control (or because you can't calm down)."

In Helper Response 2, you might have said: "You feel confused (uncertain, uneasy, reluctant) because you're not quite ready to get into this yet (or if you wanted to go a bit deeper: because you're afraid of what I might think or how I might judge you)."

In Helper Response 3: "You are feeling hesitant (frightened, anxious) because this is all new for you (or because you don't know where this will lead)."

In Helper Response 4: "You feel alone (sad, disappointed, frustrated) right now because you haven't been able to confide in anyone (or because people haven't responded the way you hoped)."

The best outcome of going through this exercise is that you realize the variety of choices you have when reflecting feelings. There are always at least a half dozen feelings that might be evident in verbalizations, as well as an equal number of content messages that you might rephrase. What this means is that you must give yourself the latitude while you are learning these skills to just say something, reflect something, and then move on. Clients will barely notice what you perceive as mistakes. Just keep the conversation going by showing how closely you are listening and how hard you are trying to understand.

Emotional Flooding

Many people who come to therapy are disconnected from their feelings and are uncomfortable with overtly expressing inner states. Others who seek help may be overwhelmed with emotions or may have surprisingly strong and unexpected reactions that frighten them. At times, this emotional catharsis can be helpful and good for the client, but not in every circumstance. For instance, some clients

Exercise in Feeling Reflections

Find a partner. One of you agrees to talk about something that has some strong feelings involved. If you can't think of something, then role-play a client who is upset about something.

During the conversation, the helper is going to concentrate only on reflecting feelings. That is the only intervention besides active listening skills (head nods, uh-huhs, attending). Use the stem sentence, "You feel _____." Several times during the conversation, say "You feel" and then insert a feeling word. If you can't think of a good one, then insert anything you can think of—it doesn't matter nearly as much as you might think. Your job is to keep the conversation going by reflecting back the feelings you perceive.

Exercise in Feeling Reflections: Round 2

Once you have gotten a little comfortable using "You feel," the next step is to add a "because" at the end that summarizes the content expressed: "You feel _____ because _____."

Take turns reflecting one another's feelings by following the steps outlined earlier: (a) listen, (b) identify the feeling underlying the message, (c) decode the meaning of the feeling and its origins, and (d) reflect back what you understand.

might be unable to pull themselves out of their pain and feel afraid to fall into a deep depression from which they can't escape. There may also be times that the session is coming to an end, and you want to make sure the client is clearheaded enough to drive home. When this happens, we attempt to prevent or moderate emotional flooding to the point that clients can more easily make the transition out the door and back into their daily lives. In the following dialogue, the therapist helps the client slowly pull back from emotional intensity by moving things back into content.

Client: (after crying intensely for thirty minutes and receiving lots of empathy) I can't believe he would leave me and the children without a goodbye.

Therapist: You have a lot to process, your feelings and how you are going to handle your finances.

Client: (still crying) He handled all the bills. I don't even know what bills to pay.

Therapist: How have you managed to handle a few of the bills so far in a way that makes you feel proud?

Client: (tears slowing down) Well, let's see. . . . (tears drying up; sighs), I mostly have received phone calls and information in the mail.

The client is redirected to think about practical matters in these last few minutes that can be useful to reduce her feelings of helplessness while also preparing her emotionally to leave the session for the day. Also note the way the therapist helps her focus on a small increment of progress so the session ends on a more positive, helpful note.

Reflecting Process

A variation on the theme of reflecting feelings is reflecting the process within the client's experience or the therapeutic relationship. Reflecting the client's process can be done in a variety of ways. One is to demonstrate any incongruence you observe: "I notice you're talking about how you've been seriously betrayed, and yet you don't seem angry about it." Another example is nervous laughter: "You're talking about something really sad, and you're laughing about it." This behavior is usually an indication that the client feels deeply about the topic, yet seeks to avoid those threatening or difficult feelings.

Another type of process reflection relates to the way someone delivers information or tells stories. Here are some examples:

- "I notice that each time you talk about your older sister, your voice gets really quiet, like you are whispering."
- "When you talk about your partner, you seem extremely animated."
- "You seem to use a lot of detail when you tell me stories."
- "Each time I reflect a feeling, you change the topic."
- "You seem to be expressing your feelings more readily now than when we first met."

When you reflect process, especially without interpretation or judgment, clients can become more aware of how others perceive them. After all, how clients behave with you is probably reflective of how they are with others. In addition, nonverbal behaviors can demonstrate underlying processes that clients experience. By enhancing awareness of this, clients can explore beliefs, feelings, or experiences about which they have been unaware. Finally, because you have noticed these nuances, you are able to communicate a deeper level understanding of what you have heard and seen.

One word of caution, though: Once you reveal observations about nonverbal behavior, clients who are not yet ready to expose themselves fully may become self-conscious and attempt to conceal and/or control those behaviors in the future. So, these types of reflections are best used after you've developed strong rapport, and only when you think the client is ready to be that exposed.

PUTTING REFLECTING SKILLS TOGETHER

In actual counseling situations, you will combine reflecting content and feelings in a natural way. Because the latter is so much harder to do, you may find yourself using two or three times as many reflections of content as you do reflections of feeling. With practice, you will do this effortlessly and naturally. Within a matter of weeks you will be able to use these skills reasonably well, although it will take years, if not a lifetime, to truly feel like a master.

Reviewing what we have covered so far: In previous chapters you learned how to listen effectively and how to attend to people when they are speaking. In this chapter you have been introduced to three very important exploration skills: (a) asking questions as prompts and probes, (b) reflecting or paraphrasing the content of communications, and (c) reflecting feelings. You might be surprised to learn that with just these three behaviors you can demonstrate a significant part of what therapists do in their work. Depending on the client, the stage in the process, and the particular issue, you might very well use these three skills for more than three quarters of your interventions and responses.

In the session that follows, the therapist uses the three skills to facilitate exploration:

Therapist: What would you like to work on today? [Open-ended question]

Client: Last time you said we could get more into things with my parents. You know, how maybe the decisions I've made really aren't my decisions but just my attempt to please them.

Therapist: Uh huh. [Attending and active listening]

Client: Do you know what I mean?

Therapist: You are talking about the approval seeking that you have done your whole life, not just with your parents, but with others. [Paraphrasing]

Client:	Well, I've just been thinking that maybe this has been a big problem for me. I mean, I'm almost thirty years old and I'm still acting as if I live at home.
Therapist:	You are feeling very uncomfortable realizing the extent you still feel dependent on your parents. [Reflection of feeling]
Client:	That's for sure. So, where do we go next with this?
Therapist:	You're hoping I will tell you what to do just like your parents. Part of you enjoys deferring to others. I wonder if you avoid making your own decisions so you don't have to be responsible for negative outcomes. [Rephrasing; reflection of feeling; interpretation]
Client:	It's just that I don't want to upset them. And they're just trying to be helpful. I mean, they're not trying to intrude or anything . . .
Therapist:	What is the latest incident with your parents that bothers you most right now? [Redirective open-ended question]
Client:	You just wouldn't believe it.
Therapist:	I can see that you are feeling really embarrassed to even talk about the situation because you realize that it only confirms the extent to which you have been dependent on them. [Reflection of feeling]
Client:	You won't believe this one. I was about to go to bed last night when the phone rang. Of course it was my mother. She calls me every night about this time.
Therapist:	You are saying that like it really irritates you. [Reflection of feeling]
Client:	Well, it does!

In just a few minutes, the client is already well on his way to exploring an important issue in his life. The therapist opened the session with a question and then used this skill only one more time to redirect the focus, when she asked him to supply a specific example of the latest intrusion. She noticed that the client was about to defend his parents, explain their behavior, and go off on a tangent, so she asked the question to help them deal with something more specific. The rest of the time, she used reflective skills exclusively, except for the one deeper-level intervention when she inserted a bit of interpretation: that the client was doing the same thing with the therapist that he does with his parents—trying to avoid responsibility. This advanced-level skill will be covered in a later chapter.

We want you to see how natural and powerful these few simple skills can be in the hands of an experienced practitioner. Within a very short period of time, you can get into some very important issues and collect all the information you might need to plan an intervention strategy. In the example above, the therapist was able to find out quite a lot about the client's situation without having to ask directly. At this early stage, she concentrated primarily on mirroring what she was hearing and understanding. By doing this, she demonstrating her understanding of the client's experience, deepened the process, obtained further information, and, most important, improved the relationship with the client.

EXPLORING THE PAST

Psychodynamic practitioners are not the only ones who honor the past as a major force that shapes present behavior and current problems. Almost anyone would agree that what we have already experienced and lived through has some influence on what we think, feel, and act today. This means that no matter what problem or issue a client brings up, you may wonder: How is this related to what he or she has experienced before?

CHECKING EXERCISE

There is one important point that we wish to make. It is absolutely critical (read: not optional) that you continuously check with clients to see how things are going and to assess how they are responding to your skills or interventions. You can do this in several ways. First, you can ask the client, but this is sometimes awkward. Second, you can watch and listen to see how the client responds to your interventions. Third, you can review the videotape or audiotape of the session afterward (often with a supervisor or peer).

Conduct a 10-minute interview with a partner, applying the skills you've learned so far. Tape the session.

Play the tape back in the company of a third partner who helps you to review what each of you was thinking and feeling, and especially how the "client" was responding after each skill or intervention. Pause the tape at appropriate times to stop the action, and ask one another questions like:

- What was going on right there?
- What did you have in mind when you said that?
- I notice an interesting expression on your face. What were you thinking at the time?
- Notice how your client is responding after you said that. What do you suppose he was feeling? Okay, let's ask him.

In this context, we are focusing not so much on your skills as on your client's responses to them. You must get in the habit of constantly checking how your clients respond to everything you say and do, or don't do.

There really isn't a set of skills related to exploring the past, as much as there is a mindset that guides you in the exploration of relevant history. This gets a little complicated from a theoretical perspective because some approaches (i.e., reality, cognitive, behavioral, strategic, problem-solving, humanistic, existential) appear to stick pretty much to the present and seem to avoid delving too far into the past. Nevertheless, in spite of espoused beliefs, most practitioners spend at least a little time collecting some basic background about what has already happened. At the very least, you might wish to know the following:

- How is what you are experiencing familiar to you?
- What does the present situation remind you of?
- What did you learn growing up that is limiting you?
- What have you already tried that has worked best?
- What have you attempted that has not worked very well?
- How might this story you shared have been influenced by others (parents, culture, gender roles) rather than your own beliefs?
- What are some critical incidents you experienced as a child that are still impacting you strongly today?
- What are some unresolved issues from the past that still plague you today?
- How might your present problem be connected to some of the issues that we have been exploring?

Exercise in Exploring the Past

Form small groups or find a partner. Have one person talk about a current, ongoing problem. Ideally, this would be of relatively little concern but still one that has been chronic.

Ask the person a series of questions, like those listed, that will help him or her to explore the ways this issue might be related to unresolved issues and entrenched patterns from the past.

After the exploration is complete, ask the person to summarize the ways this conversation was most helpful and what he or she learned as a result.

Although many of these questions may appear to be extensions of a particular theoretical orientation (i.e., psychoanalytic, narrative, individual psychology), we believe that the questions about the past (above) are fairly generic open-ended questions that are worth bringing up if there is time and the client is amenable to exploring their implications of their past. Essentially, you are operating as a historian. You want to know the context for what the client is experiencing in the present. Although you may not want to spend a tremendous amount of time delving into the past (much depends on your client's needs and interests, your own theoretical leanings, and the length of treatment planned), you will probably check out most of the areas just highlighted.

What is the best way to explore the past? Although we would like to give you the kind of specific direction we offered earlier in the chapter, this process uses a basic inquiry: "I was wondering what we need to look at from the past that might be useful or relevant?"

If you ask this question directly, the client will probably shrug. "How should I know?" the client will think, or say aloud. That is why you may often need to use a series of questions like those listed earlier to structure the search for important material. An example of this process is given in the following case where a woman is trying to extricate herself from a bad relationship with her second husband.

Client: He was telling me yesterday that he isn't going to make this easy for me, he's going to . . .

Therapist: You feel so frustrated. Now that you have finally decided to leave your husband, you believe he has only redoubled his efforts to make this as difficult as possible for you. [Reflection of feeling and content]

Client: Well, it's not his fault exactly. I mean, I've sort of encouraged him to not give up hope.

Therapist: You've given him a lot of mixed messages. [Rephrasing]

Client: Yeah. He just thinks I'll change my mind.

Therapist: You're angry at yourself for setting things up so you aren't taken seriously, especially this time when you really mean to do what you say. [Reflection of feeling]

Client: Right. I just don't know how I got myself into a mess like this.

Therapist: That's a very good question you asked. I can't help but think that this pattern might be somehow familiar to you. [Introducing influences of the past]

Client: What do you mean?

Therapist: This pattern did not just develop out of thin air. And I suspect this isn't the first time you've been involved in a relationship like this. What are some things from your past that help explain why you get yourself into these situations where you give mixed messages? [Probe and open-ended question]

Client:	I'm not sure.
Therapist:	Then let's spend some time exploring this further.

Just to summarize, the main idea is to explore with the client those influences and historical patterns that help explain and account for current difficulties.

SUMMARIZING THEMES

We demonstrated the final skill for exploring the past in the previous paragraph. After covering a number of complex topics, we pause to draw together the threads into a concise description that captures the essence of the various messages. Summary statements are inserted at various times during a session:

- When it is time to end the meeting.
- When you have completed a subject and are about to make the transition to another one.
- When the client looks confused or overwhelmed.
- When you need time to regroup and make sense of what is going on.
- When it is time to take stock of what you have been doing and talking about.
- When it might be helpful to organize or structure a conversation that has covered a lot of ground.

It may sound like it is totally the therapist's job to use a summarization when the situation calls for it, but a far better strategy is to ask the client to do the work.

Client:	I was telling you about how this situation got out of control. Oh, by the way, I ran into that friend I was telling you about, the one who gave me such a hard time . . .
Therapist:	One second. Before we get into this new topic, I wonder if we might wrap up what we've just been talking about.
Client:	Okay.
Therapist:	So, how would you summarize what this has been about?
Client:	Just that I have trouble with new situations like this because I wait until the last minute to prepare myself. You were saying that I should maybe think about things ahead of time instead of react impulsively.
Therapist:	What else?

Client: Um, that this is the way my parents made decisions too?

Therapist: True. But also that this theme of procrastinating, putting things off until the last minute, is your way of avoiding responsibility for making mistakes.

Client: Right.

Therapist: Okay, so you were talking about your friend . . .

In this brief excerpt, you can see how the therapist starts out by interrupting the client as he abruptly changed the subject. It is important that the current topic is completed before moving on, or at least that it's wrapped up a bit. Rather than doing the summary herself, the therapist asks the client to do it. Quite typically, the client is awkward and unskilled at doing this, just as you would expect from someone without training. Nevertheless, the therapist draws him out as much as possible, reviewing the main themes covered. Then she finishes the process by filling in the parts that were left out.

In this conversation, just like the previous example demonstrating how the exploration skills all fit together, you can observe the therapist using all the skills that were introduced in this chapter: rephrasing content, reflecting feelings, asking open-ended questions, and then summarizing main themes. All of this exploration leads logically and sequentially to the next stage of the therapeutic process: promoting insight and understanding.

Exercise in Summarizing

1. Initiate a conversation with a partner about some topic of mutual interest. Spend about 5 minutes talking about the subject in such a way that you each connect personally with it. In other words, don't just have an intellectual debate; talk about your feelings related to the issues raised.

2. After time runs out, each of you write down on a sheet of paper a summary of what you saw as the essence of this conversation. In just a few sentences, what was this conversation really about?

3. Exchange summaries and compare your impressions.

4. Reach a consensus between you as to a summary that includes both of your contributions.

5. Talk to each other about what this was like.

PITFALLS AND COMMON MISTAKES

In this chapter we have demonstrated ways to respond verbally to clients. You should now realize that the concepts you choose to focus on, the words you choose to say, or even your silence directs the session with your client. You might sometimes hear that person-centered therapy is nondirective. That isn't quite accurate; it's just less directive than some other approaches. Every response or lack of response will likely facilitate a particular client response. So, you must be mindful of what you say, how you say it, and why you say it. That is why we want to alert you to some common mistakes made by beginning therapists as they learn to respond verbally to clients.

A Social Demeanor

Therapist: Oh, I know what you mean. When my family gets too involved in my life, I feel really frustrated, too!

We have learned a certain way to communicate with others that is socially appropriate. For example, if someone laughs, we smile, even if the content of the information is not funny or happy. We use tenuous language such as "It sounds like . . ." or "It seems like . . ." to avoid making a mistake. We talk about our own similar experiences in an effort to join with the other person. We say things like "I understand" or "I know what you mean" when, in fact, we usually know how we would feel in their situation, not how they actually feel. We are unaware of our demeanor with others, such as whether we are usually enthusiastic and energetic or usually stoic and monotoned. We believe it's impolite to interrupt, yet we do it all the time because we're so excited about what we want to say.

The ways we behave in social situations are often not appropriate for the role of therapist. You have to present yourself as a professional who is confident. You have to be flexible in your nonverbals and in the tone of voice you use to match what the client means, not what the client presents. You have to focus on the client, not yourself. For some people, putting on a therapist hat will be easy, maybe even similar to the other professional hats they have worn. For others, however, learning to present themselves in a new way can be very difficult. When students work with clients who are the same gender, about the same age, are of similar background and social class, it's not unusual for beginner therapists to talk to clients as if they were friends. The therapist may find herself wanting to share personal information that's not necessarily helpful to the client. She may even have to restrain herself from indulging in a friendship outside of the therapeutic relationship. You will learn to be conscientious and more flexible in the way you present yourself so that you can join with all kinds of clients.

Kayleigh: Taking Me Seriously

One of the things I do worry about is working in a therapeutic setting with someone my own age. I am scared that two things are going to happen. The first concern is that I get too comfortable and start to see them as a friend rather than a client. The second concern is that they don't take me seriously because we are the same age so how would I know anything they don't? I definitely need to be careful about how I present myself so that I seem like a knowledgeable professional as opposed to a friend that they would just meet casually for coffee to talk about life.

Used with permission of Kayleigh Soto.

Freezing

Client: . . . I just don't know what to do now that I've lost my best friend.

Therapist: (painful silence)

When you first learn reflective skills, you may believe that you have to do this well, if not perfectly. There will be times when you will freeze, just draw a complete blank. In your role-plays or with real clients, the person will say something and then pause, waiting for you to respond. You will know that it is time for you to say something—if not a brilliant, deep-level, empathic reflection of feeling, then at least a feeble parroting remark—but your mind is absolutely empty and nothing whatsoever comes out of your mouth. You may start to panic and stutter. The cognitive activity inside your head will be full of self-castigation for how inept and hopeless you are as a helper.

This is a time to draw one of those cleansing breaths. You will want to remind yourself that almost anything you say, as long as it represents your best response to what you hear and understand, will encourage further conversation and deeper exploration. It does not matter nearly as much as you might think whether your reflections are poetic, articulate, profound, and perfectly accurate. Just keep the flow of conversation going by responding, saying something, almost anything. If you can't think of anything else, then you can always repeat verbatim what the person just said. This will give you some time to regroup and clear yourself for what comes next.

The most frequent mistake that beginners make when learning these skills is having expectations that are neither realistic nor even possible. You must be patient with yourself, realize that it is going to take many weeks, if not years, before these skills begin to feel natural. So, as you practice these skills in class, allow yourself to stop, take that breath, and then respond. The client will wait.

Exercise on Your Own: Listen to Yourself

About the best way to develop proficiency in all helping skills is to become far more aware of your interactive style and its effects on others. Videotape and audiotape yourself as often as possible. Review the tapes with someone more experienced (a supervisor is preferred, but even a peer can offer valuable feedback). When there is nobody else available, scrutinize the tapes by yourself, noting things you did well and poorly, behaviors you could have done differently. Take detailed notes about what you intend to change and improve.

Waiting Too Long

You can't just sit around and wait for the perfect opportunity to insert your reflective comments or probes in particular areas. Unlike role plays in which your partners will politely and considerately pause at regular intervals to give you the space to speak, clients will often just talk and talk and talk and talk until (a) the session is over, (b) they run out of ideas or energy, or (c) you interrupt and redirect them. There are many reasons why people do this. They might be rambling as a characteristic style. They might be filibustering to keep you from getting too close. They are often just doing what they think you want them to do; they think they are being cooperative by filling the time with as much as they can think of and say in the short period allotted. In any case, it is your job to make sure that things stay on course; if you wait for perfect pauses in the conversation, you may never get a word in.

Each conversation has a different pace, depending on the subject, the mood, and the client's interpersonal style. With some people, it will feel agonizing to keep the conversation going—each session can seem like it lasts days, or even weeks. With other clients, all you have to do is get things going and they will talk, nonstop, without a single pause. You are obviously after some sort of balance in most sessions, with roughly equal input and a natural exchange of ideas. Clients who speak haltingly and uneasily will have to be drawn out more. Clients who talk incessantly will need structure and clearer focus.

There are times when it is entirely appropriate—and necessary—to interrupt someone. In social situations this might be considered rude, but in the therapy arena, where time is so precious, you must provide the kind of structure that is needed. If you find yourself waiting and waiting and waiting in order to reflect back what you hear, it may be time to be more assertive and proactive.

Being Too Cautious

Student speaking   I really wanted to reflect her pain and sadness, but I was afraid
to instructor: that she would really lose it, and then I wouldn't know what
           to do.

One of the most common errors beginning therapists make is being too cautious. We have heard over and over again, "I'm afraid if I go too deep, the client won't be able to handle it." Sometimes this is just an excuse for not knowing how to go deeper. More often, though, fear is involved. The fear, however, is not really for the client, the fear is that the session will get to a point where the therapist feels unequipped to handle the situation.

What you must first understand in working with individuals is that the client will tell you when you are going too far. If you find you are bumping into some resistance, and the client is unable or unwilling to see what you present, then you have gone as far as the client will go. We assure you that most clients who have healthy boundaries and strong egos will let you know directly or indirectly when you are going too far. So push a little. Try some things out. If they don't work, just move on. We would recommend that you try taking a risk and failing rather than not taking risks at all. And if you still don't feel comfortable with pushing the client a little, then you might need to do your own work around this issue. Sometimes people need a little push, a little encouragement to move forward. They will let you know if you've gone too far. Trust your client to tell you.

Trying to Solve the Problem Too Quickly

Therapist: (in the intake session) So, it sounds like you really dislike your job,
           dislike your colleagues, and don't feel like you can promote in this
           job. I'm not sure why you won't just look for another job?

We mention this point in almost every chapter because it is such a common mistake for beginners. When you see someone who is struggling, someone in deep pain, someone who is reaching out to you, pleading for assistance, you can't help wanting to do all you can. You want to take the pain away just as fast as you can. You want to make the person feel better. You want to do this because of your own spirit of altruism, and also to make yourself feel better. Much of the time in this profession, you will feel utterly helpless. We don't know about you, but one of the reasons we got into this line of work in the first place was that we felt so helpless to resolve our own difficulties that we enjoyed taking care of other people's business. Even if this isn't the case, you will still find yourself trying to fix as many people as you can, just as quickly as possible. Whether or not it helps them, it makes you feel better.

We haven't even moved into the insight stage yet, much less the action stage, so during this exploration process you do not want to rush through the data gathering. Except in the cases of single-session therapy or crisis intervention, you will have at least one session (and often many more sessions) to do some solid exploration before you are expected to organize an intervention.

When watching beginners in action, we often hear the following remarks in the first few sessions:

- "Have you tried . . . ?"
- "One thing that has worked before is . . ."
- "What I'd like you to do is . . ."
- "My advice would be to . . ."
- "So, what are you going to do about this?"

There are times when direct action and advice are indicated (although much less often than you would imagine). Ordinarily, you will not want to push the client to take action until after you have worked your way through the exploration and insight stages.

Spending Too Much Time on the Past

Client: My parents would get so angry with me, even though my brother might have initiated the argument. I just automatically defended myself. I got tired of being blamed just because I was a year older than him.

Therapist: You felt frustrated and helpless. Talk some more about what it was like for you as a child.

Although it is theoretically consistent to talk about the past in some theories, beginners can get lost in talking about the client's past. As stated earlier, talking about the past can be helpful for finding the origins of the patterns your clients have developed. Clients, unfortunately, tend to tell their stories of the past in the same way, without really experiencing any emotion while telling them. As a result, if you allow your client to talk about the past in session after session, you might find that although you are obtaining interesting history, the client may not seem to be growing. Furthermore, talking about the past is usually merely one step toward the client's goal. Simply understanding the origins of the client's behaviors is not sufficient. A better alternative is to bring the past into the present. Reflect how the client feels right now about what happened then. Another possibility is to bring an exchange from the past into the room with an "empty chair" technique (discussed in the next chapter). So don't get caught in the trap of talking about the past, reflecting past feelings or experiences. Bring it into the present moment where the client can more fully experience his or her feelings and, it is hoped, gain depth and insight.

Asking Too Many Questions

Therapist: So, what made you respond in that way? Were you feeling rejected? How did it affect your friend when you said that? I mean, did she get angry with you?

Sometimes beginners will ask too many questions in a single response. The client may not know which one to answer and may feel confused. At other times, the client will answer only the last question. If you want to ask a question, make it a good one.

We mentioned earlier the dangers of seeming like an interrogator who asks one question after another. You can usually get the same information, or prompt the same behavior, by simply using reflective skills.

Exercise in Asking Too Many Questions

First experience what it is like to ask too many questions. One person talks about an emotionally laden topic, and the other simply responds with questions for about 3 or 4 minutes (that's all you'll be able to tolerate). Then switch roles. Talk about your experience.

This time, while one person talks about an emotionally laden topic, the other should reflect content and feelings. Switch roles. Finally, talk about your experience and note any differences.

Raising Your Voice

Client: My life has just gotten so boring and empty. I'm not sure what's wrong. I just feel lost, like there's a big hole, even though I have a great job and good relationships.

Therapist: Your life feels meaningless?

In North American English, raising your voice at the end of a statement usually turns it into a question. It also communicates an uncertainty and lack of confidence on the part of the speaker: "You're not doing very well today?" (with rising intonation on the last word) versus "You're not doing very well today" (with an even tone of voice).

The latter example communicates more power, more confidence, and thereby more influence. Remember, you are in the business of having an impact on people; that is your job. You can't help anyone if you can't get them to look at their lives in new ways and experiment with alternative ways of behaving. People are often resistant to do so because they feel familiar with old patterns, no matter how ineffective they might be. In order to get people to look at themselves more honestly, you must be able to convince them that such a task is in their best interests. Sometimes they will participate only begrudgingly.

You will need as many tools as possible to be as influential as possible. This includes using your voice to maximum advantage. If you raise your voice at the ends of your sentences—pitch, not volume—you are probably not communicating with as much power and confidence as you could even if you are trying to be more gentle and tentative in your reflections, sort of like saying, "Maybe this is what is going on?"

Clients are fully capable of correcting your reflections if they are not accurate, so don't worry about offering them in such an apologetic way that they sound "wimpy" and tentative.

Flat Reflections

In contrast to not raising your voice, it's important not to sound monotoned. The volume and tones of your voice should reflect the underlying message the client is trying to convey. For instance, if the client is talking about a sad topic, such as the death of a loved one, even if doing so in a joking manner, you will want to reflect a sad tone when you say, "You miss him very much." Your voice should be congruent with the topic. Another example would be if your client is talking in an even tone about his anger toward his father, you might want to state in a louder and sharper tone with, "You are angry at your dad!" Of course, clients are often congruent in their tone of voice and the topic. If the client is crying while stating her dog ran away last night, you would want to speak softly and slowly to match that tone. What we're trying to convey here is that words alone are not sufficient for reflection. You must reflect the emotional content, even if the client doesn't. Furthermore, you will want your facial expressions to match your voice. You could state a reflection about anger in a loud voice, but without a furrowed brow, you may seem incongruent. This is especially important in working with children. You will be surprised at how the client will match your affect.

Overuse of Summarizing

Therapist: What you're saying is that you really feel frustrated because you want your boyfriend to understand that you still have to work and go to school. And school is important to you; you want to do well. But your boyfriend doesn't seem to understand. He thinks that you're not paying enough attention to him. Then, you also have your parents who expect you to participate in family gatherings without your boyfriend. You're trying to do all this while working a full-time job. You just have too much on your plate right now.

Summarizing can be very helpful at times, but is best used infrequently. Why, you ask? Well, first of all, if all you do is summarize, then you probably aren't talking frequently enough. You're just listening to a client tell a story, which he or she can do with anyone. You should be interjecting often enough to demonstrate empathy and, you hope, to add depth. Second, if you are always summarizing, then you are talking too much when you do talk. If you go on and on and on about what the client just told you, then the client will likely get bored and/or lost in all of your talking. Finally, summarizing usually doesn't add anything to the depth of the conversation, and it can seem patronizing. Most clients seek therapy because they feel stuck, they need your help to go deeper than their current level. Your client knows what he or she just said. Therefore, your goal is not simply to parrot, but to reflect a deeper meaning behind what the client presents in order to facilitate insight.

Using Impersonal Reflections

Client: I've worked so hard to get promoted, and I just don't understand why they gave it to the new guy.

Therapist: It's frustrating.

To avoid depth of feeling in social situations we use *it* or *that*. For example, we say "That's hard" or "It's sad" instead of "You're struggling with that situation," or "You feel sad." When you state a reflection impersonally, you let the client avoid taking responsibility for what was said. The problem is somehow out there, but not part of the client's experience. Unless the client can take ownership of his feelings, he won't be able to change them. However, by simply personalizing the reflection by using "You . . . ," the client is more able to feel the feeling and own what you have just said, giving him the power to change his feelings if he wants to.

Reflecting the Experience of Others Rather Than Your Client

Client: My mother and stepfather fight all the time. I don't know why my mother won't stand up to him. He can be such a bully sometimes. She just seems so weak.

Therapist: Your mother is afraid to confront him.

Most of the time, your clients will talk about relationship issues, whether with partners/spouses, friends, family members, or coworkers. As a result, they will be making statements about how those other people feel, or think, or behave. It's important for you to remember that what clients present is only their own perceptions, not the actual way the other person might think, feel, or behave. Therefore, we recommend you do not make reflections about the other person, but rather you reflect your client's feelings, thoughts, or actions. After all, clients want your empathy directed toward them, not toward the other person. For example:

Client: My husband wants to give me advice when I just want him to listen.

Therapist: He always gives advice.

This is an example of reflecting the client's perception of the husband, which may or may not be true. In addition, you are emphasizing the husband's behavior. This would likely elicit a further elaboration of how he gives advice. A better response would be:

Therapist: You feel frustrated when he gives you advice.

In this example, you are reflecting your client's experience of frustration, which will likely stimulate your client to talk about her frustration. Therefore, check to make sure you are reflecting your client's experiences, not the experience of the other person. This allows the client to explore more depth of feeling.

Exercise in Reflecting a Client's Experience

Form pairs. The person in the client role is to talk about a real or fictional problem he or she is having with another person. The person in the therapist role will practice reflecting the experience of the other person, rather than the client's experience. After 5 minutes, discuss the direction this type of response took you. Then, using the same relationship issue, the person in the role of the therapist will correctly reflect the experience of the client, rather than the other person the client talks about. After 5 minutes, discuss how this type of reflection elicited a different direction in the conversation. Then switch roles of client and therapist and repeat the whole process.

Reflecting Projected Feelings

Client: I'm embarrassed and don't want my fiancé to meet my brother. He's sort of like white trash, and I've worked so hard not to be like the rest of my family. I don't want my fiancé to think I'm like my brother.

Therapist: You wish you could make your whole family disappear. You hate them all.

Client: Um, well not that extreme. I love my brother, I'm just embarrassed about the way he talks and the way he carries himself.

Therapist: You don't want to have anything to do with your brother.

Client: No, that's not it . . .

Sometimes it seems like your client disagrees with all of your reflections. This may be because the client is struggling to describe his or her situation. More frequently, however, the error is on the part of the therapist. Remember the exchange where the therapist seemed to be missing the core messages with every reflection?

Client: If he gets on my case one more time, just one more time, I'm going to make sure he never treats someone that way again.

Therapist: You are so upset you want to punch him.

Client: Well, not that angry. It's just that he has so little respect for me, or anyone else.

Therapist: You wish he would treat you with more respect. It pisses you off that he treats others differently.

Client: I'm not really that special, to tell you the truth. He treats everyone else the same way.

Therapist: So, you feel better about that at least.

Client: I don't feel good about any of this. I just wish I could get him to stop acting the way he does.

Therapist: You are feeling helpless because you don't know what to do next.

Client: I do know what to do, I'm just afraid to do it.

When this happens, it's usually because the therapist is projecting his or her own feelings onto the client. What's a projection? First introduced by Sigmund

Freud (Freud & Gay, 1989) and later utilized by Fritz Perls (2013) and others, projection is the identification of a thought, feeling, or behavior as someone else's when in fact it is yours. Confused? Let's see if we can make this clearer. In the preceding example, the therapist was reflecting how he or she might feel in the client's position. This happens most often when the therapist shares an experience similar to the one the client is describing. The therapist may have had a relationship where he or she wanted to kill the other person, where the therapist felt treated differently from others, and where the therapist didn't know what to do. The therapist projects his or her own experience onto the client with inaccurate reflections in an attempt to be empathic. The therapist is not reading what the client is expressing, however, and consequently is not being empathic.

Now, the fact that you make one or two inaccurate reflections does not necessarily mean that you are projecting. You will occasionally be off here and there with various clients. However, if you find that it's a pattern with a particular client or with a particular issue that more than one of your clients is experiencing, think about whether you have had a similar problem. If you have, then we recommend you do your own work around the issue so that it does not interfere with your ability to help others. In addition, getting some supervision or consulting until you feel confident your countertransferences aren't getting in the way is highly recommended.

Going in Circles

There are several reasons that you may find yourself not making any progress with the client. First, you may be reflecting only content. If you are unable to find the feelings beneath the content, then the session is not likely to progress well. Most clients (except those who are extremely emotional) are fearful of exploring feelings and may present mostly or only content. Presenting content or facts is much easier than expressing feelings. Thus, check to make sure you are including feelings in your reflections.

Another possible reason for going in circles, assuming you are reflecting feelings, is that you are reflecting at a superficial level, at the same level the client presents. A more advanced level of this skill attempts to discover what the client is saying and/or feeling beneath the words. One way to do this is to reverse the process. For example, an obvious reflection might be:

Client: In spite of what my parents say, I don't care about making better grades. That's their issue.

Therapist: You believe your grades are good enough.

Versus a deeper reflection:

Therapist: You are frustrated because your parents won't leave you alone.

If you believe that you are reflecting both content and feelings at a deep level but have reached a point where you find yourself going in circles and covering the same ground again and again, you know for sure that you've done enough reflecting and exploring. Sometimes the redundancy can begin after just a few minutes; at other times it may not occur within a single hour. When you realize that you are reflecting back the same feelings and rephrasing essentially the same content, it's time to summarize and move on. Take action. As a matter of fact, we are at that very point right now!

APPLICATIONS TO SELF: LEARNING TO REFLECT WILL CHANGE YOU

We have stated this before, and we'll state it again: Becoming a therapist will change you. In fact, it already has! You are becoming more aware of how you act interpersonally as well as intrapersonally. You are becoming aware of and working on many of your own issues as you learn new skills and see clients. Most relevant to this chapter is that you will interact with others differently.

You may think that the skill of reflecting is something you will use only while working with clients. We can assure you that this is not so. Once you begin to improve your ability to reflect, once you gain a level of mastery, reflecting will become second nature. You will reflect without thinking, without wanting to. You won't understand why everyone keeps telling you their problems when you're off work, even strangers who don't know what you do. And so there is some good news and bad news.

Let's start with the bad news. Many of your relationships are based on a pattern of interactions, a way of being with people. As you begin to reflect more, some of your relationships will start to decompensate. Your reflecting will cause others to go deeper, and they may not like it; some of your relationships will change or even end.

There's more bad news. Some of the people you choose to have in your life help you to work on your issues. This is more difficult to illustrate, but we'll attempt it with an extreme example. If an alcoholic is at a large party, and she is the only alcoholic, and a codependent type person is also at the party, and he's the only codependent, the two of them will find each other. We don't know how they do it, but it seems almost inevitable. They will not only meet, they will fall in love with each other. They will think that the other person is so wonderful! Well, guess what? At some level, we can be attracted to some people because of less healthy aspects of our own personality. So where is the other bad news? As you work on your own issues, and these reflection skills can really do it for you, those people won't seem as attractive. They might even complain that you're changing—that you're not the same person—and that would be true.

Okay, so enough with the doom and gloom. The good news! You will become healthier, happier, more balanced and confident. Oh sure, you always have stuff to work on. We can never master it all; that would be boring. But take it from us, you will find much richer relationships. You'll need them, and your newfound ability to listen, really listen to others, will have prepared you for them. You'll be happier than you ever imagined.

SUMMARY

This chapter contains some of the skills most essential to becoming an effective therapist. In fact, you must learn these skills as a foundation for helping clients. We have covered the use of questions, including what good and bad questions are and the frequency with which to use them. We have discussed the process of reflecting content and feelings; this skill is of the utmost importance. We have exposed you to information on how to explore the past as part of the initial stages of therapy. Finally, we have summarized summarizing in therapy. As mentioned at the beginning of this chapter, you will find the greatest use for these skills early in the therapeutic process, but you will use them until the last moment with every client of your career. Reflecting is especially essential to demonstrating empathy, to enhancing client awareness, and to strengthening the collaborative relationship. Practice, practice, practice.

Possible answers to the Reflective Exercise in which the therapist asks the client: "How does that make you feel?"

- "You're angry with him."
- "You're tired of fighting with him."
- "You feel exasperated."
- "You wish he would be more agreeable."

Skills in Action: Infertility

Therapist: Last week, we talked about how you felt you had no meaning in your life since you were unable to successfully have a child. We can continue talking about this unless there is something more important on your mind. [Summary review]

Client: No. Actually, the problem became more complicated when my best friend just found out she was pregnant. I feel so angry. She never really even wanted kids, and here I'm desperate to have a child. It's not fair. I know I should feel happy for her, and I do. It's wrong that I should feel so angry. I don't want to even talk with her. I can't think about it without crying!

Therapist: You feel jealous, and you feel guilty for feeling that way. [Reflection of feeling]

Client: I know it's wrong. I shouldn't feel that way. I . . .

Therapist: I want to interrupt you here. You *shouldn't* feel that way. [Challenging use of language that implies external control]

Client: Well, of course not! She is my friend and I want her to be happy too. I just can't help the way I feel.

Therapist: You're frustrated that you can't be fully happy for her without feeling some jealousy. I also hear a touch of sadness in your voice. [Reflection of content, then of feeling]

Client: (in a soft voice) Yeah. I thought I was over this. It's been well over a year, and I thought I'd cried enough about it. But my heart is breaking. I just don't know how to get over it. Tell me how to get over it. I'll do anything! I want to be supportive of my friend.

Therapist: I notice that you started to cry when I reflected sadness, and then changed the subject. [Avoiding invitation to give advice and instead reflecting process]

Client: I did?

Therapist: (silence because the client is thinking) [Therapeutic pause]

Client: I guess I don't feel I have any right to cry about this any more. I need to get over it. I can't change it. I just can't have kids, and that's it.

Therapist: You keep telling yourself that, but I notice that it's not working. What else do you tell yourself? [Confrontation, followed by an open-ended question]

Client: I should be happy for her. I'm selfish for making it all about me. That's who I am, that's who I'm being: someone selfish. I need to get over this. She's going to be pregnant for nine months, she's going to grow and have pictures of the baby, she's going to have this baby and want my support. I don't have the luxury of having a problem with it.

Therapist: You sound very angry with yourself. [Reflection of feeling]

Client: I am. Don't you think I'm being selfish?

Therapist: I think you still need to mourn this loss. I want to bring this conversation back to the beginning. You said you lost meaning in your life when you realized you couldn't conceive. Tell me about the first time you remember wanting to have a child. [Structuring summary, followed by a probe of the past]

Client: I remember as a little girl, even four or five years old, wanting to be a mommy. I played with dolls through my whole childhood. In high school, I dreamed of a beautiful wedding and getting married, and then having children. I thought that being a mother was the noblest thing you could do. I love playing with my nieces and nephews. They bring me such joy and happiness. I spent my teenage years babysitting for our neighbors, at church, anywhere that I could. I loved being around kids. That felt like my purpose in life. I was sure that's what I was supposed to do. That's why I didn't work very hard in college or ever think about a career. I didn't need to; I was going to be a stay-at-home mother. I was going to give all the love I never got to my kids. And I just love kids!

Therapist: I'm struck by what you just said. You feel like you didn't get the kind of love you needed growing up. [Reflection]

Client: No. My mother took good care of my physical needs, but she was always emotionally distant. She didn't hug me or tell me she loved me. She just felt cold. Don't get me wrong. I love my mother. She did the best she could, and knowing my grandmother, she probably got less love than me. It's just . . . (silence) . . . I would like to have been loved better. (through tears) And look at me now, married to a man who isn't affectionate.

Therapist: You're starving for love and affection. [Reflection]

Client: Yes. I need it so badly. And I've set myself up again to not get it. Why did I do that?

Therapist: I'm wondering if there is a connection between your need for love and affection and what you imagine a child will bring you. [Making connections]

REFERENCES AND RESOURCES

Beck, A. T., Freeman, A., & Davis, D. (2014). *Cognitive therapy of personality disorders* (3rd ed.). New York, NY: Guilford Press.

Cormier, S., & Nurius, P. (2013). *Interviewing and change strategies for helpers: Fundamental skills and cognitive-behavior interventions* (7th ed.). Pacific Grove, CA: Brooks/Cole.

De Jong, P., & Berg, I. K. (2012). *Interviewing for solutions* (4th ed.). Pacific Grove, CA: Brooks/Cole.

Egan, G. (2013). *The skilled helper: A problem-management and opportunity-development approach to helping* (10th ed.). Pacific Grove, CA: Brooks/Cole.

Ellis, A., & Ellis, D. J. (2011). *Rational emotive behavior therapy* (3rd ed.). Washington, DC: American Psychological Association.

Freud, S., & Gay, P. (Ed.). (1989). *The Freud reader.* New York, NY: W. W. Norton.

Gottschall, J. (2012). *The storytelling animal: How stories make us human.* New York, NY: Houghton Mifflin.

Hill, C. E. (2014). *Helping skills: Facilitating exploration, insight, and action* (4th ed.). Washington, DC: American Psychological Association.

Ivey, A., Ivey, M. B., & Zalaquett, C. (2013). *Intentional interviewing and counseling: Facilitating client development in a multicultural society* (8th ed.). Pacific Grove, CA: Brooks/Cole.

Levine, M. (2004). Tell your doctor all your problems, but keep it less than a minute. *New York Times,* June 1. Retrieved February 24, 2016, from http://www.nytimes.com/2004/06/01/health/tell-the-doctor-all-your-problems-but-keep-it-to-less-than-a-minute.html?_r=0

Perls, F. (2013). *Gestalt therapy verbatim.* Gouldsboro, ME: The Gestalt Journal Press.

Young, M. E. (2012). *Learning the art of helping: Building blocks and techniques* (5th ed.). New York, NY: Pearson.

Chapter 7

Promoting Understanding and Insight

This chapter, like this stage in the therapeutic process, acts as a bridge between assessment and exploration, which we have just discussed, and the action that follows. Some approaches advocate the promotion of insight as the main focus of therapy, believing that when this process is carried through in sufficient depth, it alone can lead to lasting changes. Person-centered therapy, psychodynamic theory, Gestalt therapy, and existential therapy are perhaps the best-known advocates from the traditional models of therapy, which hold this point of view. They structure the treatment in a way that increases self-awareness and self-understanding, believing that this is more than enough to get the job done. More contemporary constructivist and social constructionist models also make use of insight, but in a way that is designed to help clients not only understand the ways they perceive things, but also to change these stories to stories that are more helpful.

Carl Rogers was perhaps the most articulate spokesperson for an insight-oriented perspective when he commented that self-awareness and understanding were both necessary and sufficient conditions for change to occur. There is actually little empirical support for this assumption, and even some question as to whether the therapist is the one who promotes the insights or whether the client is the one who does this outside of the sessions.

REFLECTIVE EXERCISE

In small groups, or on your own, consider a time in your life when you had an epiphany—a major moment of revelation in which you gained some insight or understanding. This could have been a dramatic insight into the meaning of life, the

(Continued)

(Continued)

workings of the world, or perhaps a deeper understanding of yourself. Talk (or think) about what contributed most to this transformation. In addition, discuss what it took for you to remember this lesson and to learn from it.

It's possible that including an insight stage and using skills designed to promote greater understanding may not be part of every treatment plan or every case you see, but you will still provide some forum for exploring the meaning of issues and concerns, even if time is limited and motivation is minimal. After all, even the most problem-focused client will want to have some idea as to what happened and why, so future problems of a similar nature might be prevented.

THE USES OF INSIGHT

The need for insight will arise in a number of ways. Clients may wonder why they developed problems in the first place, or they may wish to understand the deeper meaning of these concerns in the context of their lives. For instance, someone who is depressed might very well be primarily concerned with making those awful feelings go away, but may also wish to have some idea as to the source of the condition. Any of the following explanations may be possible for a case of depression:

- The depression represents a sense of emptiness and meaninglessness in the person's life due to job dissatisfaction and social isolation.
- The person is experiencing a delayed reaction to sexual abuse suffered in childhood.
- The person has an overwhelming sense of helplessness and powerlessness that comes from being a member of a minority group that was oppressed.
- The person is the scapegoat and "designated client" for a dysfunctional family in which others are the ones who need help but will not seek it.
- The depression is a symptom of a degenerative neurological disease or head injury.
- There is an underlying "endogenous," biologically based depression.
- The person is grieving the loss of a relationship that recently ended.

This is a mere sampling of possible "causes" for the depression. Each might involve a different sort of treatment plan, and each would provoke a very different understanding of the underlying issues and what they mean for that person.

Depending on your theoretical orientation (or the one favored by your supervisor), the particular complaints brought to you by clients, your work setting, and the time you are allotted to offer help, there are a number of options available for promoting insight and understanding. Table 7.1 summarizes several of these possibilities, each of which makes use of particular skills that will be covered in this chapter.

THE LIMITS OF INSIGHT

Some theorists and therapists are critics who consider attention spent on insight in therapy as largely a waste of time, if not a potentially dangerous digression. Following Milton Erickson's lead, Paul Watzlawick (1997) wrote an article titled "Insight May Cause Blindness," in which he reported that there wasn't a single documented case he could think of in which a client ever changed permanently as a result of some understanding. Without action, without converting understanding into some form of structured practice, he believed that the time and energy were wasted.

Table 7.1   Models for Promoting Insight

Type of Insight	Theoretical Framework	Skill Employed	Example
Awareness of feelings	Person-centered	Reflection of feeling	"You're feeling angry because you don't like giving up control."
Unconscious motives	Psychoanalytic	Interpretation	"The anger you are expressing toward me seems related to feelings you have toward your mother."
Cognitive distortions	Cognitive	Guided discovery	"Even if you don't get what you want, how is that absolutely terrible?"
Inauthenticity	Gestalt	Confrontation	"You say you are really angry about this, but you appear quite calm."
Personal meaning	Existential	Immediacy	"I notice that right now you are withdrawing from our relationship just as you have done with others."
Problem redefinition	Strategic	Reframing	"When you say you have a bad temper, what you really mean is that you are sometimes very passionate."

(Continued)

Table 7.1   Continued

Type of Insight	Theoretical Framework	Skill Employed	Example
Family dynamics	Systemic	Restructuring	"I want you to move over there and sit with your wife instead of your children. Talk to one another about what this is like."
Power imbalances	Feminist	Exploring gender roles	"How have you limited yourself by the ways you have defined what it means to be a man?"
Sources of influence	Narrative	Outcome questions	"How did you manage to overcome the anger when it tried to control you?"
Social and language influences	Social constructionist	Re-story life circumstances	"Which roles have you adopted that were not of your own choosing?"
Consequences of choices	Reality	Challenge decisions	"Is what you are doing getting you what you want?"
Family constellation	Adlerian	Interpret early recollections	"Your memories seem to have a theme of withdrawal from the family."
Contingency contracting	Behavioral	Identify reinforcers for target behaviors	"What is it that sustains this behavior?"

This may be an extreme point of view, but there nevertheless is considerable evidence to support the reality that people can remain in therapy for a very long time, have a perfect understanding of why they continually make poor choices, and yet remain that way without a shred of visible movement toward changing their self-destructive behaviors.

An excellent example of how insight might be considered unnecessary, or sometimes even impossible to facilitate, is with some anxiety disorders. Some clients with panic disorder or phobias are unable to identify the reasons for their anxiety because the symptoms may be biologically triggered. Clients are often treated successfully for these anxiety disorders with medications and with therapy that may result in absolutely no understanding of the causes.

Seeking insight can also be challenging with clients from some cultural backgrounds who may view therapy as a resource to find solutions to existing problems. One example we often see with some ethnic groups is the parents' need to reduce conflict with their teenage child. The parents are not interested in exploring the sources of conflict but instead want advice on how to help their child be more agreeable and cooperative. They may send their child to therapy for us to "fix" him or her and believe that to do otherwise would be both inappropriate and disrespectful.

In contrast to other types of issues, one of the difficulties with determining whether or not insight is useful, necessary, or even productive, is that each theory can define insight in a different way. Perhaps those who criticize insight define it as a basic understanding of how and why people do what they do, while others might define insight as a deep epiphany that results in changes in thinking, feeling, and behaving. In the latter case, insight, by definition, facilitates change. You may want to keep in mind that human behavior is varied, and as a result how you treat clients must vary as well.

The skills covered in this chapter are designed to help clients develop at least a minimal level of understanding about the source of their problems and the meaning behind their problems. Although this may not be sufficient to help them make needed changes—and make the changes last—they will provide a solid grounding to help people understand themselves better, and in the best case, prevent future problems through such self-knowledge.

SELECTED SKILLS FOR PROMOTING UNDERSTANDING

It is a gross simplification to think that anything as complex as moments of startling insight can be promoted by the use of a few well-applied skills. When clients arrive at a new place of understanding it is usually the result of accumulated work that has spanned their whole lives. The therapist is merely the midwife who assists with the birth.

Even within the course of therapy, when clients do reach a point of new awareness it is almost impossible to identify what the therapist did or said (if anything) that made the greatest difference. It is usually a big mistake even to ask the client afterward. For one thing, clients don't often know or understand what happened; they will just make up an explanation to satisfy your curiosity. And second, even when they think they do know what happened, you may not like what you hear.

After a particularly moving session, the client discloses how pleased he is with the result. In the best scientific tradition, the therapist attempts to identify the critical factors so that such efforts might be replicated in the future.

Client: I just want to thank you so much for all your help. This was an amazing session. I think I finally understand what is going on now.

Therapist: So, I'm just curious. What made the most difference to you? What would you say helped you the most?

The therapist is reviewing in her head all the possible candidates that might be mentioned. She is almost sure the client will say that it was that wonderful metaphor she created, the one that included several different levels and was constructed to bypass the usual resistance. Or perhaps it was that well-timed confrontation in which she was finally able to get the client's attention to point out what he had been doing that was so ineffective. Then again, it could have been the gentle way that she had supported him in his time of need.

No matter what the client shares, we can almost promise you that it won't be what you expect to hear. All too often, clients are unable to articulate what it was that mattered most. Even when they can, it may not be one of the planned interventions but something quite serendipitous. We can't tell you how often we have asked clients this question and heard examples of what we had done that we didn't even remember.

So, humility is the order of the day. Understanding is an accumulative, complex process that builds on previous awareness. Your job is to use those skills that are most associated with helping the development along.

Confrontation

Confrontation has a very bad reputation. It is often associated with being rude or hurtful. Just imagine hearing the words, "I want to confront you about something," and it gets your pulse racing. Confrontation is associated with conflict, with war, with clashes of power.

In a therapeutic context, the best confrontations are so subtle and gentle that the client doesn't even know they took place. Sometimes, in order to get rid of the bad taste the word *confrontation* can leave in students' mouths, we call it a reflection of discrepancy, because your client is usually exhibiting some sort of discrepancy that you simply notice. In the dialogue that follows, the therapist is merely pointing out some distortion, and is doing it in a way that is unassuming, almost innocent.

Client: I'd like to be able to do something like that, but I'm just not good at that sort of thing. I've never been able to speak up like that with lots of people around.

Therapist: I see. I'm a little confused by something though.

Client: What's that?

Therapist: Well, you say that you can't speak up in front of groups, but last week you were telling me a story about how you gave a toast at your brother's wedding and how moved everybody had been. What do you make of that?

In this interaction, the therapist wished to confront or challenge the client's self-limiting statements that were neither accurate nor constructive (i.e., reflecting a discrepancy). Rather than telling the person that he was a liar, or that he was distorting reality, or that he was using this belief as an excuse to hide from taking action, the therapist used a much more subtle approach by simply noting a discrepancy between what the client was saying now and what he had said previously. Then the client was left with the task of sorting this out.

The client could, of course, attempt to ward off this confrontation by denying what he said earlier or minimizing its significance: "Well, that situation was different because it was just with family and close friends." But when the client is open to looking at things in a different way (and it is the client's readiness that matters most), a confrontation like this can go a long way to provoking changes: "I hadn't thought about it that way. But I guess you're right. It's not so much that I can't speak up as it is difficult for me to do so. But I can do it when I have to."

When using confrontation, it is best to confront the behavior, not the person. You can do this most easily by labeling the behavior that you observe or simply pointing out discrepancies:

1. Between what is said now versus earlier: "You said earlier that everything in your relationship was going well, but now you are saying that there are some problems."

2. Between what the client is saying versus communicating nonverbally: "You say that you aren't that excited about seeing your friend, but I notice that when you talk about him your voice rises and you start talking really fast."

3. Between what the client says he or she wants and what the client is doing: "I'm a little confused. You say you want to improve your grades, that it is your most important priority, yet you admitted that you spent only one hour studying this week."

There are other instances when confrontation might be indicated, such as when someone is doing something harmful or self-defeating. This is tricky, because if you confront when the client isn't ready, or in a way that the client can't hear the challenge, then he or she can become very defensive. Take the following example:

Client: I'm so overwhelmed! I just don't know what to do. I have to take care of my little sister. I have schoolwork. I have my full time job. I have my volunteer work at church. There isn't enough time for me to do everything, yet I can't let anything go.

Therapist: It seems to me that you make yourself too busy by getting overcommitted.

If you heard the therapist say something like this, you might feel defensive and misunderstood. On the other hand, if the therapist challenged the client more gently, the confrontation might not seem so harsh.

Therapist: I think you may be right that there isn't enough time for everything. [Validating the client] I'm struck by how you are interested in being involved in so many things, and how you seem driven to do each one as if it was a full-time job. It seems like there is something that drives you beyond just simple interest.

In this way, the therapist and client can begin to explore what might be driving the need to be overcommitted. In the first example, the therapist wanted the client to take responsibility for her behavior, but did so with the potential of sounding critical. The second response validates the client and then takes the point of view of curiosity rather than blame to explore underlying causes. So instead of just saying the client takes on too much, and that that's wrong, the second example assumes that something hidden is driving this behavior. There could be many reasons for this—the need to be perfectionistic, to compensate for feeling inadequate, or to feel responsible for everyone else and thus feel needed. The client may not know how to be any different.

It is far more likely that the client can hear the feedback in the second example and begin to explore motives and behavior further. Another advantage is that the therapist is modeling a way of thinking: The client is encouraged to assume that there is a good reason for her behavior. With this knowledge, clients themselves can gently explore any future issues that don't seem to be working in their lives, without creating blame. They end up confronting themselves.

Exercise in Confrontation

In groups of three, take on the roles of the helper, client, and observer. The client will talk about a situation and present some inconsistency—between verbal and nonverbal behavior or between several statements that don't fit together. The helper will then confront the person by pointing out this inconsistency in the most diplomatic way possible. The observer will then offer feedback on alternative ways this confrontation could have been implemented.

Switch roles until each person has had a chance to practice confrontation.

Disputing Beliefs

A popular contribution from the cognitive therapies is a more challenging set of skills for the repertoire of most therapists. Adler (1963) first introduced these as "basic mistakes"; since then other therapies have adopted this idea as an essential component of their theory, such as cognitive distortions from cognitive therapy (Beck, 1976) or irrational beliefs from rational emotive therapy (Ellis, 1973). When clients show evidence of thinking that is distorted, irrational, or illogical, the therapist may use the opportunity to explore underlying beliefs that lead to these self-defeating patterns.

It is not necessary to fully embrace rational emotive behavior therapy, individual psychology, or cognitive therapy in order to use disputing skills in your work. At times the level of client cognitive distortion is such that you believe that helping them to examine their underlying thinking may be profitable. This is especially the case in the following circumstances.

- When the person exaggerates: Listen for never and always. "I never get what I want." "I always end up with the worst end of the deal."
- When the person imagines the worst: Notice the prevalence of words like *awful* and *terrible*. *"This is the worst thing that's ever happened to me." "This is so awful I can't stand it."*
- When the person demands special status. Notice expressions like, *"It's not fair"* and *"Why me?"*
- When the person overgeneralizes: *"Because I didn't get an 'A' on my last paper, I'll never earn this professor's respect." "I blew the whole interview; I'll never be a good therapist."*
- When the person makes judgmental demands of self or others: Notice the use of the words *must* and *should*. *"He shouldn't have done that" "I must get this promotion."*
- When the person does not want to take responsibility: Notice the use of the words *made* and *can't* (instead of *won't*). *"He made me clean the house every week." "She made me angry every time she said that." "I can't do this homework; it's too hard."*

The first skill in this process is sensitizing yourself to notice when people use language that represents underlying distorted thinking. This isn't terribly complicated or involved but it will require a certain amount of reading on your part to master the basic concepts. You might consult some of the classic books by Glasser (1965), Ellis (1973), Beck (1976), Meichenbaum (1977), Lazarus (1973), Adler (1963), as well as more recent sources (Beck, 2011; Carlson, Watts, & Maniacci, 2006; Dryden & Neenan, 2014; Nordahl & Wells, 2016) in order to familiarize yourself with the most common beliefs to monitor.

On the simplest level, you can do this by noticing every time a client (or anyone) says something like *"He made me so upset,"* or *"That situation ruined everything."* Ask yourself what is intrinsically inaccurate about these statements.

Regarding the first case, you now realize that other people can't make one upset. Emotions are initiated internally. With a few exceptions, nobody else has the power to make you feel anything without your consent or without some underlying belief from which the feeling arises; emotional reactions are the result of interpretations made about various situations. Thus, in the second statement, no situation can ruin anything, unless that is the way the person chooses to interpret things.

If, for example, you did get a disappointing grade on an assignment; you could tell yourself any number of things about what this means:

- "This means I'm stupid."
- "The instructor is a jerk."
- "This proves that this department sucks."
- "I'll never be able to succeed in this field."

It is entirely possible, of course, that any of the preceding statements might be true, but is far more likely that you might be overgeneralizing and exaggerating. This could clearly result in rather strong emotional reactions, such as rage, depression, and discouragement.

Another set of possibilities is that you could say to yourself:

- "Gee, this is disappointing. I wonder what I could do to improve my grade on the next assignment?"
- "The fact that I received one grade that's lower than I prefer (but still not that bad) doesn't mean I'm stupid."
- "I wonder if the instructor made a mistake. I'll go talk to her to find out what happened."
- "I'm not crazy about the way some things operate in this department, but I guess that's true of almost any organization."

In this second set of responses you can appreciate that a very different kind of emotional reaction would likely take place. You may still be disappointed, and perhaps even a bit upset, but the intensity of the emotions is more appropriate given the circumstances.

When disputing beliefs, your job is to help clients examine what they are saying to themselves and then, if desired, substitute alternative self-statements that are more reality based. Some examples of these kinds of interventions might include:

- "I'm not clear on how you arrived at that conclusion. How does it follow that just because that one thing happened, it necessarily leads to your conclusion?" This challenges the client to examine assumptions about causes and effects.
- "What are you saying to yourself to cause yourself such misery?" This encourages clients to examine the ways their chosen interpretations determine how they feel. By implication, if they changed what they say to themselves, they could change the result. Instead of saying, "This is the worst thing that ever happened," the person could say, "This is annoying and disappointing. This is just one of those times I don't get what I want."
- "Where is the evidence to support that belief?" You are asking clients to do a reality check, to examine the basis for their assumptions. "You say that you don't have a chance of ever succeeding, but I'm not clear how you arrived at that conclusion."
- "What makes you so special?" People who act as if the forces of the universe have conspired against them can be challenged to see that they are not different from others. Although it may sometimes seem as if they got a raw deal, that perception is the result of excessive preoccupation with self.
- "You should do that?" When clients use "shoulds" or "musts," bring this to their attention so they can use more appropriate language. It is so much more empowering to say "I would like to do this" than "I should do it."
- "I notice you say 'always' a lot referring to your brother's behavior." Clients who use "always" or "never" are using exaggerated language that can develop into an inaccurate perception of the circumstance. Using more precise language such as "He often lets you down," may be more on target and decreases the vilifying of the brother in this example.

There is a kind of Socratic dialogue associated with the use of these skills. Although there are different styles of intervention, the main goal is to change the ways that people think about their predicaments, and thereby alter their emotional responses.

One challenge with this technique is that disputing beliefs assumes that the therapist knows what constitutes true "reality" without considering the ways that it may be socially and culturally constructed. Who determines what is rational and distorted and what is not? The answer, historically speaking, has been men from the dominant culture, which includes many inherent biases that have tended to marginalize women and minorities.

Certainly, many views can be agreed upon by most people, but there are also exceptions. For instance, a client sees his dead father and believes his father is trying to send him an important message; one therapist might see this as a psychotic episode, while another might validate the client's experience without labeling this belief as distorted in any way: "You believe he's trying to tell you something important." A delicate balance exists between these views.

If the client's belief is causing harm to self or others, then perhaps it is useful to assess the nature of the self-destructive behavior. On the other hand, the client's belief may not be harmful to anyone, and in fact, could be helpful. In this case, there is little reason to dispute this belief, even if you, personally, don't believe in ghosts. Below is another example in which a cultural conflict could occur in attempting to dispute beliefs.

Client: I just don't know what to do. My parents really want me to major in engineering, but I'm just not interested. I want to major in business. Even as I look around, the people who were signing up for business classes seemed more like me than the people in the engineering program.

Therapist: You seem really torn. You want to please your parents, but by doing so you give up something important to you. Since you are the one who has to take the classes and do that work, you may want to consider talking with your parents about your feelings.

Client: I can't do that!

Therapist: You mean you *won't* do that. You *choose* not to. I sense you're afraid.

Client: Okay, I won't do that. I have a duty to my parents and cannot displease them.

Therapist: You believe it's your responsibility to keep your parents happy, but in fact, your parents are responsible for their own happiness.

Dominant Western cultural values teach us that our lives are our own, and that our parents will support us if we can give them good reason to do so. Among many ethnic groups, however, there is a different power hierarchy between children and parents. Confronting parents or disagreeing with them may be a sign of extreme disrespect and is unacceptable. The client in this case cannot conceive of confronting her parents, but the therapist thinks that the client lacks courage. This is a huge cultural misunderstanding. A more culturally aware therapist might say, "A part of you wants to remain loyal to your parents based upon the dictates of your culture, but another part of you wants to be independent and do what you please. You feel stuck." In this way, the therapist acknowledges the client's struggle without imposing cultural beliefs. Insight is enhanced by reflecting these conflicting beliefs, and that is the beginning to discovering a resolution to the problem.

Exercise in Disputing

With a partner, take turns role-playing the following scenarios in which attempts are made to identify the distorted beliefs implicit in the statements. Once these have been identified, challenge their validity by using the skills that were introduced.

- "I can't go to the party. I'm just not good in social situations like that. I'll probably make a fool of myself the way I always do. And even if I did meet someone, things like this never work out for me."
- "There's something wrong with the car and they can't find out what the problem is. It's just not fair. There's no way that I can concentrate on anything else until this gets fixed. That's just the way I am."
- "He makes me so angry the way he is always manipulating people. He should respect people more."
- "If I only had a better education, then maybe I'd have a chance to do something with my life. But it's too late for me now. There's just nothing I can do but accept that this is the way things are going to be."

Interpretation

If disputing beliefs is part of the legacy of cognitive therapy, then interpretation is one of the major contributions of psychoanalytic therapy to generic practice. This is a very different sort of approach to promoting insight, but one that also seeks to alter people's perceptions about their situations.

Through the processes of systematic observation and analysis, the therapist develops certain hypotheses about what might be going on and why. Interpretation is the skill that is used to offer these observations to the client with the hope that this will foster a deeper level of understanding of the meaning of the symptoms and their underlying causes.

Interpretations can be made on several different levels:

- Unconscious motives and desires can be made more explicit. "Perhaps the reason why you hesitate to tell her how much you care about her is that you fear she will respond in kind. Deep down inside you don't feel you deserve to be loved."
- Connections can be made between present and past behavior. "You are struggling to establish yourself as someone who is competent and knowledgeable. This reminds me of what you said previously about how inept you felt as a child when you couldn't play any sports well."

- Underlying themes and metaphors can be highlighted. "Perhaps the argument you have been having about who should do which chores around the house is really a struggle for control in your relationship. You have mentioned previously that you used to fight over who would drive the car when you went out together."

There was a time when interpretation was the foundation for what many therapists would do in order to promote insight, especially those who were trained in a psychoanalytic background. Because it does place the therapist in the role of the expert authority who sees and knows things that are not visible to others, some practitioners and theorists are reluctant to use this power-laden skill. As you can see, there is a continuum on how to utilize interpretation.

On the one end of the continuum, interpretation is the essence of therapy. For example, in psychoanalysis (Freud, 1936) and analytic (Jung, 1935/1980) psychotherapies, interpreting is a primary function of the therapist. Both of these theories have specific symbols or concepts that the therapist can use to interpret the client's discourse, whether from a dream or from catharsis. Learning these symbols and concepts takes years of training on the part of the therapist, especially with analytic therapy.

On the other end of the continuum are Gestalt (Perls, 1969) and person-centered (Rogers, 1951) therapies where interpretation is something that the therapist tries to avoid. The assumption is that the therapist can project only his or her understanding of the problem, because the therapist is unable to fully take on the client's paradigm or be completely objective. Therefore, the client must seek his or her own interpretations. Furthermore, if the client arrives at his or her own interpretation, then it will definitely be well timed and accurate; the therapist would be at risk of providing an interpretation prematurely or inaccurately. Clients with stronger personalities can negate an incorrect interpretation. Clients who like to please or who have poor boundaries, however, may not negate it, or worse, may assume it's correct without thinking about whether or not the interpretation seems to fit (this is called *introjection*). So let's look at a specific example of these extreme positions before exploring the middle ground. A client reports part of her dream:

I'm in a big two-story house at the top of the stairs. I walk down the stairs, and at the bottom of the stairway is a table with a large vase full of tall, white flowers. I can smell the sweetness of the flowers, and I feel sad at the sight of them. I stand there frightened, unable to move.

Perhaps the psychoanalytic therapist would interpret the large vase of flowers as representative of the vessel that holds all her dreams, and the white flowers the purity and innocence of her childhood hopes that have been only marginally realized. In contrast, a Gestalt therapist would ask the client to report the dream in the present tense; once that's completed, the client might be asked to choose something that stands out most in the dream. For instance, if the client picked the flowers as the most significant part, the therapist could ask her to become that object and then describe, in the present tense, what that feels like: "I am in a vase. I am white. I am pretty. I represent death . . ." When the client begins describing herself as the flowers, she will usually come to her own awareness of what the dream means. In the first example, the therapist offers an interpretation, and in the second example, the therapist leads the client through a process that allows her to arrive at her own interpretation. There are also many other ways to use dream interpretation that take other approaches.

Exercise in Interpretation

Get into groups of four or five people. Have one person tell a recent or recurring dream for about 2 or 3 minutes; if no one has a dream to talk about, have someone tell a brief and somewhat bizarre story. Then, on a sheet of paper, take a minute or two to write down a brief interpretation of the dream or story. After everyone has finished, compare the notes among the listeners. Finally, compare what the dreamer wrote down as his or her interpretation. Discuss the differences.

A more subtle and less direct approach can be taken to help clients look beneath the surface of their behavior. In theories such as individual psychology, interpretation is essential, but is done collaboratively and with a significant amount of supporting evidence before it is submitted to the client. Interpretative interventions can thus be employed by making the client more responsible for creating meaning:

- "I wonder what it means that you are so reluctant to tell her how you feel."
- "I suspect that what you are doing now is part of a long-standing pattern in your life. What does this situation remind you of?"
- "This sounds very familiar, given some things you have described earlier. What stands out for you?"

In these instances, instead of supplying the meaning through interpretation, the therapist helps the client to do the work. Regardless of how the process is introduced, clients are taught to think in ways that uncover underlying themes, recurrent patterns, and significant metaphors that may be instructive. As with all other skills, you will be much more effective if you use the client's language rather than your own preferences when encouraging this deeper understanding. Again, if the client arrives at the interpretation on his or her own, it will be well timed and more accurate.

Providing Information

Sometimes clients struggle because there are things they don't know or understand. For instance, imagine if a couple came to see you because of sexual difficulties. When you ask them what the problem is, the wife answers meekly that sexual intercourse was so painful that she didn't want to do it anymore.

You ask them to describe the way they initiated their lovemaking. They are painfully embarrassed by this discussion, but so desperate that they do their best to be accommodating.

Husband: Well, we just do it.

Therapist: Could you be a little more specific please?

Husband: Well, I just kinda tell her that it's time and then we go upstairs and we do it.

Therapist: Maybe we could just break this down into smaller steps. First, how do you indicate that it is time for lovemaking?

Wife: He sort of nods his head, like in the direction of the bedroom.

Therapist: Okay. Then what happens?

Wife: Like he says, we go into the bedroom and then we do it.

Therapist: Again, it would help if you could be more specific.

Wife: Well, I lay down on the bed. Then he pulls down my underpants, and he shucks out of his pants.

Therapist: Go on.

Wife: That's about it. Then he gets on top and we do it. It really hurts though, so sometimes we have to stop pretty quick.

Therapist: Wait a minute. Let's back up a little. You mean to say that you just lie down on the bed, and he just enters you right away?

Husband: Yes sir. That's it. Why? Are we doing something wrong?

When asked about foreplay, the couple had no idea what the therapist was talking about (this is a true story based on one of our cases). They had little understanding about their bodies and the ways they worked and almost no knowledge about pleasuring one another's bodies. The therapist provided them with information about their bodies and made some suggestions for foreplay. The "cure" results from their applying this new knowledge.

There are several other instances in which problems could arise because clients don't understand something important. Therapists thus take on the roles of teachers and instruct people in areas that are relevant. Examples of this might include:

- Explaining how emotional responses are the result of thinking patterns or underlying beliefs.
- Instructing people in the short- and long-term effects of their favored mind-altering substance.
- Providing basic information about the best ways to interview for a new job.
- Teaching about the ways that stress can result from unhealthy lifestyle choices.
- Supplying a model for making decisions systematically.
- Giving referral sources for physicians who can do recommended medical tests.
- Introducing a systematic plan of mindful eating to help with weight loss.
- Explaining the ways that family members can become scapegoats as a result of underlying dynamics.
- Explaining to a teenager that she can choose to follow the rules and earn privileges or choose not to follow the rules and suffer the consequences; either way, she is still choosing, even if she follows her parents' rules.
- Educating about the ways in which people of color are marginalized by the majority culture.
- Explaining how reported symptoms represent normal responses and are not necessarily problematic.
- Warning about risk factors associated with suicide attempts.
- Describing the ways that self-perceptions are shaped by one's culture, gender, and family background.
- Explaining the variables that are most associated with relapses and what can be done to prevent them.

- Teaching people to recognize the signs and symptoms of trouble before the trouble occurs.
- Distinguishing among the various kinds of depression and explaining how the client's symptoms fit along this continuum.
- Directing the client to sources on the Internet that will provide additional information.
- Recommending books and movies that might highlight a relevant point.

The key component of the skill associated with giving information is doing it in such a way that you don't come across as a pedantic teacher. It is also far better to teach the client how to get needed information than for you to do all the work. For example, if a client is interested in going to college but is unsure how to proceed, rather than telling him or her what to do, it may be better to work with the person to figure out how he or she could find the needed information. This way, you are helping the client not only learn about things related to present needs, but also to learn the process by which he or she can find out things in the future.

Exercise in Providing Information

Get into groups of four or five. Discuss a situation where each of you was given incorrect information, or had little or no information about a subject that was important to you. What were the consequences of not knowing? Share how you eventually obtained the correct information and how this affected you. How do you usually go about seeking new information when you have questions?

Giving Feedback

Whenever prospective clients have asked what is so unique about therapy that it is worth the money, a favorite response is that it is the one place you can go to hear the truth. Therapists are in a unique position to observe people and then offer constructive assistance. Where else can someone go to hear how he or she really comes across to others? Who else is going to tell people why they are so annoying? Who else can give people concise and accurate input on what they are doing and understand the effects of that behavior? And who else is going to say these things in a way that the feedback can be heard?

It does indeed take considerable sensitivity, as well as honesty, to offer people things about themselves that everyone else knows but is afraid to tell them. To make this much more personal: You consistently do things that are less than effective. You sometimes put people off by the way you behave. You erect barriers that get in the way of greater intimacy. You engage in defense mechanisms that not only protect you from getting hurt but also insulate you from enjoying life. Furthermore, most of the people in your life know this about you but they will never tell you.

There are a number of very good reasons why you rarely hear the truth about your own self-defeating behavior. People don't want to hurt your feelings. They are afraid you will take things personally and hold a grudge. They don't know how to tell you in a way that you will hear them. And most of all: They are concerned that it won't do much good, so what is the point in even trying?

Among the things you will do for your clients, one of the most valuable is to give them honest and useful feedback about what they do well and not so well. It would not at all be an exaggeration to say that sometimes such comments can irrevocably change people's lives. If you can figure out a way to find the core of what people are doing to get themselves in trouble, and if you can bring this to their attention without threatening them too much, it might just be possible for them to make needed adjustments. However, it is very, very hard to offer such feedback without creating high levels of threat and defensiveness.

Giving feedback is one thing; doing it in a way that it can be heard and accepted is quite another. It's a difficult skill to learn, and we hope that as therapists-in-training you have good role models in your professors and supervisors, who provide you with constructive feedback about your counseling skill level. Notice how they do it and if you think it's done well, mimic what you see and hear.

Good Feedback Is Honest

One of the things we can do for clients is to tell them how they appear to others. It is as if each of us walks around in the world with a piece of spinach caught between our teeth. Everyone else can see this unsightly mess but nobody is willing to bring it to our attention because it is embarrassing. So they pretend to ignore it, or they whisper about it to others, leaving us in the dark.

When you notice that clients are doing something that is counterproductive or acting in ways that are off-putting, you can bring this to their attention. Here are some examples of the sort of feedback that might be offered:

- "I notice that when you talk to me you rarely make eye contact or mumble. This makes it difficult to make contact with you. I wonder if this might be one of the things that is getting in the way of some of your other relationships?"

- "One thing that might be helpful for you to know is that you continuously interrupt me before I can finish responding to you. This discourages me, and others, from feeling like we are heard by you."
- "You consistently raise your voice at the end of everything you say, communicating that you don't have much confidence in yourself. That may be one reason why you don't feel like others are taking you seriously."
- "It is your right to wear as many body and facial piercings as you want, but if you want to get a job in a traditional setting, you might want to rethink the image you project to prospective employers."
- "Next time you tell your daughter that you disagree with what she is doing with her life, you might want to do it in such a way that she doesn't feel so attacked by you."
- "You strike me as much stronger and more powerful than you give yourself credit for. There are times, like right now, when your passion and enthusiasm seem to take over."

What we attempt to do as part of our jobs is to look at our clients clearly and to tell them what we see. We do not offer this feedback as "the truth," as the way things really are, but rather as an informed, reasonably objective opinion. Certainly we have our own biases, but that is one reason why our own therapy and supervision are so important to help us remain clear-headed and objective.

The Best Feedback Is Specific

Useful feedback includes examples of what you are describing. When possible, it includes both supportive and constructive elements. Notice that we avoid using the words *positive* and *negative.* This is because what might be considered "negative" or criticism could be just the most useful thing that anyone could hear. Likewise, what might be labeled "positive," meaning a compliment, would feel good for about a minute but would actually offer very little to the person that is helpful in an enduring way. Ideally, feedback should include elements that cover both strengths and weaknesses: "I really appreciate your warm smile and giving nature. You are the first one to reach out to help others who may be in need. You also neglect yourself and don't do a very good job of taking care of what you need."

Feedback that is too general or abstract is not very useful because the person will not have a clear idea of what you are talking about. Because impressions like this are potentially threatening, people look for any excuse to devalue or ward off what they hear if it does not fit their own self-image. Your feedback will carry a lot more weight and power if it is accompanied by supporting examples:

> ### Exercise in Feedback
>
> With a partner, or in small groups, take turns giving each other feedback. First, write down each person's name. Next to the name, note several impressions of that person. Include something that you especially value and admire, as well as a few things that you think they might work on. Remember, you are not responsible for being "right," but merely offering your opinion of what you observe. Make the feedback as specific as possible, including an example of what you mean.
>
> Anyone who wishes to hear the feedback may volunteer. It is very important that nobody be forced to receive or give feedback if it is not desired.
>
> The person receiving the feedback is not allowed to respond until after everyone has finished. Then he or she may react by sharing what was most helpful.
>
> Talk about your reactions to this feedback exercise.

You don't seem to enjoy hearing anything about yourself that is positive in any way. It is almost as if you prefer to put yourself down, and have others do the same. Earlier when I tried to tell you that I liked what you said, you seemed very uncomfortable. You looked away, shuffled your feet, and laughed uneasily. It felt like you were giving me a clear message that this was definitely something you did not want to hear. I would not be inclined to tell you anything supportive like that again.

In this example, the person giving feedback supplies detailed data to support the impressions. This includes both behavioral descriptions (averted eye contact, shuffled feet, uneasy laughter) and personal disclosures (this pushed me away). As you might imagine, it is far more difficult for someone to ignore or negate feedback like this that comes with specific, supporting evidence.

It Is Easier to Digest Feedback That Is Concise and Clear

Be careful not to be too wordy when you give people feedback. The essence of your message may get lost. The experience of hearing feedback is pretty intense and emotional. Your heart is thumping in your chest. Your palms feel sweaty. After all, you are about to hear the naked truth about how others see you.

Imagine that you are sitting in the company of a therapist—an expert, a specialist in giving feedback. This person is well trained, well educated, very experienced, and licensed by the state to help people. Furthermore, this professional is a bit intimidating and seems very smart and knowledgeable. Now this therapist turns her attention toward you. She is about to tell you what she really thinks about you and what she observes about your behavior. Now, tell us you wouldn't be a little nervous.

Under such circumstances, whether in individual or group therapy, the recipient of the feedback is not concentrating as closely as you might like. That is one reason to record the feedback or have someone take notes so there is a summary of anything that's missed. This is also a reason to keep what you have to say as concise and focused as possible. If you go on too long, or try to cover too much ground, the essence of what you have to say will not be heard.

Rambling feedback: "I think you need to do a little more to get things going. I mean, you are trying and all, and I think that's good, but you have to do a little more. Do you know what I mean? Like, when you were saying last time that you want to get your grades up, you didn't really do much. You haven't done much so far. You said that your parents were putting a lot of pressure on you and that really bothered you. And you really need to ignore them and concentrate on what you want. That is, if you know what you want. And that's another thing: You should stop listening to what others say and listen to yourself more. That reminds me of one more thing . . ."

Concise feedback: "You have said several times that you want to improve your grades but I've noticed that you haven't followed through on what you claim is so important to you. You talk so much about what your parents say that I rarely hear what you really want."

Offer Feedback in a Sensitive and Caring Manner

The time and energy you spend offering feedback are wasted if the person can't or won't hear what you are saying. It is thus extremely important that you are careful, sensitive, and diplomatic in what and how you share. You may think that what you are saying is framed in words that are straightforward and honest, but the client may hear something quite different.

You don't want clients to wonder about your motives, believing for even a moment that you might be trying to hurt them. Like confrontation, feedback can be potentially hurtful if clients are not adequately prepared for it or are not able to process the input in constructive ways. In the following conversation, the therapist sets up the feedback carefully so the client can prepare himself to hear it.

Therapist: You say that you are confused about why it is so difficult for you to make friends. I wonder if you'd like to explore that further.

Client: What do you mean?

Therapist: Well, I've been in a relationship with you for the last few months. I've had the opportunity to know you and spend time talking with you about very personal things. Perhaps I could offer you some feedback on what I've observed.

Client: I guess so.

Therapist: You sound hesitant about this.

Client: I am, I guess. What did you have in mind?

Therapist: Again I sense that you are feeling uncomfortable and a little frightened about what I might say to you.

Client: No, not really.

Therapist: I think it is perfectly reasonable to be curious and a little apprehensive. After all, it isn't often that you have an opportunity to hear how you come across to others. And I think after all this time you know me well enough to realize that I will be very honest with you.

Client: Yeah, that's what I'm afraid of.

Therapist: Maybe, then, it would be best if we held off on this until you felt more open to hearing what I'd say.

Client: No, I think I can handle it. It's just . . .

Therapist: It's just that you want to make sure that I'll be gentle.

Client: Yeah, but I know you will.

Therapist: So you do trust me but you are still feeling a little nervous about this. Maybe we could take some time to talk about other times in your life when people have told you things that were difficult to hear and how you processed those experiences. That might give us some guidance as to the best way that we could proceed right now.

This therapist is being very cautious and deliberate in the way the feedback is set up. He senses that this could be a turning point in their work together, but he doesn't want to risk compromising the trust they have built between them by scaring the client away. He also knows that hearing this feedback is absolutely essential to the work they have yet to do, so he has no intention of backing off completely. He just wants to be as sure as he can that sufficient steps have been taken to prepare the client to be as receptive and open as possible.

Many students have complained that they don't want to hurt the client's feelings. They get defensive when we ask them to give constructive feedback or to offer feedback that might be construed as hurtful. This is the kind of feedback they often imagine: "Your irresponsible behavior seems to get you into a lot of trouble." If confrontation isn't your style, another way to frame feedback that can potentially be construed as negative is to reframe it using what is positive and negative about a particular quality. For instance, someone who is irresponsible can also be seen as spontaneous: "You really know how to have a good time, and I also see that your ability to have a good time can sometimes get you in trouble when you don't take care of your responsibilities." Notice how phrasing in this way compliments the client and shows how the extreme of spontaneity can also appear to be irresponsibility. Try this on your own.

Exercise in Reframing

Get into pairs and list qualities of former friends or partners (or maybe even current friends or partners) that irritate you. Have your partner reframe them in a way that is gentler. An example might be in the case of selfishness: "You seem to be really good at self-care and setting boundaries to get your needs met, and sometimes you may not be aware of how your actions are affecting your wife." You should be able to do this with virtually any negative quality. Try doing at least five each.

Silence

Silence is not something you might automatically think of as a technique or skill in any part of the therapeutic process. Yet silences are a large part of what we do. How you intervene depends very much on what the silence means. Is the client reflecting on things? If so, it might be best to wait things out. But what if the silence indicates confusion, or frustration, or anger, or withdrawal? In each case, you will have to sort out what is going on and then respond appropriately. The first step, however, is for you to become more comfortable tolerating silence.

Silence is used in all stages of therapy, and when used appropriately it can be one of your most powerful tools. There will be times when a client says something unexpected, or you state something that is profound. The client will look down and stare or have tears well up in her eyes, remaining perfectly still. You can see that he or she is really processing something. You may be tempted to respond while the client is reflecting on things. In fact, you might be eager to say something because, by now, you've had time to think of a good response. However, what you say is not likely to be as powerful as what the client may be thinking or experiencing. Keep quiet until the client makes eye contact again. This allows the client time and space to work out what's going on in thoughts or feelings, and can help build rapport. He or she will most likely tell you what was going on. If not, ask, "What was going on with you just now?"

There are times when silence is inappropriate. How will you know when? You'll know. When the client talks and then stops to look at you, it's your turn to talk but you may have nothing to say. This will inevitably happen to you. The ball is in your court, and you haven't a clue about how to return it. When all else fails, reflect.

Also, the client may be looking at you but processing information at the same time, possibly based on what was said last, or simply trying to read you in some way. The client is not waiting for you so much as doing internal work related to what just happened. The judgment call you have to make is based on the evidence available, which you use to try to assess whether the silence is productive, confusing, frustrating, or just a waste of time.

Kayleigh: The Sounds of Silence

It is a struggle for me to keep my mouth shut. When someone is telling me about a problem, I desperately want to help them and give advice or at least say something to show that I am listening. I've learned that when I do this, sometimes it comes across as me just wanting to talk too, and it also can cut them off in the middle of a thought. I have now seen how helpful silences can be. Silences do really make clients feel heard and respected because no one is talking over them or trying to relate themselves to the clients' experience. I have really become a big fan of silences.

Used with permission of Kayleigh Soto.

Self-Disclosure

This skill just might be the most challenging of all to use appropriately. It either can be used as a powerful impetus for encouraging clients to open up and take risks or can represent the ultimate in clinician self-indulgence.

You have had experiences in the past when teachers spend excessive amounts of time telling you stories about their lives and about the wonderful things they have done. In some cases, these stories might have been amusing or interesting anecdotes, perhaps even useful in illuminating a particular point. There have been other times, however, when such self-disclosures were a colossal waste of time. You sat there wondering to yourself, "Why are you telling me this? I don't really care."

There are, in fact, several reasons why you might want to use self-disclosure:

1. To bridge psychological distance between yourself and your client: "I remember feeling much the same way that you do when I was in high school."

2. To take yourself off the pedestal and make yourself appear more human: "I have also struggled with issues similar to this in my life."

3. To illustrate an example from your life of how you have successfully overcome similar problems that confront the client: "I found that what made the biggest difference was talking to close friends about my struggle as a way to recruit more support."

4. To demonstrate ways of dealing with difficult situations: "When I had a similar problem I found it helpful to stop trying so hard to make things happen."

5. To increase your stature and potential power in the client's eyes: "I have worked with similar situations many times before with great success."

6. To use immediacy to increase intimacy and trust: "After what you shared just now I am feeling closer to you than ever before."

7. To model appropriate ways of thinking, feeling, and behaving: "He made me angry . . . I mean, I made myself angry over what happened."

8. To demonstrate authenticity and genuineness in order to increase perceived attractiveness: "As I hear your story, I feel a deep sense of loss for you."

9. To remain culturally sensitive when working with ethnic groups who need to know you a little before feeling safe enough to disclose themselves.

Because self-disclosure takes the focus off the client and puts the attention on the therapist, it has certain detrimental side effects, especially for clients who are already insecure and used to deferring to others. Before you ever use the skill of disclosing yourself in session, you must be certain that there is no other way to accomplish the same goal. It is often helpful to ask yourself: How can I get this same point across without taking the attention off the client?

We don't mean to absolutely forbid the use of this valuable skill. We just wish to warn you that it can be abused by therapists who are overly self-centered and like to remain the center of attention. Using self-disclosure should not be used when working with clients who would redirect the focus off themselves and on to you to avoid something difficult or with clients who have poor boundaries.

Teaching Tales

A particular kind of self-disclosure involves the sharing of stories from your life that are designed to emphasize or illuminate some crucial lesson. These could be brief heroic stories in which you have overcome some challenge. They could also include examples from your life that illustrate some important point.

Here are some brief examples of our favorite personal stories that we often employ in our work to inspire or instruct clients, students, or supervisees.

- Failure [Jeffrey]: "For the longest time, I thought I was the only therapist who ever screwed up in sessions. Few of my teachers and supervisors would ever talk about their mistakes so I got the impression that if I didn't know what I was doing (which is my experience of doing therapy some of the time), I was incompetent. I have since learned that all of us are pretending to know a lot more than we really do."
- Belonging [Leah]: "After completing my undergrad in psychology, I needed a break before continuing to grad school to become a therapist. I worked in several jobs and found that I was miserable in each one. I was bored, unchallenged, and I wasn't able to connect with others. I thought I must have been depressed or something. I was afraid I was incapable of happiness. When I finally returned to school, I found that I felt a real sense of belonging there. The work was interesting and fun. What a relief. I wasn't depressed; I was just in the wrong job."
- Redefining self [Jeffrey]: "I was a mediocre student in school and was told by almost everyone that I would be lucky to graduate from college. Then one day I decided that I wanted to be smart. I started watching people on campus who I thought were smart and I realized that what separated them from me was that they walked around carrying books. And they read them. So I started doing the same thing. And pretty soon everyone started treating me as if I was smart. Then I started to believe it myself."
- Being supportive [Leah]: "I always liked being helpful to others. So when they told me life was bad, I told them it would get better. If they told me they couldn't do it, I told them they could. What I later learned was that I was not being supportive, but rather invalidating their feelings. Once I learned the skill of reflecting feelings and content, I found nothing could be more supportive than that."

We've got dozens, perhaps hundreds, of such stories that we've collected over the years and kept in our inventories. They are all intended to promote insight by offering our own experiences as teaching points. Interestingly, we have found that sharing personal stories about our mistakes, failures, and confusion is more helpful to students (and readers) than heroic tales about some spectacular breakthrough.

Exercise in Constructing an Inventory of Teaching Tales

On your own, or in small groups, list some of your life experiences that might be used to illustrate key points in therapy. You can think in terms of the categories mentioned by the authors, as well as generate illustrations for several other areas that might arise.

WHAT HAPPENS NEXT?

Some clients come for therapy primarily because they are in search of some deeper level of self-awareness or understanding. Although it is rare in today's climate of managed care, there will even be some cases in which the client is not necessarily interested in changing anything as much as in understanding what is going on. Some approaches, such as psychoanalytic and existential therapy, are particularly well suited for this type of work.

DIAGNOSTIC CHECKLIST

Here are some questions you might consider for checking how things are going with your client when you begin to promote insight:

- What is the cultural context for the client's experience?
- What parts of this issue may be connected to normal developmental growth?
- What is going on in this relationship that parallels other conflicted encounters that are taking place in the client's life?
- How am I feeling about this client that might inform me about how others react?
- What is the client doing that is getting in the way of my knowing, understanding, or becoming close to him or her?
- How are the life themes and current difficulties in the client's life being played out during our encounters?
- In what ways is the client's established pattern limiting?
- What recurrent issues between us might represent dysfunctional or fully functioning behavior on the part of the client?
- What interactional role and relationship position does the client take in the therapeutic relationship?
- What interactional therapist role is the client evoking?

The vast majority of your cases will consist of people who not only want to make significant changes in the ways they think and feel and behave, but desperately need to do so. Some will be referred by the courts; unless they stop their destructive behaviors, they will end up in prison. Some people will come to you with their marriages falling apart or on the verge of losing their jobs. Some will be addicted to drugs, prescription medications, or alcohol; they will need to change before they spin out of control. Some will be so depressed or anxious that they are on the verge of giving up altogether and killing themselves. Some children might behave in physically violent ways that could lead to expulsion and other long-term problems. In all these cases, it is not nearly enough to just help them to understand how they got themselves in these predicaments. You must help them to change the usual ways that they take care of business. In order to do that, you are going to have to help them make the challenging transition from understanding what might be going on to doing something about it. It is an understatement to say that is a difficult job.

PITFALLS AND COMMON MISTAKES

As we have done in previous chapters, we now introduce some common mistakes made by beginning therapists that are associated with the skills of facilitating insight. Some pitfalls that occur during this stage in the process will also be mentioned.

Forgetting to Use the Skill of Reflection

Even the best of therapists make this mistake from time to time. You have established the relationship with your client. You have seen your client for several sessions now, and she seems to trust you. You begin to feel like you are doing some work. You confront. You interpret. You give feedback. You use silence. You dispute distorted beliefs. You ask stimulating questions. But you're forgetting something. What is it? Reflecting! It is vitally important throughout the therapeutic process that you reflect content and feelings. We even teach our students that before you ask a question, reflect what the client said, and then follow with the question. Clients need to be heard, understood, and to hear what they are saying at all stages of the therapy. The relationship always needs to be fostered and tended to. As the process advances, this is the one area that some students completely forget. When you test the relationship with confrontations and honest feedback, you must also nurture it with empathy. Most important, nurture the relationship with feeling reflections. This type of response can elicit a powerful reaction in your client at later stages of therapy. Furthermore, reflecting feelings and demonstrating accurate empathy—simply stating their feelings out loud—can facilitate clients' insight. Hearing themselves often results in insight.

Following Your Own Agenda

Client: I really don't like to go to this church. It's too big and impersonal.

Therapist: You say you don't like it but you attend each week. [Confrontation]

Client: I attend because my religious views are important to me.

Therapist: But you just said you don't like this church. [Confrontation]

Client: I don't.

Therapist: And yet you go because it's important to you. [Still confronting]

Client: Yes.

Therapist: So why don't you go to a different church? [Question]

Client: Because this one is close to home, and I hate driving.

Therapist: You would rather be unhappy at this church than be unhappy driving. [Confrontation; reflection of content]

In this example, the therapist just couldn't seem to be able to gain any depth. He is so tied to keeping to his agenda that he can't seem to find a different way to approach the subject. He's not evidencing much empathy for the client's experience, either. Sometimes when we think we're on to something, we get excited and try to lead the client with too many confrontations and questions. As a result, the client gets defensive and more determined than ever to hold his or her position.

If you sense your client is getting defensive, take a look at what you are doing. Do you have an agenda? Are you asking a lot of questions? Are you confronting a lot? Are you forgetting to be empathic? If so, slow down and reflect the client's feelings. A better dialogue might go something like this:

Client: I really don't like to go to this church. It's too big and impersonal.

Therapist: You say you don't like it but you attend each week. [Confrontation]

Client: I attend because my religious views are important to me.

Therapist: You value the experience of going to church, but you wish this church was smaller and more personal. [Reflection of content]

Client: Exactly.

Therapist: Tell me more about your feelings of the church being too big and impersonal. [Directing client]

In this second example, the therapist has slowed down enough to understand the problem instead of leading the client into a personally imposed agenda. He is showing empathy and understanding so the client feels safe enough to explore deeper.

There will be times when you get excited and find yourself directing the session. Don't be too hard on yourself. It happens to the best of us. Just ask yourself why you have the need to control the session, to lead the client in your own direction. Once you answer that question, you will find that you stop following your own agenda and follow your client's instead.

Interpreting Too Much

As mentioned previously, we recommend that interpretation be used with discretion. If you find yourself working hard to make connections, or the interpretations you're giving your client are consistently off the mark, then you are interpreting too much. You could be way ahead of your client. Your client may not be ready for what you are presenting. Or you could be wrong because of your own projections. Remember, the client should do the majority of the work, not the therapist.

Another consequence of interpreting too much is that you could foster a dependency in the client, who learns to look to an authority figure to solve problems. In contrast, if the client solves the problem herself, she has added a skill she can use for the rest of her life while building self-esteem. A double bonus! In addition, the realization will be at a pace that is appropriate for the client to receive it. Obviously.

Finally, if your client has weak boundaries and likes to please others, your interpretations will mean nothing. He or she will agree with everything you say but not seem to make any progress. Your interpretation is like a false insight. It's worthless. With clients who seem to accept everything you say as truth, who are uncomfortable with disagreeing, or who want to please you too much, don't interpret at all. Let the clients do the work. You can lead them with some thought-provoking questions, but don't be overeager to give away too much information.

We believe that interpretation for some of you will be very tempting. You may have a need to share information to give you a sense of belonging or importance. If this is the case, you may find yourself getting way ahead of your client all the time. It can take years to learn how to slow down and trust that the client can do it at his or her own pace, and that the client's pace, not yours, is the right pace.

Interpreting Too Quickly

Sometimes we might feel so anxious or impatient that we would be inclined to jump in with some opinion or insight before the client is ready to hear it. In other cases, we interrupt the client in the middle of a story and see an annoyed look, as if to say, "Back off. I'm not done yet." It is important to remember that although our feedback, interpretations, and input are certainly an important part of the therapeutic process, so is allowing clients to tell their stories.

Therapist: I've really thought about your family history you shared last week in our first session. You've said your primary purpose for coming to therapy is to help you find a meaningful relationship with a man who is loving instead of someone who is charming, but self-serving. It sounds to me like your previous relationship was with a man who resembled your father in many ways. You don't seem to have a good male role model to know how to pick a good man. [Self-disclosure; Reflection of content; Interpretation]

Client: Hm. . . . Maybe you're right, but my father left us when I was two years old and hasn't really been a part of my life. My stepfather took over when I was five years old, and he was very loving and attentive.

Some beginners are so eager to offer immediate help that they introduce interpretations too quickly; it's no surprise that they would often miss the mark. This can often happen with new clients and can be especially problematic because faulty conclusions might decrease credibility before the therapeutic relationship is well established. Instead, if you take a few sessions to fully explore the client's stories and worldview first, you will be gifted with a more complete picture of the client's life while also strengthening the relationship. Consequently, you'll be in a better position to make more accurate and useful interpretations.

Teaching Your Client Too Much

Therapist: Now that we're finished with the paperwork, tell me what brought you here today.

Client: I heard you could help me lose weight. I've tried every diet. I exercise. I try to eat healthy, but I know I could do better. I'm sick of being tired all the time. I want to feel healthier, live longer, and yet I seem compelled to eat more than I should. Can you help me?

Therapist: There may be several reasons why you struggle. First, dieting is not healthy. Each time you cut your calories or deprive yourself in some way, your metabolism slows down. Then the next time you eat, your body is prepared to starve again and stores everything you eat. So the first thing we need to do is have you eating every three hours. In addition, many people don't know how much they eat. They don't pay attention and think they eat much healthier than they actually do. So, I'd like you to keep a food diary so we can discover your weaknesses. In addition, many people eat for emotional reasons. They don't listen to their bodies and eat out of boredom, depression, or anxiety. Furthermore, many people are in the habit of eating everything on their plates. They don't eat mindfully. They don't enjoy the taste of their food as they watch TV, and they don't know when to stop. Eating too quickly is also a problem because it takes some time for the mechanism in your body to process that you have eaten enough. So, I'd also like you to write down the time you started and stopped eating, what you ate, how you felt, and what you were doing while you were eating. Other contributing problems are . . .

So what is the problem with teaching clients too much? Well, when you teach, you may not be doing therapy. They are two very different roles. Let's articulate this as clearly as possible. When you teach, your job is to provide information as an expert on some subject matter to the person you are teaching. When you do therapy, you are guiding the client to find his or her own answers, not giving the client yours. When you teach, you assume that there is a correct, objective solution to a problem. With therapy, however, there's no such thing as *correct* or *objective*. Therapy is a process of discovery. So although you may need to educate your clients on occasion, as with the couple with sexual problems described above, teaching is not your primary role.

Inappropriate Use of Self-Disclosure

Client: I'm really nervous about starting graduate school. I never thought I was smart enough to get in.

Therapist: I remember when I started graduate school. It was scary for me, too, but in time I realized I belonged.

In this vignette, the therapist self-disclosed with the client to try to ease the client's anxiety, or maybe to make herself seem more human. However, a response like this can frequently have negative effects on the client. The client may not feel heard or understood. He or she may feel patronized or invalidated. Using a self-disclosure in this type of situation was inappropriate. In addition, the therapist shifted the focus off the client. Although you may feel the need to self-disclose similar situations to your client to bridge the psychological distance between you, to make yourself seem more human, or to demonstrate a way to deal with a problem successfully, you risk minimizing the client's experience. You risk invalidating the client's experience. You risk making it about you. The client in the preceding scenario could easily respond with, "Really? How long did it take you to feel like you were in the right place?" Now the focus is on the therapist. How is that helpful to the client? It's not.

So when and how do you use self-disclosure? You use it cautiously, infrequently, and after you have established a relationship with your client so that the client knows this isn't a pattern for you, to talk about yourself. The best time to self-disclose, though, is when you use the technique of immediacy. For example, if a client is having difficulty with relationships, and you experience your client as abrasive, then when the time is right, give your client the feedback as demonstrated in the feedback section of this chapter. But in all cases, you must first develop a strong relationship with your clients so they know your meeting with them will not be about you—that it will be about them.

APPLICATIONS TO SELF: YOU'RE ALREADY DOING THIS STUFF

Most people, at one time or another, feel the need to find meaning in what's happening at a given moment in their lives. It could be trying to understand something as difficult and infrequent as the death of a young family member. It could be something as familiar as trying to understand how what they are learning in a particular class is relevant to their life. So searching for meaning and consequently seeking insight are natural parts of what people do.

You may think that the skills associated with seeking insight are new (or you might not), but they are things we do naturally in our everyday conversations. The only difference here is that we are articulating each type of response, each intention of what is said with a client. When you talk with a friend, words usually flow (at least we hope they do, because you want to talk for a living). You will find that when you talk with a client, at least at first, words will not flow. You might experience awkward silences, stumble, fumble, and sound much less competent than you actually are. Why? Because now, as a therapist, you understand the power of words. How you phrase something and the words you choose impose some sort of meaning, facilitate a certain type of response from the other person. Now, as a therapist, you must choose your words carefully. In an instant, you must read the verbal and nonverbal behaviors of your client, interpret them, connect them with previous discussions, translate them into your own words, decide what direction you want to take, and then finally, still in the same instant, respond appropriately. Scared? Well, that's understandable. But you already do this to some extent, unconsciously, right now. We hope in this class you will be more conscious of what you say, when you say it, why you say it, and how you say it. We assume that you have the potential to learn all this or you wouldn't have been accepted into your program. Have patience with yourself.

You're already doing this stuff, you just aren't aware of it; you're not doing it mindfully. Let's look at each skill, again, here. Confrontation: Tell me you haven't confronted someone, ever. We didn't think you could. Surely you have been confused about mixed messages from someone. "I thought you said to meet you after lunch, not before." Or perhaps you have received bad service somewhere and complained. "I asked for my meat to be cooked well-done and this is rare." These are confrontations. What makes it different in therapy is that you have to time it appropriately and word it in a way that the client can hear it. That's the skill aspect that you need to learn.

Let's take the next one. Disputing beliefs: We're going to guess that you came to this field with a certain level of psychological mindedness. You have probably been exposed to the challenging of beliefs, whether from books or your own therapy. Sometimes you hold a certain unrealistic belief; sometimes you use language imprecisely. In either case, at some point you must have been told or told someone else that, for example, "never" and "always" are unlikely situations. We listed several of these in the chapter. Pay attention to what people say, the words they choose. If you already do this at home, it will come more easily to you as a therapist. Practicing on yourself or at home with others will make distorted beliefs sound like a loud bell in your head. In fact, if you do this enough, you'll have a hard time not confronting this type of language, even in your own head.

Next is interpretation. Now, we know you've done this one. You don't think so? Well, how many times has a friend talked about a problem with another person, and you told your friend why she said what she said, or why the other person did what he did. "I know you didn't mean it when you said you didn't love him." "When he told you what to do, he was not trying to be controlling. He was trying to be helpful." That's your interpretation. See, you are doing it. It's simply a matter of applying meaning to a situation. You probably do this every day. The difference here, again, is that as a therapist you have a greater responsibility to your client because you are in a position of power, because you are perceived as an expert. You therefore want to be cautious in making these interpretations and more mindful of when to use them.

Providing information was the next skill presented. If you have ever been a teacher or a supervisor, you couldn't escape using this skill: "You will be expected to arrive at work at 8:00 a.m." If you have a child, you do this all the time: "Don't touch the stove; it's hot." So, how is this different with your clients? You provide information for clients only when what you want to accomplish can't be done in another way. You are not your clients' teacher, you are their therapist. You want to facilitate their ability to find their own answers. In some circumstances, however, you will need to stop and teach them something. You already know how to do this, it's just *when* to do it that's new.

So far so good? You've done all the above, and we're guessing you have given feedback to someone before, too: "Does this make me look fat?" I wonder if there is a single person who hasn't had to answer that question, even if they ask it of themselves. No matter how you responded, you were giving feedback. Since you probably give feedback of some sort all the time, what makes it different in therapy? Honesty and tact. Face it. We're not always honest with our feedback. "No, that looks good on you." But as a therapist, you will need to learn this most difficult skill, and we say difficult only because being both honest and tactful can be hard. "That dress doesn't flatter you in the best way possible, but perhaps this other dress will accentuate the best attributes of your figure." Start practicing this at home, if you dare . . .

And now for some silence. . . . This skill is probably used much less frequently than the other skills presented in this chapter. Many of us feel uncomfortable with silence. Many people need to fill the space with talking or the television or with music. Even when we are silent on the outside, our minds are full of conversations. "Oh, no! I forgot to lock the door. That reminds me, I need to have the door fixed on the car. I need to call the insurance company. I wonder if my insurance will go up. I can't afford more bills. Oh, the bills. I need to pay bills today . . ." The conversation in your head can be endless. However, you probably have experienced silence, even in your own head. Think about times when you felt dead tired, and you just stared into space. While this may happen at times, it's not something we do easily in a dyad or group. You can practice this one at home, too. Try just sitting quietly for 5 minutes without any noise or distractions. Then once that seems tolerable, try it with a friend. Then when that seems tolerable, try it in the car with a friend. As you get more comfortable with it at home, you'll get more comfortable with it as a therapist.

Finally, we get to self-disclosure. This can be done in several ways. You have probably joined with a person by saying, "I had a similar experience . . ." or been genuine about your experience: "I didn't think the restaurant provided us with good food or good service." Any time you talk about yourself, you are self-disclosing. In spite of being redundant, we'll say it again: You have been using this skill in your everyday life, but as a therapist you will do it very differently. In your private life, when you self-disclose, you do so for you, to talk about yourself. As a therapist, you self-disclose only when it is helpful to your client. So, you'll have to think before you disclose to be sure you are speaking for the client's benefit, not your own.

There they are: seven skills. You have used each and every one of them. The only difference is that, as a therapist, you will use them in conscious ways to facilitate the growth of your client. We hope you are beginning to see that you already have these skills, you merely need to refine them and know when to use them as a therapist.

SUMMARY

In this chapter, we introduced some ideas about insight and whether it is necessary and/or sufficient for effective therapy. Some skills and techniques were presented to facilitate insight, although they can be used during any part of the therapeutic process. The skills included confrontation, disputing, interpreting, providing information, giving feedback, silence, and self-disclosure. The next chapter continues with more skills, ones that are more often used to facilitate the action phase of therapy.

Skills in Action: Unexplained Anxiety

Client: I'm still feeling really stressed this week. I'm just so overwhelmed with work and with school. I don't know. I used to be able to handle it, but now I just can't seem to. You know, like we talked about last week. I'm still sleeping poorly, so I'm tired all day long. I'm not hungry. I feel jittery without drinking any coffee. I have this weird thing lately, that I get butterflies in my stomach a lot, like I'm about to take an exam or something. I can't seem to do anything about it!

Therapist: You're feeling out of control, and you're worried that it won't stop. Tell me more about feeling those butterflies. [Reflection of feeling; invitation to talk more]

Client: I know this sounds really strange, but every time some strange guy walks my way, I get that bad feeling. If it's someone I know, I'm fine. If it's a strange woman, I'm fine. It's just men who I don't know. Isn't that weird? I must be crazy.

Therapist: I don't perceive you as crazy. Instead, you're feeling confused about this. Let's see if we can solve the mystery. Think back to when this started, when you first remember feeling this anxiety.

	What happened around that time? [Disputing beliefs; reflecting feelings; questioning]
Client:	Nothing. I guess it started about six months ago, maybe seven.
Therapist:	Okay, so you recall feeling this in August, when the semester started. Think about any usual events that might have happened in July or early August. [Questioning]
Client:	I can't really think of anything. Oh, well, I guess there was this one little thing. My roommate and I were robbed. Some dude knocked on the door, and when I opened it, he forced his way in. But that's it really.
Therapist:	You seem to believe this isn't a big deal. [Reflection of content]
Client:	Yeah. So?
Therapist:	You're minimizing what happened. I'm struck by that. Tell me more about what happened that day. [Confrontation; self-disclosure; invitation to talk more]
Client:	Okay. Um, well, as I said, he broke into the house and pushed me down. He was holding a knife and threatened to hurt us if we moved. He went through all of our drawers and stole our jewelry, took our purses without even looking in them, and a few other items. He pushed us around and said that if we reported him, he'd come back and make sure we couldn't report anything again. Then he left. It couldn't have lasted more than ten minutes.
Therapist:	You don't sound distressed about it at all, as if you are describing what happened to someone else. I think I would be really frightened if that happened to me. [Reflection of feeling; giving feedback; self-disclosure]
Client:	Well, I grew up in a bad neighborhood. I was scared, but you know, it wasn't the first time. I mean, when I was a kid, we had been robbed a few times, but not while we were at home. That was the freaky part.
Therapist:	I'd like to consider the possibility that maybe you feel scared now because of what happened then. I could be wrong, but the timing seems to fit. [Confrontation; interpreting]
Client:	(silence for twenty seconds as the client looks down) Yeah. I guess you're right. [Allowing for silence without interruption; client looks at therapist]

Therapist: You seem sad now. [Reflection of feelings]

Client: I guess I feel like I just got the wind knocked out of me.

Therapist: You're surprised. What you may be experiencing is called posttraumatic stress disorder. Have you ever heard of it? [Providing information; questioning]

Client: Yeah, but can you tell me what that is?

Therapist: When people experience an intense negative emotional experience, they often have symptoms like you describe. It's as if your body is preparing itself for another attack by keeping you hypervigilant so you can't sleep well or relax. [Providing information]

Client: But I don't think it will happen again. We moved to a new neighborhood where I tell myself I am safe. But the symptoms still won't go away.

Therapist: You tell yourself you're safe, but a part of you doesn't believe it. We can work on stopping the symptoms, but for the moment, at least you know what this is. (thoughtful pause) Something just occurred to me. You said you grew up in a neighborhood that was bad. What do you mean by that? [Confrontation; questioning]

Client: We had gangs and stuff. Sometimes we'd hear gunshots. I guess you get used to it.

Therapist: I'm not sure that you can get used to it, although you may learn to live with it. I'm wondering if this recent experience is somehow connected to a previous experience. [Providing information; interpretation]

Client: Hm. Maybe. (silence for a few seconds) Well there was this one time that I was in the middle of gunfire, but I didn't get hit or anything.

Therapist: It sounds like you might have been exposed to a lot of violence all your life, and now, finally on your own away from home, you're feeling more vulnerable in general. This robbery pushed you over the edge. I think that maybe the robbery experience is complicated by the lack of safety you've always felt. [Interpretation]

Client: Yes! I have never felt safe!

Therapist: The robbery only confirmed your belief that the world may not be a safe place. [Reflection of content; interpretation]

Client: Yes! That's exactly it! If I'm not safe at home or at school, then there must not be any safe place in the world.

Therapist: You're constantly on guard in anticipation of something bad happening. You can't imagine life without some level of fear. [Reflecting feelings]

Client: Right. I never thought about it that way, but it's true.

Therapist: You seem relieved that this theory fits for you. [Reflecting feelings]

Client: I do. Now what?

Therapist: Now we begin to work on helping you explore this issue of safety, or the lack of it that you feel. It will be a good place to pick up next week.

Client: Okay. Thank you!

Therapist: Thank you.

REFERENCES AND RESOURCES

Adler, A. (1963). *The practice and theory of individual psychology.* Paterson, NJ: Littlefield Adams.

Audet, C. T. (2011). Client perspectives of therapist self-disclosure: Violating boundaries or removing barriers? *Counselling Psychology Quarterly, 24*(2), 85–100.

Barnett, J. E. (2011). Psychotherapist self-disclosure: Ethical and clinical considerations. *Psychotherapy, 48*(4), 315–321.

Beck, A. (1976). *Cognitive therapy and the emotional disorders.* New York, NY: International Universities Press.

Beck, J. (2011). *Cognitive behavior therapy: Basics and beyond* (2nd ed.). New York, NY: Guilford Press.

Carlson, J., Watts, R. E., & Maniacci, M. (2006). *Adlerian therapy: Theory and practice.* Washington, DC: American Psychological Association.

Dryden, W., & Neenan, M. (2014). *Rational emotive behavior therapy: 100 key points and techniques* (2nd ed.). New York, NY: Routledge.

Ellis, A. (1973). *Humanistic psychotherapy: The rational-emotive approach.* New York, NY: McGraw-Hill.

Ellis, A. (2015). *Better, deeper, and more enduring brief therapy: The rational emotive behavior therapy approach.* New York, NY: Routledge.

Evans, D. R., Heart, M. T., Uhlemann, M. R., & Ivey, A. E. (2010). *Essential interviewing: A programmed approach to effective communication* (8th ed.). Pacific Grove, CA: Brooks/Cole.

Freud, A. (1936). *The ego and mechanisms of defense.* New York, NY: International University Press.

Glasser, W. (1965). *Reality therapy: A new approach to psychiatry.* New York, NY: Harper & Row.

Jung, C. (1980). The Tavistock lectures. In *Symbolic life: Miscellaneous writings. Collected Works* (Vol. 18, pp. 1–182). Princeton, NJ: Princeton University Press. (Original work published 1935)

Lazarus, A. A. (1973). Multimodal behavior therapy: Treating the BASIC I.D. *Journal of Nervous and Mental Disease, 156,* 404–411.

Marzaleck, J., & Myers, J. (2006). Dream interpretation: A developmental counseling and theory approach. *Journal of Mental Health Counseling, 28*(1), 18–37.

Meichenbaum, D. (1977). *Cognitive behavior modification.* New York, NY: Plenum Press.

Nordahl, H. M., & Wells, A. (2016). *Changing beliefs in cognitive therapy: A therapist's guide.* Hoboken, NJ: Blackwell.

Perls, F. (1969). *Gestalt therapy verbatim.* Moab, UT: Real People Press.

Rogers, C. (1951). *Client-centered therapy: Its current practice, implications and theory.* Boston, MA: Houghton Mifflin.

Rosen, S. (Ed.). (1991). *My voice will go with you: The teaching tales of Milton H. Erickson.* New York, NY: W. W. Norton.

Watzlawick, P., Ray, W. A., & Nardone, G. (2009). *Insight may cause blindness and other essays.* Phoenix, AZ: Zeig, Tucker & Theisen.

Yalom, I. D. (2000). *Momma and the meaning of life: Tales of psychotherapy.* New York, NY: HarperCollins.

Ziv-Beiman, S. (2013). Therapist self-disclosure as an integrative intervention. *Journal of Psychotherapy Integration, 23*(1), 59–74.

Chapter 8

FACILITATING ACTION

Not all clients are ready for or are interested in insight; the same can also be true of taking action. You may reach a point in the helping relationship where the client's increased awareness of self-understanding takes a period of time to percolate. There is a period of indwelling, or reflection, of taking stock to process what was learned. The client, at this point, may elect to stop the sessions for a while and then return later. If the degree and depth of insight generated are more than the person can comfortably handle, he or she may decide to stop treatment altogether. This does not mean, by the way, that progress ceases; on the contrary, clients accomplish some of their most important work on their own.

There are some realities of contemporary practice that you must also face. Even if your client is not yet ready to take decisive action, you will still be asked by your supervisors, agency administrators, and other third parties to demonstrate the effectiveness of your treatments as measured by client progress. This movement toward evidence-based practice emphasizes research-informed interventions, greater accountability, and measuring the outcomes of what you do. Obviously, these tasks are much easier to accomplish if there is some measurable, discernable action taking place in the client's life.

TRANSITION FROM INSIGHT TO ACTION

It will be appropriate and useful to spend some time helping most of your clients to convert their new understandings into some constructive action. This may start with a few important questions.

Therapist: So what?

Client: Excuse me?

Therapist: Now that you understand that the reason you've had so much trouble committing yourself to a long-term relationship is your fear of rejection, what are you going to do about it?

Client: What do you mean?

Therapist: I'm asking you what you intend to do to put what you've learned into action. What are you going to do now that you understand what is going on?

This client is being challenged to examine the implications of his new self-knowledge. The work can very well stop at this point, but it is highly unlikely that entrenched, chronic patterns of interpersonal behavior would be altered by a single new awareness alone. After all, lots and lots of people understand that certain things are bad for them but they keep doing them anyway. And many clients may have attained some clarity about what is wrong, and even how to fix it, but they still persist in self-defeating behaviors. This is not simply because they may be lazy or afraid, but sometimes it's because they just don't know how to convert what they've learned into action. It is your job to help them make this transition.

Exercise in Not Being Ready

In small groups, talk together about times in your life when you have realized that you needed to do something but you weren't ready to take action (perhaps such a process is going on within you right now). What did it take for you to move to the next level and follow through on what you knew you needed to do but were reluctant to do?

Exercise in Taking a Risk at Home

We all like to do what's comfortable and predictable. When you go to a restaurant, you probably order the same dishes every time. In order to understand how scary taking a risk can be, go to a really good restaurant and don't choose what you want to eat. Tell the server you will have whatever the chef recommends and to make it a surprise. Of course, if you have a small limitation (i.e., no fish), that's fine, but choose a restaurant where you will have few, if any, limitations. If that seems too scary to you, go to the movie theater without checking to see what is playing or when it is playing. Just decide to go at a certain time, drive there, and see the next movie that is on, especially if you have never heard of it. If you are too familiar with movies, see a foreign film. When you get back to class, process with the other students what that was like.

DEALING WITH RESISTANCE

We give you fair notice that the transition to action is not necessarily smooth and effortless. Clients don't just respond to our urgings for action by saying, "Okay, what should I do? Let's get going!" Even if they do say that, they probably don't mean it. And even if they do mean it (at the time), that doesn't imply that they have the skills and sustained motivation to put their desires into action.

The Gestalt paradigm suggests that all clients are resistant—that overcoming resistance is the purpose of therapy (Perls, 1969). If there is no resistance, there is no need for therapy. So, resistance is both natural and normal. Helping clients explore and, hopefully, overcome resistance is the therapist's job. Furthermore, it is one of the major challenges in doing any kind of therapy.

A case could be made that there really are no resistant, difficult clients, only difficult therapists (Kottler, 1992; Kottler & Carlson, 2002). In other words, most clients are doing the best they can to be cooperative under very threatening circumstances; it's just that the ways they are choosing to cooperate are different from what the therapist expects and prefers.

The very first thing that beginning clinicians (and many experienced ones) do when the results are not positive is blame the client for being resistant and ornery. We often call them names and assign them scary-sounding diagnoses (especially "borderline") as a way to explain their obstructive behavior. Most of the time, though, these individuals really are trying to work with us in the only

Table 8.1   Forms of Client Resistance

Withholding Communication	*Restricting Content*
Being silent	Making small talk
Making infrequent responses	Intellectualizing
Making minimal responses	Asking rhetorical questions
Engaging in rambling	Digressing
Being Manipulative	*Violating Rules*
Discounting	Missing appointments
Being seductive	Delaying payment
Externalizing	Making improper requests
Forgetting	Displaying inappropriate conduct

ways they know how. Granted, we may find these "cooperative" behaviors coun-terproductive and annoying, but they nevertheless represent the person's best efforts at the time.

This is not to say that clients do not engage in behavior that obstructs the pro-gress of therapy, because they do (see Table 8.1). They do this for several reasons: because they don't know better, because it keeps you from getting too close, because it slows the pace of progress down to manageable levels, because they feel empowered, because they aren't ready, and so on.

When dealing with any form of resistance, the first thing to realize is that clients are not doing this to make your life miserable. This is seldom about you, or even what you are doing or not doing. In fact, if the problem was easy to solve, the cli-ent would not need to come to therapy in the first place. The very nature of need-ing therapy for help with a situation means that the issue is complicated and the client lacks some sort of awareness about the problem and/or how to solve it.

It is crucial to identify the source of the resistance. Look in several areas, such as the quality of your relationship and the trust level established; a weak therapeu-tic relationship tends to inhibit the client's ability to be open and vulnerable. Consider the "secondary gains" the person may be enjoying. These are the benefits that result from remaining stuck, such as the power the person may feel from destroying things on his or her own terms or that the fear of the unknown involved in change is scarier than remaining the same. There is a certain amount of comfort in staying with what you know. Clients may need to mourn a loss, heal a wound, or to forgive themselves or others. Remember, as well, to consider the pace of progress—you may be moving faster than the client can handle.

When facing resistance in any form, you have a number of options that include some of the following:

1. Stop doing what isn't working and try something else. You may be pushing too hard or the client might not be ready.

2. Don't overpersonalize what is happening, but accept responsibility for your share of the conflict.

3. Demonstrate greater flexibility in your methods.

4. Make the resistance the topic of therapy rather than trying to work around it.

Sometimes there are very good reasons why clients resist your efforts to push them toward action. Maybe they aren't ready to go where you are guiding them. Pay attention to the signals they are giving you; unless you honor their pace and needs, you will find yourself leading way out in front. Alone.

Table 8.2   A Few Models for Promoting Action

Theoretical Framework	Skill Employed	Example
Cognitive-behavioral	Assigning homework	"Create a schedule of how you could do your homework each week to prevent procrastinating."
Behaviorism	Setting goals	"What is the first step you can take in learning to assert yourself?"
Behaviorism	Reinforcement	"You feel really good about asserting yourself last week."
Psychodrama	Relaxation	"Take a deep breath, and close your eyes right now. Tell me where you are holding tension."
Gestalt	Role-playing	"Talk to me as if I were your mother. What would you say to her now?"
Gestalt	Working with the resistance	"You are afraid you will lose control if you allow yourself to be angry. Keep holding in your anger to be safe and tell me more about losing control."
Individual psychology	Acting "as if"	"When you go to that meeting next week, act as if you are confident."
Psychoanalytic	Transference	"You are very frustrated with me, as you have been with your father, for confronting you about being constantly late."

Now that you have in mind the reality of resistance, we would like to introduce some techniques that are helpful in the action phase of the therapeutic process. Table 8.2 presents a few of the techniques, as well as the theoretical orientations from which they come. As in previous chapters, the skills here can be used throughout therapy even though these skills are more advanced than some of the others previously mentioned. For instance, in a Gestalt approach most practitioners don't see resistance as needing to be overcome but rather as an opportunity to look at something more deeply and to work with it as an ally.

You may feel overwhelmed at the idea of learning even more skills when you have already been introduced to so many, but our goal is to expose you to some of the techniques you can master while seeing clients. The goal of this text is to help you learn how to perform a good intake, become proficient at providing empathy through the use of reflections, and (probably from this chapter) learn how to set good goals with your clients. All of the other skills will develop at their own pace, in your own time. Be patient with yourself. As we said before, learning the skills to become an effective therapist is not as easy as people may think.

THE MIRACLE QUESTION

As a precursor to transition from insight to action, many therapists help clients to visualize a time in the future when they are no longer struggling with their symptoms. This helps not only to set goals, but also to plant the seeds for a positive outcome. One such strategy is called *the miracle question,* so named because it asks clients to imagine a miracle occurring: "If you could change anything about your life, how would your life be different from the way it is now?"

Another variation might be posed as follows: "Imagine that a miracle occurred. Picture a time in the future in which you no longer have the problems you are facing today. Let me know when you can picture that by nodding your head."

The client sits silently for a minute or two, brow furrowed, obviously concentrating hard, then nods head.

"Good. Now, take a guess and tell me how you managed to make the problem go away."

This strategy was first posed by the individual psychology theorist Alfred Adler, made popular by master hypnotist Milton Erikson, and later integrated into solution focused therapy by Steve de Shazer and others. The purpose is to get the client to think about the future and what might be ideal before shifting that hope or desire into a workable goal. This question asks the client to explore what she wants so that both the therapist and the client can move forward in a way that fits best with the client's hope. Another advantage of this strategy is that clients often supply the keys to their own problems when they are encouraged to guess what might have worked best. Because they are given permission to be wrong (to guess), and because this is a fantasy exercise, it is not nearly as threatening as asking clients directly, in the present, what they need to do to make things better. If they knew the answer, they wouldn't be in therapy in the first place.

Caution is indicated when using this technique because the therapist can inadvertently push toward some goal that is not at all what the client has in mind.

Therapist: You seem to have some clarity about keeping yourself safe.

Client: Yes. I realize that I feel alone, not because other people push me away, but because I push them away. I'm afraid of getting hurt again. I haven't fallen in love because of my behaviors.

Therapist: So how might we go about helping you gain the courage to try again?

Client: Are you kidding! I don't want to take that risk again. I feel relieved just knowing that I'm not being rejected. I want to find a way to have a fulfilling life without falling in love. It's okay not to be in a love relationship, right?

As you can see, the therapist projected her own assumption that the client would want to fall in love as a way of dealing with feelings of loneliness, yet the client wanted to find other ways to feel less lonely. If the therapist had asked the miracle question, she might have avoided this mistake.

FOR REFLECTION

There is no doubt that you have some aspect of yourself that troubles you. Picture a time in the future when you no longer have this difficulty. A miracle occurred and you are cured! Spend a few minutes visualizing this as vividly as you can. Picture yourself functioning in ways that, previously, had been beyond your reach. You are confident, in control, and poised, dealing with situations that previously gave you a lot of trouble.

Now, imagining yourself in this way, what did you do to make this happen?

Even though this is a challenging task, one in which your first response might be that you don't know, force yourself to guess what you might have done.

Your answer to this miracle question supplies you with guidance about what you may need to do to make this fantasy a reality.

SETTING GOALS

Setting goals can occur at two levels: (1) short-term goals that can be accomplished from session to session, and (2) long-term goals that are to be attained by the end of the treatment. Long-terms goals are often established early in treatment and will likely be changed or modified over time in light of progress that is made. Short-term goals are born out of each session. In either case, you are frequently reassessing treatment and goals, and consequently, exploring how insight can be converted into action.

There are a variety of homework tasks that you might give clients as an extension of their sessions. These might include writing assignments (keeping a journal), reading assignments (books, articles), social interactions (initiating conversations), behavioral tasks (study skills), lifestyle changes (exercise program), or other activities. (For sources, see Rosenthal's [2011] book of favorite homework assignments by the most prominent practitioners, and the *Journal of Clinical Activities, Assignments, and Handouts in Psychotherapy Practice*.)

Teaching Goal Setting to Clients

As a general operating procedure, many therapists save the last few minutes of every session for asking clients to summarize what they learned and then guiding them to declare what they intend to work on before the next meeting. Depending on how insightful and skilled your clients may be, this can take just a few minutes or half the session. There is usually some period of training involved in which clients are taught how to think in this way. Over time, they will learn to automatically ask themselves the following questions:

- What happened in the session today that was significant and meaningful for me?
- What did I learn that I didn't already know?
- What part of the discussion am I most interested in working on during the next week?
- How can I translate what we talked about into something specific that I can do this week?
- What am I prepared to report next week that I have been able to accomplish during the intervening time?

Exercise in Learning

Apply the questions listed above that clients ask themselves at the end of their sessions. Ask yourself what you have just learned in this chapter that you didn't yet know. What do you intend to do differently now that you realize these things? What are you going to incorporate into your behavior from now on? What are you going to do today that puts this into practice?

Like most of the other therapeutic strategies, setting goals is a learned skill that takes considerable practice. It is very challenging to help clients to translate what they have been talking about into constructive things that they are prepared to do. It takes a tremendous amount of sensitivity, diplomacy, and creativity to help people move beyond the talking stage to the action stage.

When helping people to set between-session goals, you might keep several factors in mind. Effectively set goals should be mutually negotiated; as specific as possible; realistically within time constraints and the client's ability; measurable, so you can determine the extent to which the goal was reached; and relevant to the core issues discussed.

Negotiating Mutually Determined Goals

The first and most important thing to keep in mind is that all goal setting is done in partnership with the client. Both of you should be actively involved in determining what will be done between sessions. This requires a degree of negotiation and subtle shaping because clients are not initially very good at this process. You must resist the urge to prescribe goals for your clients, as they will be much less committed to following through on the tasks if these seem like homework assigned by an authority figure. We start the following dialogue by assuming the client has some insight into her problems and what she stands to gain from the insight.

Therapist: What do you want to work on this week?

Client: I don't know. What do you think I should do?

Rather than falling into this trap of doing the work for the client, the therapist shifts the responsibility back.

Therapist: Let's see if we can figure this out together. First, let's review what you realized today and what you want to do about it.

Client: I'm not really sure. Maybe something about my parents bugging me too much.

Because clients are unfamiliar with goal setting in therapy, be patient when teaching them these skills. The therapist needs to help this client expand her vision of what happened.

Therapist: That's true. We did talk about your parents and how they treat you. We also talked about a number of other things, like the difficulties you have had throughout your life telling people how you feel. This has been true not only with your parents but also with your best friend.

Client: I guess so.

Therapist: So how else would you summarize the session?

The therapist avoids the temptation to do all the work and instead helps the client to share the load.

Client: Well, I did say how disappointed I am that my parents—okay—lots of people sort of walk all over me. And you pointed out that this may happen because I let it happen. I don't assert myself. I'm afraid that if I assert myself, then people won't approve of me, and I'll be all alone.

With the summary completed, the therapist next moves to convert this insight into a goal that can be worked toward.

Therapist: Back to the question I asked earlier. Given that you have difficulties asserting yourself with your parents, your best friend, and others, how could you make progress toward your goal this week?

The therapist is gently but firmly leading the client to declare something that she can do during the week that will get her closer to her ultimate goal of being more assertive. It is extremely important that this process be mutual so that the client feels invested in the outcome.

Imagine what you would say to this client if she returned the following week and said: "Um, sorry, but I just didn't have time to do what you told me to do this week."

If you prescribe homework, or it's even remotely conceived of in that way, then clients can act out, rebel, or lash out at you by failing to follow through on what you told them to do. Sometimes they just never return because they feel embarrassed about not completing the assignment. But if, on the other hand, you clearly reinforce the idea that this is *their* task that they have *chosen* to do, then you have a lot more leverage.

Therapist: No need to apologize to me. This was something that you said you had wanted to do. I guess you changed your mind.

Client: I really wanted to do it. Really. I just didn't get the chance.

Therapist: I notice that you are defending yourself to me and that is not necessary at all. Whether you follow through on your homework or not, I will continue to support you. Let's explore what you gained and lost by not asserting yourself this week.

By emphasizing the mutuality of the goal setting, the therapist makes it clear that the client is the one who is responsible for completing the task. Therapy goes as fast, or as slow, as the client is willing and able to go.

Structuring Goals That Are Attainable

Another common mistake that beginners make is allowing clients to develop goals that are not reasonable or realistic. Sometimes people become so enthusiastic about changes they wish to make in their lives that they get carried away. In other cases, a lack of experience may lead beginner therapists to declare goals that are not reasonably attainable within the time parameters established.

Let's say the young woman mentioned in the previous section decided that she wanted to become more assertive with her parents and best friend. She might easily agree that in the very next week she was going to stand up to them and not let herself be pushed around anymore. That is an admirable objective but one that is not very practical considering that she has been so chronically unassertive in the past. She would need to set intermediate steps on the way to her ultimate goal.

Her first homework assignment might be to document each time she wishes she could have asserted herself, but did not. She could journal about both her fears of becoming more assertive and her frustration with avoiding her own assertiveness. As her awareness increases, she can then attempt to begin changing that behavior.

Client: I was thinking that when my friend, Emi, tells me that we're going to a movie this weekend that I would just tell her that I won't go.

Therapist: I'm wondering if you have ever done that before with Emi, stood up to her in that way?

Client: Sure. Well, not exactly.

Therapist: So if you did all of a sudden stand up for yourself in this way, Emi might find it sort of strange. She might not understand what it is you are doing and why.

Client: I guess so.

Therapist: My question for you, then, is how could you set this up with Emi in small steps so that you might prepare her better for the new ways you want to negotiate this relationship?

The therapist is helping the client to scale down her expectations. Rather than going after her goal all at once, and perhaps setting herself up for disappointment or failure, it is often preferable to move a little at a time in the desired direction.

When you ask clients what they want to work on between sessions, they will sometimes set ludicrous goals for themselves. Someone who wants to start an exercise program will say that he intends to go to the gym every day for the next week and work out for a minimum of 45 minutes each time. He might very well be able to do this, but if for some reason he skips a day or cuts a workout short he may believe that he has failed in his commitment and become discouraged. In this case, it would be your job to get the client to agree to a much more attainable objective—perhaps going to the gym three times during the week instead of every day, and doing 20-minute rather than 45-minute sessions. If this goal is easily reached, then it can be raised slowly in the following weeks.

Kayleigh: Attainable Goals

In one of my first sessions using cognitive therapy, I came up with the following goal: I'm not going to let what my boyfriend does bother me. This was an incredibly unrealistic goal, and my therapist saw that right away. She worked with me to set a more realistic goal. Instead, we agreed on keeping a log of how I react when my boyfriend does something that I didn't like. This was an important first step for me because I would never be able to remember the specifics of why I got mad; so I always felt I was to blame.

Writing down the events and my reactions really helped me see that he wasn't treating me right, which caused me a lot of unnecessary stress. I also noticed that I justified and defended his actions, which made everything worse. It was so helpful to be able to see the event from a more objective point of view, which was what my journal allowed me to do.

Used with permission of Kayleigh Soto.

Developing Specific Assignments

Goal setting is a holdover from behavior therapy that emphasizes the importance of therapeutic tasks that are measurable, observable, and specific. Measurable and observable goals are required by third-party payers to evaluate the client's progress. Specific goals need to be developed so the client knows exactly what has to be done, when it should be done, with whom it should be accomplished, in which circumstances, and with what intended outcome. This increases the likelihood that the client will do what was agreed upon and makes it easier to hold the person accountable.

A client saying that he is going to try to do some exercise in the next week is a lot different from saying: "I will go for a twenty-minute walk at least three times during the next week. If for some reason, the weather makes it difficult to get all three walks in—and I can't imagine that it would—then I will substitute one twenty-minute session with an aerobics video." This would be a very simple commitment to check out.

Your job is to help clients take fairly complex, abstract, general struggles and convert them into specific therapeutic tasks that can be completed in weekly segments.

Exercise in Setting Specific Goals

On your own or in a small group, translate these fairly general client goals into more specific homework assignments that could be reasonably completed within a week's time:

- "I want to stop feeling so stressed and anxious all the time."
- "I want to lose weight."
- "I'm going to start telling people what I really think."
- "I'm going to start studying more."
- "I'm going to try to work more efficiently."
- "I want to feel better about my marriage."
- "I'm going to stop procrastinating."

Not all client concerns that are brought up in therapy necessarily lend themselves to specific homework assignments, or even structured goals. For instance, some clients may bring up more existential issues related to finding greater meaning in their lives or wanting more life satisfaction. These may not readily translate themselves into a homework assignment.

In other cases, you may inadvertently perpetuate continued self-defeating behaviors for those who are already overly goal oriented. Imagine you are working with a client who works as an electrical engineer in charge of quality control for a company. He attends each of your sessions with a clipboard on his lap to take notes. He brings to each meeting a list of things he wants to talk about, and as each one is covered, he puts a neat checkmark by the item. He ends every session by asking you what he should do the following week, then sits poised with a pen ready to write down the instructions and dutifully follow them through.

At first, you are impressed with his organizational skills, determination, and motivation to get the most from therapy. He is a model client, you think, ready to do almost anything you ask of him. The problem, you realize, is that he is seeking help in the first place because of impoverished relationships. His wife is ready to divorce him because she is so sick of his controlling, restricted behavior. His kids rebel against his attempts to impose his notion of an ordered universe on their lives. So when you conspire with him to develop additional structured tasks for his life, you may be inadvertently reinforcing exactly the behavior he most needs to change. For this man, the best thing might be a distinct lack of goals and homework. What he needs most in his life is to learn to live without specific objectives.

Make certain that the kinds of goals you help your clients develop are consistent with what they really need most.

Exercise in Goal Setting as a Group

1. Ask people to think of specific areas of their lives that they would like to work on and in which they'd like to make progress. Ideally, these would be the kinds of things that lend themselves to small, incremental goals: homework assignments.

2. The focus of your group is to have each member declare some goal that he or she is prepared to work on during the next week. These goals will be committed aloud to the group before it ends.

3. Make the goals realistic and attainable within the time available.

4. The goals should be reasonably specific so it can be determined whether they were reached.

5. The goals should be relevant to some core issue rather than just a goal for its own sake.

6. Make sure the goal is self-declared rather than prescribed by others. People are far more likely to follow through on something they came up with themselves. Don't let group members assign goals to others; instead they might help one another develop goals.

GENERATING ALTERNATIVES

After goals have been delineated and agreed upon, the next step is to help people make initial progress toward their objectives. One thing that gets in the way of this is the client's belief that options available are limited. Sometimes people feel stuck because they don't see other ways to get their needs met.

In the following dialogue, the therapist uses several skills you have already learned to promote greater understanding of how alternatives have been limited in the client's life. From there, structure is introduced to increase the number of options available for taking action.

Client: I don't see that I have a choice about what I can do. My job requires me to be at the office at least sixty hours per week. I work out every morning before I go in. I volunteer to work at the church on Sunday afternoons. In the morning and evenings, I've got to take care of my two dogs; they need to be walked several times a day. So I just don't see that I have any time left over for a social life.

Therapist: That's fine if this is the life you want. But we've been talking for the last several weeks about how badly you want more friends in your life, and how you'd like to be married and raise a family. I'm not sure how that can possibly happen if you aren't willing to make yourself available to meet and spend time with people. [Confrontation]

Client: Good point. But what am I supposed to do?

At this point, the client is trying to get the therapist to solve her problem, which is not going to happen. (Well, it better not.) Instead the therapist is determined to help her generate other alternatives and, if necessary, to supply prompts and suggestions that might get her to think more creatively and proactively.

Therapist: The way you have framed the problem, you don't have any extra time available. Another way to look at this is that your priorities don't reflect what you say is most important. [Reframing]

This reframing defines the problem in a way that allows for more personal control and flexibility. If there really is no time available, no place the client can cut back, then there is no sense talking about other options since none are possible. But if, on the other hand, the client agrees that she has made certain choices in her life that limit her own options, then she can make different choices.

Client: That may be so, but I still don't see what I can do.

Therapist: Let's pretend that you were starting over. You are beginning a new job. You have no commitments—no pets, no volunteer work, no appointments, no other responsibilities. You could structure your life any way that you wanted. What would this look like?

The therapist is helping the client to visualize a life with more freedom, more options. The insight the therapist hopes would be generated is the idea that being trapped is a state of mind. Once the client is willing to acknowledge that she has no time available because of the ways she has overprogrammed her life, she will be far more motivated to look at other alternatives.

Therapist: Assuming you could make some different decisions about how you spend your life, what could you do instead?

Client: I'm not sure what you mean. I can't very well stop walking my dogs. That would be cruel.

It is common for clients to resist looking at other alternatives. After all, if this were easy, they wouldn't have sought help in the first place.

Therapist: Okay, rather than looking at what you don't choose to change, let's concentrate on what is possible.

Notice the language the therapist uses to emphasize the choices involved and to focus on what can be done rather than what cannot be changed.

Client: Are you saying that I should stop going to church and stop caring about my career?

Therapist: I'm not saying that you should change anything at all. This isn't about what I want, but rather it's about what you said you want. Right now, you have yourself in a bind. On the one hand, you say your life feels empty because of a lack of intimacy; on the other hand, you don't seem willing to give up or change anything in order to get what you say you want. [Reflection of discrepancy]

The therapist refuses to accept responsibility for this "circular" discussion in which it is clear the client resists making adjustments. It is important that the client be held accountable for the choices made. A summary statement and then a confrontation are used as leverage to say to the client: It's your life. What do you want?

Client: You're right. I really have to do things differently. But I just don't know how.

Therapist: You're frightened that once you clear some space in your life, you won't be able to hide anymore from the emptiness you feel. You've been overstructuring your life so you have no opportunity to become involved in a relationship in which you might get hurt. You enjoy being in control, but also feel trapped by this predicament. [Interpretation]

This reflection of feeling, restatement, and interpretation is the transition from insight to action. The ball is now in the client's court. She is either ready to return the volley or will let the shot pass her by. At this point, the therapist doesn't care about her shot selection, but just wants her to make an effort to swing at the ball.

Therapist: Assuming that you are prepared to make some changes, let's brainstorm some things you might do. I'm not saying that you have to do these things, just that you *could* do them if you wanted to.

Working as a team, the two of them together make a list of options, some of which are more desirable and practical than others. The purpose of a brainstorming exercise is to generate as many options as possible. Decisions can be made later as to which ones are the best alternatives. There is a power and freedom that come with the notion that you have lots of possibilities open to you.

Here is a copy of the list:

- Hire a housekeeper who can walk the dogs.
- Cut back on hours at work and slow down the fast-track career plan.
- Change jobs to one that doesn't require such total devotion and leaves more room for outside interests.
- Talk to her supervisor about ways she could cut back her hours.
- Give up volunteering at church.
- Change her exercise routine from working with a personal trainer to taking a class where she would interact more with others.
- Invite people to lunch instead of eating alone at her desk.

It doesn't matter that much which options are listed, as long as they reinforce the idea that there are many possibilities for what can be done. The power of this action strategy comes from helping people to realize that they can make changes. The goal is not necessarily to find the "right" course of action, but rather to put the client in an experimental mood where lots of things may be tried until a good combination has been discovered.

Exercise in Brainstorming

Get into groups of four or five. Think about some problem in which you feel stuck because of a lack of viable solutions. Write down on a sheet of paper at least 10 possible solutions. They can be wild, crazy, or impractical; the important thing is that as many options as possible are listed.

After spending a few minutes on this private list-making, share your ideas with a group and compile a master list of possibilities (eliminating duplications). You should have at least two dozen, maybe more. The object at this stage is quantity rather than quality or practicality.

In the third step, help one volunteer to narrow the list down to the best three or four options that have the most potential to be useful.

Talk about the process of what happened, not only for the volunteer, but also for the group.

REINFORCING BEHAVIOR

We learned long ago from behaviorists that if you want behavior to continue, it is a very good idea to reinforce it. We therapists do this unconsciously and subtly in our work. When a client says something that we particularly like, we nod our heads and smile encouragingly. When clients digress or talk about things that are less interesting, we might act and look bored, hoping to extinguish this behavior. If subtle cues don't work, then we become ever more assertive in guiding clients to talk about the things we believe are most useful.

Most therapists have a list of behaviors that they think are good for most of their clients. This may include such things as sharing feelings, being honest, taking constructive risks, increasing intimacy, and so on. When clients engage in these behaviors we let them know that we are pleased, using social approval as a powerful motivator. We are attentive, involved, and engaging. We make reflections or statements that encourage directions that we think are productive.

Likewise, when a client engages in a behavior that is self-destructive, self-defeating, or otherwise counterproductive, we use reinforcement strategies to try to discourage similar future actions. Notice in the dialogue below how the therapist's response shapes the client's behavior in a more productive direction.

Client: So we went out, had a few drinks, got a little drunk, and then started trashing this place.

Therapist: (frowns, shakes his head)

Client: Well, we didn't mean anything by it. We were just having a little fun.

Therapist: [Redirecting] Tell me more about the meeting you had with your boss. You said you were going to talk to her about being reassigned.

Client: Oh yeah. I did talk to her.

Therapist: [Supporting] So what happened?

Client: Well, the bitch said . . .

Therapist: (looks startled)

Client: I mean, my boss—and you gotta admit she can be a real hardass sometimes—didn't really want to talk about it.

Therapist: You found the courage to approach her about it. You must feel good about that. Even though things didn't work out this first time, you showed that you have options other than sitting around waiting for things to happen. I wonder if there are other places in your life where you might do something similar.

Rather than allowing the client to focus on his disappointment, the therapist reinforces the effort without imposing judgment. Success is thus defined in terms of things within one's control (taking a risk) rather than the outcome (how others respond).

Whenever clients do things that you want them to continue, you must find ways to support and reward their behavior; when they do things that you don't think are good for them, it is important to let them know that as well. The best way to do this is by reflecting how they might feel good about their successes, rather than imposing your judgment or pride, which the client can become dependent on. You can also state the facts about what occurred, which often sounds like approval but isn't. In this way, the client becomes his or her own source of self-esteem and learns how to make decisions from an internal locus of control. Essentially, you are using your power and influence to guide clients in directions that are good for them.

Exercise in Guiding Your Clients

1. Talk about the ethical and moral implications of therapists deciding what is good and bad for their clients. Do you think there is a way to avoid this predicament? Would it be desirable to do so?

2. Which behaviors are you aware that your instructor attempts to reinforce in your class? Which specific actions are supported and which ones are discouraged? Supply specific supportive examples.

3. Make a list of behaviors that you would like to encourage in most of your clients and those you would hope to discourage.

RELAXATION TRAINING

Stress! Who is not familiar with it? We know that graduate students are quite familiar with stress. Relaxation training can be helpful for any client (and for you as well) to achieve many therapeutic goals. However, the need for relaxation is not only common sense, but it is also supported by a significant amount of research and data (Baer, 2006; Batty, Bonnington, Tang, Hawken, & Gruzelier, 2006; Day,

Eyer, & Thorn, 2014; Hubbard & Falco, 2015; Lazarus, 2006; Utay & Miller, 2006). Before we talk about using relaxation techniques with clients, though, we must emphasize that it is important that the client has had a physical examination to rule out any physiological illnesses or problems as sources for the symptoms indicating that stress is the problem. An approval from a physician is also helpful for clients on medications that may be affected by a reduction in stress including blood pressure medications or insulin for diabetes.

When is the best time to use relaxation with the client? When the client's symptoms could be reduced by lowered stress. And what are the effects of stress? Well, there are too many effects to list them all, but we'll name a few:

- *Makes concentrating difficult.* When you tax your body with constant stress, the chemicals in your brain don't fire the way they do when you are relaxed, thus inhibiting your ability to concentrate.
- *Increases risk of depression.* When you have experienced long, pervasive stress, or a short but very intense stressor, the cells in your brain seem to permanently change (based on MRIs) in a way that increases your chances of depression.
- *Creates problems with your health.* Chronic stress lowers the immune system and increases your chances of high blood pressure, headaches, Reynaud's disease, and other disorders.
- *Affects your mood negatively.* Think about when you feel stressed. You are crankier, have a shorter temper, and can tolerate less. That is because stress prepares your body to fight or flee a dangerous situation. Your body doesn't know that you don't need hormones that enable fight or flight when you are waiting impatiently in line. It produces them anyway.
- *Interferes with your sleep.* Your body needs to maintain homeostasis, to remain stable at all times. If you are stressed most of the time, the body will decide that stress is the new way to be. So, when you go to bed at night, your body is still wound up, ready to fight or flee from the phantom monster your body has been running from or fighting all day. Your body forgets how to relax, and you can't sleep.

And there are many others. However, because this is not a class in stress reduction, we'll spare you the details of the many consequences and their physiological bases. Instead, we'll tell you how you can teach relaxation to your clients to facilitate quicker recovery. We hope you choose to learn stress reduction for yourself too. With less stress, clients tend to be less defensive, less resistant.

Remember the deep breathing exercise in Chapter 4. That is a wonderful way to transition your body out of its normal stress state into a more relaxed state. When many clients who have stress-related illnesses go in for biofeedback therapy, they may report feeling relaxed, but the equipment that is connected to their hand tells a different story. "Relaxed" to them is still, objectively, very stressed out. Starting each session with a deep breath might at least be a good way for the client to transition from the outside world into this one hour of healing.

Without equipment, the best way to reduce stress is to practice relaxation each day. You will want to start by being relaxed yourself. If you are uptight, your client will be unable to relax. Once you have relaxed, then you can teach relaxation to your client in the therapy room. In session, keep soft lighting in your office at all times and have relaxing images on your walls. If you have a recliner, have the client recline with eyes closed. If the client is not comfortable closing his or her eyes, have the client look down to relax the eyes. You might say something like this:

Therapist: Start with a deep breath and then focus on breathing normally without changing it. Thoughts may float in and out. Pain or itches may come to your attention. Just acknowledge the distraction and return gently to focusing on breath.

This gets the client started and focusing. The next step is called progressive muscle relaxation. Tell the client when he or she tenses the muscle, not to squeeze too tight. You don't want the client to get a cramp.

Therapist: Now, starting with the feet, tense and hold, then relax them. Feel the difference when you let go. (pause) Move up to your calves, and tense and hold, then relax them . . .

You continue up through the thighs, buttocks, stomach, hands, forearms, upper arms, shoulders, neck, and face. Tense and hold each muscle group, then relax. Make sure to pause after each group is relaxed so the client can feel the difference. Speak in a slow and soft voice. After the client has relaxed the whole body, the therapist would say this:

Therapist: Now allow your body to take over your attention. If there is a particular area that still needs more attention, focus your attention there. Feel yourself letting go. You may feel very heavy or you may feel like you are floating.

By focusing attention on his or her body, the client will become more aware of tension still being held. This process does not add tension. On the contrary, it makes the client aware of the tension so that he or she can let go of the held tension. Sometimes, though, the client may have one area that won't relax. Making this assumption, do the following:

Therapist: When you focus, if you find your body remaining unchanged, send love and compassion to that part of your body, honoring its need to remain the same. Let go of judgment about it, and accept it as is.

Then give the client a minute to enjoy the relaxation:

Therapist: I'll give you one minute to enjoy the relaxation, and then I'll let you know when it's time to come out of your reverie.

After one minute, do the following:

Therapist: Take a deep breath and slowly bring your attention back into the room. Know that you can use this at any time to help you relax. When you are ready, open your eyes and stretch.

The first time or two, the client may not feel more relaxed. With daily practice, however, in a few weeks the client will notice a significant change in the level of stress throughout the day, not just after the relaxation exercise. In fact, at first, he or she may feel tired after each relaxation session. Later, though, the client will feel more invigorated.

What kind of homework can you assign? One recommendation is to purchase a relaxation tape at any bookstore. Listen to it at least three times per week for about 20 minutes. This must be uninterrupted time (no phone, no TV). This is most effective if the client does this at lunch or after work rather than when waking or going to bed each day. In addition, do not fall asleep during this time, because being awake and letting go is more relaxing than sleep for someone who is stressed. Other possible ways to relax are as follows:

- Set an alarm for each hour, and for one minute, take deep breaths with eyes closed.
- Every time you go to the bathroom, take a little time to stop and breathe.
- Each time you are stopped at a light in your car, practice breathing.
- Take five minutes of quiet time before getting up, at lunch, after work, and before bed.

As with other techniques, additional training is highly recommended before performing these in your office. However, taking a few minutes each day is recommended for anyone, with or without training.

USING REHEARSAL AND IMAGERY

Behaviorism usually gets credit for creating the techniques of imagery and rehearsal. However, the philosopher Vahinger (1925) first introduced this concept in the 18th century, and Alfred Adler brought it into the field of psychology during the time when Freud was ending his career. Adler called it "acting as if." Behaviorism probably got credit for this technique because the paradigm in behaviorism is that if you change the behavior, you have made real change in the client. Well, how do you change behavior? You just go out there and do it. If you feel artificial in your new behavior, act as if it were true. See the connection?

One criticism some therapists make about behaviorism is that you cannot create lasting changes in the client by simply extinguishing a behavior. If the client isn't ready to change, he or she will replace it with another, probably just as ineffective, behavior. Therefore, for this technique to be effective, the client must be ready. Being ready usually means the client has a good grasp of where the problem behavior originated, how it served a good purpose for a while, and why and how it isn't working now. The client must have a strong motivation to change. And then the therapist can move the client from the insight into action:

Therapist: We have talked a lot about how you have been afraid to assert yourself because you don't feel like you deserve to have your needs met. Let's now consider what it might look like if you acted as if you believed yourself to be deserving of getting your needs met.

The therapist asks the client to act, to pretend as if this were true. Most likely, the client will fail a few times before changing the behavior, and even then, he or she will feel artificial. So, a good way to ease the client into the process is to start by using imagery. Once the client has a clear picture of the new behavior, the client can rehearse it in session. When the client has built some confidence in the therapy room, he or she can go out and practice it for the rest of his or her life. During each of these steps, the therapist continues to work with the client on changing the thoughts and feelings associated with resistance to change by using myriad other techniques. By the time the client starts using it in the outside world, it will feel less and less artificial, more and more a part of who he or she is.

So, what is the best way to introduce imagery? We know that if the client's defenses are down, if the client is deeply relaxed, then the imagery becomes more vivid, and the client is able to convert that imagery more easily into action. Therefore, you will want to have already established a strong and safe relationship with your client. When you initiate a discussion of imagery, work with the client to create a script that is as full of as many details as possible, including reference to each of the senses. Make sure to include an entrance into the relaxation and an exit out of it. Work with your client to choose a place that is safe for him or her: the beach, the woods, at home, a garden, or another location that represents tranquility.

Once you have written the script together, and your client is ready, have the client sit quietly with arms and legs uncrossed, eyes closed. Start with the deep breathing exercise introduced in Chapter 4. Once the client is ready, read the script slowly in a soft but audible voice through to the end. Discuss with your client how he or she experienced the imagery. You may need to make some changes to the script to make it more accurate for the client's experience. Do this each week in session; you may even want to record the script for the client to use each day at home. The more exposure to the script, the more quickly your client will be able to accept the image. A sample script for the client just described might look something like this:

Therapist: Sit in a comfortable position with your legs and arms uncrossed, eyes closed. Inhale deeply and feel the cool air enter through your nose and fill your lungs from the bottom to the top. Then exhale slowly, feeling the warm air move out of your lungs through your mouth.

Using the deep breath tells the client's body that it's time to relax and to focus her attention.

Therapist: Now, just breathe deeply and rhythmically . . . notice the rise and fall of your abdomen with each breath . . . in . . . and out . . . in . . . and out. You may notice sensations demanding your attention, or you may notice thoughts floating in. Without judgment, acknowledge their presence and gently focus your attention back on your breath.

Breathing and focusing on breath brings the client to a more relaxed state.

Therapist: Now, I'd like you to imagine a door in front of you. What kind of handle does it have? How does it open: toward you, away from you, or does it slide? When you are ready, open the door and imagine a small staircase with ten steps . . . begin stepping down, and with each step, you become more and more relaxed . . . ten . . . nine . . . eight . . . seven . . . six . . . five . . . four . . . three . . . two . . . one . . . and now you have reached the bottom, and you walk through another doorway onto a beach.

Introducing some image to transition in and out helps the client move through this process more slowly. In addition, the suggestion of going down stairs and relaxing while descending helps the client go into a deeper trance. The therapist counts very slowly.

Therapist: On this beach, feel the sand beneath your feet and the warmth of the sun on your face. Hear the sound of the seagulls and the ocean waves crashing to the shore. Smell the fresh ocean air. See the beauty all around you.

The imagery of the beach helps bring the client to a new place to prepare for a new mindset. Notice that each of the senses is acknowledged in this section.

Therapist: In this place, you are confident. In this place, you deserve to have your needs met . . . feel what it's like to deserve to have your needs met. You feel wonderful and alive. You feel content and happy. See yourself interacting with an approaching friend. You assert yourself by suggesting you both walk along the beach. Your friend readily agrees and is happy to oblige. Feel how satisfying it is to get your needs met by someone who agrees with your suggestions . . . revel in the moment.

This is the part where you interject the work, what the client wants to accomplish. This is the part of the script where you and your client work together to use the best and most realistic wording for your client.

Therapist: Take one minute on your own. At the end of the minute, I will continue . . . (after one minute) . . .

A minute is actually a very long time for silence, and the client is given the freedom to do some of his or her own spontaneous work during this time.

Therapist: Now find your doorway to the stairs . . . open it, and as you ascend the stairs, you will feel more and more awake.

Prepare the client to return.

Therapist: Know that you can bring with you anything you would like from this experience and leave behind anything that no longer works for you.

This is an excellent statement to help the client transition the imagery into reality.

Therapist: Ascend the stairs to come back into the room . . . one . . . two . . . three . . . four . . . five . . . six . . . seven . . . eight . . . nine . . . ten.

Count very slowly and bring the client back by the same process used when he or she entered.

Therapist: When you go through the door at the top of the stairs, you will find yourself here, sitting in this room. Feel the pressure of the chair beneath you. Hear the sounds around you. And when you are ready, take a deep breath, open your eyes, and stretch.

Once the client is ready, discuss the experience and any modifications that might be needed in the script. You can use imagery without a script, but the brain seems to be more receptive to repetitive learning when the repetition can occur in each session as well as at home each day (Basmajian, 1989).

As with the other techniques, it is important that you get proper training before you use this. Therefore, take a workshop or training class to get the didactic portion and then make sure you are supervised the first few times you actually execute it. It is sometimes possible for the imagery to be sufficient to cause change, but, in other cases, imagery is only the first step. Sessions serve as rehearsals so acting-as-if can be done out of sessions. In time, your client will learn a new way to be.

USING ROLE-PLAYING

One way to conceive of the value of therapy sessions is that they provide a laboratory for experimenting with new behaviors. If talking is not enough to promote lasting changes, then opportunities must be provided for helping clients to practice what they are learning in a safe environment and to receive helpful feedback for improving their effectiveness.

Role-playing involves far more than a few skills. It actually can be classified as its own style of therapy with a complex set of procedures. Although it is beyond the scope of this book to teach you all the therapeutic techniques and strategies, there are a few generic skills that are part of this modality.

J. L. Moreno (1987) and the other creators of psychodramatic methods had in mind a vehicle that would allow clients to work through unresolved struggles and rehearse alternative ways of dealing with situations. Although often used in group formats because of the increased opportunities for dramatic enactments, interpersonal engagement, and multiple sources of feedback, role-playing can be used in any form of treatment from family to individual sessions. Here are some examples of when role-playing might be employed:

1. A client is angry at a family member and wants to work through this conflict.

2. Someone has unfinished business with a parent who died many years ago.

3. A client who is extremely intellectual and emotionally restricted wants help being more expressive.

4. A client has extreme fear of speaking in public and wants to rehearse what might be said and how she might handle things if she loses her composure.

5. A session has just been devoted to learning ways of being less aggressive and offensive.

6. A client has an upcoming job interview.

7. A client demonstrates ineffective interpersonal behavior that puts people off.

8. A client has not been able to muster the courage to ask someone out on a date.

In each of these situations, and many others that could be listed, the client would be helped to follow these basic steps:

1. Explore and understand the main problem.

2. Recognize that a situation has arisen where rehearsal and practice of new skills could be useful.

3. Define the skill(s) that will be practiced.

4. Invite the client to set the scene and describe the situation that would take place.

5. Conduct a first round of practice.

6. Debrief the client about what went well and what can be improved.

7. Model alternative ways of handling the situation by reversing roles.

8. Conduct a second round of practice.

9. Provide more feedback and debrief the sessions.

10. Connect what was learned to earlier discussions.

11. Structure homework or a therapeutic task that puts the rehearsed behavior into action.

There are many variations of this basic structure, depending on the context (group, family, individual session), the setting, the client, and the presenting problem. Here is an example of what this might look like for the case described earlier of the young woman who felt oppressed by her parents and best friend Emi.

Therapist: Let's practice how this conversation with Emi might take place.

Client: What do you mean?

Therapist: I'll be Emi and you tell me what you might say to her.

Client: (giggles) You mean right now?

Therapist: Yeah, talk to me the way you would to Emi.

This sort of reluctance to get started is natural and normal. Most people feel inhibited and uncomfortable with the spontaneous nature of role-playing. That is one reason why you must feel *very* comfortable doing it in order to put others at ease.

Client: You want me to pretend that you're Emi?

Therapist: Exactly.

Client: But you don't look like her. (laughs)

Therapist: Then show me how she acts. How would she sit? Why don't you be her and I'll be you?

This *role switching* allows the client to demonstrate the ways the antagonist behaves. This accomplishes several things simultaneously. It gives the therapist valuable data that permit a more accurate and realistic portrayal of how the client perceives the person. It also forces the client to get inside the heart and head of the person with whom he or she is having difficulty. This in itself can often spark some new understandings and insights.

After this client shows the therapist how Emi behaves, her tone of voice, mannerisms, posture, phrasing, and language, the therapist is better prepared to play the part. Another benefit of this structure is that because the therapist has seen the client for some time, it is likely that he or she can play the client very well. The client then sees herself as the therapist sees her, asking: "Is that what I'm really like?"

Therapist: What do you think?

Client: I don't know. I didn't realize that I seemed that . . . I don't know . . . that assured of myself.

Therapist: Let's see what happens when you just be yourself and I'll be Emi.

After this first round, which almost never goes well because of the client's lack of experience and practice with the new strategies, the conversation can be deconstructed, analyzed, and refined. Adjustments can be made for the next round, and then, finally, for the real-life confrontation that will take place during the week.

Exercise in Role-Playing

In small groups, select one person who will be the client. This person agrees to role-play a client who is involved in a conflict with someone (a family member, coworker, friend). The client will then briefly describe the nature of the conflict, including relevant background and contextual information. Other group members will ask a few questions to draw out the nature of the difficulty. Spend no more than 10 minutes in this exploration.

Select a cast. Someone else in the group will play the antagonist. Members may take on the roles of other characters involved tangentially or directly in the situation. Depending on the preferences of your instructor, you may also take on roles of the "auxiliary ego," which is a kind of inner voice that speaks out loud what the client is unwilling or unable to say.

Role-play a scenario in which the client confronts the antagonist by saying some things that have been left unsaid. The antagonist will respond realistically (and perhaps aggressively) to this first attempt.

Debrief and analyze what happened. Give the client feedback and suggestions on other strategies that might be attempted. Perhaps another member can model or demonstrate what is suggested by stepping into the client role and trying out the strategy with the antagonist.

After the client has again had a chance to practice alternative ways to deal with this person, everyone can process the experience. Discuss what you need to learn better in order to do this in actual therapeutic situations.

You can appreciate that this sort of action strategy requires a different set of skills from those previously learned. You might still use active listening, interpretation, and all the rest of what you've learned, but this situation requires you to use far more spontaneous, dramatic therapeutic actions. You would definitely require advanced-level training and supervision before you ever attempted to do this with clients.

USING THE EMPTY CHAIR

Fritz Perls (1969) really liked the idea of the psychodrama and role-playing we just discussed, especially because he secretly aspired to be an actor. However, because he was acutely aware of the process of projection, he created a similar technique: the empty chair. In the preceding case, he would have had the client role-play both parts at once so that the client could gain a perspective of both positions. The assumption is that the problem isn't with the friend, but rather with the client's projection of the friend, the Emi in the client's head. So what better way to reconcile it than by playing both roles? Let's assume the client's name is Kimberly; the session might go something like this:

Therapist: Kimberly, you have talked about how bossy Emi can be and, specifically, how she made the decision last Saturday to go to a movie you didn't want to see. Would you like to try an experiment in what it might be like to assert yourself with Emi?

The therapist sets this up when a specific situation arises and the client is in the midst of feeling her frustration.

Client: I don't know. That sounds kind of scary. What do you want me to do?

Therapist: I'd like you to imagine that you and Emi are in this room together. You are in one chair and Emi is across from you. (moving a chair in front of the client) I will sit behind you to be supportive of your position.

Client: Okay. That seems a little weird. I'm not sure I can talk to an empty chair, but I'll try.

Therapist: Then, where would you like to start? With Emi or as yourself?

The therapist gives the client the choice to start where she feels most comfortable.

Client: As Emi.

Therapist: Then I'd like you to close your eyes for a moment and position your-self the way Emi would sit in the chair. Imagine what she looks like, her body posture, facial expressions, what she might be wearing.

The therapist is getting the client into the role of Emi.

Therapist: Good. Now open your eyes and imagine yourself in the other chair across from you. Imagine how you sit, what you might be wearing, how you might seem to Emi. When you're ready to start as Emi, tell Kimberly what movie you are going to see this weekend.

The therapist positions herself by squatting behind the client's chair. The client may begin with a specific experience where a lot of emotion is held back. Once the client says everything she has to say as Emi, she will stop to look at the thera-pist or just start responding as herself. When this happens:

Therapist: Okay, now sit in the other chair as yourself, Kimberly. Look at Emi from your perspective. What would you like to say to Emi?

The therapist facilitates the client moving back and forth. In most cases, either the client will really see things from the perspective of the other person or she will become emotional and say something in her own position that she was not aware of before. The therapist will not have to do much work from here on, but will remain behind the client, wherever she sits.

Using the empty chair is helpful because it takes any projection on the part of the therapist out of either position. Another way to use this technique would be to have the client play out two polar opposite sides of herself. For example, in one chair she might be the part of herself that wants to assert herself, and in the other chair she will play the part of her that is afraid of asserting herself. Sometimes the therapist will suggest something for the client to parrot (or adjust a statement that fits better) when the client seems to be stuck.

There are a few important points that must be made about using this technique. First, as with role-playing, the therapist must be confident when asking the client to try this. The first time it's done, the client will very likely feel really uncomfort-able, so it's the therapist's job to allay the client's awkwardness. In fact, it's some-times helpful to focus briefly on how strange it would feel to do this, and be fully empathic to that process before proceeding with the experiment.

Second, the client must be ready to perform this exercise. When is the client ready?

- When the client has discussed the issue a lot.
- When the discussion has filtered down to something specific that can be used.
- When both positions (each chair) are fully established, whether as two sides of the client or whether the client is clear about how her own position differs from the other person's.
- When the client is ripe with emotion.

One word of warning: Using the empty chair technique can elicit a great deal of emotion. It can be a powerful process. You must therefore be prepared to deal with a catharsis that can last for moments or for the rest of the session. Before employing this technique, you may want to see it demonstrated and then practice it a few times under supervision.

Exercise in the Empty Chair Technique

Get into small groups or do this as a large class. Place three chairs in the middle and the other chairs in a circle around the inner three. One person will need to role-play the therapist and another the client. This will work best if the client has a real and current issue to discuss. All others in the group will be observers.

Allow the client to describe a specific situation that isn't working with another person or to describe a specific situation where he or she feels pulled in two apparently opposing directions. The therapist should primarily reflect and clarify at this point. The more feeling reflections the better.

Once the client has described the story, the therapist can set up the experiment with the client and try it out.

After the client has finished the process, allow the client to talk about his or her experience. Then allow the therapist to talk about his or her experience of the process. Finally, allow the observers to offer support, feedback, or describe any realizations they came to by observing the process.

USING THE TRANSFERENCE

Frequently clients come to therapy because of some unfinished business with one or both of their parents. Because the therapist is in a position of power similar to that of parent to child, sometimes the client will perceive the therapist to be like his or her parent or will react toward the therapist as if he or she were his or her parent. Freud (1936) identified this process as *transference*. In classical psychoanalysis, transference is one of the most important processes to help clients, whereas other theories acknowledge its existence with much less emphasis. Nowadays, looking at projected feelings toward the therapist is part of standard procedure in most humanistic and psychodynamic approaches.

At times, the client will transfer his or her feelings onto the therapist that are really directed toward another person, usually a parental figure. This is an excellent opportunity to use immediacy and provide the safe environment the client needs to express what has been previously held back. The therapist does this by facilitating that negative expression by the client directly onto the therapist, and subsequently, the therapist can respond in a way that is new for the client.

Perhaps, for example, the client was not allowed to be angry growing up, and at some point in therapy, the client perceives that the therapist is inhibiting his ability to be angry. The therapist would invite the client to direct his feelings, including his anger, at the therapist. Consequently, the therapist would respond by taking in the anger and reflecting back empathy. Thus, the client has a new experience of expressing anger with people in positions of power. The intention is for this process to begin to elicit some healing for the client.

You may notice that this is a form of role-playing. However, instead of being set up in a rather artificial way, this process can occur more naturally and without as much inhibition on the part of the client, if well timed. In fact, you may notice how these different theories apply a very similar technique, only slightly modified it to fit the theoretical frame. First, using the transference was created, then role-playing. The empty chair technique is a further modification. Because so many theories and therapists use this type of technique, there must be something to it that facilitates client growth. In our experience, these processes can be powerful indeed.

PITFALLS AND COMMON MISTAKES

Once again, we alert you to some of the common mistakes that may be made with the skills introduced in this chapter. In addition, some of these pitfalls may be particularly relevant to the action stage of therapy. We hope your awareness of these potential mistakes will help you avoid some of them.

Forgetting to Reflect

We said it in the last chapter, we'll mention it briefly here again. You can get so excited about taking some action with the client and meeting some goals that you forget to reflect feelings and content, but especially feelings. At every stage of therapy, empathy is needed to help clients gain insight about the current stage and to continue to strengthen your relationship with the client. Remember, you are only human, and at times your client can get mad at you or feel hurt by you. You therefore want to have lots of empathy on deposit in the emotional bank account so withdrawals don't bring the account too low.

Overpersonalization

Do you have problems taking things personally? Do you assume that someone's bad mood is your fault? Well, if you do, you are overpersonalizing, and if you have difficulty with this in your personal life, you are really going to struggle with it as a therapist. Clients will not show up, will cancel appointments, will get angry with you for no apparent reason, or will resist your brilliant interventions to foster change. You may assume it's because you did something wrong. There may be some clients who make little progress despite your best efforts. Is it you or is it them? If you always assume the undesirable behaviors of your clients are about you, you are probably wrong. Clients may not show because they are afraid of therapy. Clients can cancel because they're really having a series of challenges that do not permit them to attend. Clients get in a bad mood, and may feel safe enough with you to take it out on you. Clients may not be a good fit for your style of therapy. Clients may be fearful of changing. Regardless of the situation, there will be times when it's not about you. It's about your client. In contrast, there may also be times that it is about you. If you take it personally every time, especially without exploring the issue more, then you will feel pretty beat up as a therapist. Clients can be thoughtless, inconsiderate, or resistant, and if they are that way at home, they will most certainly be that way with you. What's important is that you check it out. Get some feedback. Collect some evidence before you take it personally.

Negotiating Irrelevant Goals

In your zeal to come up with things that clients can work on, you may develop goals that meet all other criteria but are relatively unimportant and unrelated to core issues. Some therapists so enjoy feeling reassured by the steady progress of their clients that they routinely assign regular homework assignments, whether these are indicated in every case or not. Some therapists ask *all* their clients to read the same books, complete the same journaling assignment, write the same reflective papers, or undertake the same tasks that are believed to be good for everyone. Although it may be true that most people could profit from more exercise, fresh vegetables, and mindfulness, that doesn't mean that assigning these activities will necessarily address the presenting complaints.

Sometimes it is difficult to come up with a "good" goal; if the client isn't ready for action, it's liable to be difficult to come up with a goal. Consulting with a supervisor will help you sort out whether this is the case. In the meantime, don't force goals on clients when they don't seem to fit. Doing so can actually diminish or compromise the power of what you have already done together. Instead, think of all of these action techniques as part of your toolbox, and trust that your intuition (and experience over time) will tell you when to pull one of these tools out of the box for use with a client, rather than trying to make something new work because you just learned about it.

Being Impatient

We talked about this earlier in the chapter. So, your client is not moving along fast enough. He appears resistant. He says he wants to get better, but he seems to do nothing with the insight he has discovered. He won't change.

Your supervisor may tell you to slow down. You're going too fast. Change is difficult, and there are many reasons why clients don't move as fast as we'd like.

- You are striving for the wrong goal. We discussed this earlier in the book. The goals you set should be flexible. Frequently, what the client presents as an initial goal and the goal that is reached at the end of therapy are different. Therefore, you will need to periodically make adjustments to the long-term goal to make sure you are on the same page with your client.
- The goal is inappropriate. The goal can be too big and need to be broken down into smaller parts, or maybe it's not specific enough. In either case, reassess to make sure you and your client are specific about where you are going.
- Some aspect of insight is still missing. The fact that the client reaches a level of insight does not mean that the level found is the deepest level. The most frequent error we see students make is thinking that once an insight is reached, the client should be ready to make changes; very often another layer exists below this level of insight. The deepest layers usually are related to self-esteem issues of not being good enough, not feeling deserving, not feeling valued, not feeling like a worthy person, and so on.
- The client needs to get comfortable with the insight first. Perhaps you have reached a deep-seated insight. Reaching it is not sufficient. Clients frequently need to simmer at this level, to adjust to the idea. How often have you accepted something at a cognitive level, but your heart isn't in it yet? It takes time for unpleasant insights to be fully accepted by your client. Work with the resistance, not against it.
- Your expectations are unrealistic. Sometimes you are just too darn impatient. Clients take a long time to go through this process. This is why we recommend

you go through your own therapy, so you can really understand how hard it is to change. It's hard to accept change, and it's even harder to leap into the abyss. So go at the client's pace, not yours.

- The client prefers the current pain to the pain of changing. On occasion, your client may have thought his or her old way of being wasn't working, but later may decide that it's better than changing. When the change seems to require too much effort relative to the pain of staying the same, the client is free to decide not to change. You must respect that wish.

- You are not prepared to handle this type of issue. It is possible that you will be given a client or situation during your training that you are not adequately prepared to handle. You may not even know that you're not ready. In these cases, get lots of supervision and/or refer your client to someone who is more qualified to work with that particular issue. It is better, though, to learn how to work with this type of client if you have the luxury to do so under close supervision. The more you learn, the better prepared you'll be for the next client.

In all of these possible reasons for resistance, you may hear one common theme: Slow down! The client needs more time, more space, more readiness for change. We are all impatient at times, and being a therapist will help you to face this need every day.

Reinforcing Too Much

Intrinsic risks are associated with reinforcement. First, when the therapist tries to enhance or extinguish behaviors to direct the client to act "correctly," we are assuming the therapist knows right from wrong, what is good and bad. Although the therapist may have expertise in human behavior, he or she is not infallible. For example, the client described below reports in session that he has accomplished his homework from the previous week:

Client: I did what you said to do.

Therapist: What did I say for you to do?

Client: You told me to try to start asserting myself.

Therapist: Um hmm.

Client: So when my wife asked me to take out the trash, I let her know that I couldn't because I was working. I let her know I'd have to do it later, after I finished this project.

Therapist: Good. (nodding her head) How was that for you to assert yourself?

Here the therapist is attempting to reinforce the client's behavior to assert himself more. Although this may have been a difficult task for the client to accomplish, we don't know how it was done. The therapist might be hoping that it was done in a polite and tactful way, but what if the therapist is wrong? The client could have yelled this at his wife. He could have sounded exasperated. He could have used foul language. Although we may applaud his ability to stand up for himself, we can never know exactly how it was done. Six months from now, the therapist may be seeing the couple because the way the client learned to assert himself was destructive to the relationship. Therefore, reinforcing a reported behavior may have some less-than-ideal consequences. Instead of reinforcing behavior based on assumptions, the therapist may want to get more detailed information about the entire process to look for any potential warning signs that the new behavior wasn't carried out effectively.

Another intrinsic risk associated with reinforcement is that the therapist sets up an external locus of control for the client. Most people love to receive positive reinforcement, and will do a lot to gain the approval of others. Let's face it: Are any of us really comfortable with someone disapproving of us or our behavior? We want people to approve of us, and your client is the same way. The client may behave inauthentically just to gain the therapist's approval. In other words, the client will behave one way in the session, with the intention of seeking approval from the therapist, but behave another way outside of the session. In such cases, the improvement the therapist sees is false. In addition, even if the client is performing in a way outside of therapy that is deemed positive in the therapist's eyes, who will continue reinforcement for the client when therapy is finished? No one. Therefore, the therapist has facilitated an external locus of control for the client. What's the alternative?

One of the important conditions of good person-centered therapy is that the therapist provide unconditional positive regard (Rogers, 1951). Most other theorists and most practitioners would agree that unconditional positive regard is an essential component. If the client believes the therapist thinks he or she is a good and worthy human being, regardless of behavior, then the client can feel safe to experiment with new behaviors and allow him- or herself to be completely genuine in therapy. You might argue that when the therapist uses reinforcement, the therapist is judging the client's behavior, not the client's worthiness as a human. But how does the client know that? The client may or may not, and that is a risk. So how does one reinforce behavior while providing unconditional positive regard so that the client can establish an internal locus of control? Easy. Let's take the vignette above. Instead of the therapist responding with, "Good. [nodding her head] How was that for you to assert yourself?," setting up an external locus of control, the therapist could say, "You feel really good about asserting yourself." Thus, the therapist is using the client's own internal value system to reinforce the behavior. "You feel good about . . ." "You are really proud of yourself." "You liked what you did." All of these are phrases that reinforce the client's behavior using the client's value system, not the therapist's. We might even suggest that you learn to do this as much as possible in your personal life as well, especially with children.

Not Following Up on Homework Assignments

Few things are more irritating to a client than a therapist constantly assigning or negotiating homework but not following up on it. If your client made the effort to do the assignment, he or she will be eager to share the results. If you don't follow up, your client may perceive that the homework assignment was not important, or that you don't care enough to remember. In addition, if the client does not complete the work, you may miss some important information about this potential resistance. Therefore, if you assign it, make a note to yourself to follow up the next week.

Being Culturally Insensitive

An inherent risk in the action stage is that the therapist might attempt to facilitate change by imposing what he or she thinks is the right way to be. Different cultures, however, especially with ethnicity, religion, social class, and even gender, have different rules about the proper ways to be in life. Be mindful that the action task you ask the client to undertake fits well with the client's worldview. This is one reason it is important to encourage clients to come to their own conclusions about how to take action or what action they might want to take.

For example, imagine you have a second-generation Filipino client whose issue is that he wants to live on his own. He's 30 years old, but his parents insist he remain with them until he marries. He sees all of his friends living alone and doing fine while being a bit wild. He feels restricted by his parents' oversight. He can't stay out late or do anything that would bring disapproval from his parents. The therapist could easily encourage him to move out on his own because it's his life. This is true for the dominant Western culture, but not part of Filipino culture. The therapist may want to create a role play in which he can talk with his parents, although this, too, could be culturally inappropriate. Instead, the therapist might help the client understand that this is an issue of acculturation, and because he is bicultural, he feels torn between the values of his family and his ethnic origin and those of the dominant culture, which may seem more appealing. The client would need to determine what the next step should be, whether learning to find some peace in his situation or perhaps talking with his parents. Whatever he chooses, if he makes the decision, he's more likely to have success with it.

APPLICATIONS TO SELF: SHARING YOUR CLIENT'S ISSUES

In this chapter, we looked at converting insight into action. Perhaps the best way for you to really understand how this process works is to take a retrospective look at your life. Make a list of all of the major events in your life that changed you, whether in how you now see yourself, others, or the world. For each event, write out the story of what happened. Describe who you were before the event, how you were during the worst of the event, and how you changed after transcending the event. You will find that in each case, you most likely experienced a great deal of pain. Think of how much pain it took to facilitate that change. On a scale of 1 to 10, with 1 being no pain and 10 being almost intolerable pain, write down the intensity of pain required for your change for each event.

Now consider things you know you need to change in yourself. Make a list. I'm sure you can think of three or four things that you'd like to improve. Pick the one issue that seems to interfere with your life the most. Take that one issue and further list all of the ways it interferes with your life. Did you include that it will interfere with your work as a therapist? Well, it will. You will inevitably get clients who will either trigger your issue or have the same issue. You will think, "I can't even fix this problem myself. How will I help you?" And yet you can't refer every client who shares your issue. So what do you do? You have to do something that's foreign and new to you (or at least we assume this). You have to work on it. How do you do that? When you are able to answer this question, you will be so much more prepared to help clients with their issues.

We have now given you a large toolbox for your work with clients. But before you use your tools on them, use the tools in your own life. That is what this section of each chapter is for, for you to apply these skills in your own life. You will become a better person for it. Your relationships will be enhanced. Life will be sweeter. And you will become a stronger therapist.

There are a lot of therapists working out there: counselors, psychologists, social workers, hypnotherapists, school counselors, marriage and family therapists, psychiatrists. Some are really, really good. Most are just average. We want you to be one of the really, really good ones. To do that, you must, absolutely must, do your own work.

SUMMARY

In this chapter, we introduced you to some techniques from various theories to help transform insight into action. A significant portion of the chapter was dedicated to good goal setting because that is a necessary part of therapy and must be done well in order for everything else to work. If you don't know where you are going, how can you get there? We also introduced you to reinforcement, empty chair, transference, relaxation training, and rehearsal and imagery. We are now approaching the issue of evaluating how you are doing and terminating with your client, discussed in the next chapter.

Skills in Action: Being Too Responsible

Therapist: I wanted to start our session today by talking about how your homework assignment went last week. [Following up on homework]

Client: I did what you requested and wrote down each time that I felt responsible for taking care of my mom and baby sister. I was surprised that this happened each and every time I interacted with them, especially over the weekend when we spend most of our time together.

Therapist: You're surprised at how much you feel responsible. And what did you write for comments about each incident? [Probing]

Client: I realized that I feel important taking care of them, taking the role of my dad since he won't do it. I know we talked about this before, but I really got it when I tried to avoid taking responsibility. I didn't know what to do. I don't know how else to be. I just automatically started telling them what to do or how to be.

Therapist: You feel stuck in this one role. Let's generate some ideas about other ways that you could be. Since it's hard for you to think about how you could be different, think about other people you know and how they are with their families. [Generating alternatives]

Client: (pause) Okay. Well . . . I suppose I could ignore everyone. (laughing)

Therapist: Sure, that would be one possibility; let's not rule anything out. Keep going. [Reinforcing behavior]

Client: With my sister, I could be more like a friend or confidant, the way I am with my other friends. I could also let them make their own decisions, I guess, unless they ask. With my mom, I do treat her like a mom, I just put my needs aside for her. I don't think that's a bad thing.

Therapist: I think a part of you feels good when you put yourself aside for your mother, but another part of you feels exhausted when you can't make her as happy as you'd like. [Feeling and content reflections]

Client: That is true. I don't know how else to be with her. I really want her to be happy.

Therapist: You feel responsible for your family as if your sister is your child, and your mother's happiness depends solely upon you. I have a sense that you believe you either have to give in to everything or not do anything at all. [Interpretation]

Client: Yeah. I guess I do. You're implying that maybe I could take a little less responsibility.

Therapist: Exactly. You can own your part and do what you can to help. Give me an example of a time when you felt like you gave too much of yourself and felt helpless to change things. [Providing information, setting up a potential role-play]

Client: Well, my sister isn't doing well in school right now. I keep talking to her, but each time I do, she shuts me out!

Therapist: You're hurt by her setting that boundary with you. You're confused about her cutting you off from her. [Reflections of feeling]

Client: Yeah, I can't connect.

Therapist: Let's try an experiment. First, pretend like I'm her, and you approach me with your concern. [Role-playing]

Client: That's a little weird, but okay, I'll try. Kathy, you have to get your grades up. If you don't then you will regret it later. You want to go to college don't you? You want to make something of yourself. You don't want to be like dad or disappoint mom!

Therapist: You dislike your father, and you're scared your sister will be like him. When you say that, I hear you saying that she is being like your dad. [Reflecting feelings; self-disclosure]

Client: I guess I hadn't thought of that before, but you're right. I'm really afraid she'll be just like him.

Therapist: Let's try something else. I'd like you to relax in your chair, cast your eyes down, and begin breathing deeply. Picture how you and your sister have been lately. Imagine the room you're in, the furniture you sit in, the sounds and smells. (pause) Now, see yourself talking with her, don't worry about what you say, but instead picture the type of connection you'd prefer to have with her. How might this be different from what usually happens? As those images and thoughts form, hold them for a moment. (client looks up) What did you see? [Guided imagery]

Client: I saw us talking, her listening, and then we hugged after. She felt grateful, and I felt good about helping her.

Therapist: So this is your preference. You have an idea of how she might look if she were more receptive. What do you think was the difference between your first image of what actually happens versus what you'd like to happen? [Content reflection; exploring the client's goal]

Client: I felt calmer when I approached. I think I usually feel freaked out because I'm so scared. Maybe that would help. But how do I calm myself down?

Therapist: I think the answer to your question has two parts. On the one hand, you need to trust your sister to be your sister, and not your dad, to let go of being responsible for her and let her own some of her own responsibility. She is, after all, fifteen years old. On the other hand, learning relaxation might be helpful. Take this book, *The Relaxation and Stress Reduction Workbook.* Look through some of the techniques over the next week and try at least two of them on your own. Let me know next week how it went. I think reducing your overall stress would be helpful in and of itself. Then maybe as you learn to relax more, you'll be able to approach your sister differently. [Setting a goal; bibliotherapy; relaxation]

Client: Okay. I'll do that! What about my mom? I still worry about her.

Therapist: Let's start with learning to relax first, then your sister. I think letting go of some responsibility for your sister will be a little easier than with your mom. Your sister can be the first step to helping you feel less anxious about your mom. I could be wrong, though. What do you think? [Setting goals; self-disclosure; putting responsibility back on the client]

Client: You may be right. I think it would be easier to relax more with my sister than my mom. I feel I owe my mom so much. I just want her to be happy.

Therapist: You value your mom a great deal. I can tell her happiness is very important to you. Do you have any questions before we end our session today about the homework or anything else? [Reflecting feelings and content; probing]

Client: Nope. That should do it. I'm looking forward to checking out this book. Thanks!

REFERENCES AND RESOURCES

Baer, R. (2006). *Mindfulness-based treatment approaches: Clinician's guide to evidence base and applications.* San Diego, CA: Elsevier Academic.

Basmajian, J. (Ed.). (1989). *Biofeedback: Principles and practice for clinicians* (3rd ed.). Baltimore, MD: Williams & Wilkins.

Batty, M. J., Bonnington, S., Tang, B. K., Hawken, M. B., & Gruzelier, J. H. (2006). Relaxation strategies and enhancement of hypnotic susceptibility: EEG neurofeedback, progressive muscle relaxation and self-hypnosis. *Brain Research Bulletin, 71,* 83–90.

Brito, G. (2014). Rethinking mindfulness in the therapeutic relationship. *Mindfulness, 5,* 351–359.

Cormier, S., & Nurius, P. S. (2013). *Interviewing and change strategies for helpers* (7th ed.). Pacific Grove, CA: Brooks/Cole.

Davis, M., Robbins-Eshelman, E., & McKay, M. (2008). *The relaxation and stress reduction workbook* (6th ed.). Oakland, CA: New Harbinger.

Day, M. A., Eyer, J. C., & Thorn, B. E. (2014). Therapeutic relaxation. In S. G. Hofmann, D. A. Dozois, W. Rief, & J. J. Smits (Eds.), *The Wiley handbook of cognitive behavioral therapy* (Vols. 1–3, pp. 157–180). Wiley-Blackwell.

De Jong, P., & Berg, I. K. (2012). *Interviewing for solutions* (4th ed.). Pacific Grove, CA: Brooks/ Cole.

Freud, A. (1936). *The ego and mechanisms of defense.* New York, NY: International University Press.

Hubbard, K., & Falco, F. E. (2015). Relaxation techniques. In A. D. Kaye, N. Vadivelu, & R. D. Urman (Eds.), *Substance abuse: Inpatient and outpatient management for every clinician* (pp. 337–357). New York, NY: Springer Science + Business Media.

Kottler, J. A. (1992). *Compassionate therapy: Working with difficult clients.* San Francisco, CA: Jossey-Bass.

Kottler, J. A., & Carlson, J. (2002). *Bad therapy: Master therapists share their worst failures.* New York, NY: Brunner-Routledge.

Lazarus, R. (2006). Emotions and interpersonal relationships: Toward a person-centered conceptualization of emotions and coping. *Journal of Personality, 74*(1), 9–46.

Moreno, J. L. (1987). *The essential Moreno: Writings on psychodrama, group method, and spontaneity.* New York, NY: Springer.

Norcross, J. C., Beutler, L. E., & Levant, R. F. (Eds.). (2005). *Evidence-based practices in mental health: Debate and dialogue on the fundamental questions.* Washington, DC: American Psychological Association.

O'Hanlon, B., & Beadle, S. (1999). *Guide to possibility land: Fifty-one methods for doing brief, respectful therapy.* New York, NY: W. W. Norton.

Perls, F. (1969). *Gestalt therapy verbatim.* Moab, UT: Real People Press.

Rogers, C. (1951). *Client-centered therapy: Its current practice, implications and theory.* Boston, MA: Houghton Mifflin.

Rosenthal, H. G. (Ed.). (2011). *Favorite counseling and therapy homework assignments* (2nd ed.). New York, NY: Routledge.

Shaprio, S. L. (2009). The integration of mindfulness and psychology. *Journal of Clinical Psychology, 65*(6), 555–560.

Utay, J., & Miller, M. (2006). Guided imagery as an effective therapeutic technique: A brief review of its history and efficacy research. *Journal of Instructional Psychology, 33*(1), 40–43.

Vahinger, H. (1925). *The philosophy of acting "as if": A system of the theoretical, practical and religious fictions of mankind.* New York, NY: Harcourt, Brace.

Chapter 9

MAINTAINING PROGRESS AND EVALUATING RESULTS

Y ou might not consider figuring out how you are doing with a client as a therapeutic skill, but unless you can do this effectively your efforts are not likely to be very helpful. You must devise ways to determine accurately and consistently the impact of your interventions. You must be able to tell how well things are going. In fact, one of the best predictors of positive outcomes in therapy is when the clinician seeks feedback from the client on the process and the relationship, even (or especially) when things are not going well (Duncan, 2012). This allows you to make adjustments that better suit the client's needs at any moment in time, and the client feels empowered, thereby improving the therapeutic relationship.

In this chapter we discuss the skills that are involved in evaluating the results of your helping efforts. In other words: How are you doing?

SOME ASSESSMENT CHALLENGES

There are several reasons why measuring the effectiveness of your work is far more difficult than you might imagine.

1. *Though you believe you are helping people, they might not be doing nearly as well as you think.* Therapists cannot judge accurately how well things are going. At times some of your best interventions will fall on deaf ears; other times, you will think the session went horribly yet the client reports it was really helpful.

2. *Clients tell false truths when they report on their progress.* You can't necessarily trust what clients say is going on. First, they might not really know how they are doing but they want to please you so they make something up. Second, because they may not want to let you down, they will tell you things are going a lot better than they really are. Third, they may also play down how well they are doing because they enjoy the benefits of having lower expectations.

3. *How clients are doing in sessions is not necessarily a reliable indicator of how they are doing outside.* Some clients perform like trained seals during sessions—they say and do all the right things, they thank you profusely for how much you have helped them, and they repeat exactly what you most want to hear about what they have learned. Then they leave the office and don't do a darn thing to change anything. They can remain in therapy for years like this. If this isn't confusing enough, some clients will perform miserably in sessions, acting uncooperatively and appearing resistant, yet they may be making consistent and significant progress in their lives—without you knowing what is going on.

4. *Sometimes the results of therapy don't make themselves fully known until many months later.* Some interventions can have a delayed effect that is realized only some time later. After all, how many times have you finally integrated an insight even years after you first were exposed to the ideas? Clients can even leave therapy after treatment supposedly fails and then later integrate what was learned.

What all this means is that you must have a *lot* of humility and use caution when it comes to assessing the outcomes of your work. There are certainly ways you can learn to become more proficient in measuring the impact of your skills, but part of that development includes understanding the limitations of our assessment tools. That is one reason why you will want to rely on multiple measures of therapy outcomes, including client self-reports, observations of client behavior, therapist intuition, reports by family members and significant others, and objective measurement of specific behavior and declared outcome goals. In other words, the following is *not* an acceptable means by which to measure the results:

Therapist: So, how are you doing?

Client: Just great!

Exercise in Measuring Outcomes

Your instructor has devised several ways to measure how much you have learned in this class. These could include submitting audio recordings, video recording, transcriptions, process papers, and so on. This is a challenging task for you because it is difficult to get a clear sense of how much you have developed your skills. How do you measure such a thing? Based on how much you report you learn? Based on what the instructor observes?

Meeting in small groups, discuss alternative ways your therapeutic skills could be measured and assessed accurately. Think of creative ways in addition to the more traditional methods just mentioned.

SKILLS OF EVALUATING OUTCOMES AND MEASURING RESULTS: THE CLIENT'S EFFORTS

You may assume that the only way to evaluate outcomes and measure results is through your own analysis as the therapist. However, clients can take an active role in evaluating their progress, and in doing so, they are more likely to have better outcomes than if they passively show up to therapy each week. This section offers some suggestions on how you might solicit clients' participation beyond simply talking about their issues.

Self-Monitoring Strategies

One of the most logical ways to assess how therapy is going is to make the client responsible for this task. This means teaching clients to be assertive consumers and to look objectively at how things are proceeding. This could be introduced by the therapist saying the following:

> It is your job to let us both know the extent to which the therapy is meeting your needs. Ultimately, you are the best judge of this since you must live with the consequences of what happens. After every session, you must ask yourself these questions: Did I get what I wanted? To what extent have I made progress toward my self-declared goals? Ultimately, you will want to know: Is this working for me?
>
> In order to make this assessment on a regular basis, you will want to monitor carefully the progress of our work as it unfolds. It even helps to collect some data systematically, which means that you will want to measure the results on an ongoing basis.

I must warn you that progress does not always proceed in an orderly, sequential way. There will be relapses. There will be times when progress may be slow. But there should be some improvement within a reasonable period of time.

I am dependent on your feedback in order to customize what we do in here. I don't watch you in your world outside of sessions. I can't tell what you are really thinking and feeling inside, only what you report to me. I don't know how well or how poorly things are going. We must spend considerable time in here talking about what is working for you and what is not. It does little good to complain to others about your dissatisfactions and frustrations; you must bring them in here so we can review them together and make adjustments as they are needed. I am open and eager to get your feedback.

With an introduction similar to this, the therapist is educating the client about how important it is to work together to review progress on an ongoing basis. There are several means by which clients can help with this process.

Journaling

Keeping a journal in therapy is *not* like keeping a diary in which events are merely recorded. In the best possible circumstances, journaling becomes an extension of therapy, an integral part of the process by which clients continue their work on their own. In a sense, journaling eventually becomes the therapy once regularly scheduled sessions are stopped.

Like any other skill, clients don't necessarily know how to journal effectively. It is not enough to simply ask people to do this. Remember, if it is merely an assignment you give them, they will not feel all that committed to doing it on a regular and consistent basis. You must "sell" the importance of this structure and emphasize how critical it is to the work you are doing together.

As with anything else you teach to clients, it sure helps if you practice what you preach. To encourage clients to use this self-monitoring structure effectively it is preferable that you speak from personal experience—meaning that you keep your own journal on a regular basis to process your continued growth and development.

There are several different kinds of journal entries that clients can initiate, each of which complements what you are doing in sessions.

Progress Notes

Just as therapists keep progress notes on sessions, clients can construct their own narrative about what is covered in each meeting. Clients can even be encouraged to bring their notes to the session and review them as part of the check-in at the beginning of the session.

> Today we talked about the ongoing problem I have asking for what I want. As usual, I tended to overgeneralize and say that I do this with everyone but it was pointed out that I could assert myself pretty well with my friends (except for Dorrie). The main area that I have to focus on is related to my family. We looked at how I learned to be this way and drew some connections to the way my parents were raised according to a similar pattern in which the role of women is to serve men. We looked at how this belief continues to interfere with the relationship with my husband and my son. I agreed that I would talk about this with my mother this week and find out more about these so-called family legacies.

Critical Processing

This is a further (and deeper) process analysis of what is transpiring in therapy and how the person feels about it. The objective is to be as honest and frank as possible about one's own behavior, about the therapist's actions, and about the way sessions are going. If "progress notes" are mostly descriptive, then these types of entries are much more critical.

> All in all, it was a pretty good session but a painful one. I noticed that I defer to my therapist just like I do to others. There were several times when I agreed with him just because it was easier and I didn't want to disappoint him. I can tell he gets upset with me when I don't move as fast as he wants. I realize this is part of the same pattern that we were discussing. I plan to say something next time.

Insights

Journals can be used to keep track of new understandings, new insights, things that the client wishes to remember and hold onto. Entries might include particular ideas that are memorable, metaphors that seem especially useful, quotes that are especially powerful, or anything else worthy of remembering.

> That was pretty interesting the way my therapist pointed out how my expectations set up my disappointments. As long as I have such insanely unrealistic notions about what I want from people I will never get what I want. I set them up to fail me. I need to remember the Zen idea about staying clear and centered, expecting nothing, and then being delighted with whatever life brings me.

Goal-Setting

It is often useful to write down both short-term and long-term goals as they arise in sessions. Journaling about them is a way to commit oneself, in writing, to follow through on what was declared. Clients are held accountable for what they declare they wish to do. These written goals also help them to track progress.

> For the first time, I heard myself say out loud that I am not happy in my job and want a change. So, what that means is that I need to make some changes even though they really scare me. What I told my therapist is that I want to try something else, something different from what I'm doing. But it's really much more than that. I'm afraid to say it to anyone, but what I'd really like to do is go back to school and get another degree that would finally allow me to do what I've always wanted to do. I suppose the first step would be to look into what programs are available. I've also got to figure out my expenses to see what I can afford. In the short run, though, I've got to start making plans to cut down on my expenses so I can manage to live on less income during this transition.

Recording Progress

If a journal is a narrative about the therapy experience and progress that is being made, then other more objective means can be used to record progress. Clients can be taught to graph their progress in cases where specific behaviors have been identified as in need of change. They can be encouraged to plot their weekly successes and failures as they unfold. Depending on the nature of the presenting complaint, and how specifically it may be defined, the client may be directed to monitor changes in behavior.

A couple comes to therapy because they fight a lot. In fact, they fight so much and so loudly that neighbors complain and sometimes the police are called in to intervene. Although things have never escalated to the point that any physical abuse has taken place, the verbal sparring and screaming are quite toxic. This couple is difficult for anyone to be around for very long because they bicker so much of the time.

An initial assessment determines that the couple is quite committed to staying together and neither one has entertained serious thoughts about leaving the relationship (although they quite often threaten divorce). They enjoy a satisfying sexual relationship and have many interests in common. They don't even seem particularly bothered by their fights—that is more a problem for others around them.

The therapist has encouraged them to keep a detailed record of when the fights occur and to include: (a) the time of day the fight took place, (b) how long the

---

Exercise in Journaling

If you have not already done so, begin a journal of your journey as a therapist in training. Record several times a week what you are learning, what you are struggling with, and what you want to remember. List areas of weakness that you intend to work on. Explore unresolved personal issues that are triggered by the work you are doing. Write down feedback you are hearing about your interpersonal and helping skills. Discuss what puzzles, confuses, excites, and interests you the most. Write about what frightens you. Talk about the transformations in your personality, your behavior, and your relationships that you are noticing.

Make an effort to write at least a page every day, or at least several times each week. Examine your resistance and excuses for avoiding or postponing your journaling. Talk about that with your instructor or classmates.

Remember that you cannot in good conscience ask your clients to do something that you have been unable or unwilling to do yourself.

---

skirmish lasted, (c) what they were fighting about, (d) what happened right before the fight began, and (e) how the outcome of the dispute ended. They were each asked to keep separate records and then compare them at the session. Not surprisingly, they started to fight about what constituted a fight.

The therapist intervened to keep them on track and negotiated a consensus on their record from the previous week. They found that they had a total of 41 "fights" during the previous week, averaging more than 6 per day (one of the days they hadn't been together at all so no fights were recorded).

You can appreciate that the act of looking at their fighting behavior would already have had an impact on the pattern. The process of examining carefully what they were doing made them more aware of what they were doing. Furthermore, it is hard to have a proper war with one another when one or both people are busy taking notes on what is going on.

Using 41 fights per week as a baseline, the couple was responsible for keeping score on their "performance" during the ensuing weeks. They were thus able to measure changes that occurred as a result of several different interventions that took place. For instance, when they were asked to schedule all their fighting during specific intervals of time that were prearranged, the number went down to less than 30. When they were taught other ways of handling dispute resolution, the number went down farther. After each session and a different method of disrupting their pattern, the results could be measured. This allowed both the therapist and the couple to assess what was working and what was not.

As it turned out in this case, the best strategy was actually the assessment process itself. The couple became much more aware of their behavior to the extent that they couldn't engage in fighting anymore without it being labeled. They would fight about that too, of course, but the frequency and intensity of conflicts steadily decreased to one third the previous levels (but alas, still not eliminating the fighting completely).

This technique can also be effective working with children in school settings, especially when they are referred because of declining grades or interpersonal struggles. The student, along with the teacher, can track the grades or the frequency of interpersonal conflict over time. The student can create colorful charts to track progress, which in itself can be reinforcing to improve grades or behavior. Like the example of the couples above, the act of charting can be as impactful as the counseling. Many practitioners consider what happens outside of sessions to be far more important and meaningful than anything that is merely talked about.

Video Recording Sessions

We often do not know how we sound, act, or look on a regular basis. Observing yourself in action can be quite surprising, albeit uncomfortable at times. In this class, you may have been asked to record sessions of yourself practicing skills. If so, you were probably quite surprised about several things you do: nodding your head too much, giving too many minimal encouragers such as saying uh huh, fidgeting with your hands, or even moving in your chair too much. You would have never known these things had you not seen yourself in action. The same process can be helpful for your clients, and it's called interpersonal process recall (Kagan (Klein) & Kagan, 1997). Invite your client to video record the session; with most individuals owning smart phones, clients will likely have the option to record in their pocket or purse. Encourage them to watch themselves in session. This can be done in the last few minutes of a session or in a future session with the therapist, or clients can watch privately at home. By watching themselves, clients may be more able to identify maladaptive patterns of thinking, talking, or behaving.

Evaluation Forms

Many therapists create evaluation forms for clients to complete. For example, short, five-question surveys that are completed in the last few minutes of the session can be used. Questions for a quick survey might look something like this:

On a scale from 1 to 5, with 1 being least accurate and 5 being most accurate, rate the following statements:

1. I noticed some differences in my thoughts, feelings, or behaviors from last week to this week.

2. I believe my therapist cares about me.

3. My therapist understood what I was trying to convey.

4. Today's session was especially helpful to me.

5. I am improving in a variety of ways as a result of therapy.

Comments: _____

In contrast, longer questionnaires that can be completed every month to six weeks by clients at home and brought to session to discuss. Questions for a longer form might include the following:

- What did you learn, or what insight did you gain during this session (or in the last month)?
- List the type of actions or interventions you found to be most helpful.
- What actions or interventions were least helpful?
- Discuss what is missing and you would like added to therapy.

You can choose to have a variety of these in your assessment tool kit, and match each method to the client and the presenting issue. You could also use one method for all clients to keep consistency. In some ways, the method you choose to have clients evaluate the session is much less important than the invitation for clients to assess the quality of the relationship and the progress achieved. Your willingness to solicit feedback demonstrates that you care deeply about how well things are going and are quite interested in any adjustments or changes that could make things even better.

SKILLS OF EVALUATING OUTCOMES AND MEASURING RESULTS: THE THERAPIST'S EFFORTS

Being prepared to take an honest look at your work is more an attitude than a skill. Therapists and counselors often attempt to disown their failures and negative outcomes by blaming the client for being resistant. Unless you are willing to accept some degree of responsibility for sessions that don't appear to go well, there is little opportunity to learn from the experience. In fact, bad therapy can actually be your best teacher, especially if you are willing to look at your role in the poor results.

In order for any assessment skill to be of use, you must be prepared to examine outcomes as objectively and honestly as possible. This takes training, of course, but also a degree of commitment. This is the only way you are going to improve your skills.

Discourse Analysis

Another way in which you can evaluate your progress is by completing a discourse analysis. A discourse analysis also requires that you audiotape your session on occasion and transcribe it, but this time you transcribe the session completely. After transcription, look for repetitive words, phrases, or meanings used by you or the client. You can look for trends from the client to find something you might have missed in session, or you can look for trends in how you typically respond. Evaluating what you and your client say within a single session or over two or three consecutive sessions will help you to see trends you might not see in the moment and will make you aware of how you might improve your work with your client.

Evidence-Based Practice

There are myriad ways to work with a single client, and it's often difficult to choose the best path. Evidence-based practice is a growing trend and is valued because it helps therapists determine some of the best courses of action when working with clients. The rationale behind this approach is that techniques, therapies, and theories should be tested and validated as effective before using them with clients. As you are exposed to different ways to work with clients, you obtain research about the efficacy of a method before exploring training in that area. By choosing your interventions based upon some evidence, you have a greater chance at improving client outcomes.

Research is an important part of your training because it helps you become a critical and informed consumer of the literature. It is not enough to peruse articles in professional journals; you also need to determine whether the results are indeed valid for your clients and practice. This means asking yourself questions such as whether the literature review seems balanced and comprehensive, whether the procedures provided enough detail to get a sense of what was actually done, and whether the methodology seemed appropriate, and finally, how to generalize the results in an appropriate and meaningful way.

As an example of the need to read research carefully, imagine one studying the frequency and quality of "self-talk," comparing cognitive-behavioral therapy (CBT) with psychodynamic therapy. In psychodynamic therapy, self-talk is *not* the primary focus of work like it is with CBT. Therefore, you'd expect to find much less evidence of self-talk in the psychodynamic work. The authors could state that because CBT has a higher incidence of improvement in self-talk, CBT is a better therapy, but that would be an erroneous assumption. Psychodynamic therapy would use other methods to help clients. That's not to say that CBT and improving self-talk is not effective; these results would only indicate that CBT focuses on self-talk more than psychodynamic.

If you discover your client would benefit from a different type of treatment than you currently practice, you may be able to read a book and some articles to perform that type of therapy. If so, seeking consultation (discussed below) is an important step in learning your new way of working while keeping your client safe. In contrast, you may discover that the new modality requires more intensive training. Some ways of working with clients can be harmful if not employed appropriately. In this situation, you may need to refer your client to someone who can do that type of work. Consequently, you may also want to seek training in that area.

The movement toward evidence-based practice encourages practitioners to incorporate outcome measures into their work, especially relatively objective ways of assessing progress and outcomes. Most often this includes the use of questionnaires and feedback forms of some kind.

Consultation

As just stated, one of the reasons that going to conferences and workshops can be so valuable is that you can develop relationships with other professionals in your area. You will meet people whom you respect, and you should be able to develop consulting relationships for reciprocal help when one of you becomes stuck with a client. Discussing being stuck can bring fresh insight. Consultation is helpful not only when you get stuck, however; it is also helpful for ensuring you stay on top of things with your client. We can often get into ruts in the way we do therapy or look at clients, and a fresh perspective can help us to grow and prevent burnout.

Another advantage of consultation is personal growth. When very experienced therapists feel stuck with a particular client, the reason is often because of some countertransference issue. The therapist is somehow triggered by the client. Perhaps the client's personality is similar to the therapist's parent's. Or perhaps the client expresses some quality that the therapist does not like in himself or herself. For example, if the therapist is struggling with being less rigid and dislikes his own rigidity, then a client who expresses rigidity and values that rigidity may be difficult for the therapist to see objectively. By talking with another professional about being stuck, the therapist can explore aspects of his or her own personal struggles and use the opportunity as a personal growth experience, which will also, in turn, help the work with clients.

Supervision will become a large part of your weekly professional development, not only in your skills but in conceptualizing cases. Part of that supervision is consulting on cases. The eventual goal of these consultations is for you to reach a point where you naturally and consistently engage in self-supervision to supplement your sessions with other experts.

Exercise in Getting the Most From Supervision

Just as learning to be a good client takes practice, so too does learning to get the most from supervision. Before you begin the kind of intensive supervision that will be part of your later clinical courses and field placements, it would be highly profitable for you to speak to experienced practitioners and supervisors to get their advice on the best ways to use these consultation services. This is not as easy as it sounds because you may very well feel a certain amount of ambivalence about talking to a supervisor who may serve multiple roles as your confidant, advisor, tutor, and therapist, and also as your evaluator, who decides on your continued suitability for the profession. How much should you share with your supervisor about your fears, your feelings of inadequacy, your self-doubts, your mistakes and misjudgments? It all depends on the trust you feel in the relationship and whether you believe the supervisor is acting in your best interest. So, choose your supervisors wisely.

ENDING THERAPY EFFECTIVELY

The effectiveness of how therapy ends can be viewed in several ways. First, a judgment can be made about whether it ended successfully or unsuccessfully. Another way of looking at closure is whether the ending of therapy was done according to plan or took place prematurely. You might think that successful endings are always related to how intentionally and strategically the relationship was terminated, but that is not necessarily the case.

The reality is that many clients you will see simply stop coming. They may cancel an appointment and never call back to reschedule. You can't necessarily assume this relationship ended unsuccessfully, or even that there was more work to be done. Some clients just have trouble saying goodbye so they may initiate this process by walking away without looking back. A case could be made that this is, in fact, a very successful outcome. The problem, however, is that you may never find out what happened, and you have to live with that uncertainty.

One of the things for which therapists are often singularly unprepared is how to deal with failures and disappointing endings. Yet learning from our mistakes not only presents opportunities to become better at what we do, but is actually quite necessary to prevent further misjudgments in the future. In one study of the worst mistakes of the world's best therapists, it was found that what most interferes with a clinician improving professional competence are such things as overconfidence, arrogance, narcissism, rigidity, and a marked refusal to acknowledge own one's errors (Kottler & Carlson, 2003). It is crucial for you to have a safe place to consult with supervisors and peers about what you've done that did not work and thereby learn from these failures.

In ideal circumstances, or at least according to the preferred plan, clients are prepared for termination as soon as they begin treatment. This is to minimize dependency issues that may occur, but also to equip clients to understand the natural progression that takes place in the relationship. Often the closure process may take place during the last scheduled appointment, although ideally the whole ending process takes place over many weeks.

Several distinct skills are involved in ending therapy effectively. Many of these closure strategies involve adapting skills you have already learned and applying them to this distinct stage in the process.

Exercise in Good and Bad Endings

In small groups, talk to one another about learning experiences that ended on the best and worst possible notes. Describe a class, workshop, or helping relationship that ended in such a way that the momentum of what you learned continued long after things ended. Describe another relationship where your progress ended abruptly as soon as the help stopped. Talk about what made the difference between these two kinds of experiences.

Negotiating Closure

There are several different ways to address termination issues. In one scenario, clients may state that they are ready to end; in another, the therapist suggests that sessions be stopped in the near future. Regardless of who brings up the issue, there is usually some form of negotiation involved in deciding when therapy will stop. Remember that both parties will have some difficulty letting go of a relationship that has been so significant, intense, and intimate.

Client: I've been thinking lately, that uh, um . . .

Therapist: Go on.

Client: Well, I was kind of wondering if, maybe, if I don't need to come back anymore.

Therapist: You're feeling really good about the progress you've made and thinking that you're ready to start preparing for going out on your own.

Client: Yeah. What do you think about that?

Therapist: Well, for one thing I'm feeling a bit sad because we've gotten very close to one another, but on the other hand, I'm really excited for you that you are feeling confident enough to deal with things more on your own.

Client: I'm feeling a little uneasy about this too. But I think I'm ready.

Therapist: I do too! So let's talk about how we can best bring our work to a close.

In this case, it might only require another session or two to complete the therapy and then work toward closure. With other clients, you may need many weeks to facilitate this process. It all depends on the client, the amount of work left to do, and your mutual assessment of where things stand.

Summarizing Themes and Reviewing Content

Some time is spent toward the end of the relationship helping clients to put things in perspective and reviewing what they have learned. This is a time to ask them to compare where they are now to when they started, and also to consider the extent to which they have reached their previously stated goals. Such a process would look something like the following:

Therapist: This is our last session, at least for a while.

Client: Yeah.

Therapist: I'm wondering what you have been thinking and feeling, anticipating our meeting today.

Client: Well, kind of excited actually. It has been a long haul.

Therapist: Yes, it has been a tough journey for you.

Client: I'm also feeling kind of sad.

Therapist: It's hard for us to say goodbye after having spent so much time together talking about such intimate things.

Client: I kind of wonder what it's going to be like without coming here every week.

Therapist: I'm going to miss seeing you as well. We've been through so much together.

Client: For sure.

Therapist: I'm looking at you now and remembering what you were like when we first met. You remember that first session?

Client: (laughs) I wish you wouldn't remind me.

Therapist: Seriously, what were you like then compared to what you are like now?

So far, the therapist is checking on how the client has been feeling anticipating the last scheduled session. This would provide clues as to whether the person is truly ready to move on. In this case, the client seems to be feeling a healthy balance of sadness and exhilaration. Notice that we say "seems to be," because you can't know for sure what is going on merely from listening to client reports. From observing this client, it appears as if his behavior is congruent with what he is saying.

Although the therapist touches on their feelings toward one another, before pursuing that further she would like to dig deeper into what was learned from the therapy.

Client: Well, I can hardly recognize myself now. I'm just not the same person anymore.

Therapist: Say more about the specific ways this is the case. Exactly how are you different?

By asking the client to articulate how he is different, the therapist is continuing the process of assessing the outcome.

Client: For one thing, I don't complain and whine so much anymore. I've accepted that there are some things I can't change no matter how much I would like this to be the case.

Therapist: You are referring to your previous efforts of trying to get your boss to change rather than concentrating on what you could do to respond to her differently.

Client: Absolutely.

Therapist: How else are you different?

Again the therapist presses her client to define, as specifically as possible, what is different now. This is an excellent way to get the client to articulate what has been accomplished, and does so in a way that allows them to end on an upbeat note.

Next on the agenda is to ask the client to summarize the main work that was accomplished. Clients are generally not that skilled at covering all the material, so the therapist would be free to fill in what was missed.

Client: I'd say that I have more patience now than I used to. I don't seem to get so frustrated with people when they don't do things the way I'd prefer.

Therapist: I like the way you said that: "the way you would prefer." That implies that you remember that you can't make people behave a certain way, and just because they don't comply with your preferences, that doesn't mean you can't accept this and take care of yourself.

Client: Yeah, but I still get upset when my daughter doesn't listen to me. I mean, for God's sake, she's only fifteen and already she thinks she's an adult.

Therapist: Let's hold off on that for a minute and get back to what else you've learned.

The client starts to move into other things that are not fully worked through, but the therapist redirects the discussion back to the high points first. In the next stage they can talk about further work that needs to be done.

Client: Well, that thing you taught me to do so I don't get so stressed out at work.

Therapist: You mean the relaxation training?

Client: Yeah.

Therapist: Okay, what else?

Client: I don't know. I guess that's about it.

Now it is time for the therapist to fill in what the client left out. This will prompt further review by both parties and lead to listing as many things as possible that were accomplished in their sessions together. Some therapists may take notes and write down what is listed during the review or, better yet, ask the client to do so. Some other clinicians may record this last session and give the tape to the client as a parting gift. This acts as a reminder of what they did together and what is left to do.

Identifying Unfinished Business

No matter how many weeks, months, years, or even decades spent in therapy, there will always be things left unfinished. Human beings are just so infinitely complex that it is impossible to cover everything that needs to be addressed. But if the therapy has been effective, then clients have internalized the skills to continue work on their own. It could be said, in fact, that the ultimate purpose of therapy is to teach clients to be their own therapists.

This stage of the closure process involves helping clients to assess the work that is left. It is sort of an inventory of goals that still need to be reached and of continuous work that must be followed through.

Therapist: You were saying before that you still have trouble dealing with your daughter, especially when she is so strong willed.

Client: She can be so stubborn sometimes. She won't listen to anyone. It drives me crazy.

Therapist: She sounds a lot like you in many ways.

Client: (laughs) I guess that's true.

Therapist: So, you still have some work cut out for you in handling conflict in your relationship. We've also discussed how a certain amount of disagreement between parents and their adolescent children is not only normal but also healthy. You remember why?

Client: Well, you said it's because it helps them to separate from us.

Therapist: That's what I said. What do you think?

By reviewing one unresolved issue, the therapist is giving the client a quiz of sorts, asking him to repeat what he has learned and reminding him of what he must practice doing in the future. It is usual to have several areas of unfinished business to identify.

Client: No, I agree with you. It's just that it's so hard to remember this stuff when she starts ripping into me about something.

Therapist: Of course it's hard. But that's not to say that you can't make things proceed in a way that is less upsetting to both of you.

Client: Right.

Therapist: What else is left over?

The therapist continues to dig with the client into areas that have been only marginally excavated. The goal is definitely *not* to stir things up more, especially at this late stage. Rather, the objective is to remind one another about potential trouble spots that might arise at some later time. The client may elect to return for follow-up sessions, but far better is to apply what has been learned to new situations. After all, if transfer of learning is to be successful, the client must adapt what he already knows to other challenges.

Therapist: So, let's say that your daughter comes home from school today and tells you that she doesn't feel like doing her homework and she's going out with friends.

Client: Please don't remind me. I can feel a headache coming on just thinking about it.

Therapist: Then let's stop for a moment so you can practice your relaxation skills.

Client: Very funny. I guess you're reminding me that what I do with my boss I can do with my daughter as well.

Therapist: And not just with your daughter, but with anyone with whom you find yourself in conflict.

During this phase of closure, the therapist structures time for the client to review not only what has been done, but also what is left to do. This leads logically to planning for any future work.

Constructing a Plan

Based on the nature of the unfinished business, a specific aftercare plan should be developed that provides alternative support and structure needed. You cannot just close therapy with a client and expect that the client's life will continue in a happily-ever-after way. After the initial feelings of elation and relief, there may also be strong feelings of abandonment. Even when therapy has gotten into a rut, when the conversations are repetitious, there is still the advantage of a regularly scheduled appointment to review progress. When that ceases, the client may lose momentum because he is no longer held accountable.

The therapist and client together structure a plan of action for continuing the work left to do. This might involve referral to a support group, but may also involve looking at alternative ways that the functions of therapy can be met. Examples of this might include regularly scheduled meetings with friends, journaling, attending classes or workshops, reading books of a particular nature, continuing exercise programs, and so on.

Saying Goodbye

This might sound like the simplest of steps but is actually among the most difficult. You have spent many hours together talking about the most intimate things imaginable. There is a lot of ambivalence tied up in this relationship that is now coming to an end. You want to say goodbye on an upbeat note, but also one that acknowledges the bittersweet nature of any ending.

Just think about entering into the most intimate relationships with people, learning their deepest secrets and darkest fears. You spend hours together, talking only about meaningful content. You develop emotional attachments to one another; you even come to look forward to your meetings. An even more complicating factor is that if you are in private practice, you might also be dependent on the income clients provide. Then, one day, it is time to say goodbye, perhaps forever. You may act like this is no big deal, as if this sort of thing happens all the time (which it does), but that does not stop the pain and loss associated with ending a relationship—even if it is for the best of reasons.

Scheduling Follow-Ups

You will want to leave the door open for any issues that may come up in the future. It is also considered sound practice to schedule checkup sessions that are designed to make sure the client is continuing to make steady progress. Surgeons will want to see patients a few weeks or months after a wound has healed, just to make sure that the mending has continued; therapists and counselors will do the same.

Follow-ups can be handled in a number of ways. You might schedule another session a few weeks or months later. You may have started to taper off the frequency of sessions from weekly to biweekly to monthly as a way to minimize closure trauma. Another possibility is that you could send follow-up letters or make an aftercare phone call just to check to see how things are going and to communicate your continued interest and care. You would want to be careful not to give the impression that you are pressing the person to return—merely that you want him or her to know that you are still in his or her corner.

Handling Relapses

The best way to prevent relapses is to plan for them, because some degree of backsliding is inevitable. Programs can be implemented to plan for and prevent relapses (Miller & Rollnick, 2002; Stevens & Smith, 2012). Several steps are involved in this process, each of which requires its own set of skills.

1. *Identify high-risk situations.* Help the client to recognize those situations that will be the most tempting. Example: Someone who has worked on controlling his anger may realize that he is in real jeopardy of relapsing when he drives alone in rush-hour traffic.

2. *Develop coping skills needed to deal with these situations.* Prepare clients with the behaviors they'll need to deal with the challenges they will face. In the first example, the man may need anger management and stress reduction techniques.

3. *Rehearse responses.* Whether through imagery, fantasy exercises, or role-plays, it is a good idea to help clients rehearse how they will respond in potential relapse situations. The man with anger control problems may be asked to imagine himself caught in a traffic jam and then be guided through ways he can respond as an alternative to blowing up.

4. *Practice new skills.* Before the therapy ends, you will want to structure opportunities for clients to deliberately slip backward so they can prove to themselves they have the power and skills to recover at will. We are not saying that you should urge a recovering alcoholic to have a drink, but rather that you should help the person to practice putting himself in stressful and challenging situations (going to a dinner party with alcohol) and then dealing effectively with the temptations.

5. *Generalize to new situations.* Help your clients to apply what they have learned with the presenting problem to other areas of life.

6. *Build resilience and adaptability.* The one thing that you can count on is that things will change. Clients will face new challenges they had not ever considered. They will encounter difficulties that were not planned for. Help clients to prepare for surprises so they can recover with minimum interruption in their continued growth.

7. *Increase frustration tolerance.* Help clients to deal with disappointments and setbacks in such a way that these become minor annoyances rather than major disruptions.

8. *Develop support systems.* Build in sources of support that can be available as needed. These could include self-help groups, sponsors in 12-step programs, friends and family members who will pitch in, and referrals to other professionals.

9. *Make needed lifestyle changes.* Assist clients to make alterations in their routines and habits in such a way that they encourage and support changes that were made. These might involve significant changes in friendships, social activities, spending habits, and so on.

10. *Learn from mistakes.* Remind clients that setbacks and failures are inevitable and unavoidable, yet they don't have to represent significant difficulties as long as one recognizes what is happening and learns from the mistakes.

Exercise to Reflect on Failure

In order to help clients learn the most from their mistakes and failures, it helps if you are skilled at doing the same. No matter how skilled a therapist you might be, how well prepared and trained you are, how experienced you become, how good your supervisors might be, you will still face situations where you can't help people to the extent you would prefer. Some of your clients will leave as unhappy customers. Some will even become worse no matter what you try to do to help them. And somehow you must learn to acknowledge your limitations and weaknesses as a clinician if you ever hope to get better.

In small groups, talk about some of the most disappointing failures and regretful mistakes in your life. Share what you learned from these experiences and how they made you stronger and more skilled in the future.

Talk to one another about some of your fears and apprehensions related to making mistakes in your work. How do you intend to work through these blunders when it is often not safe to admit your imperfections and lapses to others?

PITFALLS AND COMMON MISTAKES

In this last chapter before approaching work with families and groups, there are only a few common mistakes we see with beginners. Yet because endings are just as important as beginnings, you will want to attend to avoiding these pitfalls as well.

Forgetting to Evaluate Your Progress

Several reasons exist as to why a licensed therapist might cease to obtain supervision. While you are in school and during your internship for licensure, you will be required to be evaluated at least once per week individually and/or as part of a group. Sometimes these evaluations are quite formal. At other times, evaluations will be done surreptitiously while your supervisor listens to you talk about your cases and reads your case notes. Once you are licensed, however, supervision is no longer a requirement. In fact, unless you work for an agency, obtaining external supervision at your skill level is difficult at best. Even if you work for an agency, your supervisor may not be looking to help you improve so much as making sure your clients are not dissatisfied. As a result, many practitioners get comfortable working with their clients without supervision, and unless they have difficulty with a client, they cease to get supervision. They forget. What's worse is that after not having supervision for a long period of time, the practitioner may become somewhat insecure about his or her skill level and fear receiving any supervision, imagining that another professional will discover that he or she is an imposter, not a good therapist at all. And so begins a terrible cycle of not obtaining supervision.

A more dangerous situation is when therapists lose all humility and believe themselves to be excellent practitioners, not needing to improve on any skill or to become educated in any new areas. Therapists who find themselves in this position frequently burn out. They can lose why they came to this field in the first place. They can feel stagnant and bored, thankful when a client no-shows or cancels. It isn't likely that therapists who believe each client is a burden will be able to provide good therapy.

Furthermore, seeking to evaluate your performance requires that you be able to receive constructive feedback (i.e., criticism) throughout your career, which can be quite difficult at times. Therapists cycle through feeling competent and incompetent, with or without supervision. At first, you may feel incompetent because this is a new skill. You may be more forgiving of yourself as a trainee until you feel like you have finally mastered the first level of skills. Then you feel competent, feel good about your abilities. An event happens, such as you see someone else's work or you receive a new supervisor, and suddenly, you feel incompetent again. It's difficult. Students often don't realize that they are now trying to master a more advanced skill level, and feel instead that they are starting from the beginning. They are quite hard on themselves. So after cycling through this a few times and receiving a license, a therapist may feel too raw to receive any more supervision; this is especially true if the supervision was inadequate, where the supervisor offered information only about weaknesses and didn't also point out strengths.

Obviously the reverse can be just as dangerous, where the supervisor points out only strengths and disregards areas for improvement. The therapist may falsely believe he or she no longer needs to evaluate progress.

Finally, even if the therapist would like to obtain supervision after licensure, doing so requires some additional work and, consequently, time, a valuable commodity. Finding creative ways to self-supervise or to consult without losing confidentiality is difficult and time-consuming. Obtaining information from your clients in session can take time away from your client's need to talk. Assessing information outside the session takes time away from other activities. So what does a therapist do? Many therapists just don't do anything, which is rather sad for their clients. Many therapists may just become mediocre at helping clients. However, you can be different. You can become a phenomenal therapist if you continue to evaluate, if you commit to taking the extra time and effort required. If you truly intend to transform lives, you must be open to continual evaluation. Your clients will be happier, and so will you.

Terminating Prematurely

In some situations, terminating with your client may be unavoidable. For instance, while you are in school, you may have only one semester with a client, who will need to be referred to next semester's students if he or she is not ready for termination. When you leave an agency to start earning an income after your internship, you may have to terminate prematurely. These are situations that are not preventable. Yet, you can let the client know in advance and work within these limitations.

Even without these externally imposed systems, you may find yourself terminating prematurely. When?

- *When you don't particularly care for a client because he seems like a difficult case for you.* For instance, imagine a client who has a history of domestic violence and is sent to you by the probation department, for anger management. He may yell at you, take absolutely no responsibility for his outbursts, and resist your best attempts to help him. He continues to come because he is required to stay in therapy if he wants to keep out of jail, but he's not that committed to changing. As you can imagine, clients who are involuntary can be quite challenging, but you must find a way to work with them. Perhaps you won't accomplish a lot, but when you do, imagine how rewarding that progress could be: much more fulfilling than the easy client.
- *When you find the client triggers a countertransference feeling in you.* Just imagine that you are going through a difficult period in your marriage. Your

wife just can't keep a job, yet she spends money like it's going out of style. You have tried everything at home to be supportive and yet be assertive about taking care of your needs. Then a client comes in who says she is frustrated with her spouse because he won't let her spend money on new clothes for a new job she just started. Your client has always known that her husband was conservative with money, but this just feels ridiculous to her. As you listen, you find yourself aligning with the husband. Your questions are leading in a certain direction. You can't be objective; you're too angry with your own wife to even see this client's perspective. You are aware enough to know that your own issues are getting in the way. What do you do? Refer? No, you work on it. You are experiencing a countertransference, a situation that happens in therapy when your client triggers something in you similar to a relationship or other issue in your life. The best way to combat this reaction, which will happen, is for you to receive your own therapy or obtain supervision or consult with another professional. You cannot refer every client who has money problems. You must get help. So the bad news is you have to work on your own stuff. The good news is that you aren't likely to become stagnant because of this problem and may even find an acceptable solution. And by overcoming yet another challenge in your life, you will grow personally and professionally.

- *When your client has vastly different values than you that may even be offensive to you.* Let's assume you have grown up in a conservative Christian environment with strong Christian values. A client comes to you and says that he needs therapy because he can't seem to find a woman to whom he is attracted. Through the process of therapy, he comes to realize that he has always been attracted to men, even as a child. What do you do if you believe that being gay is wrong because it is against your religion? Do you try to convince the client it is a choice? No, you realize your ethical guidelines require that you not impose your values. Do you try to convince your client to become asexual? You realize that's not likely to work. Do you refer? Maybe, but we hope not, because you realize that the client may see the referral as a rejection and feel hurt because you have already established a therapeutic alliance. Instead, we hope you can learn to see the world through your client's eyes, see from his phenomenological perspective, and work with your client from that foundation, not from your own. If you can master this skill with something so extreme, imagine how much better you will be as a therapist. You will really enhance your empathy skills by limiting your own projections as much as humanly possible. And just imagine how wonderful your clients will feel and how they will foster your ability not only to see them, but to accept them as well.

Your ethical codes state that you can refer a client when necessary, and you will need to at times (AAMFT, 2012; ACA, 2014; APA, 2010; NASW, 2008). Referrals are appropriate on occasion and can be in the best interest of you and your client. However, at what point do you stop referring clients? Do you keep only the ones you like, the ones who are psychologically minded, who self-pay, who are responsible, and who work hard? Not likely, because you won't get a lot of people like that. You'll go broke first.

So rather than referring or terminating prematurely, you must continue to do your own work, as a therapist and personally. If you find yourself talking your clients into termination over and over, you may want to take a look at what might be going on. Instead of asking yourself why none of these clients wants to terminate, ask yourself what they have in common that makes you uncomfortable. You may need to take responsibility for trends and own your part in them. Most likely, you will find that you have an issue that needs some attention. If you do, get your own therapy. Therapists who obtain their own therapy are not unusual, because the nature of the work requires that they—you—be as healthy as possible. It's normal and natural for therapists to be in and out of therapy for the duration of their career. Therefore, just accept the fact that you will probably need therapy from time to time until you retire. You'll be better for it.

Not Reminding the Client of Upcoming Termination

Try to imagine this situation. You having been working with a client for 13 weeks, and it is the end of the session. Suddenly, you remember that next week is your last session together.

Therapist: Well, we have about ten minutes left, and I wanted to remind you that last week will be our last session.

Client: What? Next week? But I still have so much work to do. I'm just getting started.

You can imagine how frustrated and betrayed the client might feel. She is totally unprepared for termination. Even though she has a week to think about it, she may not return because of her anger. Worse, she may regress, knowing that her primary support will be taken away in only one week. How is she to cope with such short notice? And now she has a new issue, abandonment!

As stated earlier, sometimes you know in advance that you will need to terminate with clients on a predetermined date. When you first meet with them, you should let them know that your time together is limited. In addition, by your letting clients know in advance, they can be well prepared when the time for termination approaches. Having a predetermined date may even be an advantage because clients realize they must get the work done within a prescribed amount of time. Clients can't take their sessions with you for granted.

All clients should also be reminded of the termination date at least three sessions in advance so that they have time to process the information. During the last few weeks, you may want to give your clients sufficient time to discuss their feelings with you so that you can say goodbye well. Saying goodbye is something we don't always do well, even when you're both ready. Furthermore, if your clients have some abandonment issues (and who doesn't, to some degree?), you will want to help them find new ways to cope with the parting. By mistakenly not providing clients with sufficient notice, you may exacerbate their issues yet never become aware of the consequences.

Stringing the Client Along

So, you finally made it. You have had your license for years, and you have had a booming private practice. But then the economy changes and people are getting laid off of work right and left. Your best clients can no longer afford the luxury of therapy because they are unemployed, like thousands of others. You have only a few clients left who self-pay, and you know that most of your HMO or insurance-paid clients will have only six sessions. How will you make ends meet?

When seeing clients becomes your bread and butter, your only income, you may be tempted in difficult times to string your clients along, keeping them in therapy much longer than necessary. You may find yourself rationalizing that the client still has work to do. You may find yourself convincing many clients to continue therapy even when they think they are ready to terminate. If that happens, we recommend you become really clear about whether you want the client to continue therapy for your sake or for the client's sake. Continuing therapy because issues still exist is not necessarily in the client's best interest because, as we have stated before, your clients will always have issues. This is why setting goals (discussed in Chapter 8) can be so helpful. Goals will help you and your client know when it is time to terminate. Clients need time to go into the world with their newfound skills and use them, refine them, and, ideally build some self-confidence as a result of reaching them. Your job is to work yourself out of a job, even if that is inconvenient for you. That's not to say that you won't have some clients who want long-term therapy. You might. Yet very few clients, especially when you need them most (in economic hard times), will have this luxury. Terminate when the client is ready. Terminate because the goal has been met. It's your ethical obligation.

APPLICATIONS TO SELF: CLOSURE ON CLOSURE

One of the most difficult challenges you will face as a clinician is mastering the art and science of ending the therapy effectively. There are a lot of feelings that will be stirred up inside you as you say goodbye to people you have grown close to—sadness, loss, frustration, abandonment, relief, excitement, pride, and a dozen others. These feelings are not unlike those that parents feel when their kids leave home.

Closure is difficult to manage because the client may also be experiencing tremendous ambivalence about ending the therapy. There is relief, of course, at just saving the time and expense involved. The client may also feel a degree of pride in graduating from a very challenging program—some might say, the most painful and growth-producing structure for learning that is available.

When bringing therapy to an end, you must help clients to come to terms with their reactions, and also help them to continue their work on their own. In addition, you must learn to come to terms with your own losses after experiencing such intimacy with your client.

Think about how you have ended relationships in the past. List four or five important relationships that have ended. Write how each one ended: abruptly, slowly, on good terms or bad, willingly or unwillingly, and so on. Read back through what you wrote. Do you see a trend? We often get in the habit of doing things the same way over and over, and endings are no exception to that rule. What makes most of us especially clumsy about ending relationships is that we are not taught how to do this well, neither didactically nor by example. So, learning to be okay with ending these most intimate relationships will help you to do it in your life outside of the therapy session.

SUMMARY

In this chapter, we have covered the importance of evaluating your progress with your clients. Related to evaluating progress is deciding when to terminate therapy and how to do that effectively. We hope, at this point, that you feel like you have a foundation for working with clients in an individual setting. In the next two chapters, we introduce you to working with two other client types: families and groups. Each of these requires many of the skills you have learned up to this point but also requires some additional skills that focus on interpersonal relationships in a therapeutic setting.

Skills in Action: Closure

Therapist: As we've talked about for a few weeks, it's our last session today, and we've been wrapping things up. I would like us to take some time today to review what you've learned in the past six months, what you still want to work on, and how you'll continue the work when we are done. Last week, we agreed that you would review the journal you've been keeping during our time together. Tell me what you discovered. [Following up on homework; encouraging the client to summarize]

Client: Before reading it again, I had forgotten how frustrated I was with my sister and her family. I can't believe that I felt so responsible for her kids! I still have a hard time when I go to her house, but now I'm getting better about knowing how I can help, and what I need to let go of.

Therapist: You're really feeling a lot more confidence in your ability to handle things with your nephews, but you've also been able to generalize this to other areas of your life. [Providing encouragement and planting hope; transfer of learning]

Client: Yeah, I realized that this is not just an issue with my nephews, but that I need to take responsibility for everything and everyone.

Therapist: That is an important challenge for you. We talked about when you take responsibility that it served you in some way. [Facilitating exploration; reminding client of previous lesson related to secondary gains]

Client: It does. When I feel responsible, I learned or realized that I feel important and a sense of belonging. I also discovered that by being responsible, I could feel more in control and less helpless.

Therapist: And what's different now? [Probing]

Client: I think that by being in therapy I feel like I am important too and can have a role without having to take full responsibility. I don't know why, but for some reason, I feel better about who I am.

Therapist: You say you don't know why, yet you DO have some ideas about that. You feel a sense of belonging and see your value now. You mentioned before about feeling helpless, too. [Confronting; reflecting feelings; facilitating discussion about unfinished business]

Client: Yeah, I'm still uncomfortable with feeling helpless. I think with that awareness, I can also sense when I start feeling desperate, that I'm probably feeling helpless.

Therapist: You are still working on being comfortable with sometimes really being helpless. [Reflecting content]

Client: I am, but I've been practicing those relaxation techniques we worked on to stop myself and think before I act or speak. I'm getting really good at that.

Therapist: You look really happy and relieved as you say that. [Reinforcement]

Client: I never thought that I would be able to slow myself down. I wish I'd known how to do this a long time ago. I even use it when I get angry with my wife. She likes it, too.

Therapist: It sounds like your marriage is improving, too. You never mentioned that before. [Reflecting content]

Client: It definitely is. I guess I got so stuck on my nephews, I forgot to mention that. She really likes you because of how I've changed with her. (laughs)

Therapist: You're surprised at how this changed other aspects of your life. [Feeling reflection; transfer of learning]

Client: It's true. I am. (smiling)

Therapist: I'd like to go back to your feelings of helplessness. You're getting better coping with it by using the relaxation techniques, which you say have been helpful. We talked about what was behind the difficulty with your feelings of helplessness, the source of your frustration. [Reflection of content; probing unfinished business]

Client: Yeah, looking over my journal I discovered that it was because my mom always told me that I had to take care of my family, that I am the responsible one, the one she can always depend on. I can hear her voice in my head all the time.

Therapist: And how will you handle that belief once you're out of therapy? [Planning for relapses]

Client: I need to develop a voice that reminds me that she knows I have limits, I can't do everything.

Therapist: Exactly what would you like that voice to say? [Probing to create a plan]

Client: I would say to myself, "I can only do my part, and I'm still a good person, even if I can't fix it."

Therapist: That's what we talked about. How has that been working for you? [Clarifying the plan]

Client: Actually, it does. I just need to remember it.

Therapist: You can always look back at your journal from time to time, which should help you remember. (pauses) I just want you to know that I've really enjoyed working with you, and I'm going to miss our meetings each week. I've liked how hard you have worked and how open and optimistic you are. [Offering a suggestion; self-disclosure; saying goodbye]

Client: Thank you. I feel the same way. I'm going to really, really miss our time together. I'm . . . (starts to cry)

Therapist: (waits for client to regain composure) You were *saying* that you are going to miss me and miss our conversations. [Refection of content]

Client: (nods, dabs eyes with tissue, takes a deep breath)

Therapist: Yet you also have some fears about how you are going to do on your own. [Reflection of feeling]

Client: (nods)

Therapist: Yet most of the work you've done in here, you have done on your own. Sure, I've helped a bit. Provided you with support. But YOU are the one who has made all this progress. And everything you've learned is now part of you. [Instilling hope; reinforcing progress]

Client: You're right, of course. I do know I'll be fine. I'm actually really ready for this. But I will still miss you. Is that okay?

Therapist: I'll miss you too. And remember: I'll be following up with you in a month just to make sure that you are continuing to progress as you wish. We can always schedule a "tune-up" if it's needed. [Planning for follow up]

REFERENCES AND RESOURCES

American Association for Marriage and Family Therapy. (2012). *AAMFT code of ethics* [Electronic version]. Retrieved October 23, 2015, from https://www.aamft.org/imis15/Documents/AAMFT%20Code_11_2012_Secured.pdf

American Counseling Association. (2014). *ACA code of ethics* [Electronic version]. Retrieved October 23, 2015, from https://www.counseling.org/resources/aca-code-of-ethics

American Psychological Association. (2010). *Ethical principles of psychologists and code of conduct* [Electronic version]. Retrieved October 23, 2015, from http://www.apa.org/ethics/code/principles.pdf

DeFife, J. A., Hilsenroth, M. J., & Gold, J. R. (2008). Patient ratings of psychodynamic psychotherapy session activities and their relation to outcome. *Journal of Nervous and Mental Disease, 196*(7), 538–546.

Dillon, C. (2003). *Learning from mistakes in clinical practice.* Pacific Grove, CA: Brooks/Cole.

Duncan, B. L. (2012). The partners for change outcome management system (pcoms): The heart and soul of change project. *Canadian Psychology/Psychologie Canadienne, 53*(2), 93–104.

Falvey, J. E. (2002). *Managing clinical supervision: Ethical practice and legal risk management.* Pacific Grove, CA: Brooks/Cole.

Jones, W. P., & Kottler, J. A. (2006). *Understanding research: Becoming a competent and critical consumer.* Upper Saddle River, NJ: Prentice Hall.

Kagan (Klein), H., & Kagan, N. I. (1997). Interpersonal process recall: Influencing human interaction. In C. E. Watkins (Eds.), *Handbook of psychotherapy supervision* (pp. 296–309). Hoboken, NJ: John Wiley.

Kottler, J. A., & Carlson, J. (2003). *Bad therapy: Master therapists share their worst failures.* New York, NY: Brunner-Routledge.

Miller, S. D., Duncan, B. L., & Hubble, M. A. (2004). Beyond integration: The triumph of outcome over process in clinical practice. *Psychotherapy in Australia, 10*(2), 2–19.

Miller, W. R. & Rollnick, S. (2002). *Motivational interviewing: Helping people change.* New York, NY: Guilford.

Morrissette, P. J. (2002). *Self-supervision: A primer for counselors and helping professionals.* New York, NY: Brunner-Routledge.

National Association of Social Workers. (2008). *Code of ethics of The National Association of Social Workers* [Electronic version]. Retrieved October 23, 2015, from http://www.social workers.org/pubs/code/code.asp

Rabu, M., Haavind, H., & Binder, P. E. (2013). We have traveled a long distance and sorted out the mess in the drawers: Metaphors for moving towards the end in psychotherapy. *British Journal of Counselling and Psychotherapy, 13*(1), 71–80.

Stevens, P. & Smith, R. (2012). *Substance abuse counseling: Theory and practice.* New York, NY: Pearson.

Tryon, G. S. (2002). *Counseling based on process research: Applying what we know.* Boston, MA: Allyn & Bacon.

Vasquez, M. J. T., Bingham, R. P., & Barnett, J. E. (2008). Psychotherapy termination: Clinical and ethical responsibilities. *Journal of Clinical Psychology, 64*(5), 653–665.

PART III

SKILLS TO USE WITH MULTIPLE CLIENTS

Chapter 10

SKILLS FOR FAMILY THERAPY AND OTHER ROLES FOR THERAPISTS

This chapter and the one that follows on group leadership skills look at the ways counselors and therapists use their generic training to work in specialized treatment modalities. Family and group strategies share a number of core assumptions in that they work with several people at the same time. The main difference, of course, is that a family is a group in which all members share a preexisting culture.

Family therapists use the same basic skills favored by clinicians who see individual clients, plus a number of others that are intended for this unique situation. If you had a family in session, for instance, you would most likely reflect individual members' feelings, challenge their dysfunctional thoughts, examine underlying intrapsychic issues, and confront discrepancies in behavior, just as you would if you were seeing a single client. But you would also do a lot of other things in ways you would not dream of doing in individual therapy.

Imagine, for instance, that you are interviewing a couple and asking the husband first what he sees as the main problem.

Husband: I think it's just a matter of my wife having expectations in our relationship that I could never meet.

Wife: Now that's a lie and you know it. The real problem here is that I don't trust you. And you know why.

Husband: That's not true, dear. We've been over this before . . .

From just the first few seconds you can appreciate that merely reflecting content and feelings will not be helpful to this couple. Furthermore, you will quickly lose control of the session unless you introduce a very different structure and style of communication. This is the main challenge of family therapy (and of group therapy in the next chapter); all the while you are attending to the needs of one person, you have others present who may have very different agendas and interests.

It is beyond the scope of this introductory skills course to teach you what is most needed to conduct effective family, couples, child, or group sessions. Although you will find between 80% and 90% of things you do in such work will involve adapting what you have already learned in previous sections, there are some specialized skills and techniques that require more advanced training. This chapter and the one that follows are intended to get you started thinking about the ways you would help more than one person at a time.

A DIFFERENT WAY OF LOOKING AT THINGS

When we speak of "family therapy," it sounds like we mean a single entity exists that is universally accepted by therapists. You probably know better by now than to expect such simplicity in this field. Just as in individual therapy (and group therapy), there are dozens of different ways family therapy can be defined and structured whether as single parent, multigenerational, blended, or many other configurations.

Some family therapists believe that it is preferable to bring in as many members of the family as possible, maybe the whole clan: the more participants, the better. Other therapists like to work with only the nuclear family unit, leaving out the aunts, uncles, cousins, and extended kin. There are therapists who identify only the most powerful member in the family and initiate changes through him or her. Other therapists pick the weakest family member and attempt to bolster his or her position in the tribe. Still other therapists believe that all therapy is family therapy, even if you are doing only individual sessions, because when you change one person you change the whole family system. Regardless of which family members the therapist wants to see, and which theoretical approach is favored, there are still some universal assumptions that most practitioners share. These beliefs guide not only which skills you would select in a given clinical situation but also how you would use them.

Circular Causality

In a systemic approach, you don't subscribe to simple cause-effect phenomena in which one person *causes* another to act in a particular way. Instead, behavior is seen as infinitely more complex and interactive. One person's actions are likely to be both the cause *and* effect of another's behavior. In any conflict situation, no one person is solely at fault for the problems; instead, each contributor does something that provokes continued tension.

An adolescent boy and his father respond to the therapist's invitation to tell why they came to therapy:

Father: My son can never get home on time. He's always breaking his curfew.

Son: If you didn't have such unreasonable expectations, I could be on time.

Father: I think that being home by eleven at night on weekends is perfectly acceptable. There's nothing you can do after that that can't be done earlier. And anyway, when I have extended your curfew, you were still late.

Son: That's not true and you know it! It's not fair, my friends don't have to be in until midnight.

Father: I'm not their dad, nor do I care to be.

Son: That's it, isn't it? You just hate my friends and you'll do anything to make me lose them, like expecting me to come home at such an early hour.

Father: Your curfew has nothing to do with that; eleven is late enough. It's what my father required and it kept me out of trouble.

Son: See, you do think I'll get into trouble. You just don't trust me.

As you can see, this conversation is going nowhere. The two people clearly have made assumptions about each other's position and are responding to those assumptions. Because the father had the same curfew, he thinks it's reasonable. The son, on the other hand, may assume that his dad is just trying to keep him away from his friends because he doesn't trust him to make good decisions. This argument may also be an issue of acculturation where the father is a first-generation hyphenated American and the son is second generation; the son could be frustrated because his peers from the dominant culture have more freedom than he is given. Regardless of the reasons, the therapist is not likely to help these two by focusing on only one person's position. The therapist must explore both positions while teaching them how to communicate.

System and Subsystems

What family therapists look for are the underlying structures of family systems: This means the way the family is organized as well as how communication takes place. Within the larger family unit, there are also smaller units called *subsystems* or *coalitions*. There are also *boundaries* in place, both between the various coalitions and between the family and the outside world. There is a whole new vocabulary associated with this approach: it talks about families who are *enmeshed* (meaning overly dependent) or *disengaged* (overly isolated), the use of *triangulation* (when one person creates conflict with two others), the *multigenerational transmission process* (what we learn from our parents), whether a family is *functional* or *dysfunctional*, and many other words depending on the particular theorist. Each of these must also be placed within a cultural context. A close mother-son relationship within the dominant culture may be considered enmeshed, but within some ethnic minority cultures, the bond is considered perfectly normal.

For example, a mother may be enmeshed with her older son, creating one coalition. She gives him lots of positive attention and sometimes talks to him about her marriage problems. Her happiness or sadness is intricately interwoven with her relationship to her son and with his well-being. She feels responsible not only for his life but also for all of his reactions. The father may be closer to his daughter. He is involved with her extracurricular activities and buys her gifts spontaneously. He never sees her weaknesses but is critical of the other kids. The younger son is not close to either parent (he is disengaged) and continually gets into trouble. Both parents blame each other for their younger son's problems.

Such coalitions and subsystems develop alliances, ways for members of any family to protect themselves. While coalitions often remain stable over time, sometimes they are affected by the particular stage of the family life cycle. Just as an individual's life progresses through a series of predictable, sequential stages, so too does a family's (Carter, McGoldrick, & Garcia-Preto, 2010). That's why it's important for family therapists to know what stage a family is in, whether in the early childhood or empty nest period.

Not only must you learn to assess individual issues and development but you must also examine personal issues in their larger systemic context. That is one reason why family therapy is among the most popular treatment approaches— because it seeks to address not just individual problems but also the larger issues that may be involved.

The Family Culture

In Chapter 2, we discussed about how culture is an important component in helping people. This is important to keep in mind when working with a family, as well, so you remain sensitive to differences that will emerge in the ways members relate to one another. You will want to customize your helping relationships, based on the cultural background of the family, including levels of acculturation for ethnic minorities, socioeconomic class, geographic location, family history, and other variables.

Each family member has a particular role that he or she plays within the system; these can include distractor, scapegoat, problem child, rescuer, and so on. These distinctive roles evolve over time to keep the family in a state of homeostasis or balance, even if it appears to outsiders as rather strange or dysfunctional. We presume the family is seeking help in the first place because something is not working or some member is experiencing difficulties, which will require some sort of realignment of roles and coalitions.

The children have their different ways of competing for attention. The parents have somewhat fixed roles with each other, as well as roles toward the children as a group and toward each individual child. The more intense the dysfunction within the family, the more rigid these roles can become. It's as if each member were bound to a script in a play or a movie and cannot escape that structure; no one knows how to be different from their usual, well-rehearsed role.

Dysfunctional family cultures are especially complex. While each family is remarkably different, there are similarities among them with respect to specific problems. Examples might include an alcoholic father and codependent mother; abusive father and victimized mother; prescription-drug addicted mother and codependent father; or verbally abusive mother and silent, unavailable father. Usually, the roles within such families are quite rigid, the boundaries within the family are more enmeshed, and the boundaries around the family are closed, keeping everyone insulated and impervious to influence.

Exercise in Birth Order

Form groups according to birth order (only children, first-born children, youngest children, middle children, etc.). Keep in mind that the formula might not work as well for those born more than 5 or 6 years before or after their nearest sibling. First, note how many people are in each group. It isn't uncommon for graduate classes to have more first-born or only children. Talk to one another about some of your common issues growing up in your families. In your birth-order groups, discuss how you created your sense of belonging in your family or sought your parents' attention. Were you mostly: responsible, cute and funny, a wallflower, stirring up trouble, etcetera?

STRUCTURING A FAMILY INTERVIEW

Contrary to recommendations in earlier chapters for structuring interviews, several significant adjustments must be made in how family sessions are conducted.

For one thing, you have multiple clients present, each with his or her own agenda. For another, there is almost always a certain degree of chaos going on, especially when there are three or more people in the room and some of them are children. Unless you are prepared to exert some control and structure, the situation can spin out of control rather quickly.

There are so-called humanistic, nondirective family therapies, but we do not recommend that you try such an approach as a beginner. You must establish sufficient safety and boundaries to make sure that each family member is heard, that each person has a chance to talk, and that conversations do not deteriorate to the point of becoming disrespectful or abusive. Remember that families in distress come to you in the first place because they are conflicted, disorganized, and often out of control. It is your job to establish needed structure.

Set Up Rules and Boundaries

Some therapists choose to establish rules at the beginning of therapy, while others choose to wait until a rule needs to be established in the moment. Unlike individual therapy, and because families seeking therapy may function chaotically, you will need to set some rules of behavior for therapy sessions. This is as important with couples as it is with entire families.

Families who end up in therapy are often more interested in being heard than listening to others. Members interrupt each other and often don't even hear what another person is saying. They project meanings from the other person that are inaccurate. They struggle to gain power, and yet feel helpless and powerless most of the time. They do this by talking louder, talking more, interrupting, putting other members down, criticizing others, being patronizing, or even by *stonewalling* (not talking at all and acting apathetic). They blame each other readily, but often take little responsibility for their own behavior. They act defensive, exhibit anger freely, but often avoid showing more vulnerable feelings like sadness and hurt (see Gottman & Silver, 2015). They do this at home, and unless you set rules or boundaries in session, they will do this in your office. You will, therefore, have to establish rules similar to the following:

- Allow other people to finish their thoughts before speaking;
- reflect back what was stated before responding;
- attempt to understand the other person's perspective, even if you disagree;
- speak from your pain or sadness rather than anger; (and if you can't do that, then)
- try to speak in a lower tone of voice;
- criticize behaviors, not the other person's character;
- take responsibility for your own feelings and behaviors; or
- realize that arguments aren't meant to be won or lost, but rather negotiated.

You may even assign these rules as homework. You could ask them to say only nice things to each other or nothing at all during the week between sessions. You could ask them to write down each incident when they feel hurt or angry. You can recommend they keep a list of the times they break these rules between sessions. In this way, rules and boundaries can become the foundation for changing the ways in which family members interact with each other. Sometimes these changes are sufficient (in higher functioning families), but in other cases, these rules are only the beginning of change.

Let's examine a possible scenario. Have you ever seen an argument with the following process?

Wife: Where were you? I cooked dinner and we all ate hours before you got home last night. You knew that I would have dinner ready at six, but you had to work late.

Husband: Don't jump down my throat! I wasn't really working late, it's just that . . .

Wife: I know, I know. Your most important client called at the last minute and . . .

Husband: No, that's not it at all. When I left the office, I had to . . .

Wife: You forgot to do something absolutely urgent. I'm really tired of your excuses.

Husband: But you haven't given me a chance to even tell you what happened. [talking to the therapist] Do you see what I have to put up with?

Therapist: I can see that you are feeling really frustrated, and . . .

Wife: Oh, so you're siding with him!

Notice how neither of them will allow the other to complete a sentence, much less a thought. All too often, when people are angry, they work so hard to prepare their next argument that they don't listen to each other at all. We could probably assume that this couple does this at home, too, and if the therapist allows this to proceed, the therapist will find that they will get nowhere.

At the point where we ended, if the therapist said something about not interrupting, the wife might feel put off, unless a ground rule had been established at the beginning of therapy. Furthermore, the therapist should have allowed the husband to finish his thought at the beginning. Perhaps the sessions would have gone in this direction:

Wife: Where were you? I cooked dinner, and we all ate hours before you got home last night. You knew that I would have dinner ready at six, but you had to work late.

Husband: Don't jump down my throat! I wasn't really working late, it's just that . . .

Wife: I know, I know . . .

Therapist: Sally, remember our agreement, that we would allow the other person to finish speaking before responding?

Wife: Okay.

Husband: As I was saying, I was not working late. I was home late because I was taking care of some personal business. Something for us, for you.

Well, you can see how it might be more helpful to allow each person to finish speaking. Some practitioners set up a rule not only requiring that the first person finish speaking but that the recipient of the information has to repeat what was heard until it is perceived correctly. For instance, to continue the scenario would be as follows:

Wife: You were late because you were working, again, for me?

Husband: No, that is not what I said. I said I was taking care of personal business, something for you and me, not for the office.

Wife: You were doing work that was for us. So, you were working late.

Husband: No, it wasn't work. It was . . . well . . . I wanted to make it a surprise, but I was buying your anniversary gift, and it took longer than I expected.

As you can imagine, this conversation will take an entirely different turn than the first example. Now the explanation is much clearer than before. With this understanding, the wife's anger might be diffused.

Even more so than in individual sessions, you must establish and enforce rules for how people behave. These can be presented to clients or you can negotiate them as a collaborative exercise. Here is one way this idea could be presented:

Therapist: Before we begin our work together, I'm wondering what rules we need to agree on together.

Adolescent: Rules? Why do we need rules? I thought we were here to speak our minds.

Therapist:	Good point. So let me ask you: Why do we need rules?
Mother:	Well, for one thing so we don't end up arguing like we do at home.
Younger child:	Yeah, and so I get to talk too. You guys are always yelling so much that I don't even get to say anything.
Father:	Okay, enough of that. It's not that bad and you know it.
Therapist:	So far you've mentioned that you have problems working out conflicts at home because voices are sometimes raised, you don't listen to one another, and not everyone gets a chance to talk.
Younger child:	You can say that again.
Mother:	Hush now!
Younger child:	See that? She's doing it again. They never let me talk.
Therapist:	Another rule that might be important is not interrupting one another . . .
Younger child:	I'm for that one.
Therapist:	. . . just like you did now.

Whether you negotiate the rules or simply explain the ones you know from prior experience are critical, you will need to alert participants about (a) the importance of being respectful, (b) the need to listen before responding, and (c) the requirement that people attend sessions on time and consistently. These rules should be established at the first session and should be applied consistently so that the therapist is seen as treating everyone equally.

Join the Family

Before you can help a family, you have to develop collaborative relationships with the members to earn their trust and be able to influence them. Salvador Minuchin (1974) felt it was especially important to become part of the system that you intend to influence. This is also important when you consider that you are going to ask people to do things that they won't want to do or that they will find very difficult. Joining the family gives you the leverage to undertake the therapeutic changes that you believe are necessary to restructure the way decisions are made and the way communication takes place.

So, what does it mean to "join" a family? Essentially, this involves using all your charm, caring, and acceptance—plus your clinical skills—to get members to trust and respect you. You do this by demonstrating that you are fair and that you are concerned with everyone's welfare. You not only present yourself as caring and kind but also as firm and dependable. In a nutshell, you get everyone (or almost everyone) to like and respect you, to consider you one of them. You become an honorary member of the family as a function of the intimate time you spend together.

An area that beginners often find confusing is how to join the family, that is, to become accepted as a trusted member of the unit, yet maintain appropriate professional boundaries at the same time. This is indeed a challenge that can be discussed openly with family members as the relationship evolves. As with all forms of therapy, you must walk a line (it is not necessarily a fine line) between presenting yourself as caring, trustworthy, and dependable, and communicating that you are there as a paid professional.

Ask Yourself (and Your Clients) Some Questions

Part of your assessment process in family therapy is asking a series of questions that help you locate better what the problem is and what needs to be done to address it. Here are some questions you might consider:

1. *What is the problem?* You are likely to get a different answer from each family member. That is not only expected (and interesting) but also the varied perspectives will be useful.

2. *When does the problem occur?* Just as important, when does the problem not occur? In other words, when is the problem most and least evident?

3. *Where does the problem occur?* You are gathering more information about the specific settings and situations in which the problem takes place. This gives you information about context and reinforcers.

4. *With whom does the problem occur?* It is always interesting to discover that the problem is activated by the presence of some people and not by others. What does that mean? How does this guide your understanding of what might be going on?

5. *What are the effects on others?* Thinking systemically, you are interested in the interpersonal and reciprocal effects of behavior. You wonder what happens when the problem occurs: How do people respond? How might this behavior be reinforced inadvertently?

6. *What payoffs do the various family members enjoy?* Behavior does not persist unless it is helpful in some way. Even dysfunctional and self-destructive behavior presents some benefits to people. They get sympathy and attention. They don't have to feel responsible. They have an excuse for not getting on with their lives. They can focus on the problem and don't have to think about other things that are even more challenging.

7. *Who in the family has had similar problems?* The answer to this question will give you some clues as to how the presenting complaint is related to other family history.

Assess Family Dynamics

When you are thinking systemically (as all family therapists do), you are looking at the characteristic ways that members relate to one another. You check out who is aligned with whom. You note who has the power, and who doesn't. You assess who the *scapegoat* (the person the family identifies as creating the problem for the family) is. You look at how decisions are made. You examine the ways people communicate with one another and identify the underlying messages that are implicit in what they say and do. You identify the metaphors embedded in their behavior. You assess the stage at which the family is operating in its life cycle. The big picture is that you are looking at the family as a unit, as a system, and as a living thing.

Family therapists collect this information and form their observations using a variety of methods. They use *genograms* (or pictorial maps) to gather family history. They watch the family in action and note patterns that emerge. They observe where people sit, who talks to whom, and in what tone. They watch how the family makes decisions. They plot the communication patterns. They look for evidence of codependence. They not only search for weaknesses in the family system but also strengths: What resources are available to this family? How have they managed to keep things together in the face of their problems? What are some of the family legacies that have been passed on from one generation to the next? These would be limiting in some ways, but also helpful to the members in organizing their lives.

Form Diagnostic Impressions

You would use everything you already know to diagnose individual disorders that you observe in family members. You may notice, for instance, that the mother has a substance abuse disorder, the father an explosive personality disorder, the grandmother a chronic neurological condition, and the child a developmental disorder. All of these issues would obviously play a significant role in what brought the family into treatment.

Thinking systemically, you would also examine a number of other issues integrating cultural sensitivity into the process:

1. How are emotions expressed in the family? How do members respond to one another emotionally?

2. What is the state of individuation among members? If codependency is present, how is it present? To what extent are members disengaged from or enmeshed with one another?

3. How is power distributed?

4. What are the family rules and how are they enforced?

5. How are conflicts and disputes resolved?

6. How is information shared?

7. What are the family myths?

This last question about myths refers to the historical legacy and traditions of the family. How do members of the family view their unit? How do they describe their family to others? What rituals are used as part of the family's functioning?

In addition to these general considerations, you will want to check out the same areas you would in any interview: How are people functioning in terms of basic skills? What is the drug/alcohol use among family members?

Among partners or spouses, you will also want to look closely at how they are doing together with the "Big Three": (1) money, (2) sex, and (3) children (Goldenberg & Goldenberg, 2016). In other words, how do they make decisions in these areas? What is their degree of satisfaction in the way they handle these issues?

Exercise in Identifying Family Myths

In small groups, talk to one another about your own family identification. How would you best describe your family? What are some of the unique rituals in which you all participate? What would a therapist need to know and understand about the way your family functions in order to be helpful to you?

Use Therapeutic Tasks

Family therapists have the ambitious goal of restructuring the way a family operates; it is virtually impossible to do this working only during sessions.

Directives or therapeutic assignments are often prescribed (or negotiated) for family members to work on between sessions. These could be either direct tasks ("Do something nice for one another each day") or paradoxical directives ("I want you to keep arguing with one another, but next time I want you to do it nonstop for an hour").

Therapeutic tasks can be designed along a number of lines. Although they are part of the same action-oriented skills you might use during sessions with an individual client, in the family context, the assignments have a distinctly collaborative texture. They could be structured to change the way members communicate with one another, asking them, for instance, to use a minute timer to control how long each person speaks and to ensure more equal participation. Tasks may be created to change the power structure in the family (such as realigning the hierarchy so that parents exert more control over wayward children). Or, they may be used to address the presenting problem directly (asking the bedwetting child to help his or her father change the sheets).

It should be clear that when you are doing family therapy you are more active, directive, and initiating than you might ordinarily be in your individual sessions. You have a slightly different role, one that is intended not just to help individual family members but to help restructure the way the family functions as a unit.

Using directives in therapy is considered an advanced-level skill that is *not* intended for beginners. In fact, some clinicians prefer not to use directives at all because they may keep power and control in the hands of the therapist and could be seen as manipulative. First become comfortable with the basic skills; add directives to your repertoire later. In more advanced course work, you will also learn how to adapt these powerful skills to more collaborative methods.

Get Everyone Involved

In family sessions, you must keep *everyone* engaged in the process. Doing family therapy is not like doing individual therapy in front of an audience. Even if there is one person who is the "identified client"—the one with the supposed problem—when you look at things systemically you view the situation from a more global perspective. The systemic approach looks at the interdependence between people and the ways their behavior is affected by reciprocal, circular influences. Blame is moved away from the individual to focus instead on what the family can do to restructure itself in more constructive ways. Everyone must take responsibility for their part of family functioning.

Since there are multiple persons in the room, you must use your eyes and attending skills to keep everyone fully present. You will instruct members to speak to one another rather than to you. You will draw in members who are quiet. You will restrain those who are overly controlling or talkative. You will balance the contributions, the energy, and the pace so that things move along in a way that meets the needs of everyone present. If you think this is easy, you haven't been paying attention. That is why some family therapists elect to work with a partner whenever possible.

Kayleigh: Triggering Own Family Issues

I worry about siding with one individual during family therapy. Whenever my guy friends want advice from me and talk to me about how their girlfriends don't trust them and they are constantly calling to see where they are, I get so many red flags up and I start thinking "wow, those girls sound crazy" or "I could never be like that." On the other hand, any guy (or girl) who has cheated on his (or her) significant other, I feel that the relationship is doomed due to the lack of trust there. You can't have a relationship without trust. With those two things said, I feel that if I was doing family therapy with a couple where one of these scenarios happened, I would have trouble staying unbiased and impartial. That is definitely something I need to work on and reading this chapter reminded me of the bias that I have. I agree that I need to work out my own self-applications before embarking into family therapy.

Used with permission of Kayleigh Soto.

COUPLES COUNSELING

Many of the skills used in couples counseling come from various theoretical backgrounds, just as they do in individual theories or family theories. The first research that comes to mind is by John Gottman and collaborators who have published several books on the factors that are predictive of successful marriages versus those that end in divorce (Gottman, 2002; Gottman & Silver, 2015). Gottman recommends paying attention to how couples communicate with each other and teach them to communicate in more effective and productive ways.

A very common couples therapy skill to teach clients is reflective listening. Each person is allowed to speak until he or she is done. The other person in the couple must then repeat what was said and get it right before responding. This can be a slow and painful process for couples who hold a great deal of hostility. You will be amazed at how poorly they will follow these directions. They have difficulty articulating themselves well. They struggle to refrain from interrupting. They often misinterpret what the other person is communicating. And they prefer to share their own perspective rather than validate those of others.

Another popular theory is imago therapy, which Hendrix (2007) developed using psychodynamic principles of *attachment*. This approach helps clients identify early childhood wounds and recruit the other partner to help heal these wounds, which not only can repair the relationship but also if the relationship doesn't last, can help prevent clients from choosing the same type of partner over and over again. Another approach, emotion-focused therapy, is growing in popularity as well (Johnson, 2012, 2013, 2014). This approach uses a blend of person-centered and attachment principles to help the couple communicate more effectively while demonstrating empathy to heal childhood wounds. Finally, many of the theories we discussed in Chapter 3 have formulae for working with couples. These are just a few examples of how individual theories can be applied to a couple's system.

Doing a Couples Assessment

Before you begin the first session, you will want to discuss whether or not you are willing to hold secrets as part of your usual limits of confidentiality. Your *hold secrets policy* should be shared in the first session, before anyone reveals anything you don't want to know. Another decision to make in couples therapy is whether you are willing to see the couple separately from time to time or whether you believe that they must be seen as a system for the best possible results. Many family therapists believe that the best way to work with a couple is as a couple. Other therapists, especially those who are aligned with theories more inclined toward individual therapy, like to get to know the individuals separately and occasionally do intrapsychic work along with their interpersonal work. The theory to which you feel most aligned will probably help you determine whether or not you are willing to see the couple individually. If you do, make sure you keep in mind that the couple as a whole is your client, not one of the individuals within the couple. In addition, crisis situations such as domestic violence or addiction issues may help determine whether you see them individually or as a couple.

We've covered some of the skills and mechanics for doing family interviews, but there are some more specific strategies that might be applied to working with couples. In one sense, doing couples therapy is just a specialized form of family therapy but with only two people whose conflicts will often be related to the same "Big Three" mentioned previously (1) money, (2) sex, and (3) kids. The format below can give you an idea of how you might conduct a first session with more than one person.

1. Ask each person for presenting complaints.

2. Ask each person for expectations for treatment.

3. Hear the story of how they met.

4. Get a brief history of their relationship.

5. Assess current functioning as individuals (personality, personal issues, interpersonal skills, developmental functioning, etc.) and as a couple (communication, roles, power, intimacy, differentiation, sex and money issues, decision making, etc.).

6. Check out family configuration (coalitions, boundaries, etc.).

7. Identify significant others.

8. Dig for family-of-origin issues.

9. Ask what is going right and what is working well.

10. Determine their respective degree of commitment to the relationship (rate on a 1–10 scale).

11. Discuss goals for treatment.

12. Invite feedback and initiate summary.

13. Negotiate mutually agreed homework (if indicated).

14. Reflect on what you observed, heard, sensed, felt, and experienced.

Sex Therapy Skills

Another specialized counseling area is sexual dysfunction and personal issues related to sexual behavior. These are relatively common difficulties, as roughly one quarter of women report difficulties having orgasms and one quarter of men ejaculate prematurely (Mah & Binik, 2001). Then there are problems related to value and moral issues, inhibitions, as well as a variety of physical problems related to achieving or maintaining erections in men and responsiveness issues in women. When couples struggle in their relationship as a whole, they often also have difficulty with their sex life.

Sex therapy skills are often educational in nature, in that clients are taught to heighten their awareness of their senses and bodies, create greater intimacy in their relationships, enhance their pleasures, and eliminate thinking that is getting in the way. Although it would not necessarily be classified as a "skill," a huge part of doing sex therapy work involves monitoring your own attitudes and comfort with the subject. If clients sense that you are in any way uneasy about your own sexuality or with talking about sex, they are also likely to feel uncomfortable. That is why much of sex therapy training involves not only learning the methods for treating various sexual dysfunctions but also addressing your own unresolved issues related to sex. The goal is to get to the point where you can talk to people about any facet of sexuality and do so easily.

The actual skills in doing sex therapy are considered add-ons to the usual therapy practices of developing a solid relationship with the partners, earning their trust, exploring the context of the problem in relation to other factors, and figuring out the particular meaning of the symptoms. For instance, a man who ejaculates prematurely may be communicating anger to his wife ("Ha, ha, I got off and you didn't"). A woman who does not have orgasms with her partner may be communicating similar anger ("You are not good enough to excite me"). We are not saying this is the case, just that the presenting symptoms often say things that may not be heard because the partner doesn't want to hear.

Exercise in Sexual Values

In the margin of the book, in your journal, or on a separate piece of paper, write out what it would be like for you to respond to each of the following clients who presented their problems to you in a first session:

- "I like to dress up in my wife's underwear and I think about doing that when I am having sex with my wife. I'd like to talk about this with her but I'm afraid of what she might think."
- "I have never felt comfortable as a man; it's always seemed to me like I'm a woman in a man's body. I want to explore the possibility of having a sex-change operation."
- "I am a lesbian and involved in a long-term relationship with my partner. We would like to adopt children but first we want to get couples counseling to have us look at what might be involved in this."
- "I have been having a sexual relationship with my younger brother since we were teenagers. We still get together on occasion. Although I feel a little guilty about this, I'm not sure if it is wrong that we continue this relationship. We both like it."
- "I am having an affair but I don't want my husband to know about it. I don't think it really hurts my marriage; in some ways it takes some pressure off because my husband doesn't like sex as often as I do."
- "I can have erections to the point of orgasm only when my wife and I watch pornographic videos. She says it bothers her but I don't see what the problem is if it adds spice to our relationship."
- "My husband doesn't know this but the only way I can have an orgasm is with a vibrator. If the truth were known, I'd much prefer to masturbate instead of have intercourse."

Talk about your reactions to these presenting problems in small groups. Pay particular attention to areas where you might need to do some work in order to deal with some of your biases and unresolved issues related to sex.

SPECIALIZED SKILLS FOR WORKING WITH CHILDREN

In one sense, everything that you have already learned about therapeutic skills in general also works with kids. Children of any age respond well to being heard and understood. As long as language, communication, and strategy are adjusted and adapted to the particular age and developmental stage of the client, you can use almost any intervention. One area that is quite different, though, is dealing with limits of confidentiality and consent. Parents or guardians need to provide consent, and when parents are divorced, this can be difficult. You will want to learn the laws in your state to determine the best way to obtain consent. In addition, parents have a right to the child's client files. This is an area that will be explored in your law and ethics classes and differs from state to state.

There are differences in treatment as well. Because younger children cannot easily articulate in words what they are thinking and feeling, at least in the language that adults would prefer, play becomes their primary means of communication (Axline, 1964; Landreth, 2012; Oaklander, 1988). Play therapy is a desired method that allows children to express themselves through a variety of modalities besides speech. They may use puppets, or songs, or drawing, or building, or acting out roles, in order to "speak" through their actions and "talk" about what is bothering them. Therapists may respond at the same level of communication.

Exercise in Adapting Skills to Children

On your own, with partners, or in small groups, discuss how you would use active listening skills to respond to the following statements by children of various ages. Role-play the interaction that is begun by the initial client statement.

Eighteen-year-old honors high school student: "My parents won't leave me alone. They are always on my case. It's like whatever I do is never good enough for them."

Fifteen-year-old high school freshman football player: "My parents say I better have a good season this year or I'll never make the varsity team next year. I think I can do it. At least I hope I can. But there's some pretty big guys out there."

Eleven-year-old girl who never talks in class: "Um, my parents can't come to the conference like you asked. I think they have to work or something. Um, is that okay?"

Eight-year-old boy with chronic stomachaches: "My parents say that I'm just too nervous all the time. I get upset about things. I can kind of feel my tummy hurting right now. My mom says if I relax, it'll get better."

Four-year-old girl who throws temper tantrums: "My mommy won't let me go to playgroup today. She says I was bad. But she's the one who is bad. She's mean."

Unstructured, Semistructured, and Structured Play

Many play therapists choose to provide unstructured play therapy with young children, allowing the child to be self-directed. This is much like working with an adult, primarily allowing the client to lead the conversation. How you respond to the client, in either case, certainly directs the session, but the more you allow the client to lead, the more possibility you have of seeing what is most needed. This is especially true with children, who not only act out their issues or concerns but sometimes also work through those issues in the play. By creating too much structure, you may stifle a child's creativity, self-directedness, and sense of empowerment.

The therapists who strongly believe that play therapy should be entirely child directed will even encourage the child to direct the therapist during play sessions. In the example below, the child initiates the activity:

Susie:	Let's play dolls!
Therapist:	You're excited to play dolls! It looks like you want me to play with you.
Susie:	Yes! Which doll do you want to be?
Therapist:	(whispering) Which doll should I pick?
Susie:	(Susie points)
Therapist:	(in a loud voice) I'll be this doll.
Susie:	Let's go to the store. What do you want to buy?
Therapist:	(whispering) What would you like me to buy?
Susie:	New shoes. My mom likes shoes a lot. She comes home with new ones all the time. I like to go into her closet and play with them. It's hard to walk in them though.
Therapist:	You feel grown up when you wear your mom's shoes.
Susie:	I do! Wanna play something else?
Therapist:	Sure. Whatever you'd like to do.

In this way, the therapist allows the child to lead so that she can be empowered in the play. The child is able to direct the therapist in any way she wants. Children who seldom have the opportunity to make many decisions in their own lives (except to act out) really appreciate the freedom to direct the interaction.

Therapists will choose unstructured play for preschoolers or young elementary school age children, but may choose semistructured play with older elementary, middle school or high school children. This not only allows for some creativity and comfort but also engages the child in more conversation, which can be helpful for those who are more verbal. These activities might include sand tray therapy (using a portable sandbox); drawing specific pictures; acting some scene out with puppets, dolls, or toy animals; or using clay. The key here is to get the child started on an activity and then allow the material to emerge without anticipating what to do next. Some children will talk while they perform the activity, while others become immersed in the process. When the project is completed, therapists sometimes have the child name the artwork and describe each piece. Sometimes therapists ask children to act out different scenarios with the different objects/people/things to express thoughts and feelings. Choice of the next course of action depends on the child, his or her age, and what the child has presented to you.

Structured play can also be useful. Several games specifically for therapy are available in catalogues and on the Internet. These games often set up scenarios that allow children to express their feelings, to help them make decisions, and to reveal their thoughts. If you happen to have more traditional games around, you can modify these to be more therapeutically oriented. While playing a traditional game might help build rapport, the client would probably benefit more from a game that has a therapeutic purpose. Otherwise, you find yourself just being a friend to the child, a playmate, rather than a therapist. You will want to be aware of the games that are available. Engaging in tasks like shooting hoops or playing pool can be effective with teenagers who might feel intimated by a conversation in an office. They are more relaxed and consequently, feel more comfortable to talk about personal issues. However, you must consider and discuss the limits of confidentiality when leaving the office. Finally, inviting teens to talk about their favorite music, app, or games can be beneficial to build rapport while also revealing potentially relevant information about your clients; these topics can also be used as metaphors in therapy.

This is the briefest outline of basic skills used in the play arena. Other courses and advanced training will provide opportunities to develop your existing repertoire of skills applied to these contexts.

Specific Skills for Unstructured Play Therapy

The skills mentioned below are most powerful when working with preschool or younger elementary school age children in unstructured play therapy. However, any of these skills can be used or modified when working with older children and may have a similar effect.

Reflecting Feelings

Just as you want to reflect the feelings of adults, you also want to reflect the feelings of the child. There are several advantages to doing this. First, naming what the child is experiencing helps the child understand that he is not alone. There is a name for what he is experiencing. Second, the child can internalize that vocabulary and learn to articulate his feelings more clearly as he ages, which is far better than simply reacting to his feelings. Third, the child feels heard, understood, and validated. This, combined with your unconditional positive regard, allows the child to build self-esteem. The therapist both sees the client and accepts him and *all* of his feelings. This alone can be powerfully healing, no matter how old the client is. Finally, when you validate and accept whatever the child is feeling, the child can express that feeling more fully until he no longer feels that way. It is the responsibility of parents to socialize a child; therapists, in contrast, accept almost any behavior in the playroom unless it is somehow harmful to the child or the therapist.

Have you ever seen this happen?

Johnny: I want that candy!

Mom: No. It's not good for you.

Johnny: But, Mom (in a whiney voice), I'll be good. If you get it for me, I'll do all my chores.

Mom: Absolutely not. You'll do your chores anyway. Now, let's go.

Johnny: (wailing in misery)

Mom: Johnny, stop crying!

Johnny: (still crying, but louder now)

Mom: You better stop crying or I'll give you something to cry about!

Parents can often respond like this because they are tired or embarrassed. They feel as though they've lost control. It's probably not that they don't want to validate their child; they just feel helpless and uncertain. In contrast, a session with the therapist could go like this:

Johnny: (pouring water in the sand tray and looking guiltily at the therapist)

Therapist: You're worried I might get mad.

Johnny: Yeah. My mom would. (still looking at the therapist for a reaction)

Therapist: You're waiting for me to stop you. You enjoy pouring that water into the sand.

Johnny: (with a big smile) Yeah, I do!

Reflecting Johnny's feelings allows him to recognize and learn to give words to his experience. He feels understood, accepted, and valued. This builds Johnny's relationship with the therapist so that he's able to begin working on issues that may make him feel more vulnerable. Furthermore, he feels delighted to have such freedom to play the way he would like, which isn't always possible or even a good option when at home. And, believe it or not, he will know that the rules of the playroom are different from other places, helping him to modify his behavior to his environment.

Tracking Behavior and Empowerment

Students often find tracking a child's behavior a bit silly. Frequently, children will play with limited emotional expression, especially in early sessions before a trusting relationship is built. In order for the child to know that you are with her, you want to track her behavior. You can also use language that empowers the child so that she is aware of her decision making. Phrases may sound like this:

- "You put that right where you wanted it."
- "That's not working for you the way you want it to."
- "You've decided where that should go."
- "You chose to rearrange that."
- "You can't decide what you want to do next."

These statements are quite simple to make, but have a powerful effect on the child. She will feel her sense of responsibility and choice as you reflect these phrases. She will trust her own sense of self rather than looking outward for approval, helping her later to trust her own intuition when she is older. Of course, this comes with the assumption that people are basically good and will make good decisions under the right conditions. Even if you do not hold this assumption, empowering a child during play can build self-esteem.

You may ask, "What about a child who is constantly engaging in power strug-gles with parents, siblings, or schoolmates?" The answer is that these children feel least empowered of all. When kids act in ways to increase their power, it's often because they feel powerless. After all, being a child is a powerless place to be; you are told when to get up, when to eat, when to get dressed, when to go to school, what to do at school—much of your life is decided for you. Except for unstructured playtime, which is rare today, kids have little freedom or opportunity for self-direction. At least during play therapy time, the child can be self-directed and can enhance her creativity.

Setting Limits

When do you want to set limits on unstructured play? You want to set limits if the child will harm herself or is doing something to you that feels extremely uncomfortable. This can vary from person to person, but you want to attempt to let the child be as free of limits as possible. Depending on the child, some therapists will allow themselves to be tied up, handcuffed, shot in the feet or arms (with a gun with suction-cup "arrows"), or subjected to other manipulations that may seem socially undesirable. Keep in mind, though, that the playroom is the child's world, and as long as you both feel safe, then allowing the child as much latitude as possible can be extremely beneficial to the child.

Nevertheless, there are times when you do have to set limits. For instance, you want to set limits if the child wants to turn off the lights, wants to leave the room, wants to take off all of his clothes, or wants to engage in some activity that could be harmful (like jumping off a table onto a hard floor). Landreth (2012) has a very specific way of setting limits with children. Put succinctly, here, you first want to acknowledge the child's desire. With validation, he feels understood before acting. Then you want to establish the limit. Finally, you want to give the child at least two options for other behaviors. By creating a limited number of choices or options, you not only establish other limits but also help the child feel empowered to make his own decision. If a child wants to turn off the lights, the therapist might say, "I know you'd like to turn off the lights, but the lights are for staying on. You can choose to blindfold yourself, or you can choose to close your eyes to pretend you're in the dark." If the child is about to do something dangerous, you may need to set the limit first. "The table is not for jumping off of. I know you want to jump because you think it might be fun. You can choose to jump on the ground or you can choose to make the bear jump off the table." If you can, though, validate the child first. Most children respond very well to this type of limit setting. If you have kids in your own life, try it at home.

A Final Note About Play Therapy

You should take a specific class or go through a full training program with additional supervised experience if you want to provide play therapy; you can even become certified. You'll learn about the type of room you want (easy-to-clean floors), the type of toys to choose (a variety most conducive to therapy), how to arrange the room, and to what extent and how to involve the parents. Play therapy is fun. More important, play therapy is a well-researched method for working with kids.

THE ROLES YOU TAKE AS A THERAPIST

As a therapist, you will need to take on various roles regardless of your environment, such as mediator or consultant. Sometimes these roles will be required; the skill of mediation is frequently required of you as a family therapist, for example. Sometimes you may choose to pursue other roles in addition to your role as a therapist for extra income, such as a consultant or personal coach.

Consultation Skills

As you can readily see, the roles of a family therapist are somewhat different from those played during individual sessions. In many ways, the clinician functions as much as a consultant as a therapist. You are looking at the underlying processes and dynamics of a system rather than those of just a single individual. The same is true during those times when you are asked to intervene at the systemic level of a larger group or organization.

The consulting role is playing an increasingly important part in what counselors and therapists do in their work. Most school counselors, for example, spend far more time consulting with teachers, administrators, and parents than they do actually counseling children in ongoing relationships. Consultation skills are similar in some ways to therapeutic-type skills, especially those involved in practicing good listening and responding behaviors. Likewise, consulting activities also make use of principles and strategies that are included as part of doing family and group therapy, especially the emphasis on systemic thinking. Yet consultation skills are also quite different in some ways.

Sometimes we are called on as consultants to fill a mediation role. Also known as *alternative dispute resolution*, mediation is very different from usual counseling goals even though many of the skills are the same. Just as in individual or family counseling, the mediator uses active listening and summarizing skills, though the goal is not to stir up emotional issues but rather to calm them down so that constructive decisions can be made.

You would be functioning more in the role of consultant or problem solver rather than therapist during this professional activity. You are supposed to be the objective, neutral, impartial third party who resolves disputes and helps conflicted parties negotiate to reach a mutually acceptable solution. This could be in matters of divorce or child custody, in disputes between business partners, in conflicts between employees, or in legal problems in which both parties need help coming to an agreement.

Therapists operating in a mediator role have received specialized training and certification in this profession. Although therapist and counselor education provides a solid background in active listening and responding skills, many mediators come from very different backgrounds, such as the practice of law. Mediation requires both knowledge of the legal process and solid helping skills (see Moore, 2003; Winslade & Monk, 2000).

Exercise in Getting Unstuck

Work with a partner. One of you decides to talk about an area of your life in which you feel stuck and can't seem to resolve the problem. The other partner will function as a problem solver.

The first step is to help the person figure out what he or she is doing already that is not working very well. After the "client" gives some brief background on the problem (5 minutes), ask the person to list the things he or she has tried that have proven consistently ineffective.

Get the person to agree not to do those things anymore. At this point, there is often resistance to letting go of favored strategies—incredibly, even when they don't work. But until the person agrees to let go of methods that aren't helpful, there is little room for trying anything else. At the very least, get the person to surrender at least a few of the most ineffective behaviors.

Together, brainstorm an exhaustive list of alternative strategies that could be tried. As with any such exercise, the more options you generate the better. Creative, far-out, and innovative possibilities are especially encouraged. In an exercise like this, the specific solutions are less important than the feeling the person leaves with: that there are many, many other options available than those that are currently being used unsuccessfully.

Afterward, talk about what this experience was like for all the participants and how you might use this in your lives and work.

PITFALLS AND COMMON MISTAKES

A number of mistakes and misjudgments are common among beginning family therapists. Many of these result from failing to adapt skills intended for working with individuals to the more challenging demands of having multiple clients in the room at the same time.

Changing the Therapy Format

If you typically see only individuals, you may not think that bringing in other members of the family or friends would be appropriate; or if you work primarily with families, you may not consider that seeing one person individually would be appropriate. Yet it is sometimes not only appropriate to change your client format, but fruitful as well. Here's one example of thinking outside the box: You've been counseling a mother of four children who comes in for family therapy to deal with the recent death of the husband/father. The children seem to be coping poorly, and the mother is concerned. After making an initial family assessment, taking into consideration the particular conditions of bereavement and with such different issues of the children, you could have a 45-minute session with the family as a whole, and then see each person individually, including the mother. The family may do better with a format where they are able to get the individual attention they desperately need, especially because the mother isn't able to give each child individual attention the way she wants. At the same time, they are able to do some work as a family and learn new ways to interact with each other.

If you decide to work with children, you will find that it's not uncommon for parents to bring their child in to be "fixed." Parents, however, often need as much work in parent education or in dealing with their own stressors related to their child's problems as the child. So, if you work in a facility with others, we strongly recommend that you encourage the parents of the children to participate in parent education classes or their own therapy, or both. The best time to approach the subject is before you see the child. You might say something like this:

> I understand you are struggling with Johnny's anger outbursts. You don't know where they are coming from or how to deal with them. You must feel extremely tired and frustrated yourself, trying to cope with this new problem. [if the parent agrees] At our agency, we have found that when parents participate in parent education and/or do their own therapy, the child seems to progress much more quickly. Because you will be sitting here in the waiting room anyway, I would like to strongly recommend you see your own therapist. You can choose to undergo parent education, which may give you some skills in dealing with Johnny's particular problem, or you may choose to just talk to a therapist about your own frustration. Which do you think might be better for you now?

Notice that no blame was placed on the parent, and in fact, the therapist provided empathy and used that empathy to encourage therapy. In addition, you may have noticed that the therapist gave an either/or choice rather than asking a yes/no question, increasing the possibility that this parent might participate in something. Most parents really want their kids to get better and, if the invitation is worded correctly, will agree to participate in therapy themselves. So, you might make it a habit to encourage parents to participate in therapy too.

Another common situation arises during individual therapy when issues with another person are continually the topic of conversation. Sometimes, your client may want to say something to the other person, but does not have the courage. You may, therefore, want to bring the other person into the room so that you can provide support to your client while he or she speaks to this other person. This is especially typical when working with an adolescent who needs to confront a parent. In addition, it is sometimes helpful to allow an adolescent to bring a very close friend to therapy for one or two sessions. Watching them interact can provide you with more information than working with the adolescent alone. Usually the friend will give you more information than your client can about himself or herself, and you can strengthen the relationship with your client by joining with him or her and the friend.

Occasionally adding or removing people from the usual therapy format may create a unique experience that might otherwise not have occurred. However, it is essential that you remember who your client is (the family, the individual, the couple) and keep your primary focus on your client or client unit. As long as you keep this in mind, you are limited only by your creativity.

Aligning With One Person or Against Another Person

When working with a couple or a family, we are sometimes tempted to align with one person or work against another because of our own issues. For instance, imagine that a couple comes to see you about their marriage. He had an affair 10 years ago and is frustrated because his wife still does not trust him. If you had been in a situation similar to the husband's, you might find yourself aligning with him. Or perhaps you see a family with four children. The family consistently blames the mother for not being at home enough, and you find yourself joining with the rest of the family in berating her. You can see the implicit problems with doing this. So, you might say to yourself, "Obviously, I want to be as objective as possible" but still find that you align with or against people in session. To prevent this, you may want to ask yourself how you feel about each client. Who do you like and not like? Why? By taking a moment to reflect on this after each session, you can at least become aware of your biases. Unless you are aware of them, your biases might interfere with your objectivity.

There is one exception to avoiding alignment. Some therapists purposely align with or against a particular person as a therapeutic technique. It's a more aggressive way to get a point across and should be used with great caution. A therapist might use this technique when one member of the family bullies the other members and thus holds too much power. The therapist may choose to bully the bully so that the person feels what it's like to be the recipient of this interpersonal style. Once the bully realizes what is going on, it is important for the therapist to articulate what he or she just did so that all of the clients understand that the therapist is not for or against one person, but rather was trying to get a point across. Nevertheless, using this technique can be quite dangerous and should be used only after sufficient training and supervision.

Waiting Too Long to Intervene

One of the biggest challenges of seeing multiple clients at once is balancing the time for each person to talk. In a family system, it is not unusual for one person to dominate the conversation. Once you notice the role each person plays, you may want to intervene by inhibiting the person with the power and inviting the person who is most quiet to speak up more often.

How might a therapist allow a client to go on for too long? Well, one example might be when one party wants to talk and the other has difficulty with verbal expression. Another situation might be when the therapist gets so wrapped up in the story that he or she forgets to check out what's going on with the other members of the family. Finally, as we have stated before, our culture has taught us that interrupting is rude. As a therapist, that standard cannot be followed. A therapist must frequently interrupt, especially in family or group settings when one person monopolizes, when an argument gets too intense, or when the clients need to be reminded to treat each other with respect and not resort to name calling. Interrupting is an essential part of the process.

APPLICATIONS TO SELF: AWARENESS OF YOUR OWN FAMILY DYNAMICS

Family therapy will test you in ways that individual sessions do not. With more people in the room, more complex dynamics, conflicting agendas, long-standing battles, and overheated emotional energy, things can easily spin out of control. All your own unresolved issues will be triggered. And that is one reason why you must work through your own stuff before you attempt to do this sort of work.

You may have noticed that much of what we recommend in this section of each chapter is that you do your own work both to enhance your skills as a therapist and for your own growth. Doing your own work will help you gain better insight into your work with clients. The skills involved with family therapy are no different. You will want to evaluate your own family dynamics, look at coalitions, and identify patterns and where those patterns might have originated.

To start this process, we recommend you do a thorough genogram of your family. Start by identifying your personal issues, which should be becoming clearer by this time, assuming you've been following the other recommendations in this book. Then identify your immediate family. For some, this process might be brief; for others, where a lot of divorces or deaths have occurred, this may be a complex process. Once you have outlined the primary people involved in the process, identify the subsystems within the family by marking coalitions and enmeshed and disengaged relationships. Mark divorces and deaths. Now go back at least as far as the generation of your grandparents and do the same thing.

After you have identified the relationships, using your issue and how someone might have an opposite issue, note these for the whole family tree. For example, if you have a tendency toward particular kinds of love relationships, note others in the family who follow a similar pattern. Or if you are someone who needs a lot of control, mark all the controlling individuals and all the irresponsible individuals. Once you have completed your picture, look for patterns. How are you influenced by patterns in your family? How might those patterns affect your current or future children?

We hope you are able to identify some new information by using this technique. What do you do with this information? Well, think about how, as a therapist, you might approach your family. Where would you start? What homework might you assign to this family? How might you need to mediate the process of doing family therapy with your immediate family?

By thinking about your own family, you can gain some insight into who you are and may, therefore, be more prepared to work with similar families. If possible, attend a few family sessions just to see what it might be like before working with a family. Seeing how others do the work will give you a sense of how different family work can be from individual work.

SUMMARY

In this chapter and Chapter 11, "Group Leadership Skills," you are introduced to specialized helping behaviors that require advanced training. We present them to you now so that you can get a head start using them in your work. Because family counseling has become so universal and generic in practice, the skills included here are now part of the repertoire of every clinician.

Skills in Action: The Frustrated Couple

Therapist:	. . . in addition to these other limits of confidentiality, I need to tell you about my "no secrets" policy. I believe that honesty is important in making a relationship work. Therefore, I will not hold any secrets that I believe will have an effect on your relationship. I will help you to disclose to your partner any secret you tell me. Do you have any questions about that? [Establishing a "no secrets" policy during intake session]
Tanya and Sam together:	No.
Therapist:	Okay. I want to invite each of you to talk about what brought you here. You can choose who goes first. [Establishing the initial complaint; empowering couple; observing control and power issues in how they respond to invitation]
Tanya:	(nodding head and pointing) You go.
Sam:	Well, I'm not happy with how the relationship is going, and for the first time in twenty years, I'm considering leaving. I'm smothered by Tanya, always being controlled as if I'm a child. I just want to be treated with more . . .
Tanya:	That's not fair. I do not try to control you!
Sam:	See what I mean? I can't even finish my sentence!
Therapist:	Let's stop here. I think we may need to establish some rules. In here, I think it's very important that we allow each person to finish speaking instead of interrupting. So, I'm asking you if you are both willing to wait until the other person finishes before responding. In this way, you will both get to finish what you want to say. [Setting rules and boundaries]
Sam:	No problem for me.
Tanya:	Of course, I can do that. But I just want you to know . . .
Sam:	See. There it goes all over again . . .
Therapist:	Okay. Okay. Slow down. Take a breath—each of you. This is obviously difficult for both of you so I'll help as much as I can. Each

	time one of you interrupts I'll signal like this (holds out hand) and that will be a cue to let the other person finish speaking. [Enforcement of boundaries]
Sam and Tanya:	(both nod heads in agreement, but then smirk at one another)
Therapist:	I'm curious. What was that look you just gave one another? [Reflecting nonverbal behavior]
Sam and Tanya:	(both in chorus): Nothing. (laughter)
Therapist:	(laughing in response) What's going on? [Joining couple by drawing attention to their shared joke]
Tanya:	It's just that we don't laugh much with one another anymore so I guess we were just tickled.
Sam:	Anyway, as I was saying, I feel like I'm being controlled by Tanya. I want to be treated with respect. She must assume I'm an idiot because she thinks she needs to tell me every little thing. It gets old.
Therapist:	I want to stop you there. Rather than trying to guess Tanya's motivations, I wonder if you could talk about your own thoughts and feelings based upon Tanya's behavior. [Clarifying rules and boundaries]
Sam:	Alright. Tanya tells me to take out the trash. I'm not an idiot—I can see that it's full. I'll get to it when I have time. She tells me how to cook when I try to make her a nice meal. She even tells me when to go to bed, as if I'm a child!
Tanya:	He gets cranky.
Therapist:	So, Sam, you feel like your efforts aren't appreciated. [Ignoring Tanya's interruption and reflecting Sam's feelings]
Tanya:	(Heavy sigh) He said I tell him what to do too much, but if I didn't then nothing would get done.
Therapist:	Tanya, you get impatient with Sam because he doesn't always respond the way you would prefer and at the pace you'd like. [Reflection and summary, but also a reframing to clarify issue]
Tanya:	I guess so. He says I always tell him what to do.
Therapist:	Sam? [Inviting a response to continue the dialogue]

Sam: That part is right. But I also want her to know that I'm tired of being treated like a child.

Therapist: (pointing) Sam, talk to Tanya directly. [Encouraging Sam to talk to Tanya instead of about her when she's in the room]

Tanya: (Tanya responds instead) Look Honey, I don't mean to do that. It's just that sometimes you just don't pay attention to things. You say I treat you like a child, but sometimes you act that way.

Sam: What the hell are you talking about? If you weren't so damn controlling all the time . . .

Therapist: Hold on. Hold on. This is important so let's take it slowly. Tanya, maybe you can give Sam an example of what you mean. And Sam, before Tanya does that, maybe you can take a breath. Right now you are feeling very defensive. If Tanya does give you an example, I wonder if you can really hear that or whether you'll feel like you have to strike back. [Blocks verbal sparring; reflects defensiveness; redirects focus]

As this session continues, the therapist will try to help them understand one another's positions, as well as the patterns that have emerged in their relationship that lead to them feeling so frustrated, resentful, and misunderstood. The goal will be to help them respond to one another differently in the session and then translate this new understanding to changes in the ways they behave at home—Sam acting more responsibly and Tanya doing less blaming.

The therapist is using many of the skills you have already learned to facilitate this conversation—paraphrasing, questions, reflections—but also is using some unique skills like "blocking" and "setting and enforcing boundaries." More specialized training in family and couples therapy skills will help you manage and lead sessions like this without losing control. The next chapter, on group leadership skills, applies some of the same concepts and interventions for working with several people in the room at the same time.

REFERENCES AND RESOURCES

Axline, V. (1964). *Dibs in search of self.* New York, NY: Ballantine Books.

Brock, G. W., & Barnard, C. P. (1999). *Procedures in marriage and family therapy.* Boston, MA: Allyn & Bacon.

Brown, J. H., & Brown, C. S. (2002). *Marital therapy: Concepts and skills for effective practice.* New York, NY: Brunner-Routledge.

Carlson, J., & Kjos, D. (2001). *Theories and strategies of family therapy.* Boston, MA: Allyn & Bacon.

Carter, B., McGoldrick, M., & Garcia-Preto, N. (2010). *The expanded family life cycle: Individual, family, and social perspectives* (4th ed.). Boston, MA: Allyn & Bacon.

Gladding, S. T. (2006). *Family therapy: History, theory, and practice* (4th ed.). Columbus, OH: Merrill.

Goldenberg, H., & Goldenberg, I. (2016). *Family therapy: An overview* (9th ed.). Pacific Grove, CA: Brooks/Cole.

Gottman, J. (2002). *The relationship cure: A 5-step guide to strengthening your marriage, family, and friendships.* New York, NY: Three Rivers Press.

Gottman, J., & Silver, N. (2015). *The seven principles for making marriages work* (2nd ed.). New York, NY: Harmony.

Hendrix, H. (2007). *Getting the love you want: A guide for couples, 20th anniversary edition.* New York, NY: Henry Holt & Co.

Hendrix, H., & LaKelly Hunt, H. (2013). *Making marriage simple: Ten truths for changing the relationship you have into the one you want.* New York, NY: Penguin Random House.

Johnson, S. (2012). *The practice of emotionally focused couple therapy: Creating connection* (2nd ed.). New York, NY: Routledge.

Johnson, S. (2013). *Love sense: The revolutionary new science of romantic relationships.* London, England: Little, Brown.

Johnson, S. (2014). *The love secret.* London, England: Piatkus.

Landreth, G. (2012). *Play therapy: The art of the relationship* (3rd ed.). New York, NY: Routledge.

Long, L., & Young, M. (2007). *Counseling and therapy for couples.* Belmont, CA: Wadsworth.

Mah, K., & Binik, Y. (2001). The nature of human orgasm: A critical review of major trends. *Clinical Psychology Review, 21*(6), 823–856.

Minuchin, S. (1974). *Families and family therapy.* Cambridge, MA: Harvard University Press.

Moore, C. (2003). *The mediation process* (3rd ed.). San Francisco, CA: Jossey-Bass.

Nichols, M. P., & Schwartz, R. C. (2006). *The essentials of family therapy* (3rd ed.). Boston, MA: Allyn & Bacon.

Oaklander, V. (1988). *Windows to our children: A gestalt therapy approach to children and adolescents.* Gouldsboro, ME: Gestalt Journal Press.

Weeks, G., Odell, M., & Methven, S. (2005). *If only I had known: Avoiding common mistakes in couples therapy.* New York, NY: W. W. Norton.

Winslade, J., & Monk, G. (2000). *Narrative mediation.* San Francisco, CA: Jossey-Bass.

Chapter 11

GROUP LEADERSHIP SKILLS

I n many ways, group leadership skills are not that different from those used with individuals, families, couples, or even organizations. In all of these helping situations, you rely on active listening, reflecting feelings and content, open-ended questions, and summarizing what was heard and understood. Likewise, you bring in a lot of your general clinical training to read nonverbal behavior, to identify problem areas, and so on. Yet there is also quite a bit of specialized content and skills in group leadership, which is one reason why you will take one or more additional courses focused solely on this clinical specialty.

We don't want to replicate needlessly the content that is covered in other courses, but we briefly mention some of the added content and skill areas that you will need in your work. Nowadays, every practitioner is expected to be thoroughly competent in applying therapeutic skills in various group settings. You will want to become familiar with training manuals specifically related to group therapy and counseling skills. These books will give you an overview of core knowledge areas for understanding the stages of group development, group dynamics, and group treatment models.

GROUP STAGE DEVELOPMENT

Just as there are predictable, sequential developmental stages that individuals progress through, so too do groups follow a series of incremental steps. For closed groups, there are several names for these stages and lots of different models, but most of them refer to a beginning in which norms and trust are established, a middle stage in which members work on personal goals, and an ending stage that helps people apply what was learned to their lives.

In the beginning stage (also called the "forming" and the "norming" stage), you address trust issues, establish constructive rules and rituals, and help members create a solid working environment. You will also elicit content and establish treatment goals for each participant. This is an awkward stage because people are trying to learn to work together. They are asking themselves the following questions:

- Is this a safe place?
- Does the leader know what he or she is doing?
- Who can I trust here?
- What do these people think of me?
- What will I reveal and what will I hide?
- Do I want to come back next time?

Needless to say, during this critical beginning stage you will do all you can to make the group experience as safe, interesting, and productive as possible. You are likely to apply exploration skills learned earlier to let group members know that they have been heard and understood and to model these behaviors so that others will use them.

The middle stage is also known as the "working" stage. Once cohesion and trust have been established, it is safer for people to take risks. This is also known as the "storming" stage because members feel safer challenging the leader, confronting one another, and behaving in more natural ways. This is the stage where most of the work is done, where clients pursue their individual treatment goals. You will use almost all of your therapeutic skills in this stage, but you must adapt them to fit the rather unique circumstances of working before an audience.

In the final closing stage, members work toward letting go. Many unresolved issues are worked through. People may have to learn to say goodbye well. Codependency issues are addressed. A follow-up program is established so that clients have a structure for continuing their progress after the group ends. One of the unique challenges you will face in leading groups is that it is especially difficult for clients to keep their momentum going once the sessions have disbanded.

Consistent with most developmental models, it is fairly important to be able to assess accurately at which stage a group is operating so that therapeutic steps can be taken to facilitate progress to the next, deeper level. However, the process isn't always linear and can move among stages if members feel unsafe or if members leave.

GROUP DYNAMICS

There is an extensive body of literature and research on group behavior, much of it is summarized in some of the basic texts in the field that are listed at the end of the chapter. Contributions from sociology, social psychology, organizational development, and related disciplines describe and explain why and how people act the way they do in interpersonal situations. You will be using specialized observation skills to check some of the following areas:

- *Proxemics.* What are the physical distances between people? How close or far away do people sit or stand from one another and what does that mean?
- *Nonverbal behavior.* What are group members communicating with their posture, their eyes, facial expressions, and gestures?
- *Coalitions.* Who is aligned with whom? What are the cliques in the group?
- *Silence.* The inevitable pauses in group will have different meanings. Are people bored? Confused? Resistant? Thoughtful?
- *Conflict.* Where are the points of tension and competition? Where are struggles for power and control?
- *Group roles.* Who is playing which role in the group? Who is the scapegoat? Who are the leaders? Who has been marginalized?
- *Cultural identities.* Which ethnic backgrounds, sexual orientations, gender identities, and other cultural backgrounds shape the norms that have evolved?

Applying group leadership skills, you will constantly be observing member behavior to notice interesting or relevant patterns. At times, you will simply file away what you notice and use this information at a later time; other instances will require immediate intervention.

Exercise in Group Skills

You are in the midst of leading a group when, out of the corner of your eye, you notice that a usually talkative member has pulled his seat back and turned body to the side. He is looking down and shuffling his feet, nervously flitting his eyes around the room and then looking down again.

What are some possible hypotheses that you can generate about what this behavior might mean? Don't settle on just one possibility based on these limited data. Remember, you don't know the context for these actions, nor do you understand the relevant history. Caution and humility are in order.

Discuss some possible ways you might intervene in this situation (if you think some action is desirable).

GROUP LEADERSHIP APPROACHES

There are more than two dozen major theoretical approaches to therapy and a similar number of models applied to group leadership. Some of these approaches are virtually identical to what would be employed in individual sessions. For instance, the cognitive therapist would address the same dysfunctional beliefs in groups that he or she might when working with single clients. The existential therapist would explore universal themes of personal responsibility, freedom, and search for meaning. The behavioral clinician would still work on specific, identifiable goals.

Some therapeutic models evolved as group therapies before they were ever used with individuals. Gestalt and person-centered therapies are examples of approaches that were field tested by Fritz Perls and Carl Rogers (respectively) primarily in groups and later refined for individual therapy. Other theories have been specifically adapted from individual to group (and family) settings. Psychodynamic theory is one good example of this; it was used with individuals for many decades before systematic group approaches were introduced.

Although it is beyond the scope of this book to cover this material in depth, you should realize that certain leadership skills have their origins in various theories. For example, psychodynamic group leaders may be more inclined to use interpretation skills, humanistic practitioners would use lots of reflective skills, and cognitive therapists would favor challenging belief systems. Based on what you already understand about the influence of various theories on our profession, this should come as no surprise.

Some Differences to Keep in Mind

Although we have been emphasizing that there are indeed many similarities between group and individual therapeutic skills, there are also some distinct differences to keep in mind. For one thing, group leadership requires even more multitasking skills. There are always a dozen, a hundred, maybe even a thousand things going on at the same time. While you are talking to one group member, everyone else in the group is reacting in some way. There is a barrage of stuff going on inside you—hunches, observations, feelings, thoughts—and only some of it is relevant. You have to sort out which things to attend to, both inside you and in the group. You have to track what the person-in-focus is saying to you and respond appropriately, and yet you must also manage the experience for everyone else present. Needless to say, this is a job that will test you in ways you never imagined.

Building Cohesion

Unless you manage to create a climate and conditions that are conducive to trust and sharing, nothing much is going to happen in a group. It thus takes some effort to structure the environment so that group members feel safe enough to disclose personal material in need of work.

Cohesion-building skills are used over the life of a group and are designed to help people feel close, respectful, and caring toward one another. In a sense, you are trying to build a community in which participants support one another and feel safe enough to be honest and confrontative.

Cohesion is built by using many of the skills that follow, in addition to those you have already learned. Essentially, you are looking for every opportunity to make connections between people, to guide them from a position of "I" to a more universal stance of "we."

Specific structures and techniques are often helpful for building cohesion. One requires members to reveal something personal about themselves, something a bit risky, and is considered the "price of admission." Once you can get everyone to share a significant part of themselves, your next step is to develop what is called universality—a searching for common experience.

In the following example, the group leader uses an opportunity to build cohesion in a group:

Natalie: I can't seem to get motivated to do this. I know I keep saying it's important but I don't seem to find the time to follow through.

Candy: Then maybe it's not important.

Jose: Yeah, I remember once when I had a problem like that . . .

Leader: Candy and Jose, you are both offering something useful to Natalie but I wonder if we might go in another direction instead. I am wondering how the rest of you are relating to similar struggles in your own lives.

Jose: Yeah, well I can definitely relate.

Leader: (pointing) Tell Natalie.

You can see that the leader is moving people away from giving advice and even confrontation ("Maybe it's not important") at this early stage. Instead she is trying to get other members to lend support to Natalie by talking about similar problems they may have. This does several things simultaneously; it helps Natalie feel not so alone, and it helps other members talk about their shared issues. These are the bricks and mortar from which trust is built.

Cohesion can be facilitated further by providing opportunities for members to give support to the member-in-focus, as well as share more about their own experiences. This is how a community of caring is constructed.

Jose: I just wanted to say to you, Natalie, that I have been having a problem like that in my life. What worked for me . . .

Leader: Thanks Jose. I realize you'd like to give her some advice, but for the moment, let's focus on how common this situation can be for other people in the group. Who else would be willing to tell Natalie how you feel toward her since she shared this problem with you? Talk directly to her rather than to me.

By politely and firmly intervening after Jose's initial comment, the therapist is again trying to stop advice giving (this "blocking" skill is discussed later) in favor of promoting more personal sharing with one another. The goals here are to help Natalie feel proud of taking a risk and to help other members feel closer to one another as a result of this sharing. Cohesion and trust often result from instances when people reveal themselves in an honest and authentic way, and feel better about it afterward.

Modeling

In all forms of counseling, therapy, and teaching, some modeling takes place. This is when clients learn new skills and attitudes as a result of watching the professional and internalizing what is observed. Often this takes place unconsciously and in very subtle ways.

In groups, where a lot of vicarious learning takes place anyway as a result of some members watching others work, modeling plays a more significant role. Remember that many group members don't know what is expected of them or how to behave. They don't know how to be effective participants. Your job is to teach them this by demonstrating appropriate behavior by the ways you present yourself.

Modeling skills can take many different forms. When the therapist intervenes with someone who is talking too much, the other members are watching carefully to see how this is done; they will be inclined to imitate the behavior in the future. When the therapist uses self-disclosure or tells a personal story designed to illustrate a point, this may encourage others to follow that lead.

Although we could list a number of other specific ways that modeling can be done, the general principle is that all clients carefully watch what you do, how you behave, and who you are. If they are drawn to you, if they respect you, if they admire you, then they will be likely to imitate your style and behavior and values. What this means is that who you are is as important as what you do. Modeling is not so much a skill (although it does require being skillful) as it is a way of presenting yourself.

Exercise in Modeling

Make a list of those specific behaviors, values, attitudes, and personal characteristics that your instructor models in class. Which of them would you most like to include in your own style?

In small groups, compare notes about the features that you have identified. Attempt to come to a consensus about which modeled behaviors have been most powerful and influential for the class as a whole.

Capitalizing on Vicarious Identification

One of the remarkable things that happens in groups is that while one person is working and is the focus of attention, others are identifying strongly with what is going on. This is called vicarious identification. Imagine, for example, that someone is talking about a problem with his boss. This authority figure is reported as being arbitrary, capricious, unfair, and at times even verbally abusive and disrespectful. Time is taken in the group to help this person work on the issue, role-play a possible confrontation, understand the underlying issues, connect this problem to others in his life, and then finally to commit himself to take constructive action. The vicarious identification skill that next takes place occurs when the therapist asks other group members to talk about how they have personalized or identified with the issue that was presented. This is some of what people said:

- "I don't have a problem with my boss. In fact, I like my boss a lot. But this reminded me of the crap I get from my father, who still tries to control my life. I've decided it's time to do something about this."
- "I was thinking about the way I feel treated by an instructor. She always seems to cut me off when I make comments in class, as if she doesn't like me or value what I have to say. I'm going to talk to her."
- "Gee, I was reminded that some of the people who work for me may feel the same way that you do toward your boss. I sure hope not but I intend to check this out with them."

Like many of these leadership skills, this is less a single specific behavior that can be learned and more an overall strategy that is different from that of individual sessions where you don't have to be concerned about these additional challenges. Remember that in groups, even though you may be working with one person at a time, you are doing so before an audience in which each person is asking himself or herself: "What does this have to do with me and my life?"

Linking

Linking involves making connections between members as well as searching for common themes. As mentioned earlier, linking not only often leads to cohesion and trust building but may also be used more generally to connect material from various members to find common themes.

Cassie: I just feel so out of control lately. I can't seem to sleep or eat right. I walk around like a zombie.

Luis: I know what that's like. I've been working three jobs trying to keep my head above water.

Leader: So Luis, you can identify with the stresses that Cassie has been going through even though your pressure results from a different source. I wonder if others might say something about how they identify with what Cassie and Luis have mentioned.

The therapist is trying to universalize Cassie's disclosure so that she doesn't feel so alone and also to help members remain engaged in the process. The best way to think about linking skills is that you are trying to build as many points of connection as possible between members. This is important not only in group work but also in family counseling sessions.

Exercise in Linking

Get together in small groups. Each of you present separate personal issues that are either real or role-played. Take turns making linking statements to draw connections and find common themes in issues that were presented.

Scanning

In group and family sessions, you must juggle the needs of multiple clients at the same time. You have less control over what's going on and less time to attend to the individual concerns of each person. For this reason, it is important to monitor carefully how each person is doing and how each one is reacting to what is going on at any moment in time.

Scanning is the skill of continuously observing each member of the group, using your eyes to let each person know that you are aware of him or her. It is sort of like continuously taking each person's pulse, communicating that you are watching to make sure each one is okay.

Scanning is a safety measure but much more than that. It is what allows you to keep the group functioning as a unit, reading problems when they first manifest themselves nonverbally. Who is nervous? Who is reluctant? Who is excited? Who is about to talk? Who wants to say something but needs encouragement? Who is restless and bored? Who is sending signals to others? Who is frustrated? Who is in trouble?

Scanning involves simply periodically "making the rounds" of a group with your eyes, checking in with each person. When you are leading a group by yourself (as opposed to having a coleader), you will already have enough to do just helping individual members work on their issues. It takes additional energy to remember to scan the group to see what else was going on while you have been focused on the person who was talking.

Exercise in Scanning

Make an effort to scan periodically around your class or in other groups of which you are a member. Notice the nonverbal behavior around you, the variety of ways that people are reacting to what is going on. Notice who is bored, who is frustrated or puzzled, who wants to talk and is waiting for an opening. Who is agreeing most with what is going on? Who is disagreeing? Make scanning a habitual part of your natural behavior.

Cueing

One of the unique aspects of doing group therapy over individual therapy is that you are trying to get members to do most of the work to help each other. Initially, you may model appropriate ways of intervening, showing people how to respond sensitively, how to explore issues, how to confront someone, how to let people know that they have been heard and understood. Whenever possible, it is best to cue members to intervene rather than try to do everything yourself. There are several reasons for this: It helps clients learn helping skills, it diffuses reactions to authority, and it shares the burden of the work.

If you are scanning consistently and effectively, then you will notice members who are having strong reactions to what is going on and what is being said. You can use these observations to cue members to talk at appropriate times. Involving group members is often more effective than doing all of the work yourself.

For instance, sometimes a client in the group consistently talks too much. You know this is a problem because you want to draw out the quieter members so that this one person doesn't continue to dominate. But if you are the one to intervene, there are certain side effects. For one, the person may feel publicly censured by the authority figure. Besides, people generally need practice confronting others, and this would be a perfect opportunity.

So, when you notice this monopolizing behavior going on, rather than saying something about it, you might look around the group and see who else is bothered or disturbed. You notice that a quiet man is shaking his head and muttering to himself.

Leader: Excuse me, Dan, but I couldn't help but notice that while Melinda was talking, you were shaking your head. What's going on?

Dan: Nothing.

Leader: It might be my imagination but you seemed to be annoyed about something when Melinda was talking.

Dan: Well, it's just that she talks . . .

Leader: Don't tell me. Tell her.

The therapist has cued Dan to confront Melinda rather than doing so himself. Ironically, Melinda is far more likely to hear such a confrontation from another member, because she is likely to feel less threatened than if the therapist had intervened.

Blocking

Unlike in individual counseling situations, you are not in complete control of what happens in a group. Some members may say things that are mean or even hurtful. Some people may talk too much or act in manipulative ways. Sometimes you may even end up with severe personality disorders in a group, individuals who may wish to disrupt the process for their own sense of power or entertainment. Less severe but still challenging are those clients who simply lack interpersonal skills or socially appropriate behavior. They may disrupt proceedings and become distracting if their behavior is not checked. This means that you must set limits and enforce these boundaries consistently.

There are specific times when you must intervene to prevent people from hurting one another, or themselves.

When Someone Is Being Disrespectful or Abusive

You must prevent members from being verbally inappropriate or hurtful to others. This is part of the group norms that you would establish from the beginning. Examples of behavior that you would need to block include any instance when members are rude, hurtful, or disrespectful to one another. This might occur because the person is insensitive, ignorant of consequences, malicious, or malevolent. You can block this behavior directly by labeling what is going on and intervening to stop it:

> I realize you feel very passionate about what you are saying, but speaking to him with your voice raised and using that language makes it hard for anyone to actually listen to what you are saying. You may want to choose to take a moment to consider whether you wish to speak in a way that is more respectful and more inviting for others to hear.

Another way of handling the situation is to structure an opportunity to give the person feedback at the same time that the "victim" is given a chance to do some work.

Freda: Look, bitch, I don't give a shit about this crap. And I'm tired of listening to you and hearing you whine all the time.

Leader: Freda, I can see that you are feeling rather strongly about Teresa and what she has been saying. [Reflection of feeling] But speaking to Teresa in this way is not okay. [Blocking] Teresa, I wonder if you'd be willing to talk to Freda about what that felt like. [Cueing]

Teresa: She was mean. And that hurt. But I'm not surprised . . .

Leader: Talk to Freda. [Redirecting]

Teresa: Freda, I don't like it when you talk to me that way. It hurts. If you've got some problem with me, then . . .

Freda: Look, you talk too damn much. Nobody else can get a word in . . .

Leader: Freda, you are the truth teller of the group, which is an important role in the group. But I don't think that Teresa is hearing you when you use that language and tone of voice. [Blocking] I wonder if you could try it again but phrase it in a way, and in a way that might be easier for Teresa to hear you.

When Someone Is Incessantly Complaining

Remember, group members don't know the rules and norms for how to behave. Some members will whine and complain about all the people in their lives who they believe are making them miserable. Even if this were true (which it rarely is), there is still little you can do to change anyone else's behavior. Unless you block this behavior, it can easily eat up all the time in the group with group members going on and on about people who are not part of the group.

The best way to deflect this behavior is to reflect the feelings of the person who is speaking: "You're feeling powerless to change your supervisor's behavior." If, after several attempts to reflect the member's content and feelings and he or she continues to complain about others, you may want to reflect this process:

> Maya, I notice you often talk about how others are treating you badly. We have tried to offer you some support, but you still continue to focus on others rather than yourself. I sense you're not getting what you need from the group. How can we offer support and help to *you*?

By taking this approach, you eventually help the client recognize her part in the situation, the part that *she* can change. This process becomes an opportunity for the client (and others in the group) to take responsibility for her own part in conflict, which in turn empowers the client.

Energizing

Leading groups is considerably different from individual counseling because you must juggle so many tasks at the same time and keep so many different people (with different needs) fully engaged in the process. Sometimes the job seems overwhelming.

Use scanning and other therapeutic skills to keep the group members interested throughout the proceedings. When a client is talking about something that is not of obvious interest to others, the others may disengage. When someone rambles too much, people tend to tune out what is going on. When people are tired or when routines become too predictable, they may also lose interest and motivation. These are the times the pace of the group will slow and energy will lag.

At such times, you must take steps to use all your skills to change the energy level. There are a lot of very creative ways to do this; you are limited only by your own imagination. Sometimes, the most direct way to deal with the problem is to bring it up to the group: "I notice the energy level seems to be flagging right now. What's going on?"

By naming what you see (or feel) happening, you present the group with the problem to solve; after all, it is *their* group. If they are bored or disengaged, then it is their responsibility to do something to liven things up.

Facilitating Feedback

If a client is to receive feedback about dysfunctional behavior, the therapist is the only one who can offer it during individual counseling. But in group work, a distinct strength is that a person may receive feedback and input from multiple sources. There is nothing more useful, and exciting, than hearing how one is perceived by others. Your job is to structure things so that this can happen. This can be as simple as asking the client who received attention if he or she would like to hear feedback, or it can be a far more complex activity that involves everyone.

Giving feedback is a skill that must be learned like any other. In order to teach this skill to others, you must first be an expert yourself. This means that you must work hard at learning to hear feedback directed at you in a way that does not make you feel defensive, so that you can make changes based on what was offered. It also means that you must learn to give feedback to others so that they don't shut down or feel they must ward off perceived threats. And make no mistake—it is very scary to hear people's honest perceptions of you.

Here are some guidelines to keep in mind:

Be Honest and Frank

Solid feedback must be on target. This is not a time for watering down the truth or hedging for the sake of being polite. A group is supposed to be the one setting where participants can finally find out what others think and feel about them. Our whole lives we walk around in the world doing some stupid, ineffective, and annoying things, but few (if any) people will ever let us know. They will whisper behind our backs. They will keep their opinion of us private. They will tell others, but rarely will you hear such remarks directly from clients. It is as if the whole world knows something about you that is hidden from your own view. How many times, for instance, have you looked at people and wondered how they could not possibly realize how annoying some trait of theirs is? In groups, you have to create ways for people to hear—out loud—what others are thinking.

As we stated in the previous chapter, make sure to include both supportive and constructive elements. Ordinarily, this might be labeled as "positive" and "negative" feedback, but these terms are neither accurate nor useful. It so happens that what might be called "negative," that is, critical, might actually be the most constructive thing that could ever be offered to you. Let's say, for example, that you have some irritating trait that is off-putting and that compromises your credibility. Maybe you raise your voice at the end of each statement, turning it into a question. Or, perhaps you end every sentence by saying, "Do you know what I mean?" Or, maybe you avert your eyes from others, communicating a lack of confidence. Or, perhaps you apologize for everything, even if it has nothing to do with you. Everyone in your world knows this about you, but until you hear from others how this behavior affects them, you are not going to do much to change it. This means that what you might ordinarily think of as "negative" feedback can have quite positive and constructive results.

Likewise, so-called positive feedback, the kind that is generally supportive and complimentary, might feel good for a few minutes but may not give you anything solid to work on. If we tell you that you are a nice person, that you are smart or lovely or kind, that would certainly feel good. But what can you do with it? What does it give you to work on?

As you can see, the best feedback contains elements that are both supportive and constructive. Here are some examples:

I really like the way you assert yourself and speak up for your rights. One thing I struggle with, however, is that you sometimes come across to me as overly aggressive and self-centered.

I love the way that you are always there for all of us. You are the first one to jump in whenever anyone needs help or support. But I also notice that you don't take care of yourself. It's almost as if you are trying to hide in other people's problems so you don't have to deal with your own.

Use Descriptive, Personalized Language

Feedback is more valuable when it is adapted to the person you are offering it to. You will want to be as specific as possible and to supply examples of the behavior you are describing. Compare the following two ways that feedback could be presented to someone who is acting inappropriately intrusive in the group, pushing people to do or say things that they are not yet ready to reveal.

Although I know that you mean well, and you are just trying to be helpful, you can be pushy at times. I wish you'd back off sometimes.

You play an important role in the group by being one of the lead persons to help others explore their issues. Sometimes, however, you seem to push harder than would seem necessary. For instance, just a few minutes ago, Claire said clearly that she wasn't sure she wanted to go any farther with this, yet rather than hearing and respecting her reluctance, you continued to press her to reveal more and more. You can and should check this out with Claire, but my sense is that she shut down because you pushed her too hard.

Generally speaking, the more specific the feedback is, the better, and the more concrete the examples, the easier it is for the person to act on what is being said.

Be Sensitive and Caring

Remember that hearing feedback is often very frightening and threatening. Offer it in the most loving way possible, as if you are giving someone a precious gift (which you are).

> ### Exercise in Feedback
>
> In order to become more expert at teaching group members to give and receive feedback you will need to gain as much experience as possible—and as much feedback on your feedback as you can get. You must make this a priority, not only for improving your feedback ability but all your therapeutic skills.
>
> With partners or in small groups, practice giving feedback to one another that meets the most important criteria—that is, be sensitive, caring, supportive, honest, descriptive, and provide specific examples.
>
> Afterward, give one another feedback on the feedback. In other words, help one another to become more effective in using this skill in the future.

Checking In and Checking Out

Because members of a group receive so much less time than they would in individual therapy, it is absolutely critical that you find ways to invite and honor every voice in the room. Since some members are shy, or reticent, or even reluctant to speak, one structure unique to group work involves beginning every session by asking each member to check in and ending each group with a checkout. There are innumerable ways to make this happen, depending on the type of group and the issues at the forefront, as well as the particular leadership approach that is favored. A more action-oriented group might ask members to check out by declaring what they are going to accomplish or work on before the next sessions, making a public commitment for which they will be held accountable. Thus, the check-in for the next session might ask everyone to report on what they did. Members can also be asked to check in with questions such as the following:

- What have you been thinking about since last time we met?
- What is one thing that is particularly troubling to you today?
- What feels unfinished or leftover from last time that you want to make sure that we revisit?
- What is something significant about you that you have not yet shared with us?
- What is the best thing, and worst thing, that you experienced during the previous week?

These, of course, are just examples of the kinds of prompts that invite members to begin a session. Regardless of the particular choice, the main goal is to check the pulse of each person present, to get a feeling for where everyone stands, and to conduct an assessment of each client's current state of mind so as to best allocate time appropriately to serve those who need help the most.

Psychoeducation

In your practicum and internship experiences, you may be asked to lead psycho-educational groups where you will integrate group leadership skills with others that are often more appropriate in a classroom setting. There are many kinds of groups that are primarily instructional in nature such as those when people are referred by the court system for addiction problems. The idea is that participants are exposed to important information that is believed to be useful to better understand their problems. For example, a group focused on weight loss, or smoking cessation, or assertiveness training, might each cover a curriculum of knowledge and skills that can be learned. In the latter case, participants would be taught the differences between being aggressive versus assertive, or might learn and then practice role-plays for confronting individuals who have been experienced as intimidating or disrespectful.

You can readily appreciate that in such groups you are combining your process skills with those that are used by teachers. That means you will need to learn ways to present captivating, interesting, and engaging lectures (usually never more than 20 minutes), combined with an assortment of group activities that keep your audience engaged and interactive with one another. These same skills that are used in psychoeducational groups will also serve you well in presentations you do with any audience. In some ways, you are already an expert on this subject, as least as a "consumer" since you have been a lifelong student and know quite well what excellent and poor instruction are all about. Your job will be to eventually make yourself into the best teacher you can.

Working With a Coleader

Another unique facet of group or family therapy is working with a partner as a co-therapist. There are a number of reasons to use this format. First, it provides greater coverage of the group. While one leader is working with a client, the other leader can be scanning and monitoring the other members. Second, the coleaders can model the way cooperative partners (surrogate parents) work together. This increases the possibilities for members to have a positive identification with a therapist. And finally, it gives the therapists a forum for comparing notes and supervising one another. As you will discover, therapy can be a lonely job, especially group therapy, because there is so much to process afterward.

There is a special set of skills employed when working with a coleader. It is crucial that you work together as a team, that you synchronize efforts so as to present a consistent, unified front. That is not to say that you can't and shouldn't disagree with one another in front of the group, because that could be instructive if done respectfully.

Sit Opposite One Another for Maximum Coverage

You want to be able to scan opposite sides of the room. You also will want to see one another so that you can signal and make eye contact to communicate during the session.

Develop a Signal System

Spend some time with each other ahead of time so that you feel comfortable working together. Agree on signals that you might use during the group session to indicate when time is running out, when you are confused, or when you want to move on to something else.

Make Sure You Are Equal Participants

Coleader teams are a lot less effective when they don't work together as equal participants. Make sure you and your partner get equal time to participate in the group process.

Take Time-Outs as Needed

When you are at cross purposes or don't understand where things are going, feel free to take a time-out to talk across the group about what is going on, or not going on. Here are some examples of when this might take place:

- "I'm not sure where you are going right now."
- "I'm confused about what this silence means. Where should we go next?"
- "I don't think that Tim is ready to go much farther with this. I think we should move on."
- "I could use some help right now."
- "I really like the way you did that."

Of course, there is also modeling in that group members are seeing two partners discuss things openly and make decisions cooperatively.

Exercise to Colead a Group

Team up with a partner to practice the co-therapy model and experience what it is like to work together as part of a treatment team. One way to do this is in a role-play in which one person plays a client (or presents a part of himself or herself) and two others interview the person together. Find a couple of opportunities to take a time-out and talk to one another to make sure efforts are coordinated.

UNIQUE ETHICAL CHALLENGES

When you are applying group skills, it is important to understand the special ethical considerations involved. These are in addition to the usual things that you must be aware of in any therapeutic encounter.

Informed Consent

As with all forms of treatment, you are required to inform clients about the risks, cautions, contraindications, and dangers so that they can make informed choices about whether and how to participate. This would include not only mentioning the limits of confidentiality but also other issues like the inevitable peer pressure and possible coercion that can take place. In most, if not in all groups, participants' pressure perceived "deviates"—those who are different from the norm—to comply with the majority values. Individual rights must be protected and members given the opportunity to pass. Research on group work has shown that casualties are most likely to occur when people are pressured to do things that they are not ready or prepared to do. Once some group members take risks and reveal themselves, they want others to do so too, so that they don't feel like they're hanging out there alone. The idea is that I opened myself up to you; now you reciprocate so that I have something on you and you can't betray me without fear of retribution.

Confidentiality

Although communications can be kept private and sacred in individual sessions, there are no guarantees that this will be the case in group sessions. You can urge members to respect others' privacy. You can stress how critical this privilege is for the group to work. You can prepare members for potential violations. But you can't ensure that everyone will honor the rules. Some violations may occur inadvertently, and others may be the result of malicious motives. Open groups can sometimes be especially challenging since members may change from week to week; in these types of groups, it's essential to reiterate the importance and limits of confidentiality each session.

Cultural Differences

As in individual therapy, or any other aspect of life, cultural differences can be a source of interest or conflict. For example, during a recent session, one group member of Mexican American background shared a story about her father who was overly demanding and incredibly irresponsible in his behavior. This woman felt the need to take care of him even though she received absolutely nothing in return; he was never particularly grateful for her help and was often rather abusive. Another member of the group of Caucasian background, who had emancipated himself from his parents while still a teenager, suggested that she "fire" her father and stop taking care of him since he was so unappreciative of her efforts and the responsibility was dragging her down. Rather than feeling grateful, the woman became furious. "That's easy for you to say! But in my Mexican culture I am obligated to take care of my parents no matter how they behave." This sort of misunderstanding is all too common in groups and the leader's job is to make certain that members' cultural differences are honored and respected.

It is helpful and important to label the conflict as cultural. Many times we have our own perspectives and make incorrect assumptions about the motivations and behaviors of others. When understood from a cultural perspective, clients can not only learn to be culturally sensitive but also learn that their perceptions are simply that, perceptions, not fact. To be culturally sensitive, you will need to understand the many constructs involved in honoring diversity and will want to advocate for your clients when they are culturally misunderstood.

Control

Another ethical challenge has to do with having less control during a group process. In individual therapy, if something goes wrong it is because of your lapse or mistake, but in groups anyone present can do something hurtful. As a therapist, it can be quite difficult to take responsibility for inadvertently hurting someone. Imagine how difficult this would be for a client. That is why you must receive additional training in group work because the skills are so specialized. You have seen how the other skills you have learned must also be adapted in order to work effectively.

Exercise in Group Skills

If you have not already had experience as a group member in a therapeutic-type group, we would urge you to make this a major priority in your training and personal development. Even though you will likely take a course (or two) in leading groups, we still strongly recommend that you gain experience sitting in the client's chair. That is the only way you can fully appreciate what your clients will go through when they appear cautious, reluctant, or hesitant to go along with your planned program.

PITFALLS AND COMMON MISTAKES

Most of the pitfalls that occur with individuals and families can occur with groups as well; we cover some of these again but from a group perspective. However, as a leader of a group of strangers, you may have some unique opportunities to mess up, too, and we cover those as well.

Trying to Do Too Much

We talked about this in previous chapters, and we cover it again here with groups. As with individuals, you may find yourself working harder than the group. You may have also noticed that while working with a group, you have more information to attend to and more people to attend to. So, in a way, you will have more work to do. Once you establish the boundaries and set up the culture of the group, however, you can encourage group members to share the work. You would do this by first modeling how to communicate and behave, and then by linking, scanning, cueing, and blocking. Eventually, the members catch on and do this automatically. Sometimes a member of the group begins to act as the leader, which can sometimes be helpful for everyone. Once the group culture is established, your work should be much easier.

Failing to Establish Boundaries

Ground rules are just as important for groups as for families, and it's important to establish them early. You will want to cover confidentiality and that although you expect each member to maintain confidentiality, you cannot guarantee it. You will want to cover some of the same ground rules you did with families, such as respecting each other (not calling each other names), letting people finish what they have to say before responding, and attending on time and consistently. There may be other rules that you consider important for running the group, but many of these can be addressed indirectly, such as blocking advice giving. No matter the boundaries you establish, you must use them consistently to avoid the appearance of favoritism, just as you do with families. Without these boundaries, a group of strangers can quickly decompensate. The slightest threat to safety can set a group back for weeks.

Failing to Keep a Monopolizer in Check

More often than not, you will have at least one group member who will monopolize the session if you allow it. He or she will talk incessantly, commenting on everything anyone else says. The monopolizer will not allow silence to simmer; he or she will always want to talk. At first, the group members may like this person because he or she allows them to remain silent, with their inhibition and ambivalence about sharing. However, if you don't keep this person in check, the other members will become frustrated. They will not feel their needs are being met, and they may not return. However, if you use your scanning and subsequent cueing skills, the group can help you keep this person in check. In fact, once cohesion has been established and the group feels safe, this person will likely be confronted by other members and have a unique opportunity to understand how he or she comes across to others. In individual therapy, you don't have this advantage. Managing the monopolizer not only helps the monopolizer learn new ways of communicating but also keeps the group functioning better.

Not Dealing Well With Silence

We mentioned this with individual therapy, and if you think it's challenging to allow or facilitate silence in individual therapy, group silence will really feel like torture. In a group, nearly all silence is productive in some way. Of course, in the first few sessions, because you are establishing the group, you may want to avoid awkward silences where no one knows how to proceed. But when working in the later stages of the group, silence can be powerful. Just like in individual therapy, sometimes silence allows one person or several people in the group to process information. It will be important that you allow time for that to occur by attending to the person who is processing. If you look around the room, slowly, others might want to talk to fill in the silence. At other times, the group will feel stuck and go silent. You may want to "save" them and say something, but allowing the silence can be good for the group. It's part of the process. After these types of silences, you might want to process what that was like for each member.

Being Too Cautious

Because group work can facilitate strong negative emotions that are relatively stronger than in therapy with individuals, you may feel cautious to the point of avoiding arguments or confrontations, if you are uncomfortable with them. You may interrupt important interpersonal conflicts that involve the expression of negative emotions. If you are not comfortable with anger or tears, you will really struggle in a group. One of the most valuable advantages of group work is to have group members work through conflict. Your role as therapist is not to avoid these conflicts, but rather to teach members how to disagree or confront well. And don't be surprised if at some point, you get to be the center of attention. Sometimes this can be the most difficult group process to deal with. It is not unusual for groups to feel frustrated if they have revealed so much of themselves but you, the leader, have revealed nothing. Occasionally, they can get downright angry with you. If you can remember that your purpose is to accept the expression of their anger but in a way that is most constructive, you will not have to take it personally.

All ranges of emotions should be allowed in a group. Sometimes your job will be to facilitate feelings that are usually withheld. Try to gather the courage to allow the group to experience intense feelings so that the members can learn how to direct those feelings in a constructive way.

Pushing Too Much (Before and After Cohesion)

In contrast to being too cautious, you might err in the other direction. You can push the group or each member too much. There are two particular areas where you may want to be sensitive to pushing too hard. First, if the group has not formed cohesively enough yet, if it's not yet safe, then you probably wouldn't want to facilitate anything before the members are ready. You cannot expect in the first, second, or even third session that group members are ready to confront each other. If you notice, for example, that when Sally speaks, Jane rolls her eyes, just make a mental note of it. Once the cohesion is established you can cue Jane to tell you what her expression is about when the opportunity arises again, as it surely will.

Even when the group is fully cohesive, you still can push too hard. When you are doing individual work, pushing is a little safer in that the likelihood that the client will feel humiliated is limited. In a group, however, humiliation is more likely to occur since there is an audience. Clients have not only you to think about, but how the group perceives them as well. Therefore, you will want to push clients gently when you can. It is more likely in a group situation than in individual therapy that a member may not return if you push too hard. In addition, other members may not think it is safe to be vulnerable, either, so your group goes back to the first stage, where the members reveal little.

Not Working Well With a Coleader

While you are in training you may be assigned to group work with another leader; in fact, most agencies require that your first group experience be with a coleader who has more experience than you.

Your personal styles of running a group or assumptions about how a group should be run may differ. For example, you may find yourself working in a domestic violence agency where you are assigned to work with batterers. The group may be primarily psychoeducational, but you prefer to be more humanistic. Imagine that you are paired with a coleader who likes to be by the book in teaching this group about the cycle of violence. You find yourself talking over each other, giving each other dirty looks, and the group losing direction and focus because of your power struggle. Or because you are new, you just sit quietly and allow your coleader to dominate. How do you think this will affect the group? Remember, everything you do is a model of interpersonal communication for group members. Although some members may mimic your styles of interpersonal communication, others might just feel frustrated with the palpable tension between you.

The best way to avoid coleader problems is to start by discussing with your coleader your style of leading groups and what process you would like to facilitate. After each group session, take some time to talk about any snags, any misunderstandings, or negative feelings. You must be able to assert yourself and not fall into the passive-aggressive game. If you do, you not only hurt your growth as a therapist, you hurt the group as well. So talk it out and be honest. It's another opportunity to practice giving feedback.

Being Too Serious

As the group develops cohesion and starts doing serious work, you may find that the group suddenly stops working. You may want to facilitate a more serious conversation, but the group won't have anything to do with it. This might be because the previous session was too serious or too deep, and the group needs to lighten up a bit to balance the depth that occurred in the previous session. Another way the group can be too serious is simply if the nature of the group tends to be serious. After a while, this can be draining to the group members, and to you. We highly recommend using humor when you can to lighten the situation. The best thing we can do is learn to laugh at ourselves. Of course, this must be done at appropriate times. But if done correctly, varying the mood of the group will keep it more lively and interesting for you and the other members.

Not Balancing Individual Needs With the Needs of the Group

A challenge specific to working with groups, including families, is balancing individual needs with the needs of the group. You may remember that at the beginning of the chapter we mentioned that the group is a unit, a client unit that functions as a whole. It has its own culture, its own unique personality and identity. Therefore, you have an opportunity to focus on what is good for the group as a whole, to facilitate its movement through stages, to get the individual members to share in the work, and to keep the best interest of the larger group in mind. You can do this to a point where you forget to consider the individual differences.

For example, imagine that one of the members begins to talk about her experience of being raped in college. She describes feeling powerless and having no control. In the midst of her sorrow, you think, "Ah, a time to link using feeling powerless," and you try to link this feeling. You have begun to invalidate this one person's experience. You must let her go where she needs to in the conversation for some period of time before attempting to link. It's only when people start to monopolize that you might want to shift the direction.

In contrast, if you are primarily an individual therapist you may be tempted to do individual therapy while the other members watch. This extreme is not good either. In some counseling programs, one requirement of the group class is that each student must participate as a group member with classmates in a group led by teaching assistants. Under these conditions, it is not unusual for one member to self-disclose and all other members, including the leader, to do therapy with that person. The next week, the same process occurs, but with a different person revealing something personal. This is basically sequential individual therapy. It's therapy for one person and eight therapists. Allowing this process to go on too long negates the primary advantage of being in a group: working through interpersonal issues. If, however, you find that one member really does need individual attention, it is appropriate to recommend privately to that person that individual therapy might be helpful. This way the individual can get his or her more intense issues dealt with in a more appropriate venue and use the group for more interpersonal challenges.

APPLICATIONS TO SELF: YOU ARE ALREADY IN A GROUP

One of the first things that most group textbooks cover is that being in a group is the most natural thing in the world. You are constantly in a group whether you are with your family, with friends, in class, in line at the grocery store. You could be defined as being in a group of some kind most of the time. Therefore, you should have ample opportunity to practice these skills outside of class. Let's look at each one.

Think of a group of friends you might have made recently. You may use the students in this class as an example. What stage are you in with your group? If this is your first semester together and you haven't done a lot outside of class, you may still be in the first stage of getting to know each other and determining what and who is safe. If you have been together a lot prior to this class and/or met very often outside of class, you may be in the second phase, where you can confront each other and can survive conflict. Or because this is the end of the semester, you may be finding ways to part and say goodbye in the ending stage of the group. The stages can sometimes be quite obvious, but sometimes it's more difficult to identify them as members move between the first and second stages for a while before everyone feels safe.

Besides the observation skills you learned in Chapter 4 for working with individuals, groups have additional challenges for your attention. Think about the last time your family gathered. As that memory forms and becomes clear, think about a particular moment in the group. What were the proxemics? Did you notice the nonverbal behavior of some of the people who were not talking? Where were the coalitions and conflicts? Was there silence, and if so, what was the meaning of the silence? What roles do each of the family members typically take? How has culture influenced the norms of your family, as compared with another family you know? We imagine you might feel a bit overwhelmed by having to attend to so much, and it is difficult, but the more you practice, the more these skills will become second nature. Now let's move on to other skills.

Think back again to a new group, one that has formed recently. Perhaps you will use this class or another class of fellow students. After reading about the importance of cohesion, think about how you have formed cohesion in this group so far. What else can you do to facilitate more cohesion? Perhaps you could reveal something risky, something personal. Perhaps you already have. In fact, think of groups where you have revealed something personal as compared with groups you have not. We might make a guess that more cohesion formed in those groups where you showed some level of vulnerability by revealing something personal. This can be used as an important tool if you want to increase the cohesiveness in groups.

Think about this particular class and compare it with another class with a different instructor. We can guess that there are some differences in how you participate in the two classes, whether due to the content of the class, or to different personal styles of the instructors. How have your instructors modeled appropriate behavior? What have they done to facilitate certain behaviors and extinguish other behaviors? Think about whether the instructors seem to communicate in the way that they teach you to communicate. As you form these impressions, you can become more conscious of the ways instructors or leaders can subtly influence the class or group. Therefore, you will want to be aware of how you come across as the group leader, because whether you intend to or not, your behavior will set up a foundation for how to behave in the group.

Students can find linking to be difficult at first. It isn't necessarily something that comes naturally, but with practice it can become second nature. Everywhere you go, listen to the ways in which people talk. Pay attention not only to the content of information but the process, and how they communicate. When you focus on both content and process, you will find it easier to make connections between people. This is a skill you can practice everywhere: at school, with friends, with family, in a restaurant.

We already suggested how to use scanning. When you are in class, scan the room to check how people are responding. For instance, if you find yourself reacting to something strongly, look around the room to see if anyone else seems to be responding as well. Pay attention to the nonverbal behaviors of those around you. Your natural inclination will be to focus on the person who is talking, so this might be difficult at first. However, this, too, will become a habit with practice, and it is most essential in working with groups.

In class, notice how your instructor cues different people to talk. He or she may call names, make eye contact and nod, or say something to indicate it's appropriate for you to speak. Also, go somewhere where people gather and watch how they communicate in groups. How does each person know when it's his or her turn to speak? Sometimes one person monopolizes the conversation, making it difficult for others. At other times, members of the group intentionally elicit from quieter members. Notice the trend that if one person picks up his or her phone, others follow;

it's a cue that gives permission to look at the phone. Regardless of the situation, notice the process of who talks when and how they know it's their turn. Then use what you learn from scanning to cue group members.

Blocking can be a more difficult skill because we are inclined not to interrupt social conversations. Nevertheless, this skill is essential for group leaders so that they can prevent feelings from being hurt unnecessarily and to enhance the safety and cohesion of the group. We have a more difficult challenge for you using this skill. The next time you are with a group of friends or family members, and one person seems to be attacked, risk interrupting in some way to block the process. We realize that this will not be the same way as is done in group counseling, but try it nonetheless. Assert yourself to protect the underdog. If you can do this with your friends or, more challenging, with your family in a way that is productive, you will be a master of using blocking in a group.

Energizing a group can be important when things come to a lull. Sometimes a group just doesn't seem very energized. This can happen after a particularly intense group experience, or sometimes when the group feels less safe for a moment. You may notice that in your own longer friendships, there have been times when the energy in the friendship waned. Your natural inclination might be to just deal with it. Now, however, try something different. Bring it up. Say that you've noticed a change, and see what comes of it. A single statement is all you need to stimulate a conversation: "I've noticed we don't laugh as much anymore."

We discussed earlier how every group session should end with a checkout in which you require each member to share what they learned from the session and what they are going to work on next. So, our question for you as we end this chapter: What are YOU going to take with you from this chapter that is most meaningful or that you found most interesting?

We have now reviewed ten skills associated with running groups that you can practice in class, with friends, or with family members. If you haven't had your group class yet, getting started now will put you ahead of your class so that you can work on more advanced skills. Get the basics down. And remember, you can use these skills to help work in other environments, such as families, couples, with schoolteachers, or at home with the people closest to you.

SUMMARY

In this chapter, we introduced you to some of the ways working with groups is different from working with individuals. We briefly covered some of the major concepts associated with group work, such as group stages and terms such as *proxemics.* Several skills were included that are specific to working with groups. Finally, we covered some skills associated with working with a coleader and the unique ethical considerations involved in doing group therapy. Now we move on to the last chapter, on what's next.

Skills in Action: Giving Feedback

Leader: Welcome back, everyone, to our fifth group meeting. Let's get started with our usual quick check-in to get a sense of where each person is and then determine the direction we want to take today. [Initiating a check-in]

Ann: I'm doing okay today. My mother and I finally had that heart-to-heart conversation, and it went really well. We both took responsibility for our parts of the conflict, and I think we may be able to talk about our differences more easily now.

Leader: Linda, you look like you're agreeing with Ann. [Linking and cueing]

Linda: Absolutely! I talked with my best friend last week and had a similar experience. That thing we did last time with Mike on how to provide feedback really made a difference! [Evidence of vicarious identification]

Mike: You seem really excited about that. I'm happy to see both of you look so happy right now. [Evidence that Mike has picked up the leader's attempt to model empathic feeling reflections]

(long silence)

Leader: Mike, would you like to go next? [Energizing the group to continue]

Mike: Ah, sure. I was just thinking about how my week didn't go so well . . .

Jenny: (speaking loudly) Me, neither! I mean, I'm glad for Linda and Ann, but my week was hell! I got in a car accident and the other guy didn't have any insurance. Then, my boss laid into me for being late to work, like I did it on purpose! [Leader scans the room as Jenny talks] I'm just so tired of that woman. She's so rigid and never gets how hard I work. I work really hard for her. I put in way more than forty hours a week, but she doesn't seem to appreciate it. I don't know what to do with her. I like my job otherwise, but . . .

Leader: Jenny, I wonder if you'd pause for a moment. Mike, you look annoyed. [Scanning, blocking rambling; cueing]

Mike:	Yeah. I wasn't done yet.
Leader:	Tell Jenny, not me. [Redirecting]
Mike:	Jenny, you do that all the time. You interrupt all of us before we're done . . .
Leader:	Mike, remember we agreed that each person would speak for himself? [Enforcing norms]
Mike:	Oh, yeah. Sorry. I mean that it feels like you interrupt *me* frequently. And I'm tired of it. It wouldn't be so bad if you didn't always complain about how others take advantage of you. (angrily and loudly) You have to be the most unlucky person in the world, or you have to figure out why you have such miserable people in your life. Maybe it's because you're so rude with everyone! You're such a . . .
Leader:	Mike, I think you may be saying some important things here, and I notice you're feeling really angry. I'd like to remind you to temper what you say to be as helpful as possible when giving feedback, like we did last week. [Providing feedback, blocking]
Mike:	Okay, let me try this again. Jenny, I think the problem might be that you don't seem to listen to others well.
Leader:	Make it personal to your experience. Don't speak for the group. [Redirecting his process]
Mike:	I don't feel like you listen to me well, and when you don't, I want to hurt you back. I wonder if other people feel that way.
Don:	I do, too. Jenny, you're a real nice person, but when you interrupt like this, I feel angry. I even feel angry for Mike right now.
Ann:	Jenny, I think some of what they're saying is true. We're friends and all, but still I've never said anything to you about this because I was afraid of hurting your feelings. Or maybe I was afraid you might try to hurt me or something. You do come on kind of strong at times.
Leader:	Let's stop for a moment and check in with Jenny to see how she's doing with all this. Jenny, what part of this are you hearing right now? [Summarizing; open-ended probe]
Jenny:	To tell you the truth, I'm really embarrassed right now. I'm feeling a bit beat up. (begins to cry)

Leader: This was really difficult for you to hear. And you're feeling confused and hurt. [Reflecting feelings]

Jenny: (nods head, still crying, looking down)

Leader: Take a moment to gather your thoughts. What's going on inside you right now? [Open-ended question]

Jenny: I was just thinking that maybe there is something about me that makes people mad. I do seem to frustrate people everywhere. I'm tired of people treating me like they are exasperated. But I just don't know how to change.

Don: Have you tried taking a breath before you speak. That's something that has worked for me. I . . .

Leader: We really appreciate you trying to help, but perhaps offering advice at this point is a bit premature. Remember we talked about the role of members, that it isn't to try to fix one another but rather to offer support and feedback so that people can work on their own stuff? [Blocking; reminding about norms]

As the group continues, the group leader will assist members in offering constructive, honest, and sensitive feedback to Jenny, then help her process what was most meaningful to her. It is important for her to also hear input from members about how courageous she is to open up to these issues and work on them. So she doesn't feel so alone, and to facilitate vicarious learning, the leader will prompt other members to talk about the ways they can identify with what Jenny shared. Even if they don't have problems related to interrupting others, everyone can relate to the feeling of being misunderstood, or of having conflicts with others that are difficult to make sense of.

Other members will be invited to talk about things they might like to work on, either related to Jenny's initial problem or to other things that may have come up during the week. The group leader will balance participation, making sure everyone is heard and that each member has a chance to talk for at least a little time.

The group will close with the therapist asking each member to check out with what they learned that week or what they want to work on before the next session. Jenny, in particular, will be given a chance to talk about what she got out of the work.

REFERENCES AND RESOURCES

Corey. G. (2012). *Theory and practice of group psychotherapy* (9th ed.). Belmont, CA: Brooks/ Cole.

Corey, M. S., Corey, G., & Corey, C. (2016). *Groups: Process and practice* (10th ed.). Belmont, CA: Cengage.

Donigan, J., & DeLucia-Waack, J. L. (2004). *The practice of multicultural group work: Visions and perspectives from the field.* Belmont, CA: Thomson Brooks/Cole.

Gladding, S. (2015). *Group work: A counseling specialty* (7th ed.). Santa Monica, CA: Pearson.

Johnson, D. W., & Johnson, F. P. (2012). *Joining together: Group theory and group skills* (11th ed.). Santa Monica, CA: Pearson.

Keene, M., & Erford, B. T. (2006). *Group activities: Fired up for performance.* Upper Saddle River, NJ: Prentice Hall.

Kottler, J. A., & Englar-Carlson, M. (2015). *Learning group leadership* (3rd ed.). Thousand Oaks, CA: Sage.

Shechtman, Z. (2006). *Group counseling and psychotherapy with children and adolescents: Theory, research, and practice.* Mahwah, NJ: Lawrence Erlbaum.

Trotzer, J. P. (2006). *The counselor and the group* (4th ed.). New York, NY: Routledge.

Chapter 12

WHERE TO GO NEXT

It is perfectly reasonable, and perhaps appropriate, that you would feel a certain degree of apprehension about using your new skills in actual sessions with real clients instead of fellow students. In fact, if you are enjoying excessive confidence at this point, you might want to examine some possible feelings of grandiosity. We don't mean to imply that with solid skills training, excellent supervision, and the work experiences you may already have under your belt, you are not entitled to feel good about how far you have come in your professional development. But we do wish to stress that even with ten or more years' experience in the field, many practitioners still feel a degree of trepidation when facing a new client. This is not only normal but expected; it is part of the exhilaration that makes this job so much fun.

Soon you will not be role-playing anymore, or doing pretend exercises. You are about to see people who desperately need your help.

We remember all too clearly the terror we felt waiting to be assigned to our practica and field placements after we completed our skills training. Thus far, we had been able to fool our professors and classmates pretty well, pretending that we felt far more confident about our abilities than we actually did. But at this point, with the prospect of seeing actual live people coming in for help, the game was about up. We would have to confess that we really had no idea what we were doing and felt like frauds who were about to get caught. There was this one reoccurring fantasy that went something like this:

Client: So I was saying that I was really upset about the way this was going . . .

Me: You were feeling anxious because you weren't sure what to do.

Client: That's the best you can do?

Me: Excuse me?

Client: That is the poorest excuse for a reflection of feeling that I've ever heard. I've seen a lot of therapists in my life and I gotta tell you that you are absolutely the worst.

Me: I am?

Client: Damn right! Your attending behaviors stink. Your reflection was shallow, and besides that, it missed the mark completely. I wonder if you were even listening. You look so nervous you are making me feel worse.

Me: Gee, I'm sorry about that. But I'm just a beginner at this . . .

Client: You're sorry? That's the best you can do? I'm feeling so discouraged by your low level of empathy skills that I feel like killing myself. In fact, I think I will . . .

Okay, maybe this fantasy is a little exaggerated. But you would be perfectly entitled to have more than a few disastrous images of what could go wrong when you start seeing clients. Most of your fears are ungrounded, but it is still understandable that you will feel anxious before you start any new, challenging enterprise.

The reality of doing counseling is that clients are so involved in their own stuff that they are barely paying attention to what you do anyway. You will be your harshest critic. Besides, as we hope you have already learned, most of what you do to be helpful is not related to the perfect execution of your skills, but rather your overall presence with the people you are helping and the quality of the relationships you develop.

A number of common apprehensions and fears are often expressed by students at this point in their development.

WHAT IF I DON'T KNOW WHAT TO DO?

Time to burst *that* bubble. It is a certainty that much of the time you won't know what to do in a given situation. As you have learned, therapy is so complex, the clinical choices so limitless, that no matter what you do at any moment, you will be flooded with other paths you could have taken instead.

The question is not so much what to do if you don't know what to do, but what to do when you face this challenge every session. The answer is that you do the best you can. You trust the process. You remind yourself that the client is the one who does most of the work; you are the facilitator. The only way you will ever get better at this stuff is to be honest with yourself—and your supervisor—about what you don't know and cannot yet do. Mostly, just strengthen your ability to build the relationship with your client through attending and being empathic. Your clients will be your teachers and will do the rest.

WHAT IF MY SUPERVISOR FINDS OUT HOW LITTLE I KNOW?

Much of your continued learning and growth will be related to the quality of your supervision. If you do not trust your supervisor, you are not likely to be very open and honest with him or her about areas in which you most need help. If you feel like you have to hide your weaknesses and cover up your mistakes to win your supervisor's approval and respect, you may be able to fake your way through the experience but at a very high cost. That is why you should choose your supervisor carefully and why you should be open with him or her about the things you need to work on. We ask our students to bring us not their best tapes, but their absolute worst ones. Furthermore, we ask them to cue the tapes to the parts where they are most bumbling, awkward, and incompetent (or at least when they felt they were). This is not an exercise in humiliation; our intent is to teach beginners to get in the habit of scrutinizing their skills critically. Until you are prepared to talk about the worst examples of your work, you will make little progress improving those skills.

WHAT IF I HURT SOMEONE?

This is a legitimate concern. One of the hallmarks of our profession is that even if you don't help anyone, you want to be sure you don't hurt them. That is one reason why good supervision is so important for monitoring your progress and safeguarding your clients.

You should know that most clients are far more resilient than you might give them credit for. Even when you do make mistakes, or use your skills awkwardly, you will have plenty of time to recover. This is where a good relationship comes in handy: Clients become very forgiving of your lapses once they trust and respect you. Note in the dialogue below how it takes the therapist several tries to find the right intervention.

Client: I just don't think I'm ready to start dating yet. It has only been a year.

Therapist: You are still feeling pretty raw recovering from your last relationship. [Inaccurate reflection of feeling]

Client:	Well no, not exactly. It's just that I don't want to give up my freedom. I love being on my own right now.
Therapist:	You say that this is about freedom, but I sense that you have some concerns about putting yourself in a position to be abandoned again. [Ill-timed confrontation]
Client:	How can you think that about me? After everything we have talked about together. Do you really think I'm that weak?
Therapist:	Not at all. In fact, right now I can feel your power in standing up to me, asserting yourself, telling me that you feel misunderstood. [Effective use of immediacy]

So it goes. Perhaps half of your skills and interventions (on a good day) will fall on deaf ears, be misunderstood, or ignored. But that's okay: You have plenty of time and lots of opportunities to find the right combination of things to get through to the person, *if* you have established and maintained a strong relationship. This is why learning the skills of empathy are so critical. You can always fall back on them when you are stuck, and at the very least, buy yourself some time to figure out where to go next.

WHAT IF I DON'T HAVE WHAT IT TAKES?

This might be the scariest fear of all—that when all is said and done, you are not cut out for this kind of work. That is indeed a possibility. Once you get out in the field and start seeing clients, perhaps you will discover that this job is not for you. But we would suggest that it is just as good to learn what you don't want to do as it is to learn what you do like.

What *does* it take to succeed in this profession? You must master the basic skills learned from this book, but that mostly takes practice and solid feedback. Most students are able to do this, although more than a few elect to give up. But if you are open and determined and dedicated and persistent, you can become better and better in your skills.

What else does it take to succeed? You have to learn not to take things personally or you will burn out quickly. Your skill level is no reflection of who you are as a person. Sometimes you will simply need to practice these skills because of the novelty of listening and responding. At other times, you will feel stuck because you need to do your own work; your own issues are getting in the way of helping a client.

You must be able to metabolize the daily stresses in such a way that you don't take them home with you. You must be forgiving of your imperfections. One of the wonderful tenets of individual psychology seems most appropriate here: Your job is to learn how to accept your inferiorities. We all are inferior in many ways, and if you can acknowledge your weaknesses, personally and professionally, and commit to overcoming them, you are on the right track.

What we find, more often than not, is that beginners don't so much wash out of their training as move on to something else because they have discovered that what they are doing is not a good match for who they are. If that happens with you, so much the better; it means that you have found something better suited to your unique gifts and abilities. Nevertheless, the skills you learn in your program and even in this class will help improve your relationships, regardless of the direction you take.

One area that may negatively affect your ability to help others could be related to your own personal weaknesses that may lead to impairment. Unforeseen events, crises, emergencies, transitions, family problems, personal problems, crop up at times that reduce your ability to function at your best. There is a certain level of distress that can be tolerated and not affect your work with clients, or may only affect your work for a week or two. There are also times when life circumstance may become too much to manage. When this happens, it is imperative that you seek your own therapy to complement supervision. In cases of boundary crossings with clients, and in particular when inappropriate sexual relationships ensue, the counselor had often been impaired for quite some time and did nothing to mitigate it. We have also seen instances when therapists who have long been medicated for bipolar disorder or depression believe that they can get off their medication, but then experience a serious setback that interferes with their daily functioning. That is one reason why it is important that we continually work to improve ourselves, deal with unresolved issues, and seek help when we can't handle things on our own.

SOME ADVICE ABOUT WHERE TO GO NEXT

The transition between the skills class and your practica/internship is a critical time in which you prepare yourself for applying what you have learned to the real world. If you have been doing your work all along, we still cannot in good faith reassure you that you will be ready. In truth, you will *never* be ready.

Bet you didn't expect we'd tell you that. You thought we were going to give you a rah-rah speech about going out there and doing it for the team. You thought we would tell you that you are well prepared and can handle whatever comes your way—but that would be a lie. Even after all these years, we still don't feel as ready as we would like to be to help the people who come to us. So, welcome to the team of humility. Even so, there are still a few more things you can do to get yourself as ready as you can.

Keep a Journal

If you haven't already begun a journal to talk about your development as a therapist and to work through personal issues that come up, we would highly recommend that you do so. I [Jeffrey] began such a journal when I started my first practicum 30 years ago, and I'm still writing in it. I talk about cases that confound me. I work through personal issues that are triggered by my work. I jot down some of my best metaphors and stories that I might want to remember (and include in a book some-day). I set goals for myself about areas that I want to improve. I plot my progress in several areas that I have been working on throughout my life. I make notes to myself about things I want to hold onto. I process new insights that come up in sessions. In short, my journal has become a lifelong partner and "peer" supervisor that has kept me accountable. It has offered comfort as well during some very difficult times.

Watch Videos of the Masters

You can learn a lot by watching master practitioners in action. Thousands of such videos have been published; they present the most distinguished clinicians demonstrating their skills with real clients. Apart from getting a better understanding of their theories, viewing these demonstrations allows you to watch the ways that highly skilled practitioners use all the generic skills that you have just learned.

You will find yourself unconsciously and (almost) effortlessly imitating the behaviors you see modeled by the masters. Without having to think about it, or even plan for it, you will find yourself in the middle of a session blurting out something that seems to come out of someone else, someone not quite you. The fact is that you can learn a lot about therapy by watching very good professionals do it.

Get Into Therapy as a Client

Even better than watching therapy is to experience it as much as you can, especially sitting in the client's chair. The more different kinds of therapy you can experience—in groups, individually, in family formats, from practitioners of different approaches—the more you will learn about what works best.

As we've said before, most of the therapeutic skills are now so universal and generic that practically every clinician relies on the same basic helping behaviors.

The true beauty, however, is in experiencing how they work with you. What is the best way to respond to confrontation? When do you most appreciate people who prove they have heard and understood you? When do you find self-disclosure instructive versus indulgent? What kinds of interpretations work best with you? When do you find that you most need some sort of summary? In other words, which skills do you most appreciate as the client? The answers to these questions will go a long way toward guiding your own choices about when to use which interventions.

Another substantial advantage to getting into your own therapy is that you will start to work on issues of your own that will tend to hold you back as a therapist. You will experience fewer countertransferences or at least be aware of them when they happen. You will also realize that change is difficult, and perhaps have more realistic expectations about how quickly your clients can change. Finally, you will be a healthier person by learning more about yourself.

Get Recordings Critiqued

In preparation for your practica/internships, it would be a good idea to get used to being recorded. This is one of the best learning modalities of all for improving your skills.

It is a strange experience indeed to watch yourself continuously. You will notice your annoying mannerisms, your characteristic gestures, every nuance related to how you present yourself to the world (and to your clients). You will hear what your voice sounds like to others, and if this sounds strange to you, then consider all the other ways you are out of touch with how others hear and see you.

Your job is to become a student of yourself, as well as of others. This means that by watching your sessions you can monitor carefully all the hundreds, if not thousands, of things that you do and say that can be improved. We are not suggesting that it is possible to track everything, but just that watching yourself is an important part of this process.

In addition, you may often have an impression about how the session went. If you watch any ten minutes of the session, you will know what you may need to do differently, especially with more training. Often, you won't even need someone else to watch it. You'll see your strengths as well, become mindful of them, and build on them.

Apart from your usual supervisors, ask knowledgeable friends and coworkers in the profession, those more experienced than you are, to listen to or watch your sessions and give you feedback. Sure, this is a time-consuming imposition on them, but they will understand how important this is to your continued development. The more feedback you can get from the maximum number of good practitioners, the better. Each person will have a different take on what could be done differently or on how to conceptualize and treat each client. That diversity of feedback helps you gain clarity about the approaches that work best for you.

Exercise in Opportunities for Improvement

Make a list of five skills you think must be developed next and prioritize them. Next to each one, write how you can commit to developing that skill in order to master it. Keep this list and your list of strengths in a safe place—perhaps in the front of your new journal—and refer to it often. Share this information with at least one other person, a classmate or someone you trust. Being accountable to others will help build your resolve to make changes.

Be a Good Consumer of Supervision

You may notice that supervisors with whom you work have different styles and philosophies if you ask them to describe what good therapy looks like. We recommend that you take full advantage of the differences you experience with each supervisor. While you are with your first supervisor, master what he or she is trying to teach you. When you go to your second supervisor, someone likely to have a different style, master that style, too. You may be thinking that it could be frustrating to be a chameleon, but the only way you will develop your own style is by trying on the styles of your various supervisors. Developing your own style of therapy is something that takes time and is dynamic: It's constantly changing.

One last word about supervision: You have the right to good supervision. What is good supervision? Ideally, your supervisor will observe you or listen to actual recordings of your sessions each week. Your self-report of a session is not sufficient to improve your skills. Take the initiative and record sessions if your supervisor does not require it, and ask him or her to listen to at least 10 minutes of at least one session each week. Ask your supervisor to explain what you did well (which you will want to repeat) and what you could have done better and how (so you can change it).

You also have the right to no less than one hour per week of uninterrupted individual supervision and preferably at least one (or two) hour(s) per week of uninterrupted group supervision. In individual supervision, you can monopolize the hour for all your supervision needs and discuss countertransference reactions. In group supervision, you have the advantage of learning from other people's mistakes, "borrowing" others' cool interventions that went well, and of hearing views from a variety of people on how best to help your client.

Your supervisor should also be teaching you about professionalism. Supervisors are responsible for making sure you write accurate and descriptive case notes, especially when ethical situations arise. They should help you with advocacy, such as working with parents or teachers in school settings. They can teach you processes or procedures for dealing with suicidal clients, child abuse reporting, and other crisis situations. They should be available for emergencies so you don't have to face crisis situations alone. You should feel they have your back.

Finally, your supervision experience should provide you with information about what you do right and what can be improved. If you are getting feedback only about what's right, you won't be able to improve much. If you are getting feedback only about what needs improvement, you'll feel really beat up each week. If you are not getting any of these needs met, assert yourself by asking for what you need.

Once you earn all of your hours, you will no longer be required to have a supervisor. You may at first feel relieved. In time, though, you may feel a little burned out, or you may not have the same level of excitement you did when you were in school. Seeking postlicensure supervision is often helpful. Many therapists use their own therapists or pay someone to continue supervision, maybe not every week, but monthly. In lieu of supervision, some professionals establish collegial relationships where they consult on a regular basis. Other therapists create leaderless groups where concerns about clients or personal issues can be discussed. You will have many options once you have your license. Make use of them to prevent burnout and to continually hone your skills so that you can continue to transform lives.

Attend Workshops and Conferences

We have already mentioned the advantages of attending workshops and conferences, and we think it's worth mentioning again. First, the organizations with which your department is affiliated usually have at least one annual national conference. Many organizations also have regional (groups of states), state-level, or local groups that meet each year or more often. Join at least one, if not two organizations and get involved. Join maybe the primary national organization in your field and perhaps a group that supports the theoretical orientation you are interested in or a group that specializes in the type of client with whom you would like to work. You can meet some of the important people in your field, and you can make friends with other professionals who can offer support when you feel stuck or just need someone with whom to talk.

Another advantage to attending workshops and conferences is gaining more specific information about the areas that interest you. Perhaps your program doesn't offer a course in a particular area, or perhaps you don't have the money or time to take all the courses you were interested in while in school. You may also find you start to develop new interests as you progress through your education. Workshops and conferences are the best way to get new information about techniques, skills, research, and trends in the field.

Being involved with so many like-minded individuals also provides you with resources when you feel stuck. The people you meet can provide you with referral resources when you aren't able to see a client, or your colleagues can refer clients to you.

Finally, joining a few organizations will lead you to external training groups where you can develop your skills even further. I [Leah] noticed that the professionals who I thought did the best therapy were affiliated with a particular theoretical orientation. I got to know some people and eventually found out about a local training group that was affordable. It was one of the most growth-inducing experiences of my professional and personal life. Because of the nature of this training group and the wonderful members who participated with me, I was able to work on many of my own issues while concurrently developing my skills as a therapist. We cannot impress on you enough that the more good training and supervision you receive (and are receptive to), the better you will be at being a therapist. At this point, you may finally realize that doing therapy is no easy task. Additional training can really help.

Practice Everywhere

One of the great things about helping skills is that you can use them everywhere, in every interaction, in every conversation. You may have noticed that in each chapter we have suggested exercises for practicing these skills in class or at home. In addition, we have a section in each chapter ("Applications to Self") where we talk about how the skills can or already do apply in your personal life. Take some time to read each of them again after you finish this semester. Make a list of what you can do, and start practicing them now, every day, if you aren't already doing that. The fact that the semester ends does not mean that your learning ends. Remember that practice makes . . . okay, not perfect, but . . . practice makes progress.

Remember Your First Priority in Helping: The Relationship

If you take nothing else from all we have given you, remember that the most essential task you must accomplish with your client is to build the relationship. Developing the relationship includes improving your skills to do the following:

- Attend to nonverbal behaviors
- Attend to nuances in the client's language

- Attend to the content of the client's communications
- Attend to the process of how your client communicates
- Provide empathic responses in a genuine and caring way

If you can do these things while being sensitive to and accepting of cultural differences, you have the foundation. As we have said before, this foundation is most of what you need in all stages of therapy for your client to grow. In fact, think of it this way: If you do nothing but give the client the positive experience of being heard, understood, and accepted, you will have helped your client, even if you didn't accomplish the goals that were articulated in the early stages of therapy. A healthy relationship can go a long way.

Be Gentle With Yourself

Finally, we encourage you to be gentle with yourself. Learning the skills involved with becoming a therapist are as difficult as training for a new sport. Instead of developing your body, you are learning to attend to many aspects of your client and to your own reactions to your client, then deciding how to respond in a way that you deem is most beneficial for your client. It is a skill, not a talent. It takes practice and is not a common way of communicating interpersonally. You will have many victories and many failures; with each failure, be kind to yourself. Becoming a therapist is a difficult but rewarding process that never ends. Enjoy it.

Caring for Yourself

Many of the suggestions made in this chapter are specifically to help your skill level. One factor that is often forgotten is that you need to take care of yourself. What does that mean? Self-care means prioritizing your life so that you don't become overcommitted. Do all the things you know you should do: eat well, get enough sleep, exercise, make time for leisure and fun, focus on your own personal and spiritual growth, and nurture your relationships. If you don't take care of yourself, you won't have enough energy or psychological space to help others. Set boundaries. Learn to say no.

Students often think they will start to take care of themselves once they graduate. Life doesn't begin after graduation; you will still have to complete internship hours to earn your license. Life doesn't begin after licensure. You will start a new job or be building a business. Life is now. Start your healthy habits right this moment. There's no point in pushing yourself so hard that you get burned out. Take fewer classes. Do what you need to do to have a balanced lifestyle today. You'll be a more effective therapist and more effective as a friend/family member.

Self-care also may need to happen between sessions or at the end of each day. Some clients have tragic stories that are hard to digest. Other clients carry such heavy loads of depression that you feel drained at the end of the session. Be mindful of ending sessions on time so you can take care of yourself after a particularly difficult hour. Create a ritual either between sessions or at the end of the day to metaphorically cleanse yourself of a hard day's work. Schedule clients in a way that you can take care of yourself. Perhaps you need an hour to recover after a particularly difficult client you see each week, maybe the client needs to be placed at the beginning of the day when you are fresh, or maybe you want them at the end of the day when you have more time to engage in self-care. Self-care requires a commitment, much in the way you commit to showing up to work or doing your homework, and it's equally important.

FINAL EXERCISE

Break into small groups of three or four and discuss:

1. What aspects of this class met your expectations?

2. What did you learn that you didn't expect?

3. What do you feel you still need to learn?

4. How can you learn what you still want to learn?

5. How do the other courses in your program apply to being a better therapist?

6. How can you take advantage of your remaining courses to develop your skills as a therapist?

7. How has going through this course changed who you are?

8. How has going through this course changed your relationships?

9. How have the people in this group been supportive to you?

SUMMARY

We hope you have acquired some useful tools for your adventure as a therapist. In the process, we also hope that we haven't overwhelmed you too much, although we know you must be feeling a little anxious. Your anxiety is good. It simply indicates that you care enough to do well and will work to improve on this foundation you are building. Trust your professors (at least the ones who are trustworthy).

Trust your supervisors. Listen well and try what they suggest. Students who are open to supervision and who are open to personal and professional change will surely grow. And get into therapy. You will have the opportunity to experience what it is like, you will also learn what you would like to do or not do when in the role of therapist, and most important, you will work on yourself, your person which is a critical element in building the relationship with clients. We wish you the best in transforming lives!

REFERENCES AND RESOURCES

Corey, G., & Corey, M. S. (2015). *Becoming a helper* (7th ed.). Pacific Grove, CA: Brooks/Cole.

Geller, J. D., Norcross, J. C., & Orlinsky, D. E. (2005). *The psychotherapist's own psychotherapy: Patient and clinician perspectives.* New York, NY: Oxford University Press.

Kase, L. (2005). *The successful therapist: Your guide to building the career you've always wanted.* New York, NY: John Wiley.

Kottler, J. A. (2003). *On being a therapist.* San Francisco, CA: Jossey-Bass.

Kottler, J. A., & Carlson, J. (2005). *The client who changed me: Stories of therapist personal transformation.* New York, NY: Routledge.

Orlinsky, D. E., & Ronnestad, M. H. (2004). *How psychotherapists develop: A study of therapeutic work and professional growth.* Washington, DC: American Psychological Association.

Weiss, L. (2004). *Therapist's guide to self-care.* New York, NY: Routledge.

REFERENCES AND RESOURCES

Abendroth, M., & Figley, C. (2011). Vicarious trauma and the therapeutic relationship. In J. C. Norcross (Ed.), *Psychotherapy relationships that work* (pp. 111–125). New York, NY: Oxford University Press.

Adler, A. (1963). *The practice and theory of individual psychology.* Paterson, NJ: Littlefield Adams.

American Association for Marriage and Family Therapy. (2012). *AAMFT code of ethics* [Electronic version]. Alexandria, VA: Author. Retrieved October 23, 2015, from https://www.aamft.org/imis15/Documents/AAMFT%20Code_11_2012_Secured.pdf

American Counseling Association. (2014). *ACA code of ethics* [Electronic version]. Alexandria, VA: Author. Retrieved October 23, 2015, from https://www.counseling.org/resources/aca-code-of-ethics.pdf

American Psychiatric Association. (2013). *Diagnostic and statistical manual of mental disorders* (5th ed.). Washington, DC: American Psychiatric Publishing.

American Psychological Association. (2010). *Ethical principles of psychologists and code of conduct* [Electronic version]. Washington, DC: Author. Retrieved October 23, 2015, from http://www.apa.org/ethics/code/principles.pdf

Arredondo, P., Gallardo-Cooper, M., Delgado-Romero, E. A., & Zapata, A. L. (2012). *Culturally responsive counseling with Latinas/os.* Alexandria, VA: American Counseling Association.

Audet, C. T. (2011). Client perspectives of therapist self-disclosure: Violating boundaries or removing barriers? *Counselling Psychology Quarterly, 24*(2), 85–100.

Austin, W., Bergum, V., Nuttgens, S., & Peternelj-Taylor, C. (2006). A re-visioning of boundaries in professional helping relationships: Exploring other metaphors. *Ethics & Behavior, 16*(2), 77–94.

Axline, V. (1964). *Dibs in search of self.* New York, NY: Ballantine Books.

Baer, R. (2006). *Mindfulness-based treatment approaches: Clinician's guide to evidence base and applications.* San Diego, CA: Elsevier Academic Press.

Baruth, L. G., & Manning, M. L. (2011). *Multicultural counseling and psychotherapy: A lifespan perspective* (5th ed.). New York, NY: Pearson.

Barnett, J. E. (2011). Psychotherapist self-disclosure: Ethical and clinical considerations. *Psychotherapy, 48*(4), 315–321.

Barnhill, J. (2013). *DSM-5 clinical cases.* Washington, DC: American Psychiatric Publishing.

Basmajian, J. (Ed.). (1989). *Biofeedback: Principles and practice for clinicians* (3rd ed.). Baltimore, MD: Williams & Wilkins.

Batty, M. J., Bonnington, S., Tang, B. K., Hawken, M. B., & Gruzelier, J. H. (2006). Relaxation strategies and enhancement of hypnotic susceptibility: EEG neurofeedback, progressive muscle relaxation and self-hypnosis. *Brain Research Bulletin, 71*, 83–90.

Beck, A. (1976). *Cognitive therapy and the emotional disorders.* New York, NY: International Universities Press.

Beck, A. T., Freeman, A., & Davis, D. (2014). *Cognitive therapy of personality disorders* (3rd ed.). New York, NY: Guilford Press.

Beck, J. (2011). *Cognitive behavior therapy: Basics and beyond* (2nd ed.). New York, NY: Guilford Press.

Beecher, Henry K. (1955). The powerful placebo. *Journal of the American Medical Association, 159*(17), 1602–1606.

Bemak, F., & Chung, C. Y. (2015). Cultural boundaries, cultural norms: Multicultural and social justice perspectives. In B. Herlihy & G. Corey (Eds.), *Boundary issues in counseling: Multiple roles and responsibilities* (3rd ed., pp. 84–92). Alexandria, VA: American Counseling Association.

Berant, E., & Obergi, J. H. (Eds.). (2009). *Attachment theory and research in clinical work with adults.* New York, NY: Guilford Press.

Binder, P., Holgersen, H., & Nielsen, G. H. (2009). Why did I change when I went to therapy? A qualitative analysis of former patients' conceptions of successful psychotherapy. *Counselling and Psychotherapy, 9*(4), 250–256.

Bjornsson, A. S. (2011). Beyond the "Psychological Placebo": Specifying the nonspecific in psychotherapy. *Clinical Psychology: Science and Practice, 18*(2), 113–118.

Bohart, A. C. (2007). An alternative view of concrete operating procedures from the perspective of the client as active self-healer. *Journal of Psychotherapy Integration, 17*(1), 125–137.

Bohart, A. C., & Tallman, K. (2010). Clients: The neglected common factor in psychotherapy. In B. L. Duncan, S. D. Miller, B. E. Wampold, & M. A. Hubble (Eds.), *The heart and soul of change: Delivering what works in therapy* (2nd ed., pp. 83–111). Washington, DC: American Psychological Association.

Bowlby, J. (1978). Attachment theory and its therapeutic implications. *Adolescent Psychiatry, 6*, 5–33.

Brammer, L. M., & MacDonald, G. (2002). *The helping relationship: Process and skills* (8th ed.). Boston, MA: Allyn & Bacon.

Brito, G. (2014). Rethinking mindfulness in the therapeutic relationship. *Mindfulness, 5*, 351–359.

Brock, G. W., & Barnard, C. P. (1999). *Procedures in marriage and family therapy.* Boston, MA: Allyn & Bacon.

Brown, J. H., & Brown, C. S. (2002). *Marital therapy: Concepts and skills for effective practice.* New York, NY: Brunner-Routledge.

Brown, L. (2008). *Cultural competence in trauma therapy: Beyond the flashback.* Washington, DC: American Psychological Association.

Calhoun, L. G., & Tedeschi, R. G. (2013). *Posttraumatic growth in clinical practice.* New York, NY: Routledge.

Carkhuff, R. R. (1969). *Helping and human relations.* New York, NY: Holt, Rinehart & Winston.

Carkhuff, R. R., & Anthony, W. A. (1979). *The skills of helping.* Amherst, MA: Human Resources Development Press.

Carkhuff, R. R., & Berenson, B. G. (1967). *Beyond counseling and therapy.* New York, NY: Holt, Rinehart & Winston.

Carlson, J., & Kjos, D. (2001). *Theories and strategies of family therapy.* Boston, MA: Allyn & Bacon.

Carlson, J., Watts, R. E., & Maniacci, M. (2006). *Adlerian therapy: Theory and practice.* Washington, DC: American Psychological Association.

Carter, B., McGoldrick, M., & Garcia-Preto, N. (2010). *The expanded family life cycle: Individual, family, and social perspectives* (4th ed.). Boston, MA: Allyn & Bacon.

Capsi, O. & Bootzin, R.R. (2002). Evaluating how placebos produce change: Logical and causal traps and understanding cognitive explanatory mechanisms. *Evaluation and the Health Professions 25*(4), 436–464.

Chen, M. W., & Giblin, N. J. (2002). *Individual counseling: Skills and techniques.* Denver, CO: Love Publishing.

Ciaramicoli, A. P., & Ketcham, K. (2000). *The power of empathy.* New York, NY: Dutton.

Cooper, M. (2013). Experiencing relational depth in therapy: What we know so far. In R. Knox, D. Murphy, S. Wiggins, & M. Cooper (Eds.), *Relational depth: New perspectives and developments* (pp. 62–76). New York, NY: Palgrave Macmillan.

Corey, G. (2012). *Theory and practice of counseling and psychotherapy* (9th ed.) Pacific Grove, CA: Brooks/Cole.

Corey, G., & Corey, M. S. (2015). *Becoming a helper* (7th ed.). Pacific Grove, CA: Brooks/Cole.

Corey, G., Corey, M. S., & Callanan, P. (2015). *Issues and ethics in the helping professions with 2014 ACA codes* (9th ed.). Boston, MA: Cengage Learning.

Corey, M. S., Corey, G., & Corey, C. (2016). *Groups: Process and practice* (10th ed.). Belmont, CA: Cengage.

Cormier, S., & Nurius, P. (2013). *Interviewing and change strategies for helpers: Fundamental skills and cognitive-behavior interventions* (7th ed.). Pacific Grove, CA: Brooks/Cole.

Courtois, C. A., & Ford, J. D. (2013). *Treatment of complex trauma: A sequenced, relationship-based approach.* New York, NY: Guilford Press.

Dass-Brailsford, P. (2012). Culturally sensitive therapy with low-income ethnic minority clients: An empowering intervention. *Journal of Contemporary Psychotherapy, 42*(1), 37–44.

Davis, M., Robbins-Eshelman, E., & McKay, M. (2008). *The relaxation and stress reduction workbook* (6th ed.). Oakland, CA: New Harbinger.

Day, M. A., Eyer, J. C., & Thorn, B. E. (2014). Therapeutic relaxation. In S. G. Hofmann (Ed.), *The Wiley handbook of cognitive behavioral therapy* (Vols. 1–3; pp. 157–180). Wiley-Blackwell.

De Jong, P., & Berg, I. K. (2012). *Interviewing for solutions* (4th ed.). Pacific Grove, CA: Brooks/Cole.

DeFife, J. A., Hilsenroth, M. J., & Gold, J. R. (2008). Patient ratings of psychodynamic psychotherapy session activities and their relation to outcome. *Journal of Nervous and Mental Disease, 196*(7), 538–546.

Dillon, C. (2003). *Learning from mistakes in clinical practice.* Pacific Grove, CA: Brooks/Cole.

Donigan, J., & DeLucia-Waack, J. L. (2004). *The practice of multicultural group work: Visions and perspectives from the field.* Belmont, CA: Thomson Brooks/Cole.

Dryden, W., & Neenan, M. (2014). *Rational emotive behavior therapy: 100 key points and techniques* (2nd ed.). New York, NY: Routledge.

Duncan, B. L. (2010). *On becoming a better therapist.* Washington, DC: American Psychological Association.

Duncan, B. L. (2012). The partners for change outcome management system (pcoms): The heart and soul of change project. *Canadian Psychology/Psychologie Canadienne, 53*(2), 93–104.

Duncan, B. L., Miller, S. D., & Sparks, J. A. (2004). *The heroic client.* San Francisco, CA: Jossey-Bass.

Duncan, B. L., Miller, S. D., Wampold, B. E., & Hubble, M. A. (Eds.). (2010). *The heart and soul of change: Delivering what works in therapy* (2nd ed.). Washington, DC: American Psychological Association.

Edwards, L. M., & Pedrotti, J. T. (2004). Utilizing the strengths of our cultures: Therapy with biracial women and girls. *Women & Therapy, 27*(1–2), 33–43.

Egan, G. (2013). *The skilled helper: A problem-management and opportunity-development approach to helping* (10th ed.). Pacific Grove, CA: Brooks/Cole.

Ellis, A. (1973). *Humanistic psychotherapy: The rational-emotive approach.* New York, NY: McGraw-Hill.

Ellis, A. E. (2001). *Overcoming destructive beliefs, feelings, and behaviors.* New York, NY: Prometheus.

Ellis, A., & Ellis, D. J. (2011). *Rational emotive behavior therapy* (3rd ed.). Washington, DC: American Psychological Association.

Englar-Carlson, M., & Shepard, D. (2005). Engaging men in couples counseling: Strategies for overcoming ambivalence and inexpressiveness. *The Family Journal, 13*(4), 383–391.

Englar-Carlson, M., & Stevens, M. (2006). Masculine norms and the therapeutic process. *In the room with men: A casebook of therapeutic change* (pp. 13–47). Washington, DC: American Psychological Association.

Erchull, M., Liss, M., Wilson, K., Bateman, L., Peterson, A., & Sanchez, C. (2009). The feminist identity development model: Relevant for young women today? *Sex Roles, 60*(11), 832–842.

Evans, D. R., Heart, M. T., Uhlemann, M. R., & Ivey, A. E. (2010). *Essential interviewing: A programmed approach to effective communication* (8th ed.). Pacific Grove, CA: Brooks/Cole.

Evans, M. P., Duffey, T., & Englar-Carlson, M. (2013). Introduction to the special issue: Men in counseling. *Journal of Counseling & Development, 91*(4), 387–389.

Falvey, J. E. (2002). *Managing clinical supervision: Ethical practice and legal risk management.* Pacific Grove, CA: Brooks/Cole.

Feltham, C. (1999). *Understanding the counseling relationship.* Thousand Oaks, CA: Sage.

Fernando, S. (2012). Race and culture issues in mental health and some thoughts on ethnic identity. *Counselling Psychology Quarterly, 25*(2), 113–123.

Flentje, A., Heck, N. C., & Cochran, B. N. (2014). Experiences of ex-ex-gay individuals in sexual reorientation therapy: Reasons for seeking treatment, perceived helpfulness and harmfulness of treatment, and post-treatment identification. *Journal of Homosexuality, 61*(9), 1242–1268.

Frankl, V. (1963). *Man's search for meaning.* Boston, MA: Beacon Press.

Freud, A. (1936). *The ego and mechanisms of defense.* New York, NY: International University Press.

Freud, A. (1954). The widening scope for indications of psychoanalysis: Discussion. *Journal of the American Psychoanalytic Association, 2*, 607–620.

Freud, S., & Gay, P. (Ed.). (1989). *The Freud reader.* New York, NY: W. W. Norton.

Geller, J. D., Norcross, J. C., & Orlinsky, D. E. (2005). *The psychotherapist's own psychotherapy: Patient and clinician perspectives.* New York, NY: Oxford University Press.

Geller, S. M., & Porges, S. W. (2014). Therapeutic presence: Neurophysiological mechanisms mediating feeling safe in therapeutic relationships. *Journal of Psychotherapy Integration, 24*(3), 178–192.

Gelso, C. J., & Bhatia, A. (2012). Crossing theoretical lines: The role and effect of transference in nonanalytic psychotherapies. *Psychotherapy, 49*, 384–390.

Gelso, C. J., & Hayes, J. A. (1998). *The psychotherapy relationship: Theory, research, and practice.* New York, NY: John Wiley.

Gladding, S. T. (2006). *Family therapy: History, theory, and practice* (4th ed.). Columbus, OH: Merrill.

Gladding, S. T. (2015). *Group work: A counseling specialty* (7th ed.). Santa Monica, CA: Pearson.

Glasser, W. (1965). *Reality therapy: A new approach to psychiatry.* New York, NY: Harper & Row.

Goldberg, M. C. (2003). *The art of the question.* New York, NY: John Wiley.

Goldenberg, H., & Goldenberg, I. (2016). *Family therapy: An overview* (9th ed.). Pacific Grove, CA: Brooks/Cole.

Gottman, J. (2002). *The relationship cure: A 5–step guide to strengthening your marriage, family, and friendships.* New York, NY: Three Rivers Press.

Gottman, J. (2014). *What predicts divorce?* New York, NY: Psychology Press.

Gottman, J., & Silver, N. (2015). *The seven principles for making marriages work* (2nd ed.). New York, NY: Harmony.

Gottschall, J. (2012). *The storytelling animal: How stories make us human.* New York, NY: Houghton Mifflin.

Greenberg, L. (2014). The therapeutic relationship in emotion-focused therapy. *Psychotherapy, 51*(3), 350–357.

Grothaus, T., McAuliffe, G., & Craigen, L. (2012). Infusing cultural competence and advocacy into strength-based counseling. *Journal of Humanistic Counseling, 51*(1), 51–65.

Halstead, R. (2007). *Assessment of client core issues.* Alexandria, VA: American Counseling Association.

Helms, J. (2015). An examination of the evidence in culturally adapted evidence-based or empirically supported interventions. *Transcultural Psychiatry, 52*(2), 174–197.

Hendrix, H. (2007). *Getting the love you want: A guide for couples, 20th anniversary edition.* New York, NY: Henry Holt.

Hendrix, H., & LaKelly Hunt, H. (2013). *Making marriage simple: Ten truths for changing the relationship you have into the one you want.* New York, NY: Penguin Random House.

Hermann, M., & Herlihy, B. (2006). Legal and ethical implications of refusing to counsel homosexual clients. *Journal of Counseling & Development, 84*(4), 414–418.

Hersen, M. (2006). *Clinician's handbook of adult behavioral assessment.* San Diego, CA: Elsevier Academic.

Hill, C. E. (2014). *Helping skills: Facilitating exploration, insight, and action* (4th ed.). Washington, DC: American Psychological Association.

Hoglend, P. (2014). Exploration of the patient-therapist relationship in psychotherapy. *American Journal of Psychiatry, 171*(10), 1056–1066.

Hood, A. B., & Johnson, R. W. (2007). *Assessment in counseling: A guide to the use of psychological assessment procedures* (2nd ed.). Alexandria, VA: American Counseling Association.

Howe, D. (2013). *Empathy: What it is and why it matters.* New York, NY: Palgrave.

Hubbard, K., & Falco, F. E. (2015). Relaxation techniques. In A. D. Kaye, N. Vadivelu, & R. D. Urman (Eds.), *Substance abuse: Inpatient and outpatient management for every clinician* (pp. 337–357). New York, NY: Springer Science + Business Media.

Huebner, D., Thoma, B., & Neilands, T. (2015). School victimization and substance use among lesbian, gay, bisexual, and transgender adolescents. *Prevention Science, 16*(5), 734–743.

Hymmen, P., Stalker, C. A., & Cait, C. (2013). The case for single-session therapy: Does the empirical evidence support the increased prevalence of this service delivery model? *Journal of Mental Health, 22*(1), 60–71.

Ivey, A., Ivey, M. B., & Zalaquett, C. (2013). *Intentional interviewing and counseling: Facilitating client development in a multicultural society* (8th ed.). Pacific Grove, CA: Brooks/Cole.

Ivey, A. E., D'Andrea, M., & Ivey, M. B. (2011). *Theories of counseling and psychotherapy: A multicultural perspective* (7th ed.). Thousand Oaks, CA: Sage.

Johnson, D. W., & Johnson, F. P. (2012). *Joining together: Group theory and group skills* (11th ed.). Boston, MA: Allyn & Bacon.

Johnson, S. (2012). *The practice of emotionally focused couple therapy: Creating connection* (2nd ed.). New York, NY: Routledge.

Johnson, S. (2013). *Love sense: The revolutionary new science of romantic relationships.* London, England: Little, Brown.

Johnson, S. (2014). *The love secret.* London, England: Piatkus.

Jones, W. P., & Kottler, J. A. (2006). *Understanding research: Becoming a competent and critical consumer.* Upper Saddle River, NJ: Prentice Hall.

Joseph, S. (2011). *What doesn't kill us: The new psychology of posttraumatic growth.* New York, NY: Basic Books.

Jung, C. (1980). The Tavistock lectures. In *Symbolic life: Miscellaneous writings. Collected Works* (Vol. 18, pp. 1–182). Princeton, NJ: Princeton University Press. (Original work published 1935)

Kagan (Klein), H., & Kagan, N. I. (1997). Interpersonal process recall: Influencing human interaction. In C. Edward Watkins (Ed.), *Handbook of psychotherapy supervision* (pp. 296–309). Hoboken, NJ: John Wiley.

Kase, L. (2005). *The successful therapist: Your guide to building the career you've always wanted.* New York, NY: John Wiley.

Keene, M., & Erford, B. T. (2006). *Group activities: Fired up for performance.* Upper Saddle River, NJ: Prentice Hall.

Keeney, B. (1996). *Everyday soul: Awakening the spirit in daily life.* New York, NY: Ringling Rocks.

Kelley, F. A. (2015). The therapy relationship with lesbian and gay clients. *Psychotherapy, 52*(1), 113–118.

Keyser, V., Gamst, G., Meyers, L. S., Der-Karabetian, A., & Morrow, G. (2014). Predictors of self-perceived cultural competence among children's mental health providers. *Cultural Diversity and Ethnic Minority Psychology, 20*(3), 324–335.

Kottler, J. A. (1992). *Compassionate therapy: Working with difficult clients.* San Francisco, CA: Jossey-Bass.

Kottler, J. A. (1993). *On being a therapist* (1st ed.). San Francisco, CA: Jossey-Bass.

Kottler, J. A. (2003). *On being a therapist* (2nd ed.). San Francisco, CA: Jossey-Bass.

Kottler, J. A., & Blau, D. S. (1989). *The imperfect therapist: Learning from failure in therapeutic practice.* San Francisco, CA: Jossey-Bass.

Kottler, J. A., & Brown, R. (2003). *Introduction to therapeutic counseling: Voices from the field* (5th ed.). Stamford, CT: Brooks/Cole.

Kottler, J. A., & Carlson, J. (2003). *Bad therapy: Master therapists share their worst failures.* New York, NY: Brunner-Routledge.

Kottler, J. A., & Carlson, J. (2005). *The client who changed me: Stories of therapist personal transformation.* New York, NY: Routledge.

Kottler, J. A., & Carlson, J. (2015). *On being a master therapist: Practicing what we preach.* New York, NY: John Wiley.

Kottler, J. A., Carlson, J., & Keeney, B. (2004). *American shaman: An odyssey of global healing traditions.* New York, NY: Brunner-Routledge.

Kottler, J. A., & Englar-Carlson, M. (2015). *Learning group leadership* (3rd ed.). Thousand Oaks, CA: Sage.

Kuyken, W. (2004). Cognitive therapy outcome: The effects of hopelessness in a naturalistic outcome study. *Behaviour Research and Therapy, 42*(6), 631–646.

Lambert, M. J. (Ed.). (2013). *Bergin and Garfield's handbook of psychotherapy and behavior change* (6th ed.). New York, NY: John Wiley.

Landreth, G. (2012). *Play therapy: The art of the relationship* (3rd ed.). New York, NY: Routledge.

Lazarus, A. A. (1973). Multimodal behavior therapy: Treating the BASIC I.D. *Journal of Nervous and Mental Disease, 156,* 404–411.

Lazarus, R. (2006). Emotions and interpersonal relationships: Toward a person-centered conceptualization of emotions and coping. *Journal of Personality, 74*(1), 9–46.

Lee, C. (Ed.). (2007). *Counseling for social justice* (2nd ed.). Alexandria, VA: American Counseling Association.

Leong, F. L., Kim, H. W., & Gupta, A. (2011). Attitudes toward professional counseling among Asian-American college students: Acculturation, conceptions of mental illness, and loss of face. *Asian American Journal of Psychology*, *2*(2), 140–153. doi:10.1037/a0024172

Levine, M. (2004, June 1). Tell your doctor all your problems, but keep it less than a minute. *New York Times*. Retrieved March 10, 2016, from http://www.nytimes .com/2004/06/01/health/tell-the-doctor-all-your-problems-but-keep-it-to-less-than-a -minute.html?_r=0

Long, L., & Young, M. (2007). *Counseling and therapy for couples*. Belmont, CA: Wadsworth.

Mah, K., & Binik, Y. (2001). The nature of human orgasm: A critical review of major trends. *Clinical Psychology Review, 21*(6), 823–856.

Maroda, K. J. (2012). *Psychodynamic techniques: Working with emotion in the therapeutic relationship*. New York, NY: Guilford Press.

Marzaleck, J., & Myers, J. (2006). Dream interpretation: A developmental counseling and theory approach. *Journal of Mental Health Counseling, 28*(1), 18–37.

May, R. (1953). *Man's search for himself*. New York, NY: Dell.

Meichenbaum, D. (1977). *Cognitive behavior modification*. New York, NY: Plenum Press.

Miller, S. D., Duncan, B. L., & Hubble, M. A. (2004). Beyond integration: The triumph of outcome over process in clinical practice. *Psychotherapy in Australia, 10*(2), 2–19.

Miller, W. R. & Rollnick, S. (2002). *Motivational interviewing: Helping people change*. New York, NY: Guilford.

Minuchin, S. (1974). *Families and family therapy*. Cambridge, MA: Harvard University Press.

Moore, C. (2003). *The mediation process* (3rd ed.). San Francisco, CA: Jossey-Bass.

Moran, M. R. (1992). Effects of sexual orientation similarity and counselor experience level on gay men's and lesbians' perceptions of counselors. *Journal of Counseling Psychology, 39*(2), 247–251.

Moreno, J. L. (1987). *The essential Moreno: Writings on psychodrama, group method, and spontaneity*. New York, NY: Springer.

Morning, A. (2007). "Everyone knows it's a social construct": Contemporary science and the nature of race. *Sociological Focus, 40*(4), 436–454.

Morrissette, P. J. (2002). *Self-supervision: A primer for counselors and helping professionals*. New York, NY: Brunner-Routledge.

Moyers, T. B. (2014). The relationship in motivational interviewing. *Psychotherapy, 51*(3), 358–363.

Muntigl, P., & Horvath, A. O. (2014). The therapeutic relationship in action: How therapists and clients co-manage relational disaffiliation. *Psychotherapy Research, 24*(3), 327–345.

National Association of Social Workers. (2008). *Code of ethics of The National Association of Social Workers* [Electronic version]. Washington, DC: Author. Retrieved October 23, 2015, from http://www.socialworkers.org/pubs/code/code.asp

Nichols, M. P., & Schwartz, R. C. (2006). *Essentials of family therapy* (3rd ed.). Boston, MA: Allyn & Bacon.

Nippoda, Y. (2012). Japanese culture and therapeutic relationship. *Online Readings in Psychology and Culture, 10*(3). doi:10.9707/2307–0919.1094

Norcross, J. C. (Ed.). (2011). *Psychotherapy relationships that work* (2nd ed.). New York, NY: Oxford University Press.

Norcross, J. C., Beutler, L. E., & Levant, R. F. (Eds.). (2005). *Evidence-based practices in mental health: Debate and dialogue on the fundamental questions.* Washington, DC: American Psychological Association.

Norcross, J. C., & Goldfried, M. (Eds.). (2005). *Handbook of psychotherapy integration* (2nd ed.). New York, NY: Oxford University Press.

Nordahl, H. M., & Wells, A. (2016). *Changing beliefs in cognitive therapy: A therapist's guide.* Hoboken, NJ: Blackwell.

O'Hanlon, B., & Beadle, S. (1999). *Guide to possibility land: Fifty-one methods for doing brief, respectful therapy.* New York, NY: W. W. Norton.

Oaklander, V. (1988). *Windows to our children: A gestalt therapy approach to children and adolescents.* Gouldsboro, ME: Gestalt Journal Press.

Okun, B. F. (2007). *Effective helping: Interviewing and counseling techniques* (7th ed.). Pacific Grove, CA: Brooks/Cole.

Orlinsky, D. E., & Ronnestad, M. H. (2004). *How psychotherapists develop: A study of therapeutic work and professional growth.* Washington, DC: American Psychological Association.

Paniagua, F. A. (2001). *Diagnosis in a multicultural context: A casebook for mental health professionals.* Thousand Oaks, CA: Sage.

Pedersen, P. B., & Carey, J. C. (2003). *Multicultural counseling in schools: A practical handbook* (2nd ed.). Boston, MA: Allyn & Bacon.

Penchaszadeh, V. B. (2001). Genetic counseling issues in Latinos. *Genetic Testing, 5*(3), 193–200.

Perls, F. (1969). *Gestalt therapy verbatim.* Moab, UT: Real People Press.

Perls, F. (2013). *Gestalt therapy verbatim.* Gouldsboro, ME: Gestalt Journal Press.

Pesek, T., Helton, L. & Nair, M. (2006). Healing across cultures: Learning from traditions. *EcoHealth, 3*(2), 114–118.

Prochaska, J. O., & Norcross, J. C. (2014). *Systems of psychotherapy: A transtheoretical analysis* (8th ed.). Belmont, CA: Wadsworth.

Rabu, M., Haavind, H., & Binder, P. E. (2013). We have traveled a long distance and sorted out the mess in the drawers: Metaphors for moving towards the end in psychotherapy. *British Journal of Counselling and Psychotherapy, 13*(1), 71–80.

Razzaque, R., Okoro, E., & Wood, L. (2015). Mindfulness in clinician therapeutic relationships. *Mindfulness, 6,* 170–174.

Remley, T. P., & Herlihy, B. (2015). *Ethical, legal, and professional issues in counseling* (5th ed.) New York, NY: Pearson.

Robinson, T., & Howard-Hamilton, M. (2000). *The convergence of race, ethnicity, and gender: Multiple identities in counseling.* Upper Saddle River, NJ: Prentice Hall.

Rogers, C. (1951). *Client-centered therapy: Its current practice, implications and theory.* Boston, MA: Houghton Mifflin.

Rogers, C. (1961). *On becoming a person.* Boston, MA: Houghton Mifflin.

Rogers, C. (1980). *A way of being.* Boston, MA: Houghton Mifflin.

Rosen, S. (Ed.). (1991). *My voice will go with you: The teaching tales of Milton H. Erickson.* New York, NY: W. W. Norton.

Rosenthal, H. G. (Ed.). (2011). *Favorite counseling and therapy homework assignments* (2nd ed.). New York, NY: Routledge.

Sehgal, R., Saules, K., Young, A., Grey, M. J., Gillem, A. R., Nabors, N. A., . . . & Jefferson, S. (2011). Practicing what we know: Multicultural counseling competence among clinical psychology trainees and experienced multicultural psychologists. *Cultural Diversity and Ethnic Minority Psychology, 17*(1), 1–10.

Seligman, L. (1998). *Selecting effective treatments: A comprehensive, systematic guide to treating mental disorders* (2nd ed.). San Francisco, CA: Jossey-Bass.

Seligman, L., & Reichenberg, L. (2013). *Theories of counseling and psychotherapy* (4th ed.). New York, NY: Pearson.

Shapiro, S. L. (2009). The integration of mindfulness and psychology. *Journal of Clinical Psychology, 65*(6), 555–560.

Shechtman, Z. (2006). *Group counseling and psychotherapy with children and adolescents: Theory, research, and practice.* Mahwah, NJ: Lawrence Erlbaum.

Siegal, D., & Hartzell, M. (2004). *Parenting from the inside out.* New York, NY: Penguin Group.

Simeonsson, R. J., & Rosenthal, S. L. (2001). *Psychological and developmental assessment.* New York, NY: Guilford Press.

Smith, T. B., Rodriguez, M. M. D., & Bernal, G. (2011). Culture. In J. C. Norcross (Ed.), *Psychotherapy relationships that work* (pp. 316–335). New York, NY: Oxford University Press.

Sommers-Flanagan, J., & Sommers-Flanagan, R. (2015). *Clinical interviewing* (5th ed.). Hoboken, NJ: John Wiley.

Sperry, L. (2010). Culture, personality, health, and family dynamics: Cultural competence in the selection of culturally sensitive treatments. *The Family Journal, 18*(3), 316–320.

Sprenkle, D. H. and Blow, A. J. (2007). Common factors and our sacred models. *Journal of Marital and Family Therapy, 30*(2), 113–129.

Staemmler, F. M. (2012). *Empathy in psychotherapy: How therapists and clients understand each other.* New York, NY: Springer.

Stark, M. (2000). *Modes of therapeutic action: Enhancement of knowledge, provision of experience, and engagement in relationship.* Northvale, NJ: Jason Aronson.

Stevens, P., & Smith, R. (2012). *Substance abuse counseling: Theory and practice* (5th ed.). New York, NY: Pearson.

Stricker, G., & Gold, J. (2006). *A casebook of psychotherapy integration.* Washington, DC: American Psychological Association.

Sue, D. W., & Sue, D. (2015). *Counseling the culturally diverse: Theory and practice* (7th ed.). Hoboken, NJ: John Wiley.

Sugden, R. (2002). Beyond sympathy and empathy: Adam Smith's concept of fellow-feeling. *Economics and Philosophy, 18*(1), 63–87.

Trotzer, J. P. (2006). *The counselor and the group* (4th ed.). New York, NY: Routledge.

Tryon, G. S. (2002). *Counseling based on process research: Applying what we know.* Boston, MA: Allyn & Bacon.

Tryon, G. S., & Winograd, G. (2011). Goal consensus and collaboration. In J. C. Norcross (Ed.), *Psychotherapy relationships that work* (pp. 153–167). New York, NY: Oxford University Press.

Tseng, W. S., & Streltzer, J. (1997). *Culture and psychopathology: A guide to clinical assessment.* New York, NY: Brunner/Mazel.

Utay, J., & Miller, M. (2006). Guided imagery as an effective therapeutic technique: A brief review of its history and efficacy research. *Journal of Instructional Psychology, 33*(1), 40–43.

Vahinger, H. (1925). *The philosophy of acting "as if": A system of the theoretical, practical and religious fictions of mankind.* New York, NY: Harcourt, Brace.

Vasquez, M. J. T., Bingham, R. P., & Barnett, J. E. (2008). Psychotherapy termination: Clinical and ethical responsibilities. *Journal of Clinical Psychology, 64*(5), 653–665.

Vivero, V., & Jenkins, S. (1999). Existential hazards of the multicultural individual: Defining and understanding "cultural homelessness." *Cultural Diversity and Ethnic Minority Psychology, 5*(1), 6–26.

Watzlawick, P., Ray, W. A., & Nardone, G. (2009). *Insight may cause blindness and other essays.* Phoenix, AZ: Zeig, Tucker & Theisen.

Weeks, G., Odell, M., & Methven, S. (2005). *If only I had known . . . Avoiding common mistakes in couples therapy.* New York, NY: W. W. Norton.

Weiss, L. (2004). *Therapist's guide to self-care.* New York, NY: Routledge.

Welfel, E. R., & Ingersoll, R. E. (Eds.). (2005). *The mental health desk reference* (3rd ed.). New York, NY: John Wiley.

Werdel, M. B., & Wicks, R. J. (2012). *Primer on posttraumatic growth.* New York, NY: John Wiley.

Winslade, J., & Monk, G. (2000). *Narrative mediation.* San Francisco, CA: Jossey-Bass.

Yalom, I. D. (1980). *Existential psychotherapy.* New York, NY: Basic Books.

Yalom, I. D. (2000). *Momma and the meaning of life: Tales of psychotherapy.* New York, NY: HarperCollins.

Yalom, I. D. (2015). *Creatures of a day: And other tales of psychotherapy.* New York, NY: Basic Books.

Young, M. E. (2012). *Learning the art of helping: Building blocks and techniques* (5th ed.). New York, NY: Pearson.

Ziv-Beiman, S. (2013). Therapist self-disclosure as an integrative intervention. *Journal of Psychotherapy Integration, 23*(1), 59–74.

Zur, O. (2007). *Boundaries in psychotherapy: Ethical and clinical explorations.* Washington, DC: American Psychological Association.

INDEX

ABOUT THE AUTHORS

Leah Brew is Chair and Professor in the Department of Counseling at California State University, Fullerton. She teaches, presents, and publishes in the areas of basic counseling skills and multiculturalism. Specifically, she has several publications and projects that have been centered on working with multiracial couples, families, and individuals. She collaborated on a project to establish "Competencies for Counseling Multiracial Populations," which was endorsed by the American Counseling Association. She has a small private practice where she specializes in working with diverse clients who struggle with depression and anxiety and are survivors of trauma. She also supervises students at a community agency who are working toward their master's degrees in counseling. She is active in the profession of counseling in the state of California, and helped to obtain the Licensed Professional Clinical Counseling credential in California, the last state to license counselors. She was also appointed a gubernatorial position as the LPCC representative on the state licensure board and has taken a leadership role in improving supervision requirements in the state.

Jeffrey A. Kottler is one of the most prolific authors in the fields of counseling, psychotherapy, and education, having written more than 90 books about a wide range of subjects. He has authored a dozen texts for counselors and therapists that are used in universities around the world and a dozen books each for practicing therapists and educators. Some of his most highly regarded works include *Creative Breakthroughs in Therapy*, *The Mummy at the Dining Room Table: Eminent Therapists Reveal Their Most Unusual Cases and What They Teach Us About Human Behavior*, *Bad Therapy*, *The Client Who Changed Me*, *Divine Madness*, *Change: What Leads to Personal Transformation*, *Stories We've Heard, Stories We've Told: Life-Changing Narratives in Therapy and Everyday Life*, and *Therapy Over 50*. He has been an educator for 40 years, having worked as a teacher, counselor, and therapist in preschool, middle school, mental health center, crisis center, nongovernmental organization, university, community college, private practice, and disaster relief settings. He has served as a Fulbright scholar and senior lecturer in Peru and Iceland, as well as worked as a visiting professor in New Zealand, Australia, Hong Kong, Singapore, and Nepal. He is professor of counseling at California State University, Fullerton.